Cultural Memories

Knowledge and Space

Volume 4

Knowledge and Space

This book series entitled "Knowledge and Space" is dedicated to topics dealing with the production, dissemination, spatial distribution, and application of knowledge. Recent work on the spatial dimension of knowledge, education, and science; learning organizations; and creative milieus has underlined the importance of spatial disparities and local contexts in the creation, legitimation, diffusion, and application of new knowledge. These studies have shown that spatial disparities in knowledge and creativity are not short-term transitional events but rather a fundamental structural element of society and the economy.

The volumes in the series on Knowledge and Space cover a broad range of topics relevant to all disciplines in the humanities and social sciences focusing on knowledge, intellectual capital, and human capital: clashes of knowledge; milieus of creativity; geographies of science; cultural memories; knowledge and the economy; learning organizations; knowledge and power; ethnic and cultural dimensions of knowledge; knowledge and action; and the spatial mobility of knowledge. These topics are analyzed and discussed by scholars from a range of disciplines, schools of thought, and academic cultures.

Knowledge and Space is the outcome of an agreement concluded by the Klaus Tschira Foundation and Springer in 2006.

For other titles published in this series, go to
www.springer.com/series/7568

Peter Meusburger · Michael Heffernan ·
Edgar Wunder
Editors

Cultural Memories

The Geographical Point of View

**Klaus Tschira Stiftung
Gemeinnützige GmbH**

KTS

Editors
Prof. Peter Meusburger
Universität Heidelberg
Geographisches Institut
Berliner Str. 48
69120 Heidelberg
Germany
peter.meusburger@geog.uni-heidelberg.de

Prof. Michael Heffernan
University of Nottingham
School of Geography
University Park
Nottingham NG7 2RD
United Kingdom
mike.heffernan@nottingham.ac.uk

Dr. Edgar Wunder
Universität Heidelberg
Geographisches Institut
Berliner Str. 48
69120 Heidelberg
Germany
edgar.wunder@geog.uni-heidelberg.de

Technical Editor:
David Antal, Berlin
Davidrantal@aol.com

ISSN 1877-9220
ISBN 978-90-481-8944-1   e-ISBN 978-90-481-8945-8
DOI 10.1007/978-90-481-8945-8
Springer Dordrecht Heidelberg London New York

Library of Congress Control Number: 2011926786

Springer is part of Springer Science+Business Media (www.springer.com)

Contents

Contributors

Jan Assmann, Prof. Dr. Department of Egyptology, Heidelberg University, 69117 Heidelberg, Germany, Jan.Assmann@urz.uni-heidelberg.de

Steven D. Brown, Prof. Dr. School of Management, Leicester University, Leicester LE1 7DR, UK, s.d.brown@leicester.ac.uk

Rainer Eckert, Prof. Dr. Stiftung Haus der Geschichte der Bundesrepublik Deutschland, Zeitgeschichtliches Forum Leipzig, 04109 Leipzig, Germany, eckert@hdg.de

Brian Graham, Prof. Dr. School of Environmental Science, University of Ulster, BT52 1SA Coleraine, Northern Ireland, bj.graham@ulster.ac.uk

Derek Gregory, Prof. Dr. Department of Geography, University of British Columbia, Vancouver, BC, Canada V6T 1Z2, derek.gregory@geog.ubc.ca

Georg Kreis, Prof. Dr. Europainstitut, University of Basel, 4020 Basel, Switzerland, georg.kreis@unibas.ch

Michael Heffernan, Prof. Dr. School of Geography, University of Nottingham, Nottingham NG7 2RD, UK, mike.heffernan@nottingham.ac.uk

Claus Leggewie, Prof. Dr. Kulturwissenschaftliches Institut, 45128 Essen, Germany, claus.leggewie@kwi-nrw.de

Stephen Legg, Dr. School of Geography, University of Nottingham, Nottingham NG7 2RD, UK, stephen.legg@nottingham.ac.uk

Denis Linehan, Dr. School of Geography and Archeology, University College Cork, Cork, Ireland, d.linehan@ucc.ie

Peter Meusburger, Prof. Dr. Geographisches Institut, Universität Heidelberg, 69120 Heidelberg, Germany, peter.meusburger@geog.uni-heidelberg.de

David Middleton, Prof. Dr. Discourse and Rhetoric Group (DARG), Department of Social Sciences, Loughborough University, Loughborough LE11 3TU, UK, D.J.Middleton@lboro.ac.uk

Sandra Petermann, Dr. Department of Geography, University of Mainz, 55128 Mainz, Germany, S.Petermann@uni-mainz.de

Dirk Rupnow, Dr. Institut für Zeitgeschichte, University of Innsbruck, 6020 Innsbruck, Austria, dirk.rupnow@uibk.ac.at

João Sarmento, Prof. Dr. Department of Geography, University of Minho, 4800-058 Guimarães, Portugal; Centre for Geographical Studies, University of Lisbon, Portugal, j.sarmento@geografia.uminho.pt

Robert Tonkinson, Prof. Dr. Department of Anthropology, University of Western Australia, Nedlands, WA 6009, Australia, bob.tonkinson@uwa.edu.au

Stefan Troebst, Prof. Dr. Geisteswissenschaftliches Zentrum Geschichte und Kultur Ostmitteleuropas, University of Leipzig, 04177 Leipzig, Germany, stefan.troebst@snafu.de

Jürg Wassmann, Prof. Dr. Department of Anthropology, Heidelberg University, 69117 Heidelberg, Germany, juerg.wassmann@urz.uni-heidelberg.de

Harald Welzer, Prof. Dr. Kulturwissenschaftliches Institut, 45128 Essen, Germany, herald.welzer@kwi-nrw.de

Christina West, Dr. Chair of Economic Geography, University of Mannheim, 68131 Mannheim, Germany, west@rumms.uni-mannheim.de

Edgar Wunder, Dr. Geographisches Institut, Universität Heidelberg, 69120 Heidelberg, Germany, edgar.wunder@geog.uni-heidelberg.de

Part I
Theoretical Considerations

Cultural Memories: An Introduction

Peter Meusburger, Michael Heffernan, and Edgar Wunder

The revival of public and scholarly interest in collective cultural memories since the 1980s has been a genuinely global phenomenon and is somewhat paradoxical. Memory is a form of temporal awareness more readily associated with traditional, nonindustrialized societies rather than with the globalized, mobile, and deracinated world of today, which ostensibly floats free of all historical moorings, disconnected from earlier generations and periods. Yet the rise of a self-consciously postmodern, postcolonial, and multicultural society seems to have reanimated memory as a social, cultural, and political force with which to challenge, if not openly reject, the founding myths and historical narratives that have hitherto given shape and meaning to established national and imperial identities. This trend, initially accelerated by the lifting of the censorship and political constraints that had been imposed in both the "East" and the "West" during the Cold War, has been facilitated since the mid-1990s by the Internet, the default source of information in the global public sphere. Uncovering the historical experiences of marginalized communities, previously silenced because of their ethnicity, religion, gender, or sexuality, is now a primary objective of historical inquiry. It is inspired in part by an emerging "politics of regret" (Olick & Robbins, 1998, p. 107) but also by a desire to provide a sense of historical legitimacy and depth to newly established social, cultural, and political constituencies. This change has necessitated an increased level of systematic analysis of different kinds of nontextual evidence, from oral testimonies to the many other

P. Meusburger (✉)
Geographisches Institut, Universität Heidelberg, 69120 Heidelberg, Germany
e-mail: peter.meusburger@geog.uni-heidelberg.de

M. Heffernan
School of Geography, University of Nottingham, Nottingham NG7 2RD, UK
e-mail: mike.heffernan@nottingham.ac.uk

E. Wunder
Geographisches Institut, Universität Heidelberg, 69120 Heidelberg, Germany
e-mail: edgar.wunder@geog.uni-heidelberg.de

P. Meusburger et al. (eds.), *Cultural Memories*, Knowledge and Space 4,
DOI 10.1007/978-90-481-8945-8_1, © Springer Science+Business Media B.V. 2011

nonwritten ways in which intergenerational individual and collective memories have been articulated.

The project has been a profoundly interdisciplinary endeavor, though one in which space, place, landscape, and geography have loomed large. As French sociologist Maurice Halbwachs (1950/1980) observed over a half a century ago, collective memory "unfolds in a spatial framework" (p. 140) and is explicable only by interrogating how the past is "preserved in our physical surroundings" (p. 140). He was referring to the built environment as a repository of conscious and unconscious collective memories, but his wider argument about the intrinsic spatiality of memory can be explored through the cultural and social practices, activities, and enactments that symbolically reinforce or challenge the collective memories inherent in physical landscapes, practices that frequently provide the core emotional attachments linking communities to their environments.

Text or Image?

All senses can generate and retrieve memories, and it is moot to debate whether texts have greater significance than images do in the formation of memory or vice versa (A. Assmann, 2009, pp. 179–240; J. Assmann, 1992, 1995). Although texts are often more influential in that function, analysis clearly shows that the pictorial and spatial domains have primacy in the "memory industry," political propaganda, and the manipulation of collective memory. But why are images more suitable for manipulating public perception than complex and elaborate texts? One explanation is that the ability to perceive and interpret patterns and traces such as footprints emerged much earlier in human evolution than either language or the ability to read texts (Liebenberg, 1990). In early human history survival relied on a sleuth-like ability to grasp situations; interpret spatial configurations and colors; and judge and anticipate risk from the gestures of others humans, the body language of animals, and the color of plants.

A second reason for the superiority of images when it comes to manipulating public perception is that they can simultaneously convey wider ranges of information than is possible with oral or written language, which imparts information linearly or sequentially. Although politically loaded slogans can have an effect similar to that of a visual image, a person generally takes longer to read a text (deliberate cognition) than to grasp and interpret the meaning of a symbol or image (automatic cognition). Advertising, propaganda, and the design of monuments all draw on automatic cognition, which "relies heavily and uncritically upon culturally available schemata—knowledge structures that represent objects or events and provide default assumptions about their characteristics, relationships, and entailments under conditions of incomplete information" (DiMaggio, 1997, p. 269). These schemata are representations of knowledge and at the same time are mechanisms that simplify cognition and structure information-processing.

Third, visual images can, under certain circumstances, efface and elide language and cultural barriers to allow meanings and messages to be understood across communities otherwise divided by their abilities to comprehend written texts. In other contexts, however, visual symbols such as flags, graffiti, and murals can accomplish the exact opposite, demarcating territory, laying claim to divided space, and asserting the power of certain narratives and interpretations in proscribed arenas. Such versatility leads directly to a fourth explanation of the power of images to mold public perception: They symbolically make visible that which is otherwise hidden or inexplicable. Images are particularly well suited to rendering abstract concepts such as gods, spirits, fame; or even desirable ideals, attributes, and emotions such as patriotism, heroism, bravery, strength, dignity, joy, tragedy, pathos, and pain. As Klein (2000, p. 132) states, an early meaning of memory lies "in the union of material objects and divine presence." Kokosalakis (2001) offers, a similar reminder: "Through symbols the material becomes spiritual and the spiritual becomes empirical and is communicated in visible form" (p. 15354).

A fifth reason for the preeminence of images and monuments in the shaping of collective perception is that they are arguably more open than language is to a wide variety of interpretations. They can often subtly invoke ideas, meanings, and sensibilities that would be more difficult to represent in a simple textual narrative. Some monuments come to have multiple layers of meaning and ambiguity over time, sometimes becoming the focus of deeply ironic or subversive public demonstrations that champion values diametrical to those that the monument originally embodied. An example is London's Trafalgar Square, designed in the early nineteenth century to express the unassailable permanence of Britain's imperial power. The massive British rallies held there by the Campaign for Nuclear Disarmament during the 1950s arguably helped convert the site's built environment into a landscape now firmly associated with the late twentieth-century peace movement and public protest. A spatial ordering of images makes it possible to insinuate connections, coherence, or similarities that could never remain unchallenged in texts. As Kansteiner (2002) notes, "one of the reasons for the privileged status of images in memory construction derives from their exceptional ability to close, and at times even obliterate, the gap between first-hand experience and secondary witnessing" (p. 191).

The sixth reason why the visual and the spatial occupy such a prominent place in memory resides in the power of images to address unconscious or subliminal cognitive processes; to remind one of unfulfilled wishes and barely perceived longings; and to induce or reinforce disgust, prejudice, fear, and hatred. Simplifying a complex reality to a set of simple images and symbols makes it possible at least to attempt manipulation of the individual and collective consciousness at an emotional and subconscious level. Cultural memory is, therefore, "as much a result of conscious manipulation as unconscious absorption" (Kansteiner, 2002, p. 180). According to Merikle (2000) "subliminal perception occurs whenever stimuli presented below the threshold or limen for awareness are found to influence thoughts, feelings, or actions. ... [T]he term has been applied more generally to describe any situation in which unnoticed stimuli are perceived" (p. 497). Psychological experiments involving persons under general anesthesia have shown that unconsciously perceived information can remain in the memory for a considerable time.

This finding suggests "that unconscious perception may have relatively long-lasting impact if the perceived information is personally relevant and meaningful" (Merikle & Daneman, 1998, p. 16). Reber (1993) has even argued that implicit learning is "the acquisition of knowledge that takes place largely independently of conscious attempts to learn and largely in the absence of explicit knowledge about what was acquired" (p. 5)—a position endorsed by Merikle and Daneman (1998) in several psychological experiments on implicit learning that show how people can acquire complex knowledge about the world without consciously trying to do so. Reber (1993, p. 18) also holds that these unconscious cognitive processes tend to generate beliefs that are more robust and fundamental than those stemming from explicitly cognitive processes. Drawing on experiments on implicit memory, Anderson (1983) has distinguished between "declarative knowledge," which is self-reflective and articulable, and "procedural knowledge," which guides action and decision-making but typically lies outside the scope of consciousness (see also Reber, 1993, pp. 14–17). There is now ample evidence that implicit, nonreflective, procedural, and unconscious functions are, in terms of evolution, much older, more robust, and less age-dependent than explicit, reflective, declarative, or conscious functions. Infants are able to learn about their social, cultural, familial, physical, and linguistic environments without support from conscious strategies for acquisition (Reber, 1993, p. 97; Squire, 1986). Neuroscientific research also demonstrates that optical signals are processed in different areas of the brain and that "responses in the amygdala likely provide a quick and crude, unconsciously processed, affectively charged evaluation of the environment that prepares an organism for immediate action" (Cunningham, Johnson, Gatenby, Gore, & Banaji, 2003, p. 640).

These arguments do not mean that texts are generally less important memory systems than images are but rather that texts have different qualities and different purposes than images. The visual and the spatial are, however, probably more susceptible to simple manipulation and propaganda than texts are. A monument, by its very location in a public space, becomes an element in a wider landscape of "visible ... material objects invested with authoritative credibility" (Rowlands, 1993, p. 142). It can send its original or imputed message whenever it becomes the center of attention, though this ability depends on regular reenactments. As Robert Musil famously observed, monuments often take on a strangely invisible quality if the person or event recalled no longer resonates with current cultural or political concerns (Musil, 1987). Indeed most monuments, statues, or political architecture eventually collapse into ruins or survive only as a historical, conserved legacy of an ancient era whose values and sentiments inform the present only in the most general terms.

By contrast, texts stored in libraries or archives do not possess the same public immediacy as a memorial or monument and can be neglected for decades. But they do not necessarily forfeit their importance in the long run. Moreover, printed texts normally exist in many copies, so even if destroyed or censored in one place, they will survive at other locations. Texts have generally aided the long-term conservation of a culture, as already foreseen in ancient Egypt, whose political elites were convinced that their written documents would outlast their built environment as the ultimate legacy of their civilization (A. Assmann, 1996, p. 124). Although books are more easily destroyed than a built environment is, their sheer number provides a greater measure of permanence against the ravages of time (A. Assmann, 2009, pp. 190–197; Míšková, 2005, p. 237). Indeed, writing is about more than merely recording and maintaining. Drawing on Gadamer (1960), A. Assmann (1996) notes that a text has "the miraculous capacity not only to preserve but also to generate" (p. 125) and that

> [i]n the material process of cultural transmission, [writing] has a singular status. The remainders and ruins of past lives, of buildings, of tools, the equipment of tombs—all of this is shaken and eroded by the storms of time. Written texts, however, if they can be deciphered and read, contain a pure spirit that speaks to us in an eternal presence. The art of reading and understanding written traces is like a magic art... in which space and time are suspended. In knowing how to read what is transmitted, we are partaking of and achieving the pure presence of the past. (Gadamer, 1960, p. 156; translation by A. Assmann, 1996, p. 126).

A. Assmann (2009, pp. 138–142) has applied this distinction to *Funktionsgedächtnis* (functional memory) and *Speichergedächtnis* (storage memory), arguing that images serve the former; texts, the latter. Functional memory works as a form of legitimation, delegitimation, and distinction, and has a political potential to support both the official memory of those in power and the subversive countermemories of the oppressed. This form of memory provides genealogies and moral dichotomies and requires performance and representation in public space. Storage memory, by contrast, has a longer-term cultural authority, is less influenced by those in power, and has correspondingly less immediate political utility. The border between functional memory and storage memory is permeable, of course, for the latter has the potential to transform into the former or otherwise influence it. But whereas functional memory is connected to existing power relations, storage memory depends on institutions such as libraries, archives, universities, and museums, in which it is stored and conserved and from which it can ultimately be retrieved.

Power, Memory, and Public Space

The memory of events or historical figures can be kept alive through regularly repeated commemorative processes and through the creation of monuments, museums, parades, rituals, street names, graffiti, and murals. This observation is consistent with neuropsychology, which teaches that the memory for events is intertwined with the memory for places, a connection that largely explains why most mnemonic devices are related to places, spaces, or spatial signifiers. This relationship between memory, images as codified memories, and structured space was established in the ancient world through the concept of *ars memorativa*

(A. Assmann, 2009, pp. 158–162, 298–339), by which mnemonic devices are based on repetition, rhythm, reference points, and spatial ordering (Poirion & Angelo, 1999, p. 37). As Fiedler and Juslin (2006) remark, "[e]ven intelligent people are not very good at the metacognitive task of monitoring and correcting sampling processes. They... normally take their information sample for granted and hardly ever reason about whether their sample has to be corrected" (p. 13). Connerton (1989) and Wright (2006) argue instead that the social process of remembering requires a bodily practice of commemoration, often in the form of ritualized performances. Buildings, squares, statues, and street names "facilitate commemorative performance by reproducing and producing social relations" (Wright, 2006, p. 50). Reiterated performances and rituals inscribe meaning to places, which, in turn, give meaning and structure to action (Maran, 2006, p. 13). Place-bound rituals and cultural artifacts renew historical associations and knowledge systems, solidifying them in the conscious and the subconscious mind. For these reasons, what Smith (1996) calls the "territorialization of memory" (p. 448) can be detected in virtually all cultures. The renowned art of memory used by Australian aboriginal societies is rooted in a landscape continuously brought to life through geographical mnemonics (Basso, 1996). Most other societies—both traditional and modern—have regular recourse, both serious and playful, to sacred mountains where gods or ancestors are believed to reside or to have communicated with priests, to holy rivers as sources of purification, and to other venerated sites. Throughout the world, monuments, statues, and symbolic landscapes act as mnemonic devices; as the storage vessels of cultural identity and information; as educational and other communications media; as triggers for sensations, emotions, and sensibilities; and as "spatial anchors for historical traditions" (Foote, Tóth, & Árvay, 2000, p. 305).

But memory is always elusive. Most historical narratives are provisional: continually reshaped by new experiences and new knowledge and positioned within shifting centers and asymmetries of power. Narratives are contingent and depend on particular cultural systems of meaning that vary in space and time. As Saler (1998) has shown, provisional historical narrative can be deeply discomforting, and most political regimes always seek to stabilize these accounts: "essentialist narratives are ... highly effective politically: they are clear, unambiguous, capable of galvanizing emotional commitments and stimulating action in ways that provisional narratives often cannot" (p. 594). When new historical research endangers a predominant narrative, power elites frequently seek to counteract these developments by fixing memories associated with the previously accepted versions of events. Vested interests go to great lengths to advance their preferred version of history for future generations. Places of remembrance are, in effect, mnemonic schemes for immobilizing the past in fixed sequences (Hutton, 2000, p. 538). Monuments of granite or marble are in themselves deeply suggestive of continuity or eternity. Symbolizing a sense of immutability and a closure of history, they are prime anchors in the political manipulation of history and the invention or reinvention of cultural traditions (see, for example, Azaryahu & Kellerman, 1999; Hobsbawm & Ranger, 1983).

Because space is not homogeneous in its functions and representational meanings, and because spatial ordering and spatial arrangements inevitably imply hierarchies, political regimes and elites seek to control the distribution of emblematic images in public space. Some places are more visible, prestigious, frequented, or symbolically significant than others. To be effective, mnemonic devices need to be specifically designed and deliberately located to channel public attention to certain events and interpretations and, crucially, to prevent future generations from ever even becoming aware of selected historical events. In this sense all memorials are simultaneously about remembering and forgetting. The opportunity and ability to draw public attention to specific issues, persons, objects, historical events, or places and to divert it from others is one of the most fundamental instruments of state power. Like a well-conceived theater set, a successful commemorative landscape spotlights only certain parts of the scene, leaving some actors and events obscure. Jubilee celebrations and rituals of intimidation alike are staged at prominent public venues with the aim of impressing people, achieving a collective catharsis, demonstrating the superiority of a given political idea, revealing the powerlessness of individuals or groups, and eliciting emotions favorable to those in power. After occupying Hungary in 1945, Soviet forces chose two locations for their most important monuments in Budapest, Gellért Hill (citadel) and Szabadság tér (Freedom Square). To every historically minded Hungarian, they were (and are) potent symbols of repression suffered during the Habsburg era. The flag-carrying Soviet soldier atop Gellért Hill represented the power, ideology, and self-confidence of the new communist regime and could be seen from most major vantage points across the entire city. Szabadság tér, the most prominent square in the city's fifth district, is the traditional center of political and economic power of Hungary.

The importance of controlling the imagery and symbolism of public space is the main reason why the overthrow of a dynasty or political regime or the conquest of new territory is almost invariably accompanied by the deliberate erasure of icons and symbols associated with the former system and the creation of new ones in their place. One can interpret the entire European cultural landscape in terms of these politically motivated cycles of creative destruction and renewal, a process that has involved monuments, statues, museums, and other features of the built environment. Imposition of new street and place names, demolition of monuments and landscapes, even the exhumation of the graveyards of forcibly removed or murdered communities have been part of systematic attempts to annihilate certain facts from the memory of future generations. Most totalitarian systems use anonymous mass graves to bury executed dissidents and those killed during ethnic cleansings. The dead are stripped of their names and identities, and their burial grounds are kept secret to prevent these locations from becoming memorial sites in the future. Indeed, such regimes do not even need the dead to construct their myths about undocumented histories past or present. Fascist Italy established war memorials in regions of South Tyrol (e.g., near Mals in Vinschgau and in the Eisack Valley near Bozen) to demonstrate to the members of the local population that they had been conquered in war, even though no military action had actually occurred in that region during World War I. By inscribing the surfaces of these memorials with the names of soldiers who had "died" in action, the regime sought to give credibility and authenticity to their territorial claims and to imply that the blood of Italian soldiers had been spilled in a national struggle in this location. Birthdates were omitted to prevent observers from checking the veracity of these claims. It should be noted, however, that democracies, too, have sought to cover the tracks of their deeds. It is telling that the US Congress voted in May 2004 to raze the Abu Ghraib prison in Iraq and to replace it with a new building.

Locating Memory

The impact a monument has on emotions or cognitive processes depends not only on its artistic appearance and the observer's prior knowledge but also on the symbolic prominence of its location and the environment or architectural setting in which it is embedded. The intended message of a memorial can change radically, even invert, if its environmental setting is altered, for example, by the close proximity of a more recently erected monument with a different message or by relocation of the original monument.

Designers of monuments often face the problem that the propaganda message they intend to impart is transformed over time. A striking example is the monument to the "Soviet Union's liberation of Budapest" on Szabadság tér in Budapest, directly across from the United States Embassy. The post-Communist Hungarian government officially agreed that this Soviet monument would not be removed, but it remains a source of contention within the local population and has been vandalized several times. These circumstances have necessitated the structure's enclosure within a protective fence and the occasional deployment of guards there. Needless to say, these measures undermine the original message, which is diminished further by the clear line of sight from this spot to the more recent monument honoring Imre Nagy, the leader of the 1956 Revolution, who was executed by the communist regime. Nagy, his back turned to the Soviet monument, looks toward two symbols of liberation movements, the Hungarian Parliament and Kossuth Square, where huge demonstrations in 1956 and 1989 called for more freedom and democracy and where secret police shot Hungarian demonstrators in 1956.

Relocating rather than simply destroying statues erected by despised former regimes indicates a certain tolerance of and historical distance to former adversaries. But the strategy can have unexpected consequences, changing the meaning of the first site and the new one, for they both disclose a great deal about the status that current authorities accord a monument's original message. Moving statues or museums from peripheral areas to more prestigious central locations indicates enhanced appreciation. An instructive example is the decision to move the Museum of the American Indian from its original New York headquarters at 155th and Broadway—in north Manhattan, far from the tourist trail—to a downtown address, the George Gustav Heye Center, in 1994. Ten years later it was moved again, to the epicenter of the national system of museums on the National Mall in Washington, D.C., between the Smithsonian's National Air and Space Museum and the US Capitol Building.[1]

Communicative and Cultural Memory

Jan Assmann

The past exists, if it can be said to exist at all, in a double form: as a sedimentation of relics, traces, and personal memories and as a social construction. This dual nature characterizes the personal past that is with us human beings not only as internal memory traces and external memory symbols of every sort but also as an image or narrative that we construe and carry with us as our autobiographical or episodic memory. As the French sociologist Maurice Halbwachs has shown, even our autobiographical memory is a social construction that we build up in communication with others. Arguably, it is strictly personal only in its first aspect, as a sedimentation or unstructured archive (Halbwachs, 1925/1985). As a social construction, the past conveys a kind of connective structure or diachronic identity to societies, groups, and individuals, both socially and temporally. Memory is what allows us to construe an image or narrative of the past and, by the same process, to develop an image and narrative of ourselves. This form of memory seems to be a specifically human faculty. Clearly, animals also possess a memory, but the link between memory and identity—the "autonoetic" function of memory, which provides the connective structure that characterizes both a person and a society—seems to be a specifically human characteristic based on the exclusively human faculties of symbolization and communication. A human self is a diachronic identity "built of the stuff of time" (Luckmann, 1983, p. 69). At both the collective and the personal levels, human memory brings about a synthesis of time and identity, which may be called a *diachronic identity*. It is this identity that allows human beings to orient themselves personally and collectively in terms of the future, the past, or both. Because of our memory, we are able to think in temporal horizons far beyond our birth and our death.

This connection between time, identity, and memory operates at three levels: the inner (or individual); the social, and the cultural (see Table 1). At the inner level, memory is about the human neuropsychical system, the individual's personal

J. Assmann (✉)
Department of Egyptology, Heidelberg University, 69117 Heidelberg, Germany
e-mail: Jan.Assmann@urz.uni-heidelberg.de

P. Meusburger et al. (eds.), *Cultural Memories*, Knowledge and Space 4,
DOI 10.1007/978-90-481-8945-8_2, © Springer Science+Business Media B.V. 2011

Table 1 The connection between time, identity, and memory

Level	Time	Identity	Memory
Inner	Inner, subjective time	Inner self	Individual
Social	Social time	Social self, person as carrier of social roles	Communicative
Cultural	Historical, mythical, cultural time	Cultural identity	Cultural

memory, which until the 1920s was the only form of memory to have been recognized as such. At the social level, memory is about communication and social interaction. It was Halbwachs's great discovery that human memory depends, like consciousness in general, on socialization and communication and that memory can be analyzed as a function of social life. Memory enables us humans to live in groups and communities, and living in groups and communities enables us to build a memory (Halbwachs, 1925/1985). During those same years, psychoanalysts such as Sigmund Freud (1953–1974) and Carl Gustav Jung (1970–1971) were developing theories of collective memory but still adhering to the first (the inner, personal) level, looking for collective memory in the unconscious depths of the human psyche rather than in the dynamics of social life. At the cultural level, the art historian Aby Warburg (1925/2003) seems to have been the first scholar to treat images, that is, cultural objectivations, as carriers of memory (Ginzburg, 1983). His main project was what he called the "afterlife" (*Nachleben*) of classical antiquity in Western culture, and he termed this project *Mnemosyne*, the ancient Greek term for memory and the mother of the nine Muses.

As an art historian, he specialized in what he called *Bildgedächtnis* (iconic memory), but the general approach to the reception of history as a form of cultural memory could be applied to every other domain of symbolic forms as well (Gombrich, 1981). The literary historian Ernst Robert Curtius, for example, applied it to language, inaugurating a new field of research that he termed *Toposforschung* (topos research; e.g., Curtius, 1948). Among these early theorists of cultural memory, Thomas Mann should be mentioned for his four Joseph novels (1933–1943), which are the most advanced attempt at reconstructing the cultural memory of persons living in Palestine and Egypt in the Late Bronze Age. By the same token, the novels conjure up European cultural memory and its Jewish foundations in times of antisemitism (J. Assmann, 2006b). Neither Warburg nor Mann, however, used the term cultural memory, for it did not emerge until the late 1980s. It is, therefore, only within the last 20 years that the connection between time, identity, and memory in their three dimensions of the personal, the social, and the cultural has become more and more evident.

The term *communicative memory* has been introduced in order to delineate the difference between Halbwachs's concept of collective memory and the understanding of cultural memory presented in A. Assmann and J. Assmann (1989) and J. Assmann (1988, 1992). Cultural memory is a form of collective memory in that a number of people share cultural memory and in that it conveys to them a collective (i.e., cultural) identity. Halbwachs, however, was careful to keep his concept of collective memory apart from the realm of traditions, transmissions, and transferences that I propose to subsume under cultural memory. I preserve Halbwachs's distinction by breaking his concept of collective memory down into "communicative" and "cultural" memory but insist on treating the cultural sphere, which he excluded, as another form of memory. I am, therefore, not expanding or diluting Halbwachs's concept in a direction that for him would have been unacceptable. Nor do I argue for replacing his idea of collective memory with the notion of cultural memory. Rather, I distinguish between the two forms as two different modi memorandi, or ways of remembering.

Culture as Memory

Cultural memory is an institution. It is exteriorized, objectified, and stored away in symbolic forms that, unlike the sounds of words or the appearance of gestures, are stable and situation-transcendent. They may be transferred from one situation to another and transmitted from one generation to another. Unlike communicative memory, cultural memory is disembodied. In order to function as memory, however, its symbolic forms must not only be preserved but also circulated and re-embodied in a society. The disembodied status of cultural memory is another reason why it was not recognized as a form of memory until recently. Memory, the argument runs, requires a mind. Things like the madeleine immortalized by Marcel Proust (1931/1982, pp. 46–47) or monuments, archives, libraries, anniversaries, feasts, icons, symbols, and landscapes cannot have or carry memory, for they lack a mind.

This objection, however, rests on a complete misunderstanding. Neither Proust nor Halbwachs nor anyone else who speaks or writes of collective memory has ever asserted that collective or cultural memory "exists in something that has no mind." Dishes, feasts, rites, images, texts, landscapes and other things do not "have" a memory of their own, but they may remind their beholder, may trigger that person's memory because they carry the memories that he or she has invested them with. Groups do not have a memory in the way an individual does, but they may make themselves a memory by erecting monuments and by developing a variety of cultural techniques (mnemotechniques) that support memory or promote forgetting (A. Assmann, 2006).

Memory, which people possess as beings equipped with a human mind, exists solely in constant interaction not only with other human memories but also with outward symbols. Human memory is embodied, and it requires a brain as the material carrier of its embodiment. In addition it is embedded, and it requires social and cultural frames for its embedment. *Memory* is not a metaphor for embedment but rather a metonym for physical contact between a remembering mind and a reminding object. Halbwachs acknowledged social frames only, but it seems obvious that human memory is also embedded in cultural frames, such as the landscape or townscape in which people grew up, the texts they learned, the feasts they celebrated, the churches or synagogues they frequented, the music they listened to, and especially the stories they were told and by and in which they live. This interaction between a remembering mind and a reminding object is why the realm of these things and especially the things meant as reminders (mnemonic institutions) must be included in the concept of memory.

This institutional character does not apply to what Halbwachs called collective memory and what I propose to rename *communicative memory*. Communicative memory is noninstitutional. It is not supported by any institutions of learning, transmission, or interpretation, nor is it cultivated by specialists or summoned or celebrated on special occasions. It is not formalized and stabilized by any forms of material symbolization. It lives in everyday interaction and communication. For this very reason communicative memory is of fairly limited duration.

Change in constellations and frames brings about forgetting; the durability of memories depends on the durability of social bonds and "frames." Halbwachs, in his work before 1941, does not seem to be concerned with the social interests and power structures that are active in shaping and framing individual memories. In his last work on collective memory, however, he shows a keen awareness of institution and power (Halbwachs, 1941). That book, written and published during the German occupation of Paris, deals with the transformation of Palestine into a site of Christian memory by the erection of all sorts of memorials after the adoption of Christianity as the state religion by the Roman empire. In this work Halbwachs crosses the line that he himself drew between *mémoire* and tradition and shows to what degree this kind of official memory depends on theological dogma and how much it is formed by the power structure of the church.

Time Frames

Jan Vansina, an anthropologist who worked with oral societies in Africa, devoted an important study to the form in which they represent the past (Vansina, 1985). He observed a tripartite structure. The recent past, which looms large in interactive communication, gradually recedes into the background. Information becomes increasingly scarce and vague the further one moves into the past. According to Vansina, this knowledge of affairs that are told and discussed in everyday communication has a limited depth in time, not reaching beyond three generations. A more remote past is marked by either a total gap of information or one or two names remembered only with great hesitation. For the most remote past, however, there is again a profusion of information dealing with traditions surrounding the origin of the world and the early history of the tribe. This information is not committed to everyday communication; it is highly formalized and institutionalized. It exists as narratives, songs, dances, rituals, masks, and symbols. Specialists such as narrators, bards, and mask carvers are organized in guilds and must undergo long periods of initiation, instruction, and examination. Moreover, actualization of the most remote past requires certain occasions, such the gathering of the community for some celebration or other. This actualization is what I propose to call "cultural memory."

In oral societies, as Vansina shows, the informal generational memory referring to the recent past is separated from the formal cultural memory that refers to the remote past. Because this gap shifts with the succession of generations, Vansina calls it the "floating gap" (pp. 23–24). Vansina sums up by stating that historical consciousness operates at only two levels: time of origins and recent past.

Vansina's (1985) floating gap illustrates the difference between social (communicative) and cultural frames of memory. The communicative memory contains memories of what Vansina refers to as the recent past. They are the ones that an individual shares with his or her contemporaries. They are what Halbwachs understood by collective memory and are the object of oral history, that branch of historical research drawing not on the usual written sources of historiography but exclusively on memories elicited in oral interviews. All studies in oral history confirm that, even in literate societies, living memory goes back no further than 80 years, after which point—separated by the floating gap—come the dates from schoolbooks and monuments (rather than myths of origin) (Niethammer, 1985).

Cultural memory rests on fixed points in the past. Even in cultural memory, the past is not preserved as such but rather is galvanized in symbols, for they are represented in oral myths, conveyed in writings, and performed in feasts as they continually illuminate a changing present. In the context of cultural memory, the distinction between myth and history vanishes. What counts is not the past as it is investigated and reconstructed by archaeologists and historians but only the past as it is remembered. It is the temporal horizon of cultural memory that is important. The cultural memory of the people who share it extends into the past only as far as the past can be reclaimed as "theirs." For that reason I refer to this form of historical consciousness as "memory," not just as knowledge about the past. Whereas knowledge has no form and is endlessly cumulative, memory involves forgetting. It is only by forgetting what lies outside the horizon of the relevant that it supports identity. Nietzsche (1874/1960) circumscribed this function by notions such as "plastic power" and "horizon" (p. 213), obviously intending to convey what the term *identity* is generally accepted to mean now.

Institutions, Carriers

The difference between communicative and cultural memory expresses itself also in the social dimension, in the structure of participation. The participation of a group in communicative memory is diffuse. Some people know more, some less, and the memories of the old go farther back than those of the young. However, there are no specialists in informal, communicative memory. The knowledge communicated in everyday interaction has been acquired by the participants along with language and social competence. By contrast, the participation of a group in cultural memory is always highly differentiated, especially in oral and egalitarian societies. The preservation of the group's cultural memory was originally the task of the poets. Even today, the African griots (storytellers) fulfill this function of guardians of cultural memory.

Cultural memory always has its specialists. These carriers of memory are known under a rich assortment of names, such as shamans, bards, griots, priests, teachers, artists, clerks, scholars, mandarins, rabbis, and mullahs. In oral societies, the degree of their specialization depends on the magnitude of the demands on their memory. The highest rank is accorded verbatim transmission. This task requires use of the human memory as a "data base" in a sense approaching the use of writing. A fixed text is verbally "written" into the highly specialized and trained memory of these specialists. The approach typically applies when ritual knowledge is at stake and when a ritual must strictly follow a "script," even if that script is not laid down in writing. The Rgveda is the foremost example of a codification of ritual memory rooted solely in oral tradition. The social rank of the specialists in ritual corresponds to the magnitude of this task. They are known as the Brahmins, who constitute their society's highest caste. It is even higher than the aristocratic class of warriors (*kshatriya*), to which the rulers belong. In traditional Rwanda, the full text of all 18 royal rituals had to be memorized by specialists who ranked as the highest notables of the kingdom. Error was punishable by death. Those three notables partook even in the divinity of the ruler (Borgeaud, 1988, p. 13).

Rituals are therefore the context in which the oldest systems of memorization or mnemotechniques arose, with or without the help of notation systems like knotted chords, churingas, and other forms of prewriting. It is interesting to see how differently various religions have behaved toward writing after the development of full-fledged systems for that new cultural technique. In the Indo-European traditions, from the Indian Brahmins to the Celtic Druids, writing is generally distrusted and shunned. Memory is held to be the far more trustworthy medium for handing down the religious (i.e., ritual) knowledge to later generations. The reason normally given for this preference is that too many mistakes may creep into a text by copying. The true reason, however, seems to be that writing always implies the danger of dissemination, the divulgence of a secret tradition to the profane and uninitiated. This distrust of writing was still very prominent in Plato's works (Plato, trans. 1901a, 1901b). In the semitic traditions such as those of Mesopotamia, Israel, and Egypt, on the other hand, writing is eagerly grasped as an ideal medium for codifying and transmitting the sacred traditions, especially ritual scripts and recitations.

Even where the sacred tradition *is* committed to writing, memorization plays the central role. In ancient Egypt, a typical temple library contained no more books than may be known by heart by the specialists. Clement of Alexandria gives a vivid description of such a library, including the books that formed the stock of an Egyptian temple library—all written by Thot-Hermes himself. The hierarchical structure of the priesthood, with its five different ranks, reflected the size and importance of the literature to be memorized. The priests were not expected to read and learn all of the books but to specialize in certain genres corresponding to their rank and office.

In describing a solemn procession of these priests, Clement showed both the hierarchy of the priesthood and the structure of their library (Clemens Alex., Strom. VI. Cap. IV, §§35.1–37; see G. Fowden, 1993, pp. 58–59).[1] It was the books of the *stolistes* that served as a codification of ritual memory proper, complemented by what Clement calls "education." The books of the high priest, on the other hand, are said to have contained literature on the laws, the gods, and priestly education. The library was thus divided into normative knowledge, which ranks highest; ritual knowledge, which comes as a close second; and general knowledge about astronomy, geography, poetry, biography, and medicine, all of which occupies the lowest rung in this canon of indispensable literature.

> [Forty-two], Clement summarizes, is the number of the "absolutely necessary" [*pany anankaiai*] books of Hermes. Of those, 36 are learned by heart by the priests; these books contain the entire philosophy of the Egyptians. The remaining six books are learned by the pastophoroi. They deal with medicine, that is, with anatomy, with diseases, with the bodily members and organs, with drogues [drugs], with ophthalmology and with gynaecology.
> (J. Assmann, 2001, pp. 88–89)

There is, however, yet another sense in which the participation in cultural memory may be structured in a society: that of restricted knowledge, of secrecy and esotericism. Every traditional society has areas of restricted knowledge whose boundaries are not defined merely by the different capacities of human memory and understanding but also by issues of access and initiation. In Judaism, for example, general participation is required in the Torah, which every male member of the group is supposed to know by heart. Specialized participation characterizes the world of Talmudic and medieval commentaries, codices, and Midrash, a vast body of literature that only specialists can master. Secrecy, however, shrouds the esoteric world of kabbala, to which only select adepts are admitted (and even then only after they have reached 40 years of age).

The participation structure of cultural memory has an inherent tendency to elitism; it is never strictly egalitarian. Some individuals have to prove their degree of admittance by formal exams, as in traditional China; or by the mastery of linguistic registers, as in England; or of the treasury of German quotations (*Citatenschatz des deutschen Volkes*), as in nineteenth-century Germany. Others remain systematically excluded from this "distinguished" knowledge, such as the women in ancient Greece, traditional China, and Orthodox Judaism or the lower classes in the heyday of the German educated middle class (*Bildungsbürgertum*).

As for the media of cultural memory, there is a more or less pronounced tendency toward a form of intracultural diglossia, corresponding to the distinction between one "great tradition" and several "little traditions" as proposed by Redfield (1956, passim). Until the creation of Iwrith (modern Hebrew), the Jews always lived in a situation of diglossia, for their "Great Tradition" was written in Hebrew and their everyday communication took place in vernacular languages such as Yiddish, Ladino, or the various languages of their host countries. To a similar or lesser degree, this phenomenon is typical of virtually all traditional societies, be it in the form of two different (though related) languages such as Hindu and Sanscrit or Italian and Latin or of two different linguistic varieties such as Qur'anic and vernacular Arabic or classical and modern Chinese. In modern societies this binary structure tends to diversify into additional linguistic varieties as cultural media such as film, broadcasting, and television multiply. The clear-cut binary structure of Table 2 therefore does not do full justice to the modern situation.

Table 2 Communicative and cultural memory: areas of difference

Forms, dimensions	Communicative memory	Cultural memory
Content	History in the frame of autobiographical memory, recent past	Mythical history, events in the mythical (*in illo tempore*) or historical past
Forms	Informal traditions and genres of everyday communication	High degree of formation, ceremonial communication; Rituals, feasts
Media	Living, embodied memory, communication in vernacular language	Mediated in texts, icons, dances, rituals, and performances of various kinds; "classical" or otherwise formalized language(s)
Time structure	80–100 years, a moving horizon of 3–4 interacting generations	Absolute past, mythical primordial time, "3,000 years"
Participation structure	Diffuse	Specialized carriers of memory, hierarchically structured

Transitions and transformations account for the dynamics of cultural memory. Two typical directions have a structural significance and should at least briefly be mentioned in this context. One is the transition from autobiographical and communicative memory to cultural memory. The other direction concerns, within cultural memory, the move from the rear stage to the forefront, from the periphery to the center, from latency or potentiality to manifestation or actualization and vice-versa. These shifts presuppose structural boundaries to be crossed: the boundary between embodied and mediated forms of memory, and the boundary between what I propose to call "working" and "storage memories" or "canon" and "archive" (A. Assmann, 1999, pp. 130–145). Western society is living through a period of transition from communicative to cultural memory. The main problem is how to preserve the personal memories of holocaust survivors and other eye witnesses of the catastrophes that occurred in the context of World War II and how to transform them into durable forms of cultural memory that may be transmitted to later generations. The Biblical book of Deuteronomy offers a striking parallel. The problem with which Deuteronomy is concerned is how to preserve the memory of the generation who had witnessed the Exodus from Egypt and the revelation of the Law and turn it into cultural memory that can be handed down to an infinite number of future generations of Israelites. The aim of Deuteronomy is to teach what to remember and how to remember, that is, both the lesson that must never be forgotten and the mnemotechnique that ensures its continuous transmission. Moses outlines a full-fledged mnemotechnique of individual and collective remembering (J. Assmann, 1992, pp. 215–228).

The book of Deuteronomy is the foundation text of a religion based on a covenant between one single god and a chosen people. In this new religion, memory is to play the central role. It deals with a revolutionary change of cultural memory. Normally, cultural memory is not instituted this way; it accumulates and changes in the course of centuries instead. The mnemotechnique of Deuteronomy follows and elaborates a model that belongs more to political than to cultural memory (for this distinction see A. Assmann, 2006). Political memory is highly normative, prescribing what, in the interest of forming and belonging to a political identity, must never be forgotten. Deuteronomy closely corresponds to this concept. The model it describes is based on a ritual that Esarhaddon of Assyria had introduced to ensure that the vassals of his empire remembered their allegiance. First, they had to travel to Nineveh in order to swear an oath of loyalty to Esarhaddon and his designated successor Ashurbanipal. Then, so as not to forget this oath once they had returned to their home cities, they had to perform an annual ritual to refresh their memory. This ritual was dedicated to the goddess Ishtar of Arbela.

> Water from a sarsaru-jar, she [Ishtar of Arbela] let them drink,
> a goblet of 1 Seah [about 6 l, or 1 $\frac{1}{2}$ U.S. gallons] she filled with water from the sarsaru-jar and presented it to them[,] saying:
> In your hearts you will speak thus: Ishtar, a narrow one is she! [i.e., Ishtar is only a local deity, ignorant of what is going on far off]
> Thus: You will return to your cities and will eat bread in your districts, and will forget these contractual stipulations.
> Thus: You will drink from this water and again remember and observe these contractual stipulations which I set up concerning Esarhaddon. (J. Assmann, 2006a, p. 10)

From this ritual of memory and certainly many similar ones that were to be repeated periodically, Deuteronomy develops an entire culture of remembrance and a life form that came to be understood as "religion" and then became the model for later world religions such as Christianity and Islam. This new type of religion comprises much more than just cult. It extends to every aspect of life and focuses especially on justice and morals. It does not develop from pagan cults but rather from the political system it means to supersede as a form of liberation, emancipation, and enlightenment. It therefore represents a totally new form of both religion and sociopolitical organization, which rests primarily on memory.

Again the connection between memory and society surfaces. Memory, as stated at the beginning of this chapter, enables us human beings to live in groups and communities, and living in groups and communities enables us to build a memory. This connection between memory and belonging is not only a matter of self-regulating or "autopoietic" evolution, as Halbwachs suggests. It is also a matter of political foundation or fabrication. Both remembering and belonging have normative aspects. If you want to belong, you *must* remember: *Zakhor*—remember—is the Jewish imperative (Yerushalmi, 1982).

The Assyrian mnemotechnique, too, was meant as the foundation of a political memory where memory is an obligation. If you wanted to belong to the Assyrian empire and be safe from its political violence, you had to remember the loyalty you had sworn. If you forgot, you would be punished and expelled. But in the ancient Assyrian context the memory was still purely ritual; whereas the Deuteronomic mnemotechnique relies primarily on written and oral language.

As a form of memory, ritual is based on repetition. Each performance must follow a fixed model as closely as possible in order to make the actual performance settling accounts between his two former mentors, Bergson and Durkheim. The influence of the latter is quite explicit. Halbwachs adopts Durkheim's central dictum of the social origins of thought. For Durkheim, the fundamental categories of thinking are symbols that reflect basic historically grounded "social facts," that is, the divisions and contours of a given social structure. Thus social order becomes cohesive when it acquires a taken-for-granted symbolic form in the collective consciousness. Put crudely, the otherwise intangible aspects of social division become symbolic "things." Durkheim's much celebrated concept of "collective representations"—which has been reworked in social psychology within the study of social representations (see Jodelet, 1991; Moscovici, 2000)—is, then, an attempt to understand how thinking becomes recruited into the reproduction of social order.

Something like this line of reasoning appears in Halbwachs's efforts to reposition remembering as a collective activity that is involved in the main tenets of group identity. At times, Halbwachs (e.g., 1925/1992) uses the term "collective representation" (p. 174) to elucidate some of the processes that he considers to be at work, but his analysis operates at a finer level of detail—he is concerned with particular groups rather than the social order as a whole. At the same time, Halbwachs clearly strives to offer an account of how the individual fits into this collective arrangement. Indeed, much of *The Collective Memory* (1950/1980) is spent developing an account of the relationship between social remembering and the experience of self-identity. It is in this last respect that Halbwachs engages with Bergson. As Douglas (1980) points out, much of this engagement is implicit, as with the discussion of the relationship between various conceptions of time. Douglas also contends that much of what is said constitutes a repudiation, which repeats Halbwachs's earlier break with "Bergsonist" philosophy and turn to empirical sociology. This interpretation is certainly one plausible reading of Halbwachs's work. However, as we intend to show, if one suspends the automatic link to Durkheim, a different reading is possible—one where the links between Halbwachs and Bergson become far more sympathetic and productive.

The "Social" Subject

Halbwachs's two major statements of his approach to "collective memory" are complex texts that try to address both a sociological and a psychological audience simultaneously. Rather than simply ignore the emerging experimental psychological approach to memory, of which Halbwachs was well aware, both books offer a series of arguments and distinctions that make the case for the impossibility of an "asocial" approach to remembering. Following a traditional line in the philosophy of consciousness, Halbwachs cites dreaming as a solid candidate for an activity that might be regarded as entirely removed from sociality. People dream alone, in private, outside the norms and structures of society. However, Halbwachs (1925/1992) notes that "even when they sleep people maintain the use of speech to the extent that speech is an instrument of comprehension" (p. 44). As language is fundamentally social, the appearance of language in dreams indicates that sociality is at least required in order to organize and understand the images that proliferate in the dreaming state.

Halbwachs (1925/1992) argues that language lends *form* to subjective experience, but he does not stop there. Dreaming is often considered to be a form of escape in which individuals remove themselves from the social structures of waking life—"it is one of those rare moments when we succeed in isolating ourselves completely, since our memories, especially the earliest ones, are indeed *our* memories" (p. 49). What, though, do these memories consist of? They are of a prior collectivity, such as early family life, which we humans are contrasting with that in which we now live, often because it appears to offer less constraint. This feeling arises, of course, as Halbwachs explains, from the fact that people simply are no longer bound by whatever constraints or obligations were actually there. They flee from the perceived complexity of the present to a perceived form of simplicity in the past:

> So it is that when people think they are alone, face to face with themselves, other people appear and with them the groups of which they are members. . . . Society seems to stop at the threshold of interior life. But it well knows that even then it leaves them alone in appearance—it is perhaps at the moment when the individual appears to care very little about society that he develops in himself to the fullest qualities of a social being. (pp. 49–50)

In effect, retreating into images of the past strengthens the connections between past and present milieus. People produce an expanded version of themselves as social beings by calling attention to distinctions visible only by comparing their membership across two different social milieus. Hence, the work that people do to cut themselves off from public life becomes precisely what makes them sophisticated social characters. Put slightly differently, it is not merely the form but the content of private experiences that is thoroughly social. Sociality is not grafted onto subjective experience; it is, rather, the very basis on which one's sense of individuality is structured. People are always already social beings. Halbwachs (1950/1980) returns to the matter in the face of an intervention by psychologist Charles Blondel. In the account by Halbwachs, Blondel offers a personal childhood memory of being alone, exploring an abandoned house and "suddenly falling up to my waist into a deep hole which had water at the bottom of it" (p. 37). This memory, which apparently does not require the presence of another either for its content or recollection, suggests, according to Blondel, that "we have direct contact with the past which precedes and conditions the historical reconstruction" (p. 37). Personal memory must, then, be distinct from and prior to collective memory. Halbwachs responds with a series of subtle observations. Although the young Blondel may have been alone when the recollected events occurred, was he somehow "outside" of sociality? No. He was in fact "immersed only in the current of thoughts and feelings attaching him to his family" (p. 39). These thoughts and feelings structured the very nature of the experience:

> That memory belongs to both child and adult because the child was for the first time in an
> adult situation. When he was a child, all his thoughts were at a child's level. He was used
> to judging events by the standard his parents had taught him, and his surprise and fear were
> caused by his inability to relocate these new experiences in his little world. (p. 39)

The tenor of the experience at the time, Halbwachs writes, is provided precisely by its location "outside" and in opposition to the family. Young Blondel is testing the limits of his familial bonds. The significance of the memory for the adult Blondel is that it marks a first instance of being in an "adult" situation, forced to rely on himself. However, the sense of all this experience is given by sociality—the position in relation to the family that the child is exploring. Again, what appears to be the most "personal" of experiences turns out to be thoroughly social.

Memory "of" the Group?

If an activity such as dreaming—an evidently passive, private experience—can be understood as an active, social process, this possibility merely foreshadows the way in which memory, for Halbwachs, is itself a structured activity that is fundamentally social in character. When people recollect the past, they do not passively open themselves up to some previously forgotten image, which appears to them as ready formed, but, rather, refashion the past on the basis of their current concerns and needs. As Halbwachs, (1925/1992) puts it, "in reality the past does not recur as such,... everything seems to indicate that the past is not preserved but is reconstructed on the basis of the present" (pp. 39–40). How does this reconstruction take place? In addressing this question, Halbwachs makes his most famous proposition—that reconstruction is a process of mutual elaboration between the individual who strives to recall images and the group of which he or she is a member:

> It is not sufficient, in effect, to show that individuals always use social frameworks when
> they remember.... One may say that the individual remembers by placing himself in the
> perspective of the group, but one may also affirm that the memory of the group realizes and
> manifests itself in individual memories. (p. 40)

The activity of remembering draws on the resources that become available when we put ourselves in the perspective of the group. One may, for instance, be able to draw on the recollections of others or of key events that have become inscribed in the oral or written history of the group. In so doing, the efforts toward recollection play a part in affirming the nature of the group and strengthening its bonds between present and past. It is here in the text that Halbwachs is often taken—by readers as diverse as Bartlett (1932) and Wertsch (2002)—to be making the wider claim that, given the interdependency of the individual and the group, this latter should at least be viewed as an ontological unit in its own right. In short, Halbwachs is frequently thought to be saying that groups rather than individuals actually "do" the remembering.

> Now that we have understood to what point the individual is in this respect—as in so many
> others—dependent on society, it is only natural that we consider the group in itself as having

the capacity to remember, and that we can attribute memory to the family, for example, as much as to any other collective group. (Halbwachs, 1925/1992, p. 54)

Note the precursor to Halbwachs's claim—one can attribute memory to groups, but only once the relational foundations of individuality have been revealed. Halbwachs is not inventing a new entity whose qualities and attributes are modeled on those of the individual, as Wertsch (2002) suggests. Rather, once he has repositioned individuality as a mode of sociality, he then proceeds to unpack the processes on which this sociality itself depends. Halbwachs is not, then, offering a species of sociological determinism. There is not a thing called "society" that causally determines the actions of a thing called "the individual." Rather, there is a process of relating the present to the past by means of which the various modes of social order, including that mode called individuality, emerges. "It is upon a foundation of remembrances that contemporary institutions were constructed" (Halbwachs, 1925/1992, p. 125).

The group is neither the source of memories nor an entity with the capacity to remember. Instead, Halbwachs (1925/1992) identifies a "collective frame-work" (p. 39) of activities that become embedded—or one might say, "actualized"—within the permeable boundaries established by a group. Indeed, Halbwachs (1950/1980) often prefers to talk in terms of these impersonal frameworks rather than of the groups that impose limits on their operation. Frameworks are what persist over time, lending continuity to a group, so its "reality is not exhausted in an enumerable set of individuals" (p. 118). Groups may survive or be reconstructed when even the greatest majority of their members are absent or deceased. This prospect again militates against the idea, as Bartlett (1932, pp. 296–300) comments, that it is the group itself that is in someway endowed with a miraculous capacity to remember. What matters, asserts Halbwachs (1980), is that it remains possible for a given person to locate himself or herself within the framework that lent the group coherence, irrespective of whether that group is present or currently active:

> [W]hen I speak of the individual making use of the group memory, it must be understood that this assistance does not imply the actual presence of group members. (p. 118)

What, then, is this framework? In essence, it is a series of images of the past and a set of relationships that specify how these images are to be ordered. For instance, with regard to the collective memory of families:

> [e]ach family has its proper mentality, its memories which it alone commemorates, and its secrets which are revealed only to its members. But these memories,. . . are at the same time models, examples and elements of teaching. . . When we say, "In our family we have long life spans," or "we are proud," or "we do not strive to get rich," we speak of a physical or moral quality which is supposed to be inherent in the group, and which passes from the group to its members. . . .. [T]he various elements of this type that are retained from the past provide a framework for family memory, which it tries to preserve intact, and which, so to speak, is the traditional armor of the family. (Halbwachs, 1925/1992, p. 59)

Family memory, as a form of collective memory, consists of shared images and meanings—that is, categories, qualities, evaluative criteria. Family members use them as a common framework around which individual recollections are interwoven or, rather, such recollections are systematically fashioned around these common elements, which come to act as resources (models, examples, and elements of teaching) for making sense of the present. In this way, the framework supports and reinforces the boundaries of the family—it is like a form of armor that provides support for the fragile familial bonds. Once again, it is memory that seems to be holding together groups rather than groups determining memory processes. However, the use of the framework does not cut the family off from the wider social order, for, as Halbwachs (1925/1992) states, there are wider sets of cultural "regulations" (p. 80) (normative procedures) that inevitably insinuate themselves within given family frameworks.

The Structure of Collective Frameworks

Once in place, a framework effectively governs how remembering is accomplished within a given collectivity. It does so by means of a process Halbwachs (1925/1992) calls "localization" (p. 52). Localization involves the forging of a network of relationships of meaning, such that, when a given member attempts to recollect some fact, that person becomes aware that "the thoughts of the others [that is, fellow members] have developed ramifications that can be followed, and the design of which can be understood, only on the condition that one brings all these thoughts closer together and somehow rejoins them" (p. 54). In other words, the collective framework obliges members to locate their own recollections within this network that stands prior to any given act of remembering. The network then acquires a kind of impersonal status—it cannot be said to originate from any given member. It passes as a common-sense mentality, the shared, taken-for-granted background knowledge that makes a member what he or she is.

Halbwachs (1925/1992) identifies two particular aspects of localization. The first is the tendency to summate recollections from different periods into a composite image. For instance, when trying to remember our parents, what we recall tends not to be a particular fact or episode but rather a prototypical scene, assembled from a variety of elements drawn from different moments. Recalling this scene, "we compose it anew and introduce elements borrowed from several periods which preceded or followed the scene in question" (p. 61). He argues that this summative image more effectively conveys the reality of our past than veridical recall of a particular incident: "[T]he scene as it is represented nevertheless gives, in a gripping abbreviation, the idea of a family" (p. 60). These shared summative prototypical images may be regarded as being akin to the knots that hold the network of relationships together and through which individual acts of remembering are obliged to pass.

The second aspect made out by Halbwachs (1925/1992) is the tendency to project this ordering of relationships onto the past, such that a "singularly vivid image" appears "on the screen of an obscure and unclear past" (p. 60). For example, in the case of religious collective remembering, the past that is recalled in rites and holy texts, such as the Christian gospels, is a time usually far remote from those who are engaged in recollection. Such a past may be deemed ambiguous, as potentially affording multiple sets of historical accounts. However, the collective frameworks of a given religion work around this ambiguity by building up a core unitary account that is continuously rehearsed in rites and ritualized understanding, such that otherwise evident lacunae in knowledge are pushed into the background.

> Theological thought thus projects into the past, into the origin of rites and texts, the views of that past that it has taken in succession. It reconstructs on various levels, which it tries to adjust to each other, the edifice of religious truths, as if it had worked on a single plan—the same plan that it attributes to the founders of the cult and the authors of fundamental texts. (p. 117)

In this sense, religious thought is well served precisely by keeping the past remote, outside of the direct knowledge of any given living person. By doing so, it is able to selectively extract elements that are combined into summative images and ideas, and they, in turn, are projected onto factual events or actually existing places. Halbwachs emphasizes that this projection requires some considerable work, a continuous "adjustment" (p. 117) of heterogeneous elements that, although extracted from diverse sources, are presented as though part of "the same plan" (p. 117). He also brings to mind that this practice requires a large tolerance of ambiguity. For instance, it was common in the Christian gospels of the Middle Ages to recognize two or more apparently incompatible geographical locations as nevertheless involved in the singular story of the crucifixion.

The primary mechanism involved in localization is linguistic. It is in acts of naming and classifying that individual remembrances become linked to the common framework: "[O]ne cannot in fact think about the events of one's past without discoursing upon them. But to discourse upon something means to connect within a single system of ideas our opinions as well as those of our circle" (Halbwachs, 1925/1992, p. 53). For example, when we utter the name of a sister or brother while among fellow family members, we are not using a linguistic token in a purely representational sense to call attention to some person who is absent at the time of speaking. Rather, we are locating our present utterance in a nexus of shared background understandings that delimit the place of our sibling in our kinship network, in shared summative images of her or his character, achievements, and so on. There is a prior "agreement" among members with respect to this framework, which is indexed by uttering the proper name: "[T]he first name is but a symbol of this agreement which I can experience at each instance or which I have experienced for a long time" (p. 72). The discursive aspects of the framework then act to "enlarge my consciousness" (p. 72) by opening up a rich set of meaningful relationships and prior knowledge, simply by the invocation of proper names. These relationships persist even when the contexts in which they were originally learned have fallen away. In a now unbearably poignant section of the text, Halbwachs wonders

> [w]hat would happen if all the members of my family disappeared? I would maintain for some time the habit of attributing a meaning to their first names. In fact, if a group has affected us with its influence for a period of time we become so saturated that if we find ourselves alone, we act and think as if we were still living under the pressure of the group. (p. 73)

consciousness" (p. 125), it must necessarily have its own particular duration that is completely unrelated to anything outside of itself. This separateness renders each subject a "self-enclosed consciousness" (p. 96) that is unable to demarcate one momentary state from another as it has no external criterion to draw on to do so. In Halbwachs's view this inability creates a number of real difficulties. If the subject is unable to properly differentiate states as they occur, what hope could there be that such a subject would ever be able to recall clearly defined memories? Moreover, how could two such subjects ever hope to communicate something about a common past with one another, as the problem is then simply multiplied rather than reduced? "It is difficult to understand how two individual consciousnesses could ever come into contact, how two series of equally continuous states would manage to intersect—which would be necessary if I am to be aware of the simultaneity of two changes, one occurring in myself and the other in the consciousness of someone else" (p. 95).

Of course, people can and do speak to one another about events that they jointly recollect. To argue otherwise is plainly absurd. They are able to do so by making use of commonly held categories, such as historical dates, names of places and persons, terms for types of activities and events, and so on. As Halbwachs (1980) puts it, Bergson and James are offering a model of the psychological subject that is "sealed up" in its own consciousness and, therefore, "cannot go outside" (p. 95) its own duration. If it cannot do that, then there is no way of explaining how these commonly held categories emerge, meaning not only that communication between subjects is impossible but, moreover, that it is difficult to imagine how the subject could ever turn around and reflect on its own past.

In contrast to Halbwachs's assertion, the Bergsonian subject is most definitely not sealed up inside itself. And Bergson has a comprehensive account of the emergence of common categories that is grounded in the nature of life and adaptation (see Middleton & Brown, 2005, for further discussion). Nevertheless, Halbwachs's solution to the problem of creating common frameworks is significant on its own grounds. Halbwachs (1950/1980) posits that the precondition for any kind of memory is the joint creation, by subjects, of an external form of duration that is abstracted from the flow of individual consciousness: "Individual durations are able to establish a larger and impersonal duration encompassing them all because they have themselves separated from their foundation in a collective time that provided their very substance" (p. 98). This abstract and "impersonal duration" is social in character. It is produced in and by collectivities. In this way, any "natural" division of time that one might inductively discern by observing the rhythms and cycles of the natural world becomes reformulated within a generalized social conception of time—"astronomical dates and divisions of time have been overlaid by social demarcations as to gradually disappear, nature having increasingly left to society the job of organizing duration" (p. 89). Now, as Halbwachs holds that people are always already social beings and that their very individuality is, in essence, a mode of a prior sociality, it follows that it is this collective time that forms the "substance" (p. 89) of one's personal duration. Put simply, a person's own individual duration and sense of time passing is but a modulation of the "abstract and impersonal" collective time that governs the community into which he or she has been born.

What forms might this "larger and impersonal duration" take? The most obvious is that supposed authoritative record of past events called "history." However, Halbwachs makes a clear distinction between time as it is defined by history and duration that is proper to collective memory. The historian, according to Halbwachs (1950/1980), thinks in terms of firm distinctions: "History divides the sequence of the centuries into periods, just as the content of a tragedy is divided into several acts[,]... simple demarcations fixed once and for all" (pp. 80–81). Yet, such temporal divisions are in stark contrast to everybody's daily, lived experience as members of collectivities. The world people wake to each morning usually appears fairly stable. They are simply unaware of the epochal differences being introduced by the unfolding of history. To think otherwise is to act like the "character in the farce who exclaims 'Today the Hundred Years' War begins!'" (p. 82). Human thought is marked not by "clearly etched demarcations," but, instead, by "irregular and uncertain boundaries" (p. 82). These boundaries originate from the collective frameworks in which people dwell and reflect the relationships and images that are sewn together there.

However, Halbwachs (1950/1980) notes that this perspective does not mean that our thought is ahistorical. When we members of collectivities try to recall something about our parents or grandparents, we tend to flesh out this remembrance with historical significance. History, in other words, acts as a resource for us that tends to shroud our memories: "We see radiating from and about the remembrance its historical significance" (p. 61). However, this resource is necessarily worked up within the immediate context of the collective frameworks that are available to us. It is these frameworks that are primary in relation to memory—an observation that Halbwachs famously underscored with the claim that "general history starts only when tradition ends and the social memory is fading or breaking up" (p. 78). This primacy arises because, given the inherently collective nature of our existence, our personal fates are tied to the continuity of the groups in which we dwell. The persistence of a group is, in turn, governed by its capacity to "perpetuate the feelings and images forming the substance of its own thought" (p. 86). This thought is, as we have shown, made up of a system of relationships and meanings that establishes resemblances and familiar patterns. Thus, in a sense, continuity is inbuilt within collective frameworks.

The "Implacement" of Frameworks

The inbuiltness of continuity within collective frameworks appears to depend on the collective survival of the individuals who make up the group. However, as discussed above, Halbwachs insists that the essence of the group is not constituted by enumerable individuals, but, instead, by a collective framework of shared images and meanings (localized in discourse and physiognomy).

How, then, might this framework itself persist in the absence of any living group members? This question is subtler than it appears because, as Halbwachs

(1950/1980) puts it, the very fact that the framework is collective means that it is detached from the duration of given individuals. It constitutes a kind of semidepersonalized medium in which the common concerns of the group are "not identical with the particular and transient figures traversing it" (p. 120). It is this depersonalized aspect that provides the key, as "what is impersonal is also more stable" (p. 120). Stability arises because collective frameworks, although imper- sonal, are not wholly abstract. They have a "spatial and physical dimension" (p. 124) that is found in the places and domains within which the group dwells and works. Collectivities inhabit and shape place in such a way that they leave their imprint on it:

> Our physical surroundings bear our own and others' imprints. Our homes—furniture and its arrangement, room décor—recall family and friends we see frequently within this frame- work. If we live alone, that region of space permanently surrounding us reflects not merely what distinguishes us from everyone else. Our tastes and desires evidenced in the choice and arrangement of these objects are explained in large measure by the bonds attaching us to different groups. (p. 129)

The design of personal spaces is, then, marked by the systems of value, tastes, and desires that arise from the collective frameworks in which people participate. In this way, the framework is effectively cut into a distinct spatial locality. The abstract is made concrete in one's activities. This effect makes it possible to read the character of groups and their collective frameworks from their efforts at domesticating and fashioning their local environments. Hence, it is possible to discern a social type or category from the description "Balzac provides of a family lodging or the home of a miser" or "Dickens gives of a study of a notary public" (Halbwachs, 1950/1980, p. 129).

What makes such descriptions truly compelling is the sense that the relationship between humans and their environment is not unidirectional. One intuits that what makes the miser miserly or the notary public officious is partly the nature of the places they inhabit—the tiny damp, ill-lit houses or the offices spilling over with countless files and sharpened quills. Halbwachs (1950/1980) presents this relation- ship as mutually responsive—people fashion their personal spaces, but are, in turn, shaped by the structure of place:

> The group not only transforms the space into which it has been inserted, but also yields and adapts to its physical surroundings. It becomes enclosed within the framework it has built. The group's image of its external milieu and its stable relationships with this envi- ronment becomes paramount in the idea it forms of itself, permeating every element of its consciousness, moderating and governing its evolution. (p. 130)

Place, once fashioned as such by a group, reciprocally acts on the collective. For example, the urban geography of cities, which divides space into distinct districts and communities, reinforces boundaries between groups. Similarly, the distribution of roads and forms of transport powerfully affects patterns of communication and neighborhood relationships. The image of the local environment then comes to dom- inate how group relationships are thought of. In some extreme or remote cases, Halbwachs (1950/1980) postulates, collectivities have a "social body with subdivi- sions and structure" that directly reproduces or doubles the "physical configuration of the city" that encloses them (p. 134). Hence, the impersonal aspect of a collective framework is reinforced by the sense group members have that it arises from the very environment itself and not from anything at all social, so deeply embedded does it appear to be in the very things around them: "This shows us the extent to which a whole aspect of the group imitates the passivity of inert matter" (p. 134).

Halbwachs (1950/1980) refers to this relationship between group and environment as "implacement" (p. 156). A group that dwells within a space on which it has "engraved the form" of its own collective framework is then "held firm" (p. 156) by the space, which supports and reinforces that framework to the point that it appears erroneously to be its very origin. The process of implacement acts to stabilize the collective by slowing down its common duration. To members, the group appears to exist in a seemingly timeless state where changes occur very slowly, if at all. This stability comes from the solid presence of the fashioned environment within which their collectivity is implaced. In this way, implacement is an essential support for collective remembering: "Each group cuts up space in order to compose, either definitively or in accordance with set methods, a fixed framework within which to enclose and retrieve its remembrances" (p. 157).

Objects as Markers of Relationships

It might be objected that Halbwachs goes too far in his theorizing of implacement. To what degree do the lived spaces of the group actually serve as the framework for collective remembering? More to the point, precisely *how* do the mundane features of the environment, such as objects and artifacts, "hold" the memories of the group? Common sense experience tells that objects may serve as useful prompts for acts of remembering—the proverbial knotted handkerchief or the credit card bill left near the telephone, for example. It is more difficult, though, to imagine how things themselves may be "engraved" with the "forms" of collective frameworks of memory.

Halbwachs (1950/1980) moves between at least three different accounts of how to think of this process. First of all, he posits, in line with the then emerging European phenomenology of the time, that all experience of space is primarily social—that is, space is "lived" as it is "perceived." An object is always seen to be surrounded by a penumbra of meanings and relationships. Recognition of an object as such has to do with experiencing the object in the context of these relationships— a table as something at which a meal might be taken; a cup as something that might be filled with water, tea, or wine, for example. It is, of course, possible to "divest objects of the many relationships that intrude into our thought" (p. 141), but to do so does not mean that viewers see the object "as it really is." Rather, they adopt the particular "attitude of another group, perhaps that of physicists" (p. 141). However, this latter experience of the object is no more real than that of any other group, merely differentially structured.

Next, Halbwachs (1950/1980) turns to a Durkheimian reading of objects. As "things are part of society" (p. 129), it makes sense to consider the way in which they act as symbols for particular sets of values. For example, "furniture, ornaments, pictures, utensils, and knick-knacks 'circulate' within the group: they are the topic of evaluations and comparisons, provide insights into new directions of fashion and taste, and recall for us older customs and social distinctions" (p. 129). Objects, then, are vehicles for the negotiation of social values (the classic modern rendering of this argument is to be found in Pierre Bourdieu's (1979/1986) work on taste). A piece of furniture or clothing becomes a symbolic token that is recognizable as such to all group members who are "in the know." In this way, objects carry with them a set of associations that resource remembering. The classic instance in this context is the kind of nostalgic remembrances that are evoked by encountering objects (say, sweets, toys, or clothes) from childhood or adolescence.

It is the final account, however—found in fourth chapter of *The Collective Memory*—that is most suggestive. It occurs during a discussion of "economic space." The particular problem for Halbwachs here is how financial value can be attributed to an object by a collective when there "is no relationship between an object's physical appearance and its price" (1950/1980, p. 146). Now, in order for a price to be assigned, it is necessary for a common memory of previous prices and the fluctuations to be established, to which both buyer and seller may refer. This memory of previous prices is indexically linked to the particular places where it is worked out—typically, shops and markets, but also the whole chain of sites where the goods are grown or manufactured, processed, and packaged and, furthermore, in the financial centers where companies themselves are valued and markets regulated (in whatever fashion). There are, then, established social practices grounded in particular spatial locations that take charge of economic memory, with merchants occupying the most visible position: "Merchants, then, teach and remind their customers of current prices. Buyers as such participate in the life and memory of the economic group only on entering merchant social circles or when calling to mind previous contacts" (p. 148).

How do merchants achieve this? Halbwachs (1950/1980) observes that the merchant's shop front acts "like a screen that prevents the customer's peering into those areas where prices are formulated" (p. 149). Prices may fluctuate substantially within the length of the infrastructure where they are fixed (think of the way crude oil prices feed forward in forecourt petrol station prices). But unlike the motion of prices, that of the merchant is spatially restricted, for he or she is required to stand and wait for the customer. This spatial immobility suggests to the customer that prices themselves are similarly stable. However, Halbwachs notes, "not only the merchant but at the same time the merchandise awaits customers" (p. 150). In order to sell a good, it usually must be on hand, on display, and available for immediate purchase. Now, as the goods must stay in one place, before the watchful eye of the customer, it is necessary for the seller to maintain a stable price:

> In effect, because the merchandise waits—that is, it stays in the same place—the merchant is forced to wait—that is, stick by a fixed price (at least for the duration of a single sale). The customer is actually encouraged to make a purchase on the basis of this condition, because he [*sic*] gets the impression of paying for the object at its own price, as if the price resulted

from the very nature of the object, rather than at the price determined by a complex play of
continually changing evaluations. (p. 150)

The intransigence of the object that is being sold—the fact that it rests immobile
between buyer and seller—acts to slow down the erratic process of setting prices.
That is, the whole social practice of remembering and setting prices is captured
and stabilized (even if only provisionally) by the object. If the problem is how the
memory of the buyer and the memory of the merchant—as the representative of
an entire commercial infrastructure—are coordinated, then the solution arises when
both parties are forced to organize their own memories around the intransigence of
the object by which they are forced to wait. It is this object that effectively mediates
between the parties and reflects their own experiences of prices back to them "as if"
they originated from the object itself.

We can extend this line of reasoning beyond the issue of price. Objects act
not merely as symbolic tokens on which are projected the desires and concerns of
groups, but also as mediators of relationships between people. They are markers of
social relationships. In other words, objects serve as the means of coordinating and
stabilizing social practices and the remembering activities that are threaded through
them. The fluidity of social relationships, then, borrows something of the solidity
and stability of the object.

When Halbwachs talks of collective memory being "localized" in place, what he
is advocating is not simply that there is a relationship between a sense of place and
the contents of memory, but something altogether more robust. Collective memory
is possible only when social relationships are slowed down and crystallized around
objects.

Displacement, Disposal, and Forgetting

Halbwachs (1950/1980) discussion of the inbuiltness of social memory in objects
and place has an obvious reverse side: What happens when those objects (or even
place itself) is destroyed? The answer is "displacement"—the destruction of the
material supports of collective frameworks—and it occupies a central position
in Halbwachs's thought. He claims that the collective memory can survive such
displacement by virtue of active resistance:

> Urban changes—the demolition of a home, for example—inevitably affect the habits of a
> few people, perplexing and troubling them. The blind man gropes for his favorite spot to
> await passers-by, while the stroller misses the avenue of trees where he went for a fresh
> breath of air and is saddened by the loss of this picturesque setting. Any inhabitant... who
> has many remembrances fastened to these images now obliterated forever feels a whole part
> of himself [sic] dying with these things. ... In contrast, a group... resists with all the force
> of its traditions, which have effect. It searches out and partially succeeds in recovering its
> former equilibrium amid novel circumstances. It endeavors to hold firm or reshape itself in
> a district or on a street that is no longer ready-made for it but was once its own. (p. 134)

The collective responds to displacement with more than a "mere display of its
unhappiness" (Halbwachs, 1950/1980, p. 135). It sets itself the task of remolding the

this continuous passage of individuals is a necessary feature of how frameworks are organized in relation to one another. The circulation of members between groups allows frameworks to communicate with and enrich one another. The person who participates in numerous frameworks will

> look for analogies, current notions, and the whole bundle of ideas prevalent in their period outside their group but displayed around it. It is in this way that history does not limit itself to reproducing a tale told by people contemporary with events of the past, but rather refashions it from period to period... to adapt it to the mental habits and the type of representation of the past common among contemporaries. (p. 75)

In passing between frameworks, the member imports novel ideas—the "mental habits" of other groups. This is even—or perhaps especially—the case with social figures whom Halbwachs (1925/1992) refers to as "men without a past" (p. 134). Such figures have long fascinated sociologists (see Simmel's classic 1908 work entitled "The Stranger" in Frisby & Featherstone, 1997, pp. 221–232; and Bauman, 1998 discussion of "the parvenu"). The value of this character, for Halbwachs, is that such a person acts as a kind of blank canvas on which the group may project and reflect on its own concerns. However, such "strangeness" is not merely confined to men without a past. It is, Halbwachs maintains, a common experience for us all. It typically occurs at those moments when we experience a distance between two or more groups to which we belong. For example, moments when we feel distanced from the others with whom we are sharing some experience, lost in thoughts and concerns that they are "neither aware of nor interested in" (Halbwachs, 1980, p. 42). The temptation is to consider that such moments make for an intensely personal, highly individual experience, but, for Halbwachs, what actually occurs is better understood as an especially complex social experience. We get caught between the collective frameworks of two groups—the one in which we are currently participating, and another in which the concerns that so preoccupy us were originally forged.

This experience, then, is a restatement of Halbwachs's claim that our most personal and supposedly private experiences are actually entirely social and collective in character. However, Halbwachs (1950/1980) expands this claim into a model of selfhood. We members of collectives are never outside of collective life—being alone, being with others, and passing between groups are all modes of sociality. We are then always "multiple," our selfhood consisting of a heterogeneous mixture of social elements: "in reality we are never alone. Other men [*sic*] need not be physically present, since we carry with us and in us a number of distinct persons" (p. 23). It is this fundamental multiplicity of self that is expounded in the most routinely cited and infamous passage of *The Collective Memory* (see, for example, Wertsch, 2002, p. 22): "Often we deem ourselves the originators of thoughts and ideas, feelings, and passions, actually inspired by the group. Our agreement with those about us is so complete that we vibrate in unison, ignorant of the real source of the vibrations" (Halbwachs, 1950/1980, p. 44).

The language of this passage is, admittedly, difficult to follow. The term *vibration* is sometimes used in a similar way in Bergson's work, where it denotes the manner in which the appearance of stability can mask the reality of movement and change. For instance, Bergson (1991) uses the image of a "chrysalis," which appears to be solid but nevertheless "vibrates" (p. 204) with the inner transformation of the larvae. Halbwachs (1950/1980) seems to be using the word vibration in a similar way here. As human beings, we feel that our unique and unchanging character structures our personal experiences, our thoughts and passions, whereas, in fact, they emerge by virtue of the varying currents of the social milieu in which we dwell and that rise up within us. Moreover, we mistakenly interpret our discovery that other people think in the same way as we do as further confirmation of the truth of our subjective experience:

> How often do we present, as deeply held convictions, thoughts borrowed from a newspaper, book or conversation? They respond so well to our way of seeing things that we are surprised to discover that their author is someone other than ourself. "That's just what I think about that!" We are unaware that we are but an echo. . . . How many people are critical enough to discern what they owe to others in their thinking and acknowledge to themselves how small their own contribution is? (pp. 44–45)

We fail to recognize that this miraculous agreement comes about because of our common location in a collective framework that is not of our own making. We agree because we are standing in the same place, so to speak, and have available to us the same stock of cultural resources, so we "echo" the same material. The point is that, so long as we regard the group as relatively "enclosed" on itself, this echoing effect, where each member reflects back the same ideas and concerns, will pass unnoticed as we will mistake the echo for intrinsic similarity. We focus only on the chrysalis and overlook the character of the movement. Halbwachs's use of the metaphor of "vibration" neatly captures this sense of people transmitting a signal to one another at precisely the same pitch and intensity.

The overlooking of movement is central to personal identity. We feel ourselves to be unique, coherent, relatively unchanging beings and, in so doing, forget the essential multiplicity that is derived from the set of locations we occupy across numerous collective frameworks. The more we immerse ourselves in one given framework, the easier this forgetting becomes. However, it is in the process of recollection that strangeness properly returns, that is, the gap between our sense of speaking or acting in a self-consistent manner and the awareness of the heterogeneous social currents that make us what we are. This concept of a gap in our experience of identity is crucial for a social psychology of remembering and forgetting (see also Bartlett, 1958), but, unfortunately, Halbwachs fails to expand further on it.

Summary

Despite his reputation as a theorist of how *groups* remember, Halbwachs's real contribution to the study of social memory is his comprehensive account of the structure of the collective frameworks in which recollection is situated: a project that finds voice in the work of Denise Jodelet. Halbwachs (1925/1992) describes how shared

References

Knowledge, Cultural Memory, and Politics

Peter Meusburger

Knowledge and memory are complexly related. They intricately merge and interact with each other. Just as deeply rooted memories affect how individuals perceive and assess certain kinds of information and evaluate a situation, the knowledge an individual possesses confers upon places, signs, objects, persons, and events particular symbolic meanings, which may, on specific occasions, trigger memories and emotions. The link or glue between an object (or place), its cultural meaning, and the memories it may entail is always generated by the knowledge of individuals. The emotional and cultural commitment or aversion to a place or symbol is constructed through the knowledge about the events that are connected with it. If a person has no knowledge about the cultural meaning of a given sign or object or about the history of a certain place, then this sign, object, or place cannot spark or refresh memories in that individual.

In this chapter I discuss how these memories are socially constructed and manipulated. I focus on the discrepancies and tensions between remembering and being reminded. Well-informed individuals are often stunned by the incongruities between their knowledge based on their personal experience or their own scientific research on one hand and the collective memories constructed and celebrated by hegemonic elites on the other. Because memory is not knowledge *of* the past but rather knowledge *from* the past (Margalit, 2002, p. 14), both collective and individual memories are susceptible to forgetting, distorting, forging, manipulating, and silencing. Hegemonic elites have the power to restrict countermemories; to manipulate cultural institutions, exhibitions, and media; and to control the access to archives and the distribution of monuments and rituals in public space. They therefore frequently try to elevate their subjective narratives to the level of public or "official" memories that supersede local and personal memories. Some of these publicly decreed memories are immediately replaced after the collapse of a political system; others remain stable for a long time and finally transmute into myths that need not be true in order to have the desired effects.

P. Meusburger (✉)
Geographisches Institut, Universität Heidelberg, 69120 Heidelberg, Germany
e-mail: peter.meusburger@geog.uni-heidelberg.de

P. Meusburger et al. (eds.), *Cultural Memories*, Knowledge and Space 4,
DOI 10.1007/978-90-481-8945-8_4, © Springer Science+Business Media B.V. 2011

people as possible. The second and third types are created bottom-up and encompass only a clearly defined collectivity. When certain groups of people come to power, the second and third category of memories can be transformed into the hegemonic memory represented by the first type. In some cases, such as the highly privileged top levels of former communist nomenclature or the first settler generation in Israel, the three types of collective memories may coincide or overlap, at least for a certain period of time. In other words, personal experience conforms to the stories told in the family and the narratives (ideologies) propagated by state authorities. But the increasing fragmentation of modern societies means that the second and third type of collective memories in most instances do not fully correspond to the state-ordered memories.

Paradoxically, the first type of memory, though supported by state power, frequently proves to be much more fragile and ephemeral than the other two. It may be quickly abandoned whenever a regime falls and new power asymmetries evolve. By contrast, intergenerational transfer of family memories or collective memories of ethnic or religious minorities are remarkably consistent. They are able to withstand heavy oppression and censorship and can survive for many generations no matter which regime rules. The traumata of slavery, colonialism, Gulag, Auschwitz, forced expulsions in Eastern Europe, or the Naqba (the systematic ethnic cleansing of Palestine) do not disappear with the death of the last witness.

Because almost any cultural knowledge can be used for political purposes in some way, it seems problematic to draw a line between cultural memory and political memory. Nevertheless, in the discussion about collective memories one should discriminate between two categories: the first, called cultural memory by some authors, is politically uncontested, enduring, and often based on cultural elements such as language or traditional styles of the arts and architecture. The second category is politically contested and short-lived. It is constructed or invented by hegemonic elites and connected with political ideologies and reason of state.

Collective Memories and Politics

Memory as a Component of Orientation Knowledge and Identity

The importance of collective memory as part of identity, social cohesion, communality, and solidarity makes it vital to politics. Collective memory is basic to what Scheler (1926) called *Heilswissen*, or orientation knowledge. Orientation knowledge consists of religious beliefs, ideological convictions, stereotypes, and historical myths. It bears on cognitive schemata, offers social systems a reference point, lends those systems order, and provides the emotional, spiritual, and cultural aspects that hold the social fabric together. Representatives of orientation knowledge motivate people, legitimate actions, strengthen self-assertion, and stiffen resistance to adversaries. Unlike professional competence or scientific knowledge, orientation knowledge need not be empirically proved by scientific methods. It is believed to be true by its adherents, but may be ridiculed or despised by the group's adversaries.

In traditional societies orientation knowledge is produced and taught by sorcerers, dream interpreters, oracles, and priests. Over time, the production center of orientation knowledge has shifted from the temple and its priesthood to propaganda departments, political parties, the media, and those scholars of the humanities and the social sciences who deliberately serve the interests of political power (see Olick & Robbins, 1998; Smith, 1996). Indeed, the "clustering of quasi-religious terms around collective memory" (Klein, 2000, p. 145) documents that some collective memories approach the status of religious convictions. Most of the politically deployed collective memories draw on Manichean classifications that help create asymmetries of moral standards and that legitimate domination and aggression. The dichotomy of *we* (us, our) and they (*them, their*) is equated with good and bad, civilized and barbarian, truth and lie, religion and superstition, and chosen people (holy nation) and terrorists (J. Assmann, 2003, 2004; Jewett & Lawrence, 2003). These mental classifications are used not as mere labels but as "methods for organizing perceptions, knowledge, and moral relationships" (Brown, 1993, p. 659). Once pigeon-holed in this way, the individuals, groups, organizations, or institutions so labeled are regarded as being governed not by experimental contingencies "but by maxims of conduct inherent in the categories themselves" (p. 658).

Concepts that one is predestined to fulfill God's will on earth, that one belongs to God's chosen people and has an innate superiority have been prevalent since medieval times in both European and Asian cultures (see Smith, 1996, pp. 452–453). This idealization of the self is often accompanied by a demonization or devaluation of the other. The others are homogenized into a collective having negative traits or representing a standard national or racial character. The others are viewed as being collectively responsible for their deeds. By contrast, war crimes committed by one's own nation are downplayed as being exclusively the fault of misguided individuals. If a nation is portrayed as acting in the name of God and as fighting against evil, then war crimes and atrocities are euphemized or legitimated as unavoidable means for achieving just ends. Manichean dichotomies and their entrenchment in collective memories and ideologies build the foundations of imperialism, colonialism, racism, slavery, military aggression, exploitation of minorities, and propaganda wars. Debate is often silenced through redirection of public attention to other topics. The construction of the "black legend" of Spanish atrocities in the New World became a way for English imperialists to distinguish their supposedly benign project of colonialism from the destructive one of the Spanish (Brown, 1993, p. 666).

Purveyors of orientation knowledge and key persons of the memory industry help select, stretch, and spin news. They try to shape the presentation and interpretation of history; they manipulate images (see King, 1997) and media (e.g., embedded journalists in the Iraq War), invent myths, organize rituals, fake documents, and reinterpret events. They decide on the facts that should be remembered and celebrated and those that should be forgotten. When the boundary between scholarship and the creation of myths becomes uncomfortably fuzzy, an impressive number of archaeologists, historians, and geographers is mobilized to promote nationalist ideology and deliver the "scientific" proof for claims such as "this is our land," "this is a natural border," or "we brought civilization and democracy to this underdeveloped area."

Agents of the memory industry also try to convince people which events may be compared and which should be regarded as unique. To catch public attention and generate emotion, they dramatize certain events:

> The public spectacle... constructs an issue in black and white. It makes it easy to know who the bad guys are, what is right and what is wrong, what is morally virtuous and what is morally reprehensible.... The political spectacle is considered a cultural opiate—it dulls the intellect but quickens the senses. (Lisus & Ericson, 1995, p. 12)

Because memory is unreliable, partial, allusive, fragmentary, and transient, it makes an easy target for political propaganda and manipulation. It is therefore in the interest of each party in a conflict to mold the representation of its own history and the history of the other(s), to bring certain topics to closure and keep others open, and to stabilize certain memories. The desired effect of propaganda and the asymmetry of moral standards between us and them are achievable only if some events are tabooed or kept secret. The culture of secrecy, discretion, reticence, and of not telling the whole truth equivocation are inherent in politics (for details see Minkley & Legassick, 2000). This characteristic largely explains why some states deny journalists access to certain areas of conflict, confiscate cameras used to document certain events, and destroy files. One of the most egregious mass killings of modern times, King Leopold's colonial exploitation of the Congo, which relied on slave labor on a massive scale and cost millions of lives, is largely forgotten in Belgium (Braembussche, 2002, pp. 43–44; Hochschild, 1998). This dark episode has been wiped out of collective memory for many decades because most documents relating to it were incinerated: "[I]n August 1908, shortly before the colony was officially turned over to Belgium, the Congo state records burned for eight days in a furnace of the Royal Palace.... At the same time, the Palace ordered the destruction of the state records that were in the Congo" (Braembussche, 2002, p. 45). "Seldom has a totalitarian regime gone to such lengths to destroy so thoroughly the records of its work.... Hitler and Stalin in some ways left a far larger paper trail behind them" (Hochschild, 1998, pp. 294–295).

The "Congolese Holocaust" was not revealed to a broad public until fairly recent times (Braembussche, 2002, pp. 43–44; Hochschild, 1998). However, the Royal Museum of Central Africa in Brussels, which contains one of the world's largest collections of Africana, makes no explicit reference to the Congolese mass killings:

> In order to silence the Congolese Holocaust another past has been invented, or at least amplified into an emotionally appealing myth. In this myth the civilizing and Christianizing role of Belgium in the Congo is time and again celebrated, not only in Belgian education and in Belgian textbooks, but also in the textbooks that circulated in the Congo and were written by the colonizers themselves. (Braembussche, 2002, p. 46)

Asymmetries of moral standards are reflected in the collective memories of most nations. Israel, which is preoccupied with mnemonic practices, maintains silence about its Palestinian citizens and their memories of the Naqba (Vinitzky-Seroussi,

2002, p. 49). Israel's foreign minister Lieberman even wanted to forbid public memorials of the Naqba. Another example is found in France, perhaps the "queen" of work on national memory. In that country the Algerian War was virtually nonexistent in the Gallic collective memory for many decades (Vinitzky-Seroussi, 2002).

Power Elites as Ordainers of History

The selection and interpretation of sources are always arbitrary, and memory knowledge, and interpretations of historical events are forever in flux. Nonetheless, hegemonic power elites are keen on having their narratives and representations remain unchanged and "freeze time into a crystalline image" (Remensnyder, 1996, p. 884) in order to derive legitimacy and motivation from the past (see also Azaryahu & Kellerman, 1999, p. 110). Political regimes prefer a secure and uncontested basis from which to operate and therefore try to prevent interpretive ambiguity and polyphony. Totalitarian systems in particular try to create "an eternal present" (J. Assmann, 1992, p. 75) and strive for an immutable canonization of texts and histories.

Memoropolitics (Crews, 1995), that is, power struggles over claims to truth, are as old as political power itself. Rulers, hegemonic elites, and political parties have always tried to prescribe what should be commemorated and celebrated and what should be silenced and forgotten. According to Arendt (1967, 1972a, 1972b), the deliberate falsehood and the outright lie have been used as legitimate means to achieve political ends since the beginning of recorded history. Truthfulness has never figured as a political virtue; lies, always as justifiable tools in political dealings (see Minkley & Legassick, 2000, p. 5). Prominent vehicles of memoropolitics are monuments, physical objects to which a commemorative meaning is attached. They are erected in public space in order to ingrain certain memories and historical interpretations (Remensnyder, 1996, p. 884). Another such medium is public commemoration, "a calculated strategy for stabilizing collective memories that are otherwise protean and provisional. In this respect, it draws upon the ancient art of memory. In its monuments and shrines, it locates memorable places on the landscape of memory" (Hutton, 2000, p. 537).

In the newly emerging nation-states of the eighteenth and nineteenth centuries, the meshing of power and public (collective) memory acquired new priority. Their tight intertwinement and the strategies of commemoration through which nineteenth-century European state administrations fabricated traditions to bolster the prestige and authority of the nation-state are noted, for instance, by Hobsbawn and Ranger (1983) and Hutton (2000). The process of nation-building has always been accompanied by a "purification" of culture, a homogenization of memory, an exclusion of minority languages from the school system and public administration, and a silencing of regional memories. However, scientific progress, newly released documents, resistance by minorities, and shifts in power relations perennially lead to revision or reinterpretation of historical events.

Countermemories as Resilient Alternative Narratives Under the Pressure of Hegemonic "Public" Memory

Underprivileged and suppressed minorities or losers of conflicts try to hold firm against the official political narratives by cultivating their countermemories and advocating re-interpretations of history. Recent history has frequently demonstrated that counternarratives and countermemories of individuals, families, and larger groups can defy the pressure of publicly enforced memories to a remarkable extent. They survive much longer than most power elites are ready to admit. The more a political system tries to impose a contested "official" history and collective memory on its population, the more it is that counternarratives and countermemories will survive and that jokes about the system will flourish. One of the most recent and impressive illustrations of this reality was the end of the communist regimes in Eastern Europe, a demise that gave these countries their own history back. Even 70 years of oppressive communist rulers completely controlling all media, museums, libraries, and the whole educational system; faking thousands of documents; monopolizing the distribution of memorials and rituals in public space; banning the "visible" dissidents to the gulags; and threatening opponents with the death penalty were not sufficient to create a collective memory that was accepted by more than 30% of the population. All these measures could not prevent people from developing their private memories, their own historical narratives and interpretation of events. Few people in communist countries believed the official versions of the massacre of Katyn (1940), the uprising of East German workers in 1953, the Hungarian revolution of 1956, or the Prague spring in 1968.

Citizens in communist countries became admirably adept at disrupting master narratives of the regime, reading between the lines, and interpreting weak signals. It was a matter of survival to live with two identities, one demonstrated in public and one lived and shared in private. The fact that the overwhelming majority of the population in communist countries had such divided identities and countermemories was one of the main reasons why central and eastern European communist systems, despite their military power and seemingly almighty secret services, collapsed within weeks after the development of mass public opposition in 1989. The astounding persistence of countermemories, passed on from one generation to the next, is another key reason why conflicts continually erupt in some regions, such as the Balkans, the Middle East, and Northern Ireland, It is also why native people in North America are experiencing a cultural revival after centuries of oppression and why certain cultural characteristics of African slaves have survived in Brazil for more than three centuries.

Variations of Historical Narratives and Collective Memories in Space and Time

The reasons for global-scale spatial disparities of collective memories are quite obvious. States and regions have different histories to be remembered, and language barriers and power interests may impede the spread of controversial information.

The jurisdiction of state power and, hence, the possibility of withholding information or affecting the curricula of public schools are more or less restricted to the state's territory. There is a strong relation between ideological domination and cultural representation.

But why are there spatial disparities in collective memories at the regional or local level? One reason is the multiplicity of memories that usually exists in a society, with the dominating elites supporting some of them and suppressing others. Social environments, spatial contexts, and spaces of personal experience offer different opportunities for learning processes, choice, and variation. Social environments and local power structures influence prevailing discourses and thus the validity of claims to truth and the credibility of narratives. They also assess the political correctness of arguments, molding cognitive schemata, stereotypes, personal interests, and the interpretation of events. Social environments thereby impart biased and incomplete information and fail to tell the whole story. However, the interaction between agent and social environment or milieu is never static or fixed. For individuals who are able and willing to learn, remembering is an active and constructive process rather than reproduction. In a modern information society people have the chance to gain access to new information and new interpretations, to acquire new knowledge, and to correct earlier interpretations.

Second, all societies have wide spatial disparities in educational attainment (Meusburger, 1998), foreign-language mastery, information-seeking skills, and other attributes that shape the perception, evaluation, and interpretation of new information. Third, group pressure or emotional solidarity may impinge on the definition and interpretation of events. In some areas bigotry or the dominating ideology may be so numbing, inflexible, and fanatic that irritating new information is just ignored by a certain proportion of the population. At times, even educated elites refuse to accept the progress of historical research because a revision of "official" narratives would jeopardize their power and privileges. A spatial heterogeneity of memories may also stem from the fact that "historians and citizens frequently... exercise self-censorship in order to escape the risk of being excluded, stigmatized, or punished" (Braembussche, 2002, p. 40). In the United States Griffin (2004) found regional divergence in cohort recall of civil rights. People had different memories of that issue, depending on the region where they lived during their adolescence. Groups of people who fought for a particular change or who were its direct beneficiaries recalled the event with greater frequency than did those for whom gradual change had less structural and psychological impact (p. 548).

Lastly, prejudice has a topological character. "For example, the feelings of... superiority in one group place members of subordinate groups *below*; feelings of alienation place others *beyond*; feelings of moral right in relation to group privileges place others *outside*; feelings of fear place others *too close*" (Brown, 1993, p. 660).

Collective memories vary not only in space but in time as well. One facet of collective memories that is affected by time is the credibility of truth claims. What was claimed to be true at the moment it was written down may no longer be regarded as true when it is read many years later. What was meant as a purposeful lie and propaganda may eventually ripen into "truth" (see also A. Assmann, 1996). An exhibition may leave a deep impression on schoolchildren; however, the same

Fig. 1 An image in the Chronicle by Johannes Stumpf (1547–1548) depicting the origin of Switzerland. It shows the leaders of the emancipation movement swearing the oath of liberty on the Rütli in a civilized setting, as suggested by the fence in the background. From *Mythos Rütli. Geschichte eines Erinnerungsortes* [The myth of the Rütli: History of a memorial site], by G. Kreis, 2004, Zurich: Orell Füssli

Fig. 2 The real landscape, with the mountains and their real silhouettes in the background, is as important as the men swearing the Rütli oath of liberty on this 1881/1888 postcard. Source: Kreis 2004

Fig. 3 Charles Giron. *Wiege der Eidgenossenschaft* [Cradle of the Swiss Confederation]. 1902. Panorama mural, 39′4¾″ × 16′4¾″ (12 × 5 m). Swiss parliament. ©Archive BBL, Berne

independence" (Kreis, 2004, p. 109).[1] This declaration stresses the unpretentious- ness of the national monument and the inspiring force of a sacred place. Only one plain Swiss flag flies over the site. It is strictly forbidden to hoist additional flags or to erect crosses or monuments on the grounds of the Rütli. The Rütli is understood today as a tract of natural, pristine wilderness, and transformation of that landscape is expressly prohibited. But what is now untouched and untouchable nature was cre- ated in 1860 by architects of the Swiss Federal Institute of Engineering after the site became official property of the Confederation.

What Is the Status of This Specific Place in the Larger Field of Cultural Memories?

Swiss cultural memory encompasses historic persons, historic events, and a com- bination of both. The places themselves can never be an object of remembrance. Indeed, the places of important past events are in many cases rather banal. They are known in German as *Tatorte*, with the stress falling on the *Tat* (the act), not the *Orte* (the places). Another term is *Schauplatz* (scene, arena, or theater), but there is often nothing to look at if no monument exists there (Mittler, 1987). Often, people are not really sure where the significant events took place. The site of the Swiss Battle of Morgarten in 1315, for example, was difficult to pinpoint. Consequently, the two cantons vying for it around 1900, Schwyz and Zug, became locked in a bitter public dispute over the question of where the event had occurred. They each asserted that it had been on their own territory, and they pressed their rival claims by erecting specific monuments to the battle.

It was during the nineteenth century that the Rütli received its status as the most central point of the Swiss nation. The site was consecrated as the national birthplace in 1891, with a jubilee celebrating 600 years of Switzerland's existence dating from the "Magna Carta" of 1291.[2] This gesture was a kind of compensation offered to the traditional Catholic conservative part of Switzerland, which lost the civil war of 1847–1848 and was subsequently subjugated by the Swiss factions that created Berne as the center of the modern and rather liberal, Protestant Switzerland. The building that houses the central institutions, which was constructed in about 1900, is not a *lieu de mémoire*, it is only a popular attraction for tourists, Swiss and non-Swiss alike.

What Does the Rütli Stand for?

To answer the question of what people take the Rütli to symbolize, it is first necessary to ponder how to go about the task. One can, of course, take the traditional route of analyzing references to it in schoolbooks, newspapers, and political speeches given on the national day. Another approach is to observe how the Rütli figures directly in celebrations and other activities on its grounds. Vastly different, even opposed, groups convene there: right-wing extremists and pacifists, army formations and family gatherings, factory staffs and retired people, and so on. The Rütli is polyvalent; it is without specific content. It is akin to a nearly empty box that is to be filled. In the 1980s Queen Elisabeth came to the famous site. In 2001 the Rütli was a destination for official state guests as well, such as the President of the Czech Republic at that time, Vaclav Havel. By the late 1990s, the Rütli had become a preferred venue among right-wing extremists, one of whose gatherings was covered by a Swiss tabloid newspaper (Fig. 4).

The Rütli has not been sought out to an equal degree over time. From the 1930s up to the 1950s, it was probably more frequented than it was before and after. In a 2001 survey 51% of the respondents reported that they had been on the Rütli, 29% of that cohort as part of a school field trip. The moving image, possibly from the 1950s, shows a school class in an open post-office bus, the children gazing at the camera. Only the caption "Trip to the Rütli" explains where they are headed, but in Switzerland most viewers can identify with the experience anyway because the Rütli is a shared place, and many of them, too, have made the trek. Every year about 70,000 people visit the small meadow. The Rütli is open to a large variety of uses: official celebrations and private demonstrations; school field trips, national pilgrimage, and international tourism (especially by Japanese, probably after they have been to Heidelberg); and declarations of military defense and pacifist convictions. But on the whole, the purposes to which the Rütli is put tend to be more right-wing than left-wing. The common feature is the intention to imbue the activities with the allure of national importance.

Fig. 4 "Disgracing the Rütli!" August 2, 2000, *Blick* (Zurich), p. 1. By the end of the 1990s, right-wing extremists had begun holding meetings on the Rütli. Source: Kreis 2004

The current openness of the Rütli derives from two ingredients: first, the openness of nationalism itself; and second, the variety of functions the Rütli has had in its long history. Under the conservative Catholic regime before the French and Helvetic Revolutions, for instance, it was used by the rather church-based local governments. In the years of revolution, this same place served the sponsors of the secular or biconfessional and centralist national State. All these manifestations give activities on the Rütli added value in the eyes of the participants and the media. What happens on the Rütli matters and is registered by the media and the nation. It is linked to the whole country; it provides Swissness (Kreis, 2010).

Like most *lieu de mémoire*, the Rütli draws its power from the media and is something of a mass phenomenon. But the place is also used by lone individuals, such as the pilgrim who makes his or her way alone to a solitary place (a chapel, a landmark, or a cave). There are testimonials strongly recommending that experience on the Rütli to the individual visitor or member of a small group. They disclose a vast narrative about going alone to experience the Rütli, encouraging others to do so, too.

From the Swiss point of view, this odd place is the center of humanity, for Europe is located at the center of the world; Switzerland, at the center of Europe; and the Rütli, at the center of Switzerland. But even the center needs a center, and it is where the three confederates gave their oath. According to myth, three springs rose to mark

Fig. 5 Myth has it that three springs spontaneously bubbled up at the place where the leaders of the Swiss emancipation movement swore their oath of liberty on the Rütli. Early nineteenth-century painting. © Kantonsarchiv Uri

that very spot immediately after the historic event: springs as origins of pure truth (Fig. 5).

All in all the Rütli is simultaneously the center and the periphery, and it benefits from this dual nature for three reasons: because it is the center, because it is the periphery, and because it is both. The Rütli myth lives from such contradictions. The first attribute, the attraction of the meadow's remoteness, does not vanish from the collective imagination, for the second attribute, easy accessibility, prevents it from disappearing. The Rütli is present in people's minds only because of its presence in the media (e.g., texts, pictures, and songs), and it is stronger in the imagination than in the real world. In other words, the image is the reality.

Another paradox is that the Rütli is far away and therefore near. It is difficult to get there and yet can be easily reached by means of the many organized boat trips specifically targeting such remote destinations. There are many pictures illustrating both realities—the distance and the accessibility by boat—in Romantic manner. In the nineteenth century the Rütli was present in every classroom of Swiss primary schools.

The Rütli enables people to easily imagine Switzerland, Swiss history, and the essence of history. The country is represented as an entity composed of and created from common will, trust, and solidarity. In a certain dimension the Rütli stands for Swiss history as well (though not completely), affording concrete examples of what Switzerland is. It performs this function as a real monument that has proven far stronger than an artificial one, as when those schoolchildren and the Swiss Society of Common Welfare spectacularly joined forces in 1859 to save this meadow from profane tourism by buying the land and offering it to the Confederation as national property. In July 1940 the grounds again showed their effectiveness as a monument when Swiss military officers assembled there in an initially clandestine and later publicly well-known meeting to demonstrate the will to defend the country against its totalitarian neighbors. As for the essence of history itself, the Rütli is like a deep well, a font that both reveals its very depths and reflects the heavens above. Unsurprisingly, it is said that the ancient Celts used the meadow for their sacred heliocentric ceremonies (Vouga, 1988) and that an eremite was once lived there in medieval times.

In 2007, Micheline Calmy-Rey, President of Government in that year, delivered an official speech on the Rütli on August 1 (see Fig. 6). Embodying three special qualities as a woman, a citizen from the French-speaking part of Switzerland, and a member of the socialist party, she sparked an animated debate about a couple of questions, but the historic and present-day meaning of the Rütli itself was not the focus. The most important part of the discussion had its roots elsewhere. There was a certain need for political discussion, and the gathering at the Rütli was only the welcome occasion for it. The official speech was understood as a rebuttal to the concurrent traditional demonstration conducted by right-wing groups on the Rütli

Fig. 6 Micheline Calmy-Rey, the President of Government, giving an official speech on the Rütli meadow on August 1, 2007. She was strongly supported, especially by young women. From "1291 oder 1307 oder: Das Datum als Quelle. Zum Streit über das richtige Gründungsdatum" [1291 or 1307: Dates as sources in the dispute over the correct date of Switzerland's creation], by G. Kreis (2007)

and raised the matter of patriotism. The rally turned out to be a major success for the liberal movement. Half a year later the whole story was a core issue during the Carnival period, especially in Basel. But the complex event was reduced to two main messages. First, a clever women had defeated a clumsy man (main political antagonist Christoph Blocher). Second, a woman had wanted to show off out of highly personal ambition and had abused the place that belongs to everybody.

The Rütli allowed Swiss citizens to discuss all the issues in specific and general terms. But the questions at hand received undue attention, and the serious questions were discussed only indirectly and unconsciously. Of course, substantive topics also existed, and still do: To whom does the Rütli effectively belong? After all, it is located in the Canton of Uri but is the property of the Confederation. Who must guarantee access to the Rütli and who must therefore be paid for doing so? The meadow can be reached especially from the Cantons of Lucerne and Schwyz, both of which are supposed to protect this access with special police forces. Who is responsible for the organization, security, and costs entailed by the Rütli?[3] In 2007 two private sponsors finally financed the ceremony that took place on August 1, prompting criticism by citizens who believed that the state should finance such events. These questions are all exceedingly complicated because the Swiss political system itself is.

As a reaction against the left's success on August 1, 2007, right-wing supporters in the Canton of Uri tried to collect signatures for a bill intended to forbid national ceremonies on the Rütli on August 1. Because the Rütli lies in the tiny Canton of Uri, which has a population of only 35,000 inhabitants, the collection of 1,000 signatures is sufficient to bring the petition for legal interdiction to a general vote. Although such a proscription has since been declared unconstitutional, only the future will tell the outcome of this episode in the Rütli's endless story.

Several major questions were touched on directly or indirectly on the occasion of the Rütli ceremony on August 1, 2007. What is the nature of the power-sharing between the 26 cantons and the federal center? Does patriotism belong only to the conservative and right-wing forces? Has the left discovered the Rütli only because it wants to win the elections? Are the extremists of the right acceptable because there are extremists of the left, too? What can be said in an official speech at a national ceremony? Is it really a provocation that justifies undemocratic protest if the official speaker addressing an audience at such a holy location explicitly recognizes the contribution of foreigners to Switzerland or the importance of the European Union (EU) for Switzerland? The Rütli is a real battlefield for rhetorical clashes, but it is also a ground for real action. As might be expected, Swiss supporters of the EU have already tried to replace Switzerland's flag—a white cross with arms of equal length against a red background—by the EU's blue flag bearing twelve yellow stars. On August 1, 2008, the discussion on the nature of the Rütli celebration obviously continued, albeit less intensely than the year before. One newspaper carried a photomontage of Barak Obama, then still a US presidential candidate, addressing an audience on the Rütli—an amalgamation thus of two very famous references (see Fig. 7).

Fig. 7 A juxtaposition of two famous names: the photomontage showing US President Barak Obama as a Rütli speaker. From "Obama als 1.-August-Redner" [Obama as a speaker on August 1], by P. Hartmeyer, July 31, 2008, *Tages-Anzeige*r (Zurich), *116* (177), p. 1 (Copyright 2008 by *Tages-Anzeiger*)

All these recent debates about the Rütli confirm the highly ambiguous nature of this place. On the one hand it has the reputation of a very special site; on the other hand it is treated like a very normal place. When it comes to the celebrations on August 1, the federal government refuses to give the Rütli privileged status. On that day every village and region is considered equally important, as are the approximately 2,500 birthday celebrations in every town square around the country, in parks, in the mountains, on the shores of the lakes and the banks of the rivers—at all of Switzerland treasured places. On the occasion of the national celebration, they all become a small Rütli. On the evening of August 1, all of Switzerland is one common Rütli.

Postscript

At the end of the Rütli celebration in 2007, a bomb buried beneath the grass exploded. The presumed perpetrator, who was arrested, had also placed explosives in several mailboxes of members of the Rütli Commission, and that in peaceful Switzerland! More than three years later, the suspect has yet to be named, and that despite Switzerland's rules of due process. People are whispering about a "man of Asian origin who had been keen on becoming a Swiss citizen, even a Swiss soldier." On August 1, 2010, the case was still pending because the Swiss secret service became involved and key files disappeared (Knellwolf, 2010). Since 2000, media coverage has focused each year on the question of whether the Rütli has been disgraced, and 2010 was no exception.

Notes

1. "Das Rütli soll bis in die entfernsten Zeiten ein reines und bescheidenes Denkmal unserer Freiheit bleiben und mit seinem Quell den Schweizer immerfort begeistern, für das Vaterland und dessen Unabhängigkeit Gut und Blut mit Freuden hinzugeben."
2. That unique event on the Rütli had a parallel in the signing of the Magna Carta, or Great Charter, on June 15, 1215, by King John on Runnymede meadow on the bank of the Thames river.
3. The overprotected ceremony of August 1, 2006, cost 1.25 million Swiss francs; that of August 1, 2007, only 300,000 Swiss francs.

References

Assmann, J., & Hölscher, T. (Eds.). (1988). *Kultur und Gedächtnis* [Culture and memory]. Frankfurt am Main: Suhrkamp.

François, E., & Schulze, H. (Eds.). (2001). *Deutsche Erinnerungsorte* [German places of memory]. Munich: Beck.

Knellwolf, T. (2010, July 31). Aktenzeichen Rütli ungelöst. *Tages-Anzeiger* (p. 4). Zürich.

Kreis, G. (1991). *Der Mythos von 1291. Zur Entstehung des schweizerischen Nationalfeiertages* [The myth of 1291: On the origin of the Swiss national holiday]. Basel: Reinhardt.

Kreis, G. (2004). *Mythos Rütli. Geschichte eines Erinnerungsortes* [The myth of the Rütli: The history behind a place of memory]. Zurich: Orell Füssli.

Kreis, G. (2007). 1291 oder 1307 oder: Das Datum als Quelle. Zum Streit über das richtige Gründungsdatum [1291 or 1307: Dates as sources in the dispute over the correct date of Switzerland's creation]. *Die Erfindung des Tells. Der Geschichtsfreund, 160*, 53–66.

Kreis, G. (2010). *Schweizerische Erinnerungsorte. Aus dem Speicher der Swissness* [Swiss places of memory: From the storehouse of Swissness]. Zurich: NZZ-Libro.

Mittler, M. (1987). *Schauplätze der Schweizer Geschichte* [Theaters of Swiss history]. Zurich: Ex Libris.

Niethammer, L. (2000). *Kollektive Identität* [Collective identity]. Reinbek bei Hamburg: Rowohlt.

Nora, P. (1984–1992). *Les lieux de mémoire* [Realms of memory] (7 vols.). Paris: Gallimard.

Nora, P. (2002). The reasons for the current upsurge in memory. *Transit–Europäische Revue, 22*. Retrieved November 15, 2010, from http://www.eurozine.com/articles/22-04-19-nora-en.html

Vouga, J.-P. (1988). *Les Helvètes au Grütli* [Helvetians on the Rütli]. Lausanne: Les Editions de l'Aire.

Sharing Space? Geography and Politics in Post-conflict Northern Ireland

Brian Graham

> [T]hey will give up anything—their wives, their money, their self-respect—before they'll give up on their past. And that makes constructing the future a little difficult.
>
> D. Park (2008, p. 256)

Whereas the concept of *lieux de mémoire* (Nora, 1984–1992) was formulated largely in the national domain, this chapter employs the example of Northern Ireland to examine the role of memory work in a society in which the state has abdicated responsibility for the meanings of the past in the present. As in other unagreed societies, it is commonly and unquestioningly assumed—not least by both the British and, though perhaps to a lesser extent, Irish governments—that the conflict in Northern Ireland can be solved through political processes and injections of public and private-sector economic capital. Indeed, the resumption of a devolved administration in Northern Ireland during 2007 was accompanied by a considerable amount of hyperbole such as the "end of history," "new beginnings," and "the end of centuries of British–Irish conflict" and the supposition, not least of the two governments and the media, that the conflict in Northern Ireland had ended.

The core thesis of this present argument, however, is that political assumptions that politics are placeless and that identity contestation can be elided stands in marked contrast to the "everyday reality" of a contested society in which possession of territory, at a variety of scales, is all-important and in which the past is constantly invoked to legitimate present narratives of belonging and place. This contrast reflects the wider issue that the political realm and, as Marston (2004) has pointed out, political geography often do not engage with cultural questions in theorizing the state and thereby fail to recognize that state processes are both symbolic and material, that they are as much about invocations of meaning and performance as about policy and legislation (Painter, 1995). I contend that the Peace Process in Northern Ireland has largely elided both the role of culture and its cognates—memory and identity—and the symbolic realm of meaning, which, ultimately, is the force that

B. Graham (✉)
School of Environmental Science, University of Ulster, BT52 1SA Coleraine, Northern Ireland
e-mail: bj.graham@ulster.ac.uk

P. Meusburger et al. (eds.), *Cultural Memories*, Knowledge and Space 4,
DOI 10.1007/978-90-481-8945-8_6, © Springer Science+Business Media B.V. 2011

validates the notion of citizenship and thus the legitimacy of any polity. The only exceptions to this generalization have occurred when investment in culture is seen as being politically expedient for parity-of-esteem reasons, the most notable example being the creation of an Ulster-Scots Agency as a Protestant/loyalist counterweight to the republican embrace of Gaelic culture.

The intractable conflict in Northern Ireland, which began (or escalated, depending on one's political perspective) in 1969, has, however, been one in which contested and contesting representations of identity stemmed from—and then reproduced—an embittered human geography of territoriality that is supported by competing memory discourses and is fundamental to the prolongation of contested identities (Shirlow & Murtagh, 2006). I maintain that the relative political invisibility of the cultural domain and a lack of understanding of its spatial underpinning is compromising and undermining the attainment of a postconflict society in Northern Ireland that might develop beyond the limitations of a power-sharing or power-splitting coalition between two antipluralist and arguably ethnocratic political parties, the Democratic Unionist Party (DUP) and Sinn Féin, with their diametrically opposed political endgames.

Insofar as it is possible to discern the DUP's ideology, linked as it is to fundamentalist Protestant religious discourse and general right-wing socioeconomic attitudes, it stands for "the achievement of a stable devolved government[, which] is but a staging post in our strategy to strengthen Northern Ireland's place within the United Kingdom and build robust democratic structures which can prevail for future generations" (DUP, 2007, p. 10). Sinn Féin, meanwhile, describes itself as "the only all-Ireland party. . . committed to achieving a 32-County democratic socialist republic and the end of British rule in Ireland" (Sinn Féin, 2007). The installation of the power-sharing administration and its First and Deputy First Leaders, Rev. Ian Paisley (formerly reviled as "Doctor No") and Martin McGuinness (Chief of Staff and then Northern Commander of the Irish Republican Army), was widely trumpeted as the shared legacy of Tony Blair, then Prime Minister of the United Kingdom (UK), and the Irish *Taoiseach* (Prime Minister), Bertie Ahern. Paisley's subsequent demise in 2008 underscores interpretations that he was a means to an end, Blair appealing to his egotistical lust for power as the only way of facilitating a deal.

If it is assumed that Northern Ireland is not merely the exercise in postmodern irony that this mandatory coalition suggests, and if its society has to negotiate a postconflict memory narrative that underpins a new present, then one requires a much more dynamic understanding of identity and its relationship to space and place and of the potential alternatives to the legacy of sectarianism and ethnic conflict that spawned both the DUP and Sinn Féin. As in the wider context of this book series entitled *Knowledge and Space*, space is conceptualized in this chapter through its social practices and relations. The functions of space relate to factors such as control of, manipulation of, and influence on activities of individuals and social systems; a means of perceiving and displaying difference; a nexus of ritual and ceremonies; the recognition, practice, and memorialization of social structures; and the built environment as a medium of communication of cultural norms, identities, memories, and values. Place (within space) is not merely physical but primarily symbolic, as in the way that built environments stabilize social life by giving material form to the intangible. In this sense, place is a meaningful segment of space, a location "imbued with meaning and power" (Cresswell, 2006, p. 3).

Both the 1998 Belfast and subsequent 2006 St. Andrews Agreements depend on a political negotiation of Northern Ireland's future that sets aside the difficult questions of contested identity. Segregation, sectarianism, and racism are largely ignored, the implicit hope of the British and Irish governments feasibly being that political agreement and consumerism will ultimately subsume such expressions of division. Hence, the negotiations surrounding political structures have been accompanied by an official rhetoric of a "shared future" and "shared space," of "moving on" to a shared, reconciled future defined by "good relations" and characterized by cultural diversity, pluralism, and the creation of "neutral" space. But space and place are never neutral. They are socially constructed and will always embody political power, values, and symbols. Moreover, they will be contested between different voices and interpreters. Not least, of course, consumer space is capitalist space with its own geography of inclusion, exclusion, and inequality.

In pursuing the idea that cultural memory is central to the recognition that any present must shape a past, the remainder of this chapter is divided into three sections. First, I explore the question of identity politics and territoriality before moving on to examine the rhetoric of a shared future and of shared space. Second, the example of the past-that-is-not-the-past is used to illustrate something of the limitations of this rhetoric. Third, I hold that the political invisibility of geographical and cultural processes—and especially memory work—is compromising and undermining the attainment of a peace process that might extend beyond the limitations of a Sinn Féin–DUP coalition of mutual interest.

Identity Politics

Physically, Northern Ireland is a remarkably small space, reaching, at its maximum, 120 km (74½ miles) east to west and 100 km (62 miles) north to south. It has, however, a conspicuously fragmented physical geography that encourages strong local identities and a noticeable propensity toward the physical exaggeration of actual distance. In 2007 it had a population of approximately 1.7 million, including a rapidly growing and now numerically significant immigrant population that has notably diversified the formerly monolithic "two traditions": Protestant loyalism and unionism versus Catholic nationalism and republicanism. The establishment of Northern Ireland in 1921 resulted from an attempt to guarantee an electoral majority for those who wished to remain in the UK, but the separation created a large minority for whom the existence of Northern Ireland violated what they believed to be the natural unity of the Irish nation. Ostensibly, this constitutional issue was resolved by the 1998 Belfast Agreement, which stipulated that Northern Ireland remain part of the UK until a majority agrees otherwise and that the Republic of Ireland repeal its constitutional claim to the "six counties." Yet although unionists, or loyalists, believe that the national question is now settled, nationalists, especially republicans, can regard both Northern Ireland and the Peace Process as interim arrangements on the road to a united Ireland. The struggle continues by other means.

I submit that there are at least four principal dimensions to the ways in which identity politics still have to be addressed in Northern Ireland. First, in the interests of forging a consociational political consensus, issues concerning responsibility for the past were deliberately left out of the 1998 Agreement, which was "fashioned so as to avoid the need for a societal narrative" (Bell, 2003, p. 1097). It contains "no mechanism for dealing with past abuses, or 'truth-telling'" (p. 1097), either at the level of the polity or in a more localized context. Despite Lundy and McGovern's (2005) contention that there is a "high degree of skepticism of formal, institutionalised 'top–down' recovery processes" (p. 86), the result is a plethora of unofficial and exclusive practices of commemoration, imprinted in the landscape by a material geography of memorialization (McDowell, 2006). Simultaneously, however, the 1998 Agreement has exacerbated other problematic elements of Northern Irish politics, most notably the reification of the hegemonic status of the two-traditions paradigm in a mandatory, bipartite coalition of interests focused on equality legislation.

Second, a significant, though unforeseen, result of the 1998 Agreement has been a "depoliticalization of society" at the "expense of the old contesting politics of national sovereignty, self-determination and independence" (Tonge, 2005, p. 7). It is matched by an escalating stress on identity and culture and, in particular, the problem of sectarianism. The attempt to deal with substate patterns of ethnosectarian antagonism through principles of parity of cultural respect and esteem has inadvertently created a legitimating vocabulary of "culture" and "cultural rights" for antagonistic expressions of separatist difference. What could be seen as an "exemption for one group [has been translated]. . . into a universal right that applied to all" (Little, 2004, p. 81). The obvious example is the "right" to communicate in a language other than English, both Irish and Ulster-Scots now having equal status so that there are "alternative languages for everyone" (p. 81) (unless, that is, one belongs to the immigrant ethnic minorities utterly invisible in the political process).

Third, although both the 1998 and 2006 Agreements tackle the political geography of Northern Ireland in terms of state jurisdiction, they fail to attend to the territoriality embedded in Northern Ireland politics and society and the ways in which identities remain firmly vested in places that are ethnically defined, often very local, or both.

Lastly, the concept of equality between the two traditions embodied in the Belfast and St. Andrews Agreements is undermined by the inability of fragmented unionism and loyalism to match the ideological certainties and confidence espoused by republicanism and particularly by Sinn Féin. Although the history of republicanism does not necessarily conform to the smooth, linear narrative often professed by the movement, it clearly has benefited more from its centrally controlled ideology and coherent infrastructure than has loyalism.

Thus, irrespective of the rhetoric of the British and Irish governments, cultural memories often remain vested in traditional principles of ethnonationalism that locate cultural belonging and citizenship in a "living space" delineated by clear boundaries and zero-sum models of space and place. Senses of belonging correspond to a geography of territoriality in which the microgeographies of segregation and struggles for territorial control exist between communities that are themselves differentiated by class, lifestyle, and gender and by internal fragmentation, particularly of unionism and loyalism, but also of nationalism and republicanism.

Accordingly, the conflict in Northern Ireland in the post-1998 Agreement era has remained inherently territorial; the ground, a key political resource. Territoriality reflects the continuing importance of place to social networks and mental and emotional bindings, and control of space is still regarded as being crucial to identity, power, and politics. It also remains a key factor in a conflictual society in general, "a symbol of political domination and political practice" (Shirlow, 2001, p. 69). The legacy of interfaces and "chill factors" and their influence on the minutiae of daily routine, travel patterns, and social networks (Shirlow, Mesev, & McMullan, 1999) still remain important. Despite some lessening of tension, identities in Northern Ireland still remain constructed around territoriality, essentially replicating ethnonationalist ideologies at the local scale (Gallaher, 2007; Shirlow & Murtagh, 2006). Since 1998, the rival territorial ideologies—most especially Sinn Féin and republicanism—have reinforced this geography by inscribing their own narratives of time, place, memory, and commemoration onto the cultural landscapes of Northern Ireland (Graham & McDowell, 2007; Graham & Whelan, 2007; McDowell, 2007). These processes have become institutionalized as inadvertent outcomes of single identity work and funding for community building capital, policies premised on the idea that meaningful alternatives to division depend, first, on building up community confidence and self-understanding (Nash, 2005). Thus, the key question remains: How can policies advocating pluralism and diversity be implemented when territoriality defines the dominant set of values within the divided communities and manifests their irreconcilable or, at best, intractable differences (Graham & Nash, 2006)?

Shared Future, Shared Space

The essential terminology used in this chapter stems from *A Shared Future: Improving Relations in Northern Ireland*, which was launched by the Community Relations Unit of the Office of the First Minister and Deputy First Minister (henceforth, OFMDFM) in January 2003 (OFMDFM, 2003). Over five-hundred written responses from groups and individuals were received during the following nine months. These responses, together with the proceedings of a conference that took place in January 2004 to discuss them, later informed *The Policy and Strategic Framework for Good Relations in Northern Ireland* (OFMDFM, 2005a), which was made available in draft form in December 2004 before final revision in 2005. The keystone statement in the latter document is that Northern Ireland lacks a "culture of tolerance," culture being about "education, planning and the arts" but, intriguingly, not about memory and identity. Curious, too, is that little has been heard of this policy agenda since the establishment of the DUP–Sinn Féin Executive in early spring 2008, conceivably because of partial incompatibility with Sinn Féin's wider goal: the monolithic control of its territory—a "state within a state."

Northern Ireland is not a state per se but a devolved constituent region of the UK. However, it does have certain similarities with ethnonational states or ethnocracies elsewhere (Graham & Nash, 2006). Yiftachel and Ghanem (2004) assert that ethnocracies are driven "by a concerted collective project of exerting ethnonational control over a territory perceived as the *nation's (exclusive) homeland*" (p. 651). Similarly, Paasi (2003) points to the ways in which the interconnection of identity and territory is fundamental to dominant political orders and their mechanisms of control. Although such writers focus on the level of the state, Northern Ireland is characterized by the functioning of ethnonationalism at the substate level as competing microethnocracies attempt to carve out exclusive territories that essentially function as alternative worlds, each with its own myth of homogeneity. Whereas the hegemony of ethnocratic control is complicated by class, being most starkly apparent in working-class areas, both Sinn Féin and, less coherently, the DUP espouse antipluralist, ethnocratic ideologies.

Arguably, therefore, the idea of a shared future is a state-led and elitist initiative toward a pluralist society and stems from a political process that, inadvertently, has concretized ethnonational allegiances. One result of privileging universal group rights in the 1998 Agreement is that attributes of individual identity such as culture, nationality, and religion, which are understood to be a matter of choice in pluralist societies, are being reinforced as determining public identifiers in Northern Ireland. Moreover, when interpreted through this prism of ethnonationalism, the term *shared society* is shaded by ambiguity, for it refers equally to agreement on living apart and agreement on living together but differently. This point is illustrated, perhaps unintentionally, by the iconography illustrating *A Shared Future*. It centers on Maurice Harron's statue, *Hands across the Divide*, situated at the western end of the Craigavon Bridge, which connects Londonderry's Protestant Waterside to Derry's almost entirely Catholic Cityside. This dramatic depiction of two figures almost, but not quite, touching their outwardly stretched hands sums up the ambiguity of division in Northern Ireland. Conventionally, it is interpreted as an optimistic, if guarded, step toward reconciliation by the people of this divided city. Equally, though, it can be read as saying "this far and no further" by people who regard their differences as irreconcilable but who agree to seek a means of living together, but apart, on the state, substate, and individual levels, a means that eschews the violence of the Troubles. Nevertheless, living apart is specifically excluded by the British government, not least because of economic imperatives: "Separate but not equal is not an option. Parallel living and the provision of parallel services are unsustainable both morally and economically" (OFMDFM, 2005a, p. 15).

The terminology of shared future and shared space owes its provenance, of course, to the broader realm of New Labour rhetoric in Britain. This vocabulary has been explored extensively by Levitas (2005) who points out the ubiquity of the language of social inclusion and the need to privilege the idea of a homogenous national identity. She holds that the "double shuffle" of "governing in the interests of capital while engaging in just enough redistribution to keep [Labour's] traditional supporters on board" requires a "conceptual ambiguity" in which "ambiguous rhetoric plays a crucial part" (p. 234). When the New Labour project is transferred to Northern Ireland, the shared-future documentation follows the "constructive ambiguity" of the "key documents of the peace process," which "could be interpreted in various ways to suit the receiving audience" (Dixon, 2002, p. 736). There is a bundling together of positive words and expressions, many distinctly ambiguous and none defined: *reconciliation, tolerance, mutual trust, human rights for all, peaceful, inclusive, prosperous, stable,* and *fair.* A shared future "will be founded on partnership, equality and mutual respect as a basis of good relationships" (OFMDFM, 2005a, p. 3). The goal is "the establishment over time of a normal. . . society," which, unlike the "culture of intolerance," is defined as a "civic society in which all individuals are treated as equals, differences are resolved through dialogue in the public sphere,. . . people are treated impartially[,]" and in which for "most of the time, most people rub along in their everyday lives" (OFMDFM, 2005a, p. 7).

It may well be, however, that the apparently inclusionary, pluralist concept of a shared future can be read as being indicative of an ethnic cast of mind that precludes those who do fit or do not want to fit into the two traditions. Although their existence is recognized in the documentation, ethnic minorities and relatively recent immigrants from central and eastern Europe are almost undetectable in the rhetoric, as are the patterns of discrimination, and sometimes violence, to which they are exposed. Thus the shared-future documentation foregrounds ideas of bilateral cultural diversity, pluralism, and the creation of "public" and "safe" neutral space, neutral, that is, in the sense that it is not "two-tribe" space. As envisaged in the documentation, neutral space can be achieved by strategies that include removing the signs of territoriality (e.g., statues, flags, murals, and other visible symptoms), reclaiming city and town centers as safe and welcoming places for all, and reducing tensions at interfaces.

But space is never neutral. It will always embody values and symbols, which, moreover, will be contested between different voices and interpreters. As Mitchell (2003) has observed, landscape is

> a concretization and marker of memory. . . more than a way of seeing, more than a representation, more than ideology—though it is very deeply all of these. It [is] a substantive, material reality, a place lived, a world produced and transformed, a commingling of nature and society that is struggled over and in. (p. 790)

Not least, of course, what is envisaged in Northern Ireland is less neutral space than principles of consumer, capitalist space applied to a society that, socioeconomically, is already strikingly unequal. According to a large-scale study for the Joseph Rowntree Foundation (New Policy Institute, 2006), Northern Ireland compares unfavorably with all other UK regions on almost all measures of poverty and is in the lower half of the European Union league. Within Northern Ireland, there is a pronounced spatial disparity, with the proportion of disadvantaged people being higher in the west than in the east, except for parts of Belfast. But the idea of a shared future also elides the role of economic disadvantage in politics. Heavily underlining Levitas's (2005) warning that "[c]onceptual ambiguity. . . is less easy to disguise when it translates into policy" (p. 234), the documents identify a set of fundamental principles that underlie the objectives necessary to establish a shared society which can be defined by a culture of tolerance. There are nine of them related to sharing space, education, workplaces, and services. I want to focus, however, on the one stating society has to deal with the legacy of conflict and violence.

The Past that Is Not the Past

In the general euphoria surrounding the restoration of devolution, but also in the disquiet at the numerous and increasingly grotesque press photographs of Paisley and McGuinness grinning broadly and sharing jokes, some commentators have pointed to the obvious questions: Why did 3,700 people have to die in the Northern Ireland Troubles after 1969? And why did several generations have to endure a state of perpetual conflict and violence with the outcome being a government of formerly sworn enemies? The evidence suggests that no one can come to terms with the legacy of conflict and violence by trying to forget it ever happened, as in post-Civil War Spain with its *"pacto de olvido,"* the "pact of forgetting." Time may elapse, for as Grayling (2006) acknowledges in his forensic study on the morality of the Allied bombing of and targeting of civilians in German cities during World War II,

> [e]veryone wants to move on as quickly as possible after such immense trauma; the immediate post-war years were not a time for self-examination and a clear-eyed adjustment of accounts. Even in the much larger and more significant matter of the Holocaust, time had to pass before survivors and witnesses were able to recover enough, after a period of forgetting and silence, to address the experience and its profound meanings. (p. 207)

But the past does eventually resurface as cultural memory. Even in Spain, the pact of forgetting has broken down. On October 31, 2007, the Spanish Parliament passed the "Law of Historical Memory," which, after some 39 years of dictatorship and a further 30 years of democracy, honors Franco's Republican victims of the Civil War (1936–1939).

Presumably, therefore, Northern Ireland will have to confront its past at some point. How might it do so? And who might shape the cultural memories? Resolutely ignoring the collected work of several decades of revisionism of Ireland's essentialist narratives of identity, the shared-future documents see the role of state-funded cultural institutions—museums, libraries, and archives—as being to explore the "complexity of history" and to create a "culture of tolerance" in sports, ritual, and language. To tease out what these words might mean, it is useful to try and conceptualize the issues through the processes and practices of heritage as memory work. Heritage is about the meanings and representations placed upon the past in the present; it is part of the process of remembering through which present identities and values are continuously being negotiated or renegotiated (Graham, Ashworth, & Tunbridge, 2000; Smith, 2006). The content of heritage is commonly seen as embracing both the material, or tangible (natural landscapes, settlements, buildings, monuments, and the like), and the intangible, which is expressed in a number of ways, including oral traditions and social practices. If the core content of heritage is defined by meaning, this is something of a false distinction because no heritage value is completely tangible; even the "tangible can only be interpreted through the intangible" (Deacon, 2004, p. 311). The shared-future documentation in Northern Ireland displays very little understanding of the legacy of the past or of heritage as a discursive practice. There are multiple dimensions to this lack of understanding, but three, in particular, are worth emphasis.

First, preservation in itself is a way of sacralizing place through its reconstitution as material heritage. An example is what has been proposed for part of the former Maze prison site, also known as Long Kesh, where paramilitary prisoners were held during the Troubles. (Prisoner release, completed in 2000, was one of the most contentious dimensions of the 1998 Belfast Agreement.) The idea is to create an International Centre of Conflict Transformation sited in key preserved structures of the former prison complex, including the hospital where nine republican hunger strikers died in 1981. These buildings are stripped and empty, whereas the *factual information* advanced by the International Centre of Conflict Transformation would "be inclusive" and should not "be perceived as being the exclusive view of any one section of society" (OFMDFM, 2005b, p. 17). But taking this interpretation is to misunderstand the idea of heritage as meaning. In zero-sum circumstances heritage sites like the Maze cannot be read as neutral arbiters of the past; inevitably, they form part of the struggle to achieve the hegemony of one particular memory discourse at the expense of others (Graham & McDowell, 2007).

Second, since 1998, the studied refusal of the state to address the commemoration of the Troubles (in the interests of attaining a political settlement) has resulted in it essentially surrendering this high ground to the paramilitaries and their political parties. Whether these actors are perpetrators, protagonists, or combatants, republicans in particular have seized the commemorative landscape, erecting fixed and permanent memorials to their partial, selective, ethnonationalist narratives that integrate the Troubles into a linear discourse of the struggle of an oppressed people against the state. For both republicans and loyalists, the ideological and discursive domains of public space have become manifested in chauvinistic commemorative landscapes that help mark and bound space and reinforce territoriality. These landscapes are also, incidentally, an important tourist attraction for the new Northern Ireland. Conversely, the state's own dead are commemorated either in closed institutional space (as with the Royal Ulster Constabulary memorial located within the grounds of the Police Service of Northern Ireland headquarters in East Belfast) or indeed elsewhere altogether (as at the National Memorial Arboretum in Shropshire, England, where the military dead and, somewhat bizarrely, personnel of the Northern Ireland Prison Service are commemorated). The state portrays itself as an "honest broker" between the two warring tribes rather than an active participant in the "war." Accordingly, overt and public memorialization of the Security Forces' dead is not seen as being in its own best interests. Ignored in this interplay of the combatants' priorities, the civilian noncombatant dead are memorialized sporadically and largely privately. The public monuments tend to call attention to those incidents that caused multiple deaths rather than single, sectarian murders.

Third, there is thus a hierarchy of victimhood and the moral approbation that goes with it in commemoration and a parallel process of obliteration and forgetting of the less valuable dead. The dissonant narratives that the state sought to avoid have been written perforce, and they point, at best, to accepting another party's right to be different while using commemoration as one means of continuing the conflict by other means. The meanings attached to the past have thus been given a materiality that cannot be easily ignored and will have to be integrated into the narratives for a new present. The British government has set up an independent entity, the Consultative Group, under the cochairmanship of Lord Robin Eames and Denis Bradley on the legacy of the past and how it might be reconciled with a shared future. Its report was published in 2009 (Consultative Group on the Past, 2009) but was rejected by all political parties in Northern Ireland and by the British Government. The issue of how to deal with the past remains unresolved.

Toward Sharing Space?

The academic conceptualization of cultural memory points to its polyvalency and dispersal of meaning through a play of different scales. This quality of polyvalency means that *lieux de mémoire* are also implicated in subaltern memory (Legg, 2005) as sites of countermemory, and in the private (domestic) as well as public realm. Thus, to a significant extent, official memory exists to discipline the extent of that dispersal. It is often the case that the first acts of memorialization of an event are ephemeral—as in the act of creating instant shrines from flowers and other everyday *memoria*—but they may eventually be superseded and replaced by official constructs of memorialization. Although Legg calls for a sense of collective memory and community in which to situate individual memories, he also observes that fragmented efforts to mark an event will be taken over and, as in natural disasters, the "small voices" ignored (Simpson & Corbridge, 2006). Above all, memory is not synonymous with "truth"; it cannot be normative. Again, in contrast to the conceptualization of space through its social practices and relations, the shared-future documents regard space as being both a "normative" and a passive "container." Again, forgetting by decree or through "constructive ambiguity" does not mean that memorycide will occur.

Thus, a succession of difficulties can be identified in any attempt at summarizing the relationships between the shared-future and shared-space rhetoric in Northern Ireland and the conceptualization of research questions about cultural memory. First, cultural memory is positioned squarely in the public realm, a space of projected unity, consent, and equality. Conversely, what little is known about private space suggests that it may be very different. There is a concealment of the private statements on the past and an embarrassment about public ones, but there may also be less a sense of sharing than of separation. Second, the rhetoric lacks definition and contextualization, perhaps deliberately as a reflection of the studied ambiguity of New Labour-speak. Nevertheless, despite this studied openness to multiple interpretations, shared space is certainly conceptualized as two-tribe space in which ethnic and other minorities are elided and largely assumed as masculine space (McDowell, 2008). Thirdly, the debate is singularly ill informed. There is little or no cognizance of how social interaction occurs in space—as in the idea of defensible space. There is no understanding of the meaning of the past in the present or of the broader debate on the intangibility and materiality of heritage. Nor is there speculation on ways in which a shared space or future can be imagined and represented through heritage and other ordering principles. The shared-future documentation fails to recognize a generation of historical and geographical academic revisionism of Ireland that has created nonessentialist explanations and representations of Irish space and place. Beyond opting for "interculturalism," it does not engage with the global debate on multiculturalism as a spectrum of possibilities that shifts through time rather than being a settled state.

In sum, there seems to be an exceptionalism to the idea of a shared future that reifies the banal introspective assumptions of the former combatants about the unique importance of Northern Ireland's conflict. Not surprisingly, perhaps, this policy agenda reflects an institutionalized mindset figuring itself through the ambiguity of New Labour-speak, state-controlled and funded cultural institutions, and NGOs and academic data-collection projects with funding dependent on adherence to the state agenda (and thus raising questions of state "capture"). Indeed, the whole process is a salutary reminder of the invisibility of qualitative evidence to legislators who are willing to access academia only as a source of quantitative data upon which they can paint their own policy agendas.

The shared future and its shared space will still be contested. Essentially, what people are seeking is a means of contesting that future and space without overt conflict. In the conceptualization of *A Shared Future*, identity is seen as an individual quality linked by a "common humanity": The state must be "neutral" between competing cultural claims. But how can the state be neutral if Northern Ireland is part of a UK whose government speaks openly of oaths of allegiance to Queen and country as a condition of British citizenship ("Pupils", 2008)? It is not the first instance of dissonance between the government's concern over multiculturalism in Britain (particularly, the role of Islamic minorities) and its apparent goals for Northern Ireland, where the aim is not assimilation or homogenization but rather "a ring of diverse cultural expressions where interactions can thrive" (OFMDFM, 2005a, p. 8). If anything, this aspiration seems to imply a Canadian salad-bowl multiculturalism but offers no means of attaining it. What does seem far more applicable to Northern Ireland as a pluralist society is a pillar model that preserves an overall unity while satisfying the fissiparous tendencies of the constituent groups. In this model, society is conceived of as a set of "pillars," each self-contained and having little connection with the others. Collectively, however, all the pillars support the superstructure of the unified state, which imposes a minimal uniformity allowing each group to manage its own cultural, social, educational, political, and even economic institutions. It depends on the idea of maintaining separation and minimal contact between the groups without privileging any particular group (Ashworth, Graham, & Tunbridge, 2007).

The British government, conversely, sees such an arrangement as a form of mutual solitudes, an unacceptable expression of voluntary apartheid. But this stance raises the question of the human rights of people to make their own claims to identity. In sum, the New Labour glibness and ambiguity of the shared-future rhetoric is actually an impediment to achieving the goal of a society beyond sectarianism. As is characteristic of innumerable societies, "sharing" is never going to be more than an imperfect process. In Northern Ireland it could naturalize a model of society where "normal" class stratification replaces the current intersections of class and ethnonationalism. Capitalist space may simply replace ethnonationalist territorial space, creating different, but still profound, axes of inclusion and exclusion.

Above all, however, there is always both the resurgence of the past that is not the past and the reemergence of the key point that every present and future must have a past. As in Serbia and Croatia, the processes of democratic transition are laden not only with a sense of being caught between the past and the future but also with the problem of negotiating a state or polity in the context of criminal pasts, of the killings by some in the names of all. The current invisibility of the shared-future rhetoric within the public utterances of the devolved administration is indicative of the tensions embedded in this morass. Memory and forgetting are inextricably implicated in political processes because those processes are not normative, either. They are about emotional geographies of reconciliation, anger, and the lust for personal power. Whatever the shape of this shared future in Northern Ireland, it will require a renegotiated memory and a materiality to translate the symbolism of that memory into some concept of what citizenship might mean. There are thus a number of salient questions: Who will shape the representations of that past and its materiality through memorialization? How will they do it and what social practices are to be involved? What are their motivations and how do those motivations relate to power structures? There are also questions about incorporating previous memorializations and their materialities, the best examples being the built forms, practices, and spectacles of war commemoration (Switzer, 2007) and the unofficial, but potent, paramilitary memorializations. There are questions, too, as to the heritage potential of the past (the material artifacts of Britishness, of paramilitarism, of the older layers of British and Irish occupation and society, and of Ulster-Scots) and the various ways in which it can be co-opted, disavowed (e.g., the destruction of the British military landscape), or perpetually contested. Above all, it is understood that this recovery of memory cannot be a normative process. It is ideologically constructed within this still bitterly conflictual society.

References

Ashworth, G. J., Graham, B., & Tunbridge, J. E. (2007). *Pluralising pasts: Heritage, identity and place in multicultural societies*. London: Pluto Press.

Bell, C. (2003). Dealing with the past in Northern Ireland. *Fordham International Law Journal, 26*, 1095–1145.

Consultative Group on the Past. (2009). *Report*. Belfast: Consultative Group on the Past.

Cresswell, T. (2006). *In place/out of place*. Minneapolis, MN: University of Minnesota Press.

Deacon, H. (2004). Intangible heritage in conservation management planning: The case of Robben Island. *International Journal of Heritage Studies, 10*, 309–319.

Democratic Unionist Party (DUP). (2007). *Manifesto.* Belfast: DUP. Retrieved November 15, 2007, from http://www.dup.org/pdf/dupmanifesto.pdf

Dixon, P. (2002). Political skills or lying and manipulation? The choreography of the Northern Ireland peace process. *Political Studies, 50*, 725–741.

Féin, S. (2007). Retrieved August 16, 2007, from http://www.sinnfein.ie/introduction.

Gallaher, C. (2007). *After the peace: Loyalist paramilitaries in post-accord Northern Ireland.* Ithaca, NY: Cornell University Press.

Graham, B., Ashworth, G. J., & Tunbridge, J. E. (2000). *A geography of heritage: Power, culture and economy.* London: Arnold.

Graham, B., & McDowell, S. (2007). Meaning in the Maze: The heritage of Long Kesh. *Cultural Geographies, 14*, 343–368.

Graham, B., & Nash, C. (2006). A shared future: Territoriality, pluralism and public policy in Northern Ireland. *Political Geography, 25*, 243–278.

Graham, B., & Whelan, Y. (2007). The legacies of the dead: Commemorating the troubles in Northern Ireland. *Environment and Planning D: Society and Space, 25*, 476–495.

Grayling, A. C. (2006). *Among the dead cities: Is the targeting of civilians in war ever justified?* London: Bloomsbury.

Legg, S. (2005). Contesting and surviving memory: Space, nation and nostalgia in *Les Lieux de Mémoire. Environment and Planning D: Society and Space, 23*, 481–504.

Levitas, R. (2005). *The inclusive society? Social exclusion and new labour* (2nd ed.). Basingstoke, UK: Palgrave Macmillan.

Little, A. (2004). *Democracy and Northern Ireland: Beyond the liberal paradigm?* Basingstoke, UK: Palgrave Macmillan.

Lundy, P., & McGovern, M. (2005). *Community, "truth-telling" and conflict resolution.* Belfast: Community Relations Council.

Marston, S. (2004). Space, culture, state: Uneven developments in political geography. *Political Geography, 23*, 1–16.

McDowell, S. (2006). *Commemorating the Troubles: Unraveling the representation of the contestation of memory in Northern Ireland since 1994.* Unpublished Ph.D. thesis, University of Ulster.

McDowell, S. (2007). Armalite, the ballot box and memorialization: Sinn Féin and the state in post-conflict Northern Ireland. *The Round Table: The Commonwealth Journal of International Affairs, 96*, 725–738.

McDowell, S. (2008). Commemorating dead "men": Gendering the past and present in post-conflict Northern Ireland. *Gender, Place and Culture: A Journal of Feminist Geography, 15*, 335–354.

Mitchell, D. (2003). Cultural landscapes: Just landscapes or landscapes of justice? *Progress in Human Geography, 27*, 787–796.

Nash, C. (2005). Equity, diversity and interdependence: Cultural policy in Northern Ireland. *Antipode, 37*, 272–300.

New Policy Institute. (2006). Monitoring poverty and social exclusion in Northern Ireland. Retrieved August 14, 2007, from http://www.jrf.org.hk/knowledge/findongs/socialpolicy/1968.asp

Nora, P. (1984–1992). *Les lieux de mémoire* [Realms of memory]. 7 vols. Paris: Gallimard.

OFMDFM. (2003). *A shared future: A consultation paper on improving relations in Northern Ireland.* Belfast: OFMDFM. Retrieved November 1, 2006, from http://www.asharedfutureni.gov.uk/nwhealth.pdf

OFMDFM. (2005a). *A shared future: Policy and strategic framework for good relations in Northern Ireland.* Belfast: OFMDFM. Retrieved November 1, 2006, from http://www.asharedfutureni.gov.uk/policy-strategic.pdf

OFMDFM. (2005b). *Maze consultation panel:Final report.* Belfast: OFMDFM.

The Concept of Culture—An Analytical Instrument

As the memory of society, culture makes it possible both to remember and to forget (Luhmann, 1995, 1997, pp. 576–594). Culture can thus be described as the sum of conscious and unconscious moral concepts (Schein, 1985). But culture is also the only way people are able to challenge these moral concepts, albeit never completely (Baecker, 2010, p. 8). The key question of my approach is therefore no longer what culture is but rather what the conditions are for production and reproduction of culture and what the potential is for identification. This process-related view allows one to address the matters of practice and positioning in social, normative, spatial, and communicative contexts: The connection between knowledge, recollection (or reference to the past), identity, and cultural continuation (see Fig. 1) creates belonging, which permits the individual to say "we." Thus, the key question is how culture evolves. It becomes apparent that the concept of "culture" should be conceived of as an analytical implication, not an empirical category (Hastrup, 1989). Culture is, hence, not an institution objectively definable as determining the action and thinking of the particular bearers of culture. Culture is an analytical instrument that emerges from the observer's description. Observing that others live and think differently than people do in one's own way of life—that is, using the concept of culture in a self-referenced manner—requires meta-level abstraction, an exercise that reveals the concept's complexity and inherently process-related character.

Fig. 1 How culture evolves?
Source: Christina West

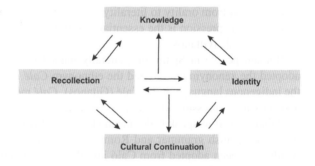

Knowledge, Recollection, and Memory as the Foundation of Cultural Identity

Identity always has two dimensions, which, paradoxically, correlate at first glance. The first is the me-identity, which consists of the individual identity and the personal identity; the second is the we-identity, or collective identity, the awareness of social belonging. The me depends on the we and finds its identity in the role it plays in the we. The we arises through its interrelation with the particular me. The we-identity is based on participation in a common implicit and explicit knowledge (Polanyi, 1985) as part of a common memory, a sharing that takes place through communication and interaction (J. Assmann, 1992, p. 139). Identity is always a social construct, and thus also always implies cultural identity and cultural continuation (Fig. 1). The development of the we-identity coincides with the emergence of distance, or distinction, from the "other" (West & Griesbeck, 2009).

Collective, Communicative, and Cultural Memory

In speaking of collective memory, Halbwachs (1877–1945) does not focus on the physiology of the brain or the heritable basis of memory. Instead, he exposes the social conditionality and the social frame of reference that are essential for the formation and preservation of the individual's memory. The individual's conscious remembering and forgetting are possible only through participation in communicative processes—recollection is always social reconstruction (see chapters by Meusburger et al. and Assmann, this volume). The abstract "truth" of a group (e.g., the Christians) must appear concretely as a happening, which is tied mostly to persons or places but also to words or forms of language and considerations (Halbwachs, 1925/1966, p. 71) in order to establish itself in the recollections of the group. Consequently, ideas, apperceptions, and all individual recollections and unexpressed thoughts and feelings have to be set in meaningful references and balanced with existent content. They are linked to the intellectual and material life of the groups to which the individual belongs. Concept, image, cognition, and idea conjoin inextricably, and a group-specific, culturally shaped type of recollection is developed. It becomes apparent in narrations, myths, and iconic forms (*Erinnerungsfiguren*; J. Assmann, 1992, p. 38), lending a sense of community and identity, and can be defined in the frames of reference of space, time, and group through a process of reconstruction (see the chapter by Assmann, this volume).

Collective memory operates in two modes: that of establishing recollections that refer to the origin of a collective; and that of compiling biographical recollections that refer to personal recollections and the basic conditions giving rise to them. In this vein, J. Assmann (this volume) divides collective memory into two categories, communicative memory and cultural memory, both of which can be a function as well as a reservoir (A. Assmann, 2004, p. 48). To facilitate analysis of the transformation from communicative memory, which is lived and typified by contemporary witnesses, to cultural memory, which is institutionally formed, supported, and archived (i.e., cultural mnemonics), two things must happen. First, one must sharpen the definition of the concepts of communicative memory and cultural memory. Second, they must be subdivided at the functional level (active mode) into individual and collective (generational) recollection of the communicative memory and into collective and cultural recollection of the cultural memory (Fig. 2). Individual recollection and cultural recollection both are linked to a passive mode that has the function of a reservoir. The individual memory is latent or unconscious: According to Proust's "episode of the madeleine," remembering is structures, too, as in case of elites who dominate them exclusively and can thus make use of them in a multiplicative way. The conditions for second-order observations and for the semantic self-description of society are thereby changing. The script and evolution of technical media are mnemonic tools that are affecting the significance of collective memory. The emphasis is not on storage capacity or authentic conservation of the past but rather on a reregulation of the balance between remembering and forgetting.

The importance of implicit and explicit knowledge and, thus, of the different types of recollection and memory in the formation and change of culture and cultural identity is demonstrated by the identity construction of the Calé (Gitanos) in Spain, most of whom are making a transition from orality to literality. Increasing literacy and education are slowly altering the kind, content, and dissemination of cultural memory and thus of Gitano cultural identity. The major anchor point of their identity construction is flamenco (see Fig. 3)—a form of expression that was

Fig. 3 Flamenco en vivo—Flamenco live. Photograph by Christina West, uwe-philips.com

originally passed down orally, that is, through direct personal interaction, producing a sense of belonging. At both the macroscopic and microscopic levels, flamenco is changing and diversifying as a result of specific social or political movements, the increasing literality of the Gitanos, and the development of new storage and diffusion media. Some forms of flamenco that have emerged have found their way into the Gitanos' cultural memory. But despite such canonization and fixation, despite the general accessibility that it has enabled and the shift of meaning it has caused, the relevance of the original flamenco—namely, the everyday affirmation and manifestation of cultural identity—partially lives on in a clan's oral communicative memory (Fig. 2).

Sinti, Roma, and Calé—From India to Europe

Punjab and Sindh in the northeast of today's Pakistan and Rajasthan in the northwest of India are the regions of origin of the Sinti, Roma, and Calé (Fig. 4). Famines, invasions, and expulsion led the Dom (or Rom), Jat, and Sindhi clans to Persia and Syria. They were known as the Luri, Koli (or Kale), and Zott, and they hired themselves out as musicians, drummers, and dancers. In the following centuries wars forced several groups to migrate westward across Armenia and the Bosporus to Greece and to fan out over all of Europe from there. However, the initial allure of their foreignness; the tales about their origins in legendary so-called Little Egypt; the acknowledgment of their musical and handcraft abilities; and their knowledge in the niche businesses of metal-processing, horse trading, and basket-making soon gave way to fear and distrust of their differentness. Members of settled society stigmatized them as atheists, invaders, vagabonds, and thieves. Persecution, banishment, enslavement, deportation, and oppression ensued. The end of serfdom and slavery in Wallachia and other parts of Europe in the mid-nineteenth century and the beginning of industrialization initiated the second major migration of the Sinti, Roma, and Calé (Fig. 5).

Sinti, Roma, Calé (or Gitanos), Manush, Kalderash, and Lovari are different groupings within the same ethnic group. They differ in the characteristics of their traditions, rites, clan structures, ways of living, laws, regional spread, and specific dialectal language variant. These distinguishing attributes account for the development of separate identities, even at the clan level, which sets the members apart from foreign tribes as well as from clans with common descent and strengthens the dependence of the members on their own group, clan, or kin. The distinguishing attributes also imply security, stability, and confidence. Although these people do not constitute a homogenous group, Germany and other European countries increasingly subsume them officially as *Roma* or *Sinti and Roma.* Such a generalized designation is controversial among the different pressure groups because the members perceive it as being equivalent to losing their identity. Present in most European countries, Sinti and Roma living as an ethnic minority on the continent today number 6–8 million and some 12 million worldwide.

The Spread of the Gitanos in Spain

The first documented reference to the Calé (1425), who had migrated across the Pyrenees to the Iberian Peninsula (Fig. 4), described them as "condes de Eyipto Menor" (the counts of Little Egypt), from which the common Spanish term *gitanos* derives. They arrived in Jaén in Andalusia almost 40 years later, on November 22, 1462. About 300,000 of the 500,000–600,000 Gitanos living in Spain today (approximately 1.4% of the Spanish population) reside in Andalusia, making up 4% of the population there (Junta de Andalucia, 2006; Unión Romaní, 2006). Most of the remaining Gitanos live in the autonomous regions: Madrid, Catalonia, and Valencia.

Most of Gitanos live as an unprivileged and marginalized ethnic minority on the fringes of society, spatially isolated in illegal shanty towns on the outskirts (*chabolas*), alongside arterial roads, under bridges, in undeveloped inner-city areas or on brownfields, between ruins, and in huge peripheral and rundown public housing of the 1950s through 1970s (*barracas verticals*). In addition to poor housing, their situation is marked by extremely high unemployment or casual employment, low life expectancy, daily discrimination, and, because of truancy, a low formal education level. Around 60% of the Gitanos are illiterate. In short, their life circumstances are precarious.

Unlike modern Spanish society, which revolves largely around economics, politics, and individual lifestyles in lieu of concepts such as family and generational cohesion, Gitano life centers on kin and family as the key forms of organization. Is clan tradition thereby a problem, and is Gitano culture a factor that leads to disadvantage? The problem is not the current social situation but rather stigmatization, which stems from a long, shared history with the *payos* (non-Gitanos) and which affects the opportunities of Gitanos in a technological society.

The Identity Construction of the Gitanos

Because the Gitanos have always been a people with an oral rather than a written tradition, their identity is not subject to any fixation in the reservoir of cultural memory in the sense meant by J. Assmann (1992). There is, then, scarcely any personal reconstructivity and no reference to the past beyond the communicative memory (Fig. 2). A Gitano inhabitant of Polígono Sur in Seville, for example, answered a question about his identity by explaining that the Gitanos are the only people who do not know about their ancestry, that they have always moved around and have never had neighbors who were able to tell them where they were from (personal communication, September 2004; my translation). Because the ancestors of the Gitanos lived nomadically and because everyday Gitano reality is always one of potential forced relocation, there is no place recognition, no bonding to given area, and, consequently, no documentation by means of accumulated material cultural assets.

Gitanos regard themselves as clearly distinguishable from the *payos*. This self-image is especially strong with respect to the importance the Gitanos attach to family membership and their fixation on the role of gender and gender identity, and their livelihoods (e.g., as itinerant traders, flamenco musicians and dancers, blacksmiths, toreros, fortune-tellers, or agricultural day laborers). It also applies in particular to their region of origin in Spain, which is synonymous with clan membership, and to their religion. Persons who adapt their lifestyle in the relevant ways can switch their membership from *payos* to Gitanos.

But community, solidarity, and cohesion refer exclusively to the clan, not to all Gitanos as a group. Gitanos outside the clan are avoided in order to prevent any misunderstanding that may end in a vendetta, but they and *payos* alike are regarded as moral beings. The *ley gitana*, the catalogue of formalized laws and moral codes that have been orally passed down, regulates the coexistence between unrelated Gitanos.

Identity construction, ongoing reconstruction, and collective cultural continuation (Fig. 1) are part of the oral communicative memory (Fig. 2). Although this direct face-to-face communication spans a maximum of only three or four generations, rituals, myths, and other factors can preserve collective recollection and identity construction over much longer periods. Thus, procedurality or institutionalization can lead to a shifting of collective recollections from communicative to cultural memory. Singing, music, and dance are essential anchor points for the identity construction of the Roma. They survive as an individualized form of expression in the oral communicative memory and as ritualized myth in the oral cultural memory. The musical form of expression of the Gitanos is flamenco, which saves, promotes, develops their culture.

At the same time singing, dancing, and music can serve as it were as a holiday from everyday life. They constitute a ritually formed, spatially and temporally limited time-out in which codes commonly used in the routines of everyday life are temporarily suspended. Through emotional compression, the tension of a *juerga* (flamenco in an intimate circle) leads to a potentially cathartic flush and allows other concerns or questions to be forgotten or shifted to the background. In this way flamenco also helps one cope with life (see Fig. 3).

Collective identities are expressed and created. At flamenco's unique creative, communicative, and crucial moment of emergence, both the me- and the we-identities are created through the specific performativity. The individual character of the performative act symbolizes the position of the Gitanos in Spanish society. The individual, by placing his or her self-confidence in the foreground, reflects the self-confidence of the entire minority in the majority society. Flamenco as a whole thereby acquires a symbolic character for a specific social milieu. As a paradigmatic event, flamenco allows people to deal with everyday affairs in a non-everyday manner.

The performative act does not proclaim a truth in the sense of preserving an aesthetic ideal or performing an academically creative act of high culture. It is not about the substance of the myth called "flamenco" but about the effect of flamenco on all participants. The actors gain their authority not through the repetition or repeatability of performative expression but through deferment that leads to change in what is quoted. In terms of language, Derrida (1988) calls this process "iteration" (pp. 298–310). The effect of the performative expression should not be attributed to the authority of the flamenco actors but to the quotations of a code that was not created by an individual. The achieved effect can never be controlled or anticipated, for all participating actors or witnesses may change the performative act by deferment or restatement. The highly individual character of flamenco and the impossibility of replicating the performative act is one important reason for the *flamenco gitano*'s high resistance to canonization or fixation in cultural memory (Fig. 2).

The Origins of Flamenco—The Phase of Coexistence and the Dark Period

Just as there are different theories about flamenco's origins, there are different positions on the question of whom flamenco belongs to. According to most scholars (e.g., Infante, 1980; Molina & Mairena, 1971; Pohren, 1962/2005), flamenco as *cante flamenco gitano-andaluz* (Fig. 6) is not the Gitanos' own creation; it is indigenous to *Baja Andalucía* (Fig. 7), from where it spread to Andalusia and parts of Spain (Fig. 8). It contains musical elements from various cultures and emerged from the interaction between the ethnic groups living in this region (Andalusians, Moriscos, and Gitanos).

The specific breeding ground arose from the fall of the Alhambra in Granada in 1492 and the following expulsion of the Moors from Andalusia by Catholic kings or illegalization and forced Christianization of any Moors who stayed in Andalusia (and who subsequently became known as Moriscos).

In the same year, a sedentary way of life was imposed on the Gitanos by decree, an act that divorced them from their traditions and language and became synonymous with conversion to Christianity. The region around Seville and Cádiz seemed suitable for settlement by the Gitanos because Moriscos already lived there as agricultural laborers for irrigation. Thus, Gitanos, Moriscos, and Moors shared the same fate of expulsion, suppression, and illegalization. But the Moriscos were expelled by decree in 1609, the goal being to drive all of them from Andalusia or kill them. Many of the persecuted Moriscos found support among the Gitanos, who let the Moriscos pose as Gitanos, live with them, and escape banishment by changing identity. During this time the *gitanerias developed*—suburbias, or peripheral quarters such as Triana in Seville, Santa María in Cádiz, Santiago in Jerez de la Frontera, and Sacromonte/Albaicín in Granada, which were inhabited mostly by Gitanos and which became places for the crystallization of flamenco (Fig. 7).

But what consequences did this development have for the identity construction of the Gitanos? The period up to 1609 can be described as the phase of coexistence (though not actually coequality) and mutual interaction of Andalusians, Moriscos, and Gitanos, a time when they lived side by side. Until at least the fifteenth century, Moorish-Andalusian music was shaped by musical elements from different cultures (Fig. 6), with its polyphony and lyrics being adapted to choral or group singing (Infante, 1980). Flamenco, by contrast, requires personality and individuality in order to produce the typical heaviness, dramatic spirit, and profundity that, in turn, symbolizes recollection and reconstruction of the me- and we-identity.

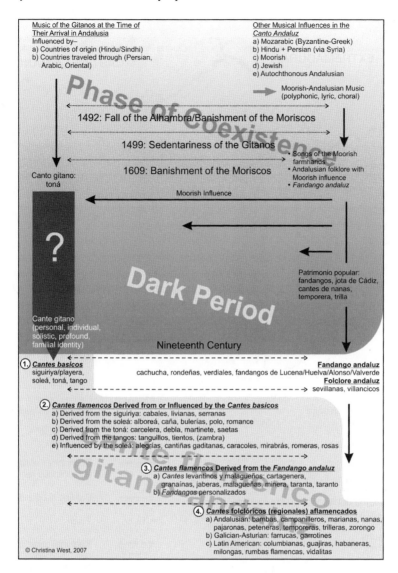

Fig. 6 *Cante flamenco gitano-andaluz*—origin, influences, types. Source: Christina West

Although a tendency toward reduction in the musical variety is likely to have already begun in the sixteenth century, the early seventeenth century marked the onset of what may be called a "dark period." With the expulsion or illegalization of the Moriscos in 1609, the main sources of the Moorish musical elements disappeared from official historiography, which according to J. Assmann (1992) means that their activities did not become set in cultural memory. The Moorish musical elements were increasingly absorbed by the Gitanos as Andalucia's remaining

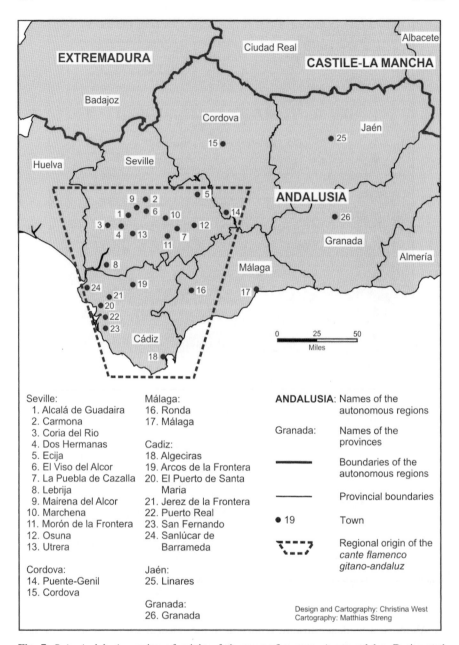

Seville: Málaga: **ANDALUSIA**: Names of the
1. Alcalá de Guadaira   16. Ronda   autonomous regions
2. Carmona   17. Málaga
3. Coria del Rio   Granada: Names of the
4. Dos Hermanas   Cadiz: provinces
5. Ecija   18. Algeciras
6. El Viso del Alcor   19. Arcos de la Frontera ─────────   Boundaries of the
7. La Puebla de Cazalla   20. El Puerto de Santa   autonomous regions
8. Lebrija   Maria
9. Mairena del Alcor   21. Jerez de la Frontera ─────────   Provincial boundaries
10. Marchena   22. Puerto Real
11. Morón de la Frontera   23. San Fernando   ● 19   Town
12. Osuna   24. Sanlúcar de
13. Utrera   Barrameda   ⌐ ̶ ̶ ̶ ̶ ⌐   Regional origin of the
                                                           ⌎ ̲ ̲ ̲ ̲ ⌎   *cante flamenco
Cordova: Jaén: gitano-andaluz*
14. Puente-Genil   25. Linares
15. Cordova
                                  Granada:
                                  26. Granada   Design and Cartography: Christina West
                                                            Cartography: Matthias Streng

Fig. 7 *Baja Andalucí—* region of origin of the *cante flamenco gitano-andaluz*. Design and
cartography: Christina West. Adapted from Grande (1999)

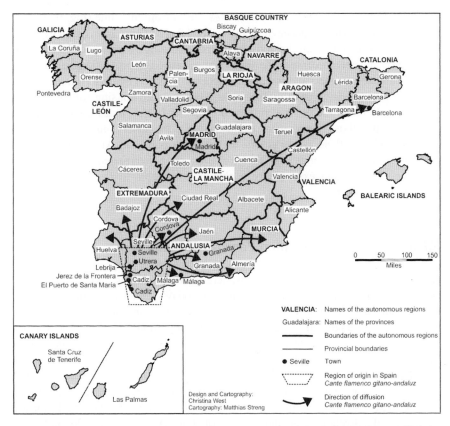

Fig. 8 Origin and spreading of the *cante flamenco gitano-andaluz* in Spain. Source: Christina West

Moriscos adopted Gitano identity (see Fig. 6). And because the Gitanos themselves had to live as a stigmatized, suppressed, persecuted, and disadvantaged group, they, too, were deleted from collective and cultural recollection of the canonized cultural memory of the society's majority population. The early musical development of flamenco therefore remains obscure. However, the profundity, importance, and functions that this form of expression has had for the orally shaped culture of the Gitanos can be understood from this condition of the society at large.

In the period when the Spanish *payos* began to show interest in the Gitanos, it became apparent that a development must have occurred in the familial environment. As of the early eighteenth century, resistance to the new dynasty (the Bourbons) and fear of French centralism and assimilation into the French way of life had given rise in Spain to a wave of evoking everything "authentic" or "originally Spanish." This folklorism piqued curiosity about regional traditions and rites, the Moorish past, and marginalized groups (Molina & Mairena, 1971). In 1783 the Gitanos were made equal to the Andalusian proletariat before the law. Knowledge about the first *cantes gitanos*, the *martinetes*, stems from that time (Fig. 6, pt. 2c). Through their form and expressivity they revealed that a mature art inspired by many sources had appeared, an art that must have ripened during extreme social exclusion. In the early nineteenth century the first Gitanos started to professionalize as *cantaores* (flamenco singers) and *bailaores* (flamenco dancers) by performing for food or money during festivities of higher society. But they did not sing *cantes basicos,* which strictly retain the original profound character of the *cantes gitanos* (Fig. 6, pt. 1), because those forms were exclusively for the inner family circle. Until approximately 1850 no *cante gitano* was sung in public in Andalusia. Instead, Andalusian folkloric songs and the *fandango* were interpreted, for their tone sequence, rhythm, and expressivity enabled most people to relate to them and perform them (Fig. 6).

Edad de Oro—The "Golden Period" of Flamenco

Andalusia gradually acquired an atmosphere in which singing and dancing could develop. The first *cafés cantantes*, similar to today's *tablaos*, a sort of cabaret, but specialized in singing, dancing, and guitar-playing, appeared in 1842, giving the Gitanos, especially the female dancers, the opportunity to earn money independently. In addition to the folkloric styles, *cantes basicos* were established step by step. The first singers began to specialize in a few styles, and the *cante* was classified by its authenticity and profundity. As the *cante gitano* opened to other groups and spread, however, the *cafés cantantes* also promoted an accommodation to the broader audience and thus a certain folkloristic profanity. Stage performance accelerated the diversification and creation of styles (Fig. 6, pts. 2d, 2e; 3; 4), and even a considerable number of *payos* as professional singers eventually emerged. Professionalization of the singers intensified the exchange between *cante gitano* and Andalusian folklore, rivalries sprouted, elements of the repertoire moved from one performer to another, and personalization brought forth new styles (Fig. 6, pt. 3b), which diffused with the *cantes gitanos* under the name *cante flamenco gitano-andaluz*. The *cafés cantantes* not only accelerated the development but also made this young art—flamenco—accessible to a wide audience.

Further Development in the Twentieth Century

Toward the mid-twentieth century flamenco became increasingly detached from its original context, being adapted to the needs of big theaters and losing the profound character of the *cante jondo*. *Zarzuela* (musical comedy) and flamenco opera were dominated by *fandangos*, which are closest to folk melodies, and the *cantes de ida y vuelta*, which with their Latin-American influence conformed well to the spirit of the age (Fig. 6, pt. 4c). From the 1950s through the 1970s, the attempt to regain the original characteristics of flamenco in small performances without use of stagecraft or background stories ushered in a return to the roots of this art form. Political flamenco, the lyrics and stage performance of which deal critically with society, appeared at the same time.

After four decades of dictatorship and with Franco's death in 1975, the *movida madrileña* emerged. It can be described as a countercultural movement that reflected the atmosphere of change during Spain's transition to democracy (*transición democrática*) (West, 2007b), particularly in Madrid. Liberation from censorship made it possible to break new ground, giving rise to *flamenco nuevo*. Ketama, a band of young musicians who grew up with the tradition of *flamenco gitano* in their families, was the first group to mix Pop, Reggae, Caribbean, and Brazilian rhythms and, later, Rap and House into the structures of flamenco. In the post-Franco era flamenco nuevo was supported politically to avoid a split between the democratic movement and the rest of post-Franco society, and multinational labels sold it outside Spain to demonstrate the nation's modernity to the world.

How Writing Changes Communicative and Cultural Memory

The assimilation and integration of folkloristic styles (Fig. 6, pts. 3, 4) and their diversification and commercialization on stage and, later, in recording studios have partially sacrificed the original profundity, importance, and function of the *cante gitano* (Fig. 6, pts. 1, 2). Nevertheless, some of the family's hermetically isolated domain has been conserved to this day. It provides the intimacy in which flamenco is still practiced for recollection, knowledge transfer, and identity construction (Fig. 1). The focus is not on rhythmic and technical perfection combined with show elements. Far more elemental is the family gathering itself; the participation of all family members regardless of age or ability; and the remembrance of ancestors, which is linked to the process of transferring, of handing down, the unique proprietary familial flamenco tradition to youth. Proprietary rhythmic, melodic, and dance structures and interpretations can be explicitly related to a person or a family and are passed on exclusively as highly specialized identifiable clan knowledge in oral communicative memory.

The opportunity to set, to establish, these proprietary familial structures by means of new media (audio and visual recording) allows flamenco to be learned outside the family context as well and, hence, without the attendant mental models, mind sets, convictions, and views on reality. The structures may be selected in any way one wishes and are beginning to mix and spread worldwide, globalizing flamenco and opening it to partial reinterpretation and embedment in new contexts. The commercial transfer of family knowledge makes that knowledge ubiquitous and decouples it from its collective identity. Recollection is becoming possible through fixed, archived artifacts in the reservoir of the cultural memory (Fig. 2). The number of retained variations or structures is increasing, whereas fixation only by oral procedurality was inevitably erasing an old variation or structure for each new one. Originally implicit knowledge is transforming into apparent explicit knowledge.

As the influence of formal education, literality, religion, and emancipation increases, identity construction among group members of this traditionally patrilinear society is gradually changing. Today, for example, the leading innovators are *Gitanas*—women—and not just where flamenco is concerned.

In conclusion, cultural memory is basically definable by the performance of the culture's recollection modes and no longer, as J. Assmann (1992) states from his theoretical perspective, exclusively by that which is remembered. The ascendant question is "how," not "what." In terms of flamenco, the foremost aspect is not its "true core" or "true substance" but rather the spiritual and emotional significance that the performative act has for the individual's awareness and identity construction with respect to the group and vice versa.

References

Assmann, A. (2004). *Zur Mediengeschichte des kulturellen Gedächtnisses* [On the history of media of the cultural memory]. In A. Erl & A. Nünning (Eds.), *Medien des kollektiven Gedächtnisses. Konstruktivität—Historizität—Kulturspezifität* (pp. 45–60). Berlin: Walter de Gruyter.

Assmann, J. (1992). *Das kulturelle Gedächtnis. Schrift, Erinnerung und politische Identität in frühen Hochkulturen* [Cultural memory: Writing, remembering, and political identity in early advanced civilizations]. Munich: C. H. Beck.

Baecker, D. (2010). *Was ist Kultur? Und einige Anschlussüberlegungen zum Kulturmanagement, zur Kulturpolitik und zur Evaluation von Kulturprojekten* [What is culture? And a few additional thoughts on the cultural management, cultural policy, and evaluation of cultural projects]. Retrieved June 30, 2010, from http://www.dirkbaecker.com/WasistKultur.pdf

Bundesministerium für Bildung, Wissenschaft und Kultur, Österreichisches Sprachen-Kompetenz-Zentrum (Eds.) (2002). *Der Zusammenhang von Sprache und Kultur am Beispiel der Burgenland-Romani* [The relation between language and culture among the Romani in Burgenland]. Graz, Austria: Österreichisches Sprachen-Kompetenz-Zentrum.

de Andalucia, J. & Instituto de Estadística de Andalucía. (2006). *Revisiones del padrón municipal de Andalucía* [Revision of the municipal registry of Andalusia]. Retrieved January 1, 2006, from http://www.juntadeandalucia.es/institutodeestadistica/padron/revpad.htm

Derrida, J. (1988). *Signatur Ereignis Kontext* [Signature event context]. In P. Engelmann (Ed.), *Randgänge der Philosophie* (pp. 291–362). Vienna: Passagen.

Foucault, M. (1978). *Dispositive der Macht. Über Sexualität, Wissen und Wahrheit* [Dispositives of power: On sexuality, knowledge and truth]. Berlin: Merve Verlag.

Grande, F. (1999). *Memoria del Flamenco* [Flamenco memoirs]. Madrid: Alianza Editorial.

Halbwachs, M. (1966). *Das Gedächtnis und seine sozialen Bedingungen* [The social frameworks of memory]. Berlin: Luchterhand. (Original work published 1925)

Hastrup, K. (1989). *Kultur som analytisk begreb* [Culture as an analytical concept]. In K. Hastrup & K. Ramløv (Eds.), *Kulturanalyse. Fortolkningens forløb i antropologien* (pp. 11–25). Copenhagen: Akademisk Forlag.

Hübschmannová, M. (2002). *Herkunft der Roma* [Origins of the Roma]. Prague: Rombase.

Infante, B. (1980). *Orígenes de lo flamenco y secreto del cante jondo* [Origin of Flamenco and the secret of the cante jondo (deep song)]. Seville: Junta de Andalucía, Consejería de Cultura edition.

Kenrick, D. (1998). *Sinti und Roma: Von Indien bis zum Mittelmeer. Die Wanderwege der Sinti und Roma* [Sinti and Roma: The migration paths of the Sinti and Roma from India to the Mediterranean Sea]. Interface Connection 3, Berlin, Germany: Parabolis.

Luhmann, N. (1995). *Kultur als historischer Begriff* [Culture as a historical concept]. In N. Luhmann (Ed.), *Gesellschaftsstruktur und Semantik: Studien zur Wissenssoziologie der modernen Gesellschaft* (Vol. 4, pp. 31–54). Frankfurt am Main: Suhrkamp.

Luhmann, N. (1997). *Die Gesellschaft der Gesellschaft* [The society of society] (Vol. 1, pt. 1). Frankfurt am Main: Suhrkamp.

Molina, R., & Mairena, A. (1971). *Mundo y formas del cante flamenco* [World and forms of flamenco singing]. Seville: Librería Al-Andalus.

Pohren, D. E. (1962/2005). *The art of flamenco*. Westport, CT: The Bold Strummer.

Polanyi, M. (1985). *Implizites Wissen* [Implicit knowledge]. Frankfurt am Main: Suhrkamp.

Proust, M. (1979). Auf der Suche nach der verlorenen Zeit [In search of lost time *or* remembrance of things past] (E. Rechel-Mertens, Trans.) (Vol. 1). Frankfurt am Main: Suhrkamp. (Original work published 1913)

Rishi, W. R. (1996). *Roma-The Panjabi emigrants Europe, Central and Middle Asia, the USSR, and the Americas*. Patiala, India: Punjabi University.

Schein, E. H. (1985). *Organizational culture and leadership*. San Francisco: Jossey-Bass.

Teichmann, M. (2001). *Geschichte der Vlach-Roma* [History of the Vlach-Roma]. Graz, Austria: Rombase. Retrieved July 5, 2010, from http://romani.uni-graz.at/rombase/index.html

Unión Romaní. (2006). *El Pueblo Gitano* [The Rroma people]. Retrieved November 30, 2006, from http://www.unionromani.org/pueblo_es.htm#distribucion

West, C. (2007a). *Gedächtnis—Kultur—Raum. Zur Identitätskonstruktion der Roma ("Gitanos") in Spanien* [Memory—Culture—Space: Identity construction of the Roma ("Gitanos") in Spain]. *Geographische Rundschau, 59*(7–8), 44–52.

West, C. (2007b). *Barcelona—Ciutat Inovadora. Innovation und Tradition in der Stadtentwicklung der katalanischen Metropole* [Barcelona—innovative city: Innovation and tradition in the urban development of the Catalan metropolis]. In T. Esser & T. D. Stegmann (Eds.), *Kataloniens Rückkehr nach Europa 1976–2006: Geschichte, Politik, Kultur und Wirtschaft* (pp. 239–262). Berlin: LIT-Verlag.

West, C., & Griesbeck, J. (2009). *Die andere Dimension des Spiels: Streetfootballworld festival 06—zur Rekonstruktion der Verknüpfung von Gewalt, Verwundbarkeit und Identität über Erinnerung, Gedächtnis, Kommunikation und Raum* [The other dimension of the game: Streetfootballworld festival 06—Reconstruction of the link between violence, vulnerability, and identity by recollection, memory, communication, space, and place]. In S. Bogusch, A. Spellerberg, H. H. Topp, & C. West (Eds.), *Organisation und Folgewirkung von Großveranstaltungen—Interdisziplinäre Studien zur FIFA Fussball-WM 2006^{TM}* (pp. 191–225). Wiesbaden: VS Verlag für Sozialwissenschaften.

Part III
World War II in European Cultural Memories

Seven Circles of European Memory

Claus Leggewie

The Holocaust as Europe's Negative Founding Myth?

Supra- and transnational memory in Europe can be visualized as a series of concentric circles, each exemplified by historical dates and memorial sites. The first circle, pertaining to the Holocaust, is tied to January 27, 1945, the date of the liberation of the Auschwitz extermination camp, observed as Holocaust Remembrance Day in many European countries.[1] This common recourse to the mass murder of the European Jews as a crime against humanity is unique for many reasons and provides Europe with a *negative* founding myth. The template for this shared response is Germany's "coming to terms with the past" (*Vergangenheitsbewältigung*), a process that initially concentrated selectively on World War II. Since the 1970s, however, and to a great extent because of US prompting, it has emphasized the centrality of the Holocaust. "This is where it happened," say German memorials, many of which are located at "authentic" sites of National Socialist crimes. "It can happen anywhere," reply observers today, taught better by the televised images from Cambodia and Rwanda, by the witnesses of other historical massacres, by Stalin's crimes, and by the wars on the territory of former Yugoslavia.

To Europeanize German memory politics might seem pretentious (H. Schmid, 2008). But it is a fact that anti-Semitism and fascism were pan-European phenomena: The murder of the Jews would have been impossible without the broad collaboration of European governments and citizens. In France, it took a long time for a thorough acknowledgement of the close involvement of the Vichy government (1940–1944) in Nazi crimes, not to mention the collaboration of French citizens in

C. Leggewie (✉)
Kulturwissenschaftliches Institut, 45128 Essen, Germany
e-mail: claus.leggewie@kwi-nrw.de

This chapter is a work in progress. Earlier versions were published in the journals *Eurozine*, *Blätter für deutsche und internationale Politik*, and *Social Research*. I would like to thank many colleagues for their constructive critique, especially Stefan Troebst, Siobhan Kattago, Heidemarie Uhl, and Wolfgang Schmale. The chapter was translated by Simon Garnett, s.garnett@eurozine.com

P. Meusburger et al. (eds.), *Cultural Memories*, Knowledge and Space 4,
DOI 10.1007/978-90-481-8945-8_8, © Springer Science+Business Media B.V. 2011

the murder of the Jews and the deep-rootedness of anti-Semitism at all levels of society. Yet there is nothing extraordinary today about there being a *Mémorial de la Shoah* in Paris. Poland, too, is undergoing similar processes, now that the debate concerning the pogroms in Jedwabne and Kielce[2] has brought to light the existence of a tenacious home-grown anti-Semitism throughout the whole of Eastern Europe (see, for instance, Gross, 2006).

The Europe forcefully unified by the Nazis was simultaneously opposed to Bolshevism, the Jews, and the politicocultural West. The degree to which the Nazi regime was supported by convinced fascists and opportunists in other European countries remains a controversial issue in many nations, above all in connection with the treatment of collaborators and forced laborers after 1945 (Basic & Welzer, 2007). Addressing the German parliament on January 27, 2009, Feliks Tych, Director of the Jewish Historical Institute in Warsaw from 1995 to 2007, spoke of the fact that many of the defendents sentenced in the "last Nazi trials" were collaborators from the East and the West who voluntarily participated in the work of annihilation carried out in the concentration camps (Tych, 2010). John Demjanjuk, who has been facing trial in Munich since 2009, is the most famous example. According to a list published by the Simon Wiesenthal Center, the Hungarians Sandor Kepiro and Karloy Zentai, the Croat Milivoj Asner, the Dutchman Klaas Carl Faber, the Dane Sören Kam, the Lithuanian Algimantas Delide, and the Estonian Mikhail Gorshkov are among the most sought-after Nazi war criminals (Hillenbrand, 2010).[3]

Remembrance of the Holocaust has always possessed a contemporary, politicopedagogical facet directed at the present and the future: Adorno's (1971) famous plea that the Holocaust be remembered so that Auschwitz is not repeated. From the Jewish perspective, the most important precaution against a recurrence of the Holocaust was the creation of a strong Israeli state. The United Nations Interim Force in Lebanon (UNIFIL) in 2006, extended until 2010,[4] gave rise to a scenario that had hitherto never needed to be anything other than imaginary: German military engagement in the Middle East. Edmund Stoiber (Christian Social Union, CSU) ruled out German participation in UNIFIL for historical reasons; others, including Chancellor Angela Merkel (Christian Democratic Union, CDU), argued that it was precisely for historical reasons that Germany had to participate. The importance of special relations with the Israeli state was, and is, a basic political tenet in the Federal Republic of Germany, yet one that is increasingly being questioned both subjectively and objectively.

The successor state to the "Third Reich" assumed legal and moral responsibility for the National Socialist policy of annihilation; however, the incantation "Never again Auschwitz" received an adjunct: "Never again war!" It was this postulate that led to Germany's resolute refusal to engage in military intervention beyond its borders, a policy that reunified Germany has overridden on numerous occasions, as in Kosovo in 1998, when it also lacked a UN mandate. Israeli prime minister Ehud Olmert's request in 2006 for the robust deployment of the German military to protect Israel and the Jews put the "special relationship" to the test because it might have suggested: "Never again Auschwitz, therefore war."

Then, as now, the politicians in Berlin went further than German society. The Germans did not want to die for Jerusalem any more than the French and the English wanted to die for Prague or Danzig in 1938. With public opinion today no longer as supportive of Israel as it was during the Six Day War in 1967, an intervention would certainly have been unpopular. The continuing occupation of the Palestinian territories has caused a change in the climate of opinion, interestingly at the same time that the recognition of German responsibility for the Holocaust has grown. Today, with Israel probably more threatened than at any other time since its foundation—in great measure a situation of its own making—the majority of Germans consider Israel to have overreached itself. Criticism of the Israeli settlement and foreign policy is also legitimate in Germany, of course, but the special relationship is degenerating.

At the same time, anti-Semitic prejudices have increased and are now attached less to traditional hatred of Jews than to the policies of the state of Israel. Anti-Semitism today is apt to be cloaked in the anti-Zionism that is a feature of radical left- and right-wing demonstrations throughout Europe. "Anti-Semitism *despite* Auschwitz" and anti-Israeli-ism *because* of Auschwitz has become a hatred of Jews *after* Auschwitz (see Rabinovici, Speck, & Sznaider, 2004). Israel does not have many lobbies at all in Germany any more, be it in the Bundestag, in either the popular or the serious press, or among intellectuals, let alone within Germany's multicultural youth. Nor has Germany ever been the guardian of Israel, a role that has fallen to the United States. Critics of the "Israel lobby" in the United States, among them Jews, have taken issue with US Middle East policy for focusing too narrowly on Israel and with the preference that the George W. Bush administration showed for purely military "antiterrorism" strategies. The European Union (EU) pursues another route. Good relations with Arab governments notwithstanding, there is no doubt as to whose side Europe would take were Hezbollah, Hamas, or Islamic Jihad and their supporters to strike at the heart of Israel. It is the Iranian president Ahmedinejad in particular who challenges the right of Israel to exist and who has taken Holocaust denial to a new, transnational level.

Can the Holocaust serve as a political yardstick for contemporary Europe? Racial discrimination and xenophobia are widespread phenomena, both in the core EU countries with their longer democratic traditions and in the transformation societies with their fledgling democracies. At first glance it seems obvious to counter these phenomena with the lessons of the past—as practiced civic political education. In January 2000, however, this technique turned out to be less than appropriate when the Stockholm International Forum on the Holocaust attempted to apply it to Austria after Wolfgang Schüssel, the leader of the conservative Austrian People's Party (ÖVP), formed a coalition with the far-right populist party (Austrian Freedom Party, FPÖ), led by the notorious Nazi trivializer Jörg Haider (1950–2008). Austria felt itself to have been publicly reprimanded, and the EU had been scared to offend Silvio Berlusconi's right-wing government in Italy.

Another way in which the Holocaust can become a current issue is the legal prosecution of denial (negationism) and trivialization (revisionism). They often appear in scholarly garb (and thus purport academic freedom and freedom of speech) and have become a core motif of neo-Nazi, far-right, and national populist movements throughout Europe. Since the mid-1980s, there have been initiatives to make such "opinions" criminally liable. According to article 130 (3) of the German Penal Code, "anyone who denies or trivializes, whether in public or before an audience, an act committed under the National Socialist regime of the kind described in the Code Offences under International Law [*Völkerstrafgesetzbuch*], in a way intended to disturb the public peace," is liable for a prison sentence of up to five years or a fine.

In 1994 the Federal Constitutional Court of Germany ruled that Holocaust denial was a matter of "claiming as fact something that, on the basis of countless witness accounts and documents, the statements of the court in numerous criminal cases, and the findings of historical research, has proven to be untrue. In itself, the assertion of this content does not therefore enjoy the protection of freedom of opinion" (Az. 1 BvR 23/94, see BVerfGE 90, 241). Other EU states, including France, Austria, Belgium, and later also Romania and Hungary, have passed similar laws; others have amended general laws against racial discrimination; and still others (such as the United Kingdom) have seen no need for action on the part of the legislature. Article 607 (2) of the Spanish legal code states that "the dissemination of any kind of idea or doctrine that denies or justifies crimes as defined in the previous paragraph of this article, or attempts to reinstate regimes or institutions that protect or guarantee these ideas or doctrines, will be punished with a prison sentence of 1–2 years." In November 2007 the words "denies or" in this law were declared to be unconstitutional by the Spanish Constitutional Court and were deleted. Interestingly, Luxembourg does not single out Holocaust denial for punishment, but rather war crimes, crimes against humanity, and genocide. In 2008, the EU passed the Framework Decision on Combating Racism and Xenophobia. In the future, the following offences are to be made criminally liable in all EU member states:

(a) publicly inciting to violence or hatred directed against a group of persons or a member of such a group defined by reference to race, colour, religion, descent or national or ethnic origin;

(b) the commission of an act referred to in point (a) by public dissemination or distribution of tracts, pictures or other material;

(c) publicly condoning, denying or grossly trivialising crimes of genocide, crimes against humanity and war crimes as defined in Articles 6, 7 and 8 of the Rome Statute of the International Criminal Court, directed against a group of persons or a member of such a group defined by reference to race, colour, religion, descent or national or ethnic origin when the conduct is carried out in a manner likely to incite to violence or hatred against such a group or a member of such a group;

(d) publicly condoning, denying or grossly trivialising the crimes defined in Article 6 of the Charter of the International Military Tribunal appended to the London Agreement of 8 August 1945, directed against a group of persons or a member of such a group defined by reference to race, colour, religion, descent or national or ethnic origin when the conduct is carried out in a manner likely to incite to violence or hatred against such a group or a member of such a group (Council, 2008, pp. 55–58).

Was Soviet Communism Equally Criminal?

There are good reasons to doubt whether bringing the Holocaust into the present in this way is morally and ethically necessary and whether its instrumentalization for contemporary ends has an effect in practical political terms. Now that the ban on the denial of the Holocaust is binding, the question arises as to whether the denial of Soviet communist crimes also deserves to be criminalized (see "MEPs ban", 2005). This topic constitutes the second circle of European memory. The Lithuanian members of the European Parliament and the former head of the Lithuanian parliament, Vytautas Landsbergis (1990–1996), have for the time being been unable to get anywhere with a motion to this effect, having found barely any advocates among western politicians. The central perspective of the Holocaust becomes problematic when it is imposed as the matrix for dealing with communist state crimes and crimes against humanity across the whole of eastern Europe. On the other hand, it is consistent when states that formerly belonged to the sphere of Soviet rule (e.g., Poland) give fines and even prison sentences as long as three years to anyone who contests communist crimes and other politically motivated repressive actions carried out by functionaries of Polish criminal authorities, the legal authorities, or persons acting on their orders up to December 31, 1989.

The origins of the EU lie in its function as a market and as an economic community, so it constantly strives to attain "harmonization." It is not easy to carry this principle over into political fields as symbolic as European history. The latter is overshadowed by two interconnected, though not simultaneous, totalitarian experiences that left millions dead or traumatized, with issues of legal and moral "atonement" remaining poisonous today. Nationally minded Europeans wish to have the national, regional, or local level control the form that these sensitive issues take (the subsidiarity principle). Under no circumstances do they want to hand them over to Brussels. However, the fact that the European Court of Human Rights has on numerous occasions found it necessary to rule on the legality of sacking politically tarnished public servants and on restrictions of voting rights in postcommunist eastern Europe indicates a certain harmonization of the way history is dealt with.

If the denial of the Holocaust is punishable across much of Europe, then this sanction quite logically encourages demands to deal with the horrendous aspects of communism in an equivalent manner. Nations that used to be occupied by the Red Army do not want to and will not celebrate May 8 and 9 as a liberation. To them the end of the Nazi regime was the beginning of another totalitarian regime that many contemporary representatives of central eastern Europe rank as "equally criminal" (Kalniete, 2004). In other words, they suspect it of genocide. The representatives of post-Soviet Russia have neither apologized nor paid reparations for the mass deportations and murders, loss of freedom, and forced Russification to which the eastern European satellite states had been subjected under their communist governments. No one any longer seriously disputes that the formerly occupied nations were victims of the Soviet empire. It would be controversial, however, if those nations were to use that past to extenuate or conceal their participation in the murder of the Jews. Attempts to offset one memory against the other occurred in the postwar era in the conflict over German history and served as propaganda for the far-right fringe; the Jewish victims, it was alleged, had been awarded an exclusive status, whereas the victims of the communist dictatorship had been deliberately neglected (Kalniete, 2001/2006).

The fact that crimes were hushed up and offset against each other was primarily due to the polemic constellations of the Cold War, which should have been overcome but which in fact continue to exist. That survival is one reason why a shared European memory and cross-border commemoration is still difficult. Nonetheless, a collective form of commemoration does seem to have been at least partially achieved (see Greiner, 2010) at commemorative sites such as Buchenwald or Sachsenhausen, where in 1945 the Nazi concentration camps were immediately transformed into "special camps" and used by the Soviet occupiers (some people even found themselves imprisoned twice in the same place). Especially at Buchenwald, it has been possible, after much negotiation, to find aesthetic architectural and historical, didactic solutions that do not ignore anyone's suffering and yet avoid false generalizations.

If Europe has—or is developing—a collective memory, it is just as diverse as its nations and cultures. Memory cannot be regulated mnemotechnically, let alone through official acts of state or routinized commemorative rituals such as May 8 and 9 or January 27. The only facets that can be European are the way in which the crimes are collectively remembered and the way in which the most cautious of lessons are drawn for contemporary European democracy. Competition between and ranking of what are contradictorily called "Holocaust memory" and "Gulag memory" are probably the most important challenge (Troebst, 2010). Detaching the "Holocaust" from specifically German perpetrators and Jewish victims universalizes it, and, in turn, reveals the superficiality to which both dogmatic singularization and "undogmatic" globalization (or Europeanization) can lead (see Levy & Sznaider, 2001). By the same token, not every kind of violence may be brought into connection with the Holocaust as an icon of the negative. Allowing comparison and analogy to deprive that mass murder of its historical depth and turn it into an ethical vaccination against genocide (via western popular mass culture) is just as problematic as particularizing it and thereby placing it beyond the realm of historical process and comparison.

Insofar as the goal is to arrive at a complete picture of the crimes committed against humanity in the twentieth century, the Holocaust memory—the core of western European memory—becomes a semicircle from the perspective of the Gulag memory. These two memories join to form the totalitarian experience of the twentieth century.

However, crude variations of the totalitarianism thesis quickly lead down the slippery slope of relativizing or even justifying one's own crimes by pointing to another's actions that were allegedly just as bad or even worse. The challenge of European commemorative culture therefore lies in establishing what was singular about the rupture to civilization constituted by the industrial, bureaucratic annihilation of the European Jews, without in the process dogmatically rejecting historical comparison or downplaying the systematic attrition of the "class enemy"

and "enemies of people" in the Soviet sphere of influence. Speaking on the six-
tieth anniversary of the liberation of the Buchenwald concentration camp, Jorge
Semprún, once a member of the communist party and a prisoner at Buchenwald
from 1943 to 1945, formulated the hope that

> at the next commemorative occasion in ten years' time, the experience of the Gulag will
> have been incorporated into our collective European memory. Let's hope that by then
> Varlam Shalamov's *Kolyma Tales* will be sitting alongside the works of Primo Levi, Imre
> Kertész, or David Rousset. For one thing, it would mean that we are no longer crippled
> down one side; but it would also mean that Russia has taken a decisive step in the direction
> of democracy. (Semprún, 2005)

"Eastern central Europe" as a single entity is a western fiction (see Schmale, 2008).
Troebst (2005) has distinguished four zones according to their memorial modes: (a)
In the Baltic states, Croatia, and Slovakia a clear anticommunist consensus predomi-
nates. (b) In Poland, Hungary, the Czech Republic, and Ukraine, the interpretation of
communism is controversial (even increasingly so). (c) Bulgaria, Romania, Serbia,
Macedonia, and Albania share an ambivalence or indifference to the communist
past. And (d) Russia, Belarus, Moldova, and other countries in the Commonwealth
of Independent States exhibit a high degree of continuity in terms of elites and ideology. In this final set of countries Stalin is often seen as the sole general of the "Great
Patriotic War," an apologist view that sometimes even extends to his repressive and
murderous characteristics within Russia itself (Gudkov, 2005). The authoritarianism
latent in post-Soviet power structures reveals the extent to which an unaddressed
criminal past undermines the path to democracy. Not only is Russia's possible self-
exclusion from Europe *expressed* in an affirmative and apologetic politics of history,
it may also have its deeper causes there.

   I have identified three reasons for the asymmetry of European memory. First, the
assumption of the singularity of the Holocaust (above all from the German perspective), combined with the acknowledgement of Russian suffering in World War II,
has caused a blindness to "red totalitarianism." This effect includes the way the history of the German Democratic Republic (GDR) has been addressed in Germany
(Sabrow, 2010), which partly clings to the foul antifascist consensus that the GDR
was antifascist, a notion that tends to extenuate the crimes of the Socialist Unity
Party (SED) just as was done with Nazi crimes in West Germany after 1945. Second,
the asymmetry between the perception of the Gulag and that of the Holocaust can be
accounted for by the far greater visibility of the latter, the murder of the European
Jews. A comparable iconization of or media attention to the crimes of communist
regimes (which in China and North Korea have cost the lives of around 100 million
people since 1917) has clearly not resulted. To put it another way, the Nazi Germans
predominantly killed other people, the Communists in Russia and China predominantly killed their own. Yet this account is also wrong if one is properly to take into
account the persecution of the populations of eastern central Europe, central Asia,
and Tibet by Russian and Chinese "colonial powers." The third reason often cited
for the asymmetry of European memory is that this murderous experience remained
eastern European at its core. Yet western Europe cannot seriously claim to have been
unaffected by Stalinism; the sheer size of communist parties west of the Iron Curtain

contradicts would contradict that denial. So would the identity-forming function that anti-anticommunism had in western Europe for many years. Although it may have provided the basis for the peaceful coexistence with the so-called people's republics and may have overcome the division of Europe, it did so, as is now clear, at the expense of human and civil rights groups (see Brumlik, 2010).[5]

Expulsion as a Pan-European Trauma?

In the collective mind of Europe, the dominant memory (one kept alive by the media) is of large-scale forced "population transfers," the third circle of European memory. Ethnic cleansings, mass expulsions, and genocides began with the collapse of the major empires in the nineteenth century and provide the background against which the Holocaust appears as an especially extreme and systematic "special case." The American historian Norman Naimark (2001) has referred in general terms to "ethnic cleansing"[6] that has occurred from the nineteenth century onward wherever emergent nation-states have succumbed to the madness of believing that political legitimacy and domestic and foreign sovereignty is attainable only on the basis of ethnically homogenous national communities.

Democratic systems, too, have been susceptible to this irrationality. The particular problem the Czechs have with the politicomoral recognition of the expulsion of the Sudeten Germans from 1945 to 1947 may lie in the fact that the decree for their expulsion was issued by a bourgeois democratic government under Edvard Benes. Similarly, the biggest hindrance to addressing the catastrophe in the former Yugoslavia as of 1991 might be that the authoritarian regime under Tito kept a better grip on the historically fissiparous Serbs, Croats, Bosniaks, and Kosovo-Albanians than did the illiberal democracies after Tito, which succumbed to an ethnonationalist furor and religious war.

More than anything else, it is this legacy of ethnic cleansings and acts of genocide that—often because they are not yet "over and done with"—obstructs the development of a pan-European memory. A counterexample would be the Europeanization of the subject of the expulsion of Germans at the end of World War II. Initiatives such as the European Network of Memory and Solidarity campaign against a purely national and backward-looking commemoration of the sort supposedly advocated by the German Zentrum gegen Vertreibung (Centre Against Expulsion). In the course of the controversial debate over this organization (see Zeitgeschichte, 2004), its initiators, notably the League of Expellees, were obliged to integrate a European and global dimension into events and exhibitions. The 1950 "Charter of Expellees from the Homeland" is now retroactively interpreted as a transnational document (Ausstellungen, 2006). Ultimately, the Centre has succeeded in becoming a hub within a European network, though it will probably be a long time before the Germans and the Poles or the Germans and the Czechs are able to issue jointly authored upper-secondary school textbooks with the same degree of normality as is now possible (albeit after a 40 years of reconciliation) between the Germans and the French (see Bernlocher & Geiss, 2006; Le Quintrec, Geiss, & Bernlocher, 2006).

The expulsion of the Germans, a bone of contention between the German and Polish governments that seems gradually to have outlived itself, illustrates how sensitive common memory can be both for domestic and foreign policy. In the West the matter of expulsion is used to revive an outdated Left–Right schemata; in the East nationally oriented (and primarily left-wing) forces stand opposed to liberal, pro-European ones. Of course, Polish intransigence on expulsion has to do with the long-suppressed and then almost hysterically debated communist past. In all postcommunist societies the heirs of the nomenklatura and the descendents of an authoritarian Right (often with a history of collaboration with the Nazis) compete for historical legitimacy, the lack whereof they attempt to compensate for with ethnonationalist sentiment.

The geopolitical and geostrategic divisions of the "Old Europe," frozen by the bloc confrontation between the Cold War superpowers, have thus reappeared. Yet it is hardly the case that old conflicts are hindering a unification of the new Europe; rather, they serves as distractions from new conflicts—over security, energy, freedom of movement within the EU, and the like. The abiding traumatization suffered by victims of expulsion and the extreme vulnerability of societies with a high share of expellees, not to mention the shocking resurgence of ethnic cleansings in the Balkan wars of the 1990s and the volatility of the refugee issue outside Europe, together call for universal norms and definitions. *Article 7, par. 1(d)* of the Rome Statute of the International Criminal Court[7] defines every forcible transfer of population as a crime against humanity, making expulsion criminal under international law. This ruling applies to the expulsion of millions of Germans after the period from 1944 to 1945. However, like all other expulsions, this one needs to be seen in its historical context, which includes the national territorial policies of the Third Reich in eastern Europe, the widespread disloyalty of many Sudeten Germans to the Czechoslovak Republic, the unstable position of the Polish and Czech governments after the German occupation, and the obligations imposed by the Soviet occupation regime.

Viewing the normative and historical levels together precludes any attempt either to automatically equate different types of population transfer or to qualify them on the grounds of contingent historical circumstances. In Europe the controversial question is which acts of expulsion and ethnic cleansing are to be categorized as "genocide." Article II of the 1948 Convention of the United Nations on the Prevention and Punishment of the Crime of Genocide defines genocide as

> any of the following acts committed with the intent to destroy, in whole or in part, a national, ethnical, racial or religious group:
>
> (a) Killing members of the group;
> (b) Causing serious bodily or mental harm to members of the group;
> (c) Deliberately inflicting on the group conditions of life calculated to bring about its physical destruction in whole or in part;
> (d) Imposing measures intended to prevent births within the group;
> (e) Forcibly transferring children of the group to another group.[8]

Despite the clarification of these offences in international criminal law and the toughening of the prosecution of these offences in line with the principle of universal jurisdiction, which obliges the United Nations to intervene in severe cases, major controversies between nations have arisen in recent decades over the existence and effects of events categorized as "genocide," including the persecution it involves. Both the moral and the legal seriousness of the charge of genocide means that perpetrators wish to dissociate themselves from it as far as possible. It is also a charge that is often made falsely, and genocide accusations have become a weapon in the battle for global recognition and international democracy.

The clearest example is the "Armenian question." A majority of liberal and secular Turks resolutely refuse to acknowledge historical responsibility for the "genocidal murder" (if not the genocide) of hundreds of thousands of Armenians in 1915. The question thus morphs into an informal criterion for EU membership, one clearly articulated both in national and supranational parliaments. The French and the Swiss have taken up the Armenian cause as their own and, seeing "the Auschwitz lie" as a precedent, have outlawed the denial of the genocide; Germany has taken a more cautious approach, issuing statements geared to consensus (see Antrag, 2005; Manutscharjan, 2005; Protokoll, 2005[9]). In terms of commemoration, the wider Europe will be divided over the Armenian question before it can start coming together. Yet consensus can be achieved only when the issue is approached the other way around—in other words, when Turkish society deals with the Armenian issue in a *European* fashion, both domestically and with old allies and enemies at the international level.

The conflict raises in exemplary fashion the question as to where Europe's borders lie, for supranational EU intraidentities extend transnationally at the European and non-European levels. Many opponents of EU membership for Turkey have hinted that, because of the country's "different" cultural and religious history, it can never share Europe's "common destiny" (see Leggewie, 2004). Even Britain, the strongest advocate of Turkish membership, indirectly endorses this view by conceiving of the Union as a free-trade zone without a cultural memory. No other complex more clearly evidences the divisive dimensions of a shared memory than the supposed cultural boundary between "Islam" and "secular" Europe. Regardless of the actual degree of de-Christianization in Europe, public opinion surveys show that many people see in Europe a historical community of memory and destiny that is opposed to Islam and Turkey. They hold this view, despite the fact that Kemalism was the prime example of a westernization process and that the secular Turkish Republic has been the best proof that such a course could be taken by what essentially remained a very Islamic country. If Europe took its secularity seriously, religious affiliation would not pose an unassailable obstacle to integration, either within immigration societies or in terms of Europe's relations with other countries.

The other contemporary point of contention concerns the mass death of millions of so-called kulaks in the Ukraine as part of the Stalinist repressions of the 1930s. Whereas many Turks deny the occurrence of the "Armenian genocide" (refutation of which stands in the way of Turkish accession hopes), western-tending Ukrainians energetically claim the term *genocide* for the famines of the 1930s. One of the major reasons that Ukrainians do so is to define themselves in a way that sets them apart from their Russian neighbors, who continue trying to relativize the crimes of Stalinism. By using the term *genocide*, Ukraine attempts to garner maximum attention for the so-called Holodomor[10] at the European and international levels, not least in order to use it as an entry ticket to the EU. However, despite Ukraine's numerous efforts to raise awareness about the famines in western Europe, the tragedy—one of the most dramatic of Soviet Communism and one that claimed millions of victims—is largely unknown in the West.

Another reason why the Ukrainian case needs to be considered is that, once again, it raises the question as to whether systematic racial and ethnic repression is the only crime that meets the definition of genocide and whether the targeted persecution of social classes and strata—in this case defined as exploitative farmers—also deserves to be counted. The catastrophic famine in Ukraine was not a natural phenomenon but rather the result of the Soviet collectivization of land, a not unintended side effect of Stalin's assault on rural private property, which, in turn, was intended to accelerate industrialization. The Holodomor was a case of *political* cleansing based on liquidation and deportation just as systematic, and on an ideology just as murderous, as that of ethnic cleansing. Even if it is necessary to introduce an objective and heuristic distinction between classical genocide and other, class-war motivated forms of democide, it will not mean that any one of these atrocities is less of a crime than the other.

War and Wartime Memory as a Motor of Europe?

The fourth circle of European memory encompasses the experience of dictatorship and genocide, one that goes back to wartime and economic crises. The mass attendance at exhibitions and the high numbers of viewers tuning into historical television programs and clicking onto websites reveal how strong the interest is in this subject. The memory of World War I, associated with the name of Verdun, plays an extremely important role, above all in England (The Great War), France (*La Grande Guerre*), and Belgium (*De Groote Oorlog*). In Germany and Austria the memory of hyperinflation, the collapse of the banks, and the Great Depression is very much alive even among members of subsequent generations. The memory of World War II is keen in all these countries and is immensely important to Russia (The Great Patriotic War) and eastern European societies as well.

An interesting case is the emergence of the so-called Christmas Truce of 1914 as a western European site of memory of World War I:

> The example of the popularization of the Christmas Truce shows that World War I has become a European site of memory in recent years. It allows the European nations to meet in common sorrow, without accusations of guilt, and serves to create a European identity and to legitimate a (western) European mission of peace. This tendency is manifested both in the "informal" media of historical culture, that is, in the tenor of the numerous Internet sites on the Christmas Truce or films on the subject, and in the formal institutions of historical culture, such as museums. (Paletschek, 2008, p. 216)

Pop-culture examples of the active European memory of the Christmas Truce are internationally broadcast television documentations and the German–English–French–Romanian coproduction *Merry Christmas*, which ran simultaneously at German, English, and French cinemas during the Christmas season in 2005. Various memorial media (nonfiction, film, memorials, and commemorative events) interconnect with one another at different levels from the local to the European and the global, as do academic historical research, oral history, and pop culture.

While in exile in London, Charles de Gaulle coined a phrase describing the whole period between 1914 and 1945: "the second thirty years' war." He wanted to highlight the profundity of the rupture, the connection between the wars, and, notably, the memorial potential of a period of terror during the seventeenth century—one that influenced Europe's national structure, society, and culture just as much as the two world wars of the twentieth century had. Initially, the justification for the existence of the European Economic Community was based not on the Holocaust, and even less on the systemic competition with communism, but on the traumatic experience of two "total wars" and the Sword of Damocles represented by mass unemployment, which destroyed the European nation-state system, de-democratizing it and robbing it of its pivotal position in the world.

Most Europeans probably associate even Sarajevo with the assassination that triggered World War I rather than with a massacre during the Balkan Wars less than 20 years ago. It is no coincidence that the icon of German–French reconciliation—the handshake between French President François Mitterand and German Chancellor Helmut Kohl over the war graves of Verdun (1984)—was preceded by the equally impressive gesture of peace between Konrad Adenauer and Charles de Gaulle in Reims (1962). It marked the point at which the hostility that had dominated relations between the two European powers was transformed into a hitherto unimaginable degree of political cooperation and sociostructural and cultural convergence. Because many readers are certain to be skeptical about the notion of a pan-European memory, it is worth emphasizing that such political processes have always been accompanied by historico-political measures such as city twinning, student exchanges, and the joint authorship of history books, which are now taken with former wartime enemies in eastern Europe as well. Even a name like Katyn, which used to imply never-ending feud, has lost some of its volatility in Russian–Polish–German relations, and there are signs that it, too, may be the starting point for a less antagonistic community of memory between the former wartime opponents.

As evident from interest in the Battle of Stalingrad, in World War II aerial bombing (e.g., Rotterdam, Coventry, and Dresden), and in the fate of the prisoners of war, wartime experiences and traumas have once again formed the collective expectations and mentalities of Europeans across borders. Another crucial place is occupied by the memory of the "Cold War" and that period's confrontation between the eastern and western blocs, especially the threat of the human race's nuclear self-annihilation, which is experienced in central Europe as a virtual Ground Zero. It is recalled with particular intensity in Great Britain and has had an impact on the civilian use of nuclear energy. In Germany the central sites of memory of the East–West division are not so much Buchenwald and Hohenschönhausen (the site of the former Stasi headquarters in Berlin) as places like the Fulda Gap (a corridor east of Frankfurt am Main that was considered a likely invasion route from East to West Germany), and the Berlin Wall, which, however, function only to a limited extent as European sites of memory (see Drechsel, 2010).

Postwar events such as inflation and depression, which caused social insecurity, impoverishment, and mass unemployment, have been re-evoked as frames of reference and models of crisis in the financial crisis of 2008. Like the two world wars, they were pan-European experiences whose severity gave cause to base European reconciliation and integration in politicoeconomic steps such as the creation of the European Coal and Steel Community and the construction of the European welfare state—in the latter case, with each country following its own national model. Despite a considerable residue of mutual stereotypes and grudges, Europe has, remarkably enough, gained distance from images of the enemy within and from national arch-enmities, and the East-West division in the mind has gradually dissolved. In some areas images of the external enemy have become more pronounced than they used to be, above all with respect to Islamist terrorism, which has fostered a general Islamophobia in Europe and elsewhere. In the face of supposed and factual external threats, it remains to be seen how resilient the "democratic peace" that has marked Europe since 1945 really is and which normative and moral demands the EU is able to bring to bear in its foreign policy.

The Black Book of Colonialism

Occasionally, victims and deniers of the Armenian genocide gather at Steinplatz in Berlin, near to where Talat Pasha was assassinated by an Armenian survivor in 1921. At either end of this rather unkempt park, one finds a memorial erected in the early 1950s—one to the victims of Stalinism and one to the victims of National Socialism. Steinplatz could, then, almost come to symbolize the history of European memory outlined above. However, a further memorial site would be missing: one that recalled European colonial crimes, the fifth circle of European memory. If one wanted to pursue this idea, the occasion commemorated might be the Berlin West Africa Conference of 1884–1885, which took place a couple of miles away on Wilhelmstrasse. Under the aegis of the Germans, almost all of Africa was divided up between European interests. In Germany, the colonial crimes committed primarily against the Herero and Nama came to be discussed relatively late in the twentieth century, in the course of the more general process of coming to terms with the past. In other countries the colonial past has been the subject of greater attention, such as recent attempts to pass laws that would require school curricula to include the "positive aspects" of colonialism (see B. Schmid, 2008).

This broad field encompasses a historical period from slavery to the neocolonial economic policies of the present. The Congolese case facilitates a politics of memory not solely limited to the European space, but it also shows the limits and pitfalls of the globalization of commemoration and memory under the aspect of a Holocaust divorced from time and space. Again, the argument that the mass murder of the Jews was singular in history must not be allowed to narrow the perspective and underpin what is ultimately a hierarchy of victims that assumes racist stereotypes. The nonaffirmative comparison between the Shoah and colonial genocide is no longer taboo; during the reign of Leopold II, king of the Belgians (1865–1909), up to ten million people in the Congo were brutally murdered—there, too, "the unthinkable" became reality. Biographical continuities between the colonial crimes and the murder of the Jews are also impossible to ignore: The racial anthropologist Eugen Fischer began his lethal career in "German Southwest Africa" and ended it on the ramp at Auschwitz.

Colonialism emerges in three historical forms: the trading company, which was based on the exploitation of raw materials and human labor and which was active above all in southern Africa; the military conqueror, which lent economic exploitation territorial form and satisfied the imperial hunger for a "place in the sun" for the elites and the masses alike; and clergymen and the pedagogues, who added a civilizing mission to colonial and imperial expansion. The proselytizing impact of this mission was negligible; the destructive and racist dimension, far more lasting. However, what has not been discussed much is how this peripheral memory rebounded on European social history. The governing classes in postcolonial societies have been pervaded by a comfortable, anticolonial ideology of justification that conceals the role of autochthonous elites in the continuing exploitation and underdevelopment of the South, a combination that has greatly slowed the progress of democratization, the rule of law, and transitional justice.

It is impossible to employ a kind of counterfactual history to represent, let alone quantify, the developmental possibilities hindered by colonization and exploitation. Nonetheless, in terms of what is required for a symbolic as well as factual atonement, Europe has done little in comparison to its reaction to the consequences of wars and genocides in Europe. These inadequacies begin with the restitution of cultural artifacts decorating the museums of major western cities today and extend to reparation payments to the descendents of the originally colonized inhabitants who suffered from slavery and the countless massacres carried out in the course of imperial wars. If one were to apply the standards of the reparation payments awarded after the two world wars or of the entitlements granted Holocaust victims and forced laborers, the sums would be enormous (Vuckovic, 2003). However, the sheer unfeasibility of such an arrangement does not have to mean that a blanket apology of the type expressed in Africa by US President Bill Clinton or Pope John Paul II is perceived to be sufficient.

This point can be illustrated by the still unsatisfactory ruling on the claims of the Herero, a people living in the northern part of what is now Namibia, who are pressing for recognition and compensation for victims and for damage caused by the colonial policies of the German Empire. The colonization of German Southwest Africa occurred along the lines described above. In 1883, the merchant Franz Adolf Eduard Lüderitz signed a contract with the clan leaders of the Herero, and one year later the region became a German protectorate. Shortly afterward, conflicts broke out over land and water rights (mainly in connection with the construction of the Otavi railway), sexual assaults on Herero women, and the draconian attempts to convert the locals to Christianity. In 1897 a cattle plague and locust swarms resulted in the loss of almost three quarters of the cattle stock, forcing the Herero to sell their land and to work as hired labor on German farms. The German administration's failure to manage the crisis prompted the 1904 Herero uprising, in the course of which farms and villages were burned down and about 250 German settlers murdered. When the governor, Theodor Leutwein, was unable to quell the uprising, the German Empire sent in an expeditionary corps of approximately 15,000 men under Lothar von Trotha. After they arrived, their plans radicalized, and they resolved to wipe out the Herero people. The following words have been ascribed to von Trotha: "It was and is my policy to carry out violence using crude terrorism and even cruelty. I annihilate the rebel tribes in streams of blood and streams of money. Only from this seed can something new arise" (as quoted in Drechsler, 1984, p. 156).[11] The result was the first genocide of the twentieth century. Up to 80,000 people died; after the battle at Waterberg, troops surrounded many Herero in the waterless Omaheke Steppe, leaving them to die of thirst. Only around 1,000 Herero were able to escape, some of whom later fought at the side of the rebelling Nama (Wegmann, 2010).

Over time, official and private attitudes toward this episode in history have somewhat changed in Germany. On the centenary of the slaughter of the Herero in 2004, the German government, via the then minister for development aid, Heidemarie Wieczorek-Zeul, acknowledged the political and moral guilt of German colonial politics and asked the Herero for forgiveness. Until that point, all formulations relevant to reparations had been avoided. The financial reparations previously sought by the Herero and pursued without success by the American courts were rejected by the German and Namibian governments. Instead, development aid in the region assumed particular importance. In 2004, members of the von Trotha family invited the leader of the Herero, Alfons Maharero, to Germany and asked forgiveness for the crimes of Lothar von Trotha.

Sensitive issues are still open, however. An apparently marginal aspect of Germany's still unresolved colonial history concerns demands from initiatives by Herero victims to release and return Herero skulls from the archives of Freiburg University, the Linden Museum in Stuttgart, and the State Museum of Natural History (also in Stuttgart), where they had ended up as trophies of the Herero uprising. Though in principal willing to act on this matter, German authorities have done little. They underestimate the meaning of the skulls for the Herero, who believe that the souls of both of the living and the dead will not find peace until these remains are returned. The intention is to exhibit the skulls in Namibia's museum of independence.

In Germany there is no complementary monument specifically to the memory of German colonial *crimes*, whereas many streets are named after Lüderitz and other former colonial figures once considered heroes in Germany. It was not until 2006 that the Munich city council, contrary to the vote of the CSU and the Free Democratic Party of Germany (FDP), decided to change the name of the city's Von-Trotha-Strasse to "Hererostrasse." The CSU justified its opposition to the proposed change by arguing that the name of the street had long since come to apply to the entire von Trotha family (Evangelischer Pressedienst Mitteilung, October 6, 2006).

If acknowledgement of responsibility for colonial crimes is insufficient at the national level, it is all the more so at the pan-European level. To the European public humanitarian catastrophes, civil wars, border conflicts, state collapses, terror attacks, and environmental and climatic disasters appear to have nothing to do with this history. Yet metaphors of the "dark continent" and "the white man's burden" are back in circulation, especially in connection with immigrants from sub-Saharan Africa.

Europe as a Continent of Immigration?

Europe's colonial history leads directly or indirectly to the sixth circle of European memory: the transnational migration to Europe in the nineteenth and twentieth centuries, and above all since the 1950s. The fact that this flow of people is also a story of asylum and escape from poverty means that there is a close connection to Europe's colonial history. However, immigration has greatly diversified in the last 60 years, leading to the present situation in which 25% of the population of western European societies will soon have an "immigrant background" (and 40–50% in the urban agglomerations).

Still relatively new, Europe's museums on migration throughout the western part of the continent raise further issues regarding cultural globalization. One question is the extent to which these museums examine merely the success or failure of migration from the perspective of the migrants and/or explore merely the difficulties with their social integration, political naturalization, and cultural assimilation from the perspective of the "majority society." Or do these museums also address migration's connection to the criminal and catastrophic history of the Shoah and the Gulag? The Shoah and the Gulag did not affect migrants and their parents directly, but the second and third generations find themselves posed with the question of how they should approach these histories and how, in light of them, they should observe and evaluate their "own" history, from which they have become alienated.

Former European sites of memory, starting with the Roman heritage and the relics of the Middle Ages, can no longer be adequately communicated without strategies for making them comprehensible to migrants, strongly confronted as they are with non-European identity options from the Islamic *umma*, for example. Hence, a European memory will become transnational only when migrant Europeans (insofar as they are recognized as citizens!) take on responsibility for crimes and events that lie outside their own sense of their ethnic origins and when, at the same time, European human rights and asylum policy can be applied in an international crisis without their being used as a normative shield for protecting Eurocentric interests.

Today, Europe has a pronounced "migration background" that is barely reflected in the public sphere and in policies on immigration and integration. Immigration is nevertheless perceived in most countries as a legacy of conflict, with critical advocates categorizing it alongside other traumatic episodes or aspects of European history. However, migration is not a collective trauma for either the receiving societies or the immigrant communities; rather, it represents a remarkable success story—with significant dark sides. On the plus side are economic prosperity and social advancement, as well as transcultural innovation, which has had a positive influence on more than just European cuisine. On the minus side are aspects of social segregation and ethnoreligious discrimination.

In this respect Europe is clearly standing at a crossroads. In many countries an open rejection of ethnic minorities is emerging, and more or less serious conflicts are being instrumentalized by politicians either to gain or to maintain power, as shown not only by far-Right and neo-Nazi parties but also for populist parties and mainstream parliamentary parties. They foment resentment, stigmatize scapegoats, and violate legal guarantees and conventions that have effectively protected minorities since 1945. The connection with the permanent economic crisis has been clear since the 1970s, raising the question as to whether European tolerance is a mere fair-weather phenomenon that could vanish abruptly with the end of the economic success story. This uncertainty is also fed by far-Right and far-Left hostility to Europe, positions that are strongly represented in the European parliament.

Europe's Success Story After 1945

To summarize, Europe's collective memory after 1989 is just as diverse as its nations and cultures. It is also just as divided—in the sense of "shared" as well as "split"— as its national and social world. The strong and recurrent impulse to believe that forgetting is better than remembering in and for Europe is understandable and has attracted prominent advocates—in postcolonial France as in post-Franco Spain and postsocialist Poland. On the other hand, there is the slogan of the prominent former dissident Adam Michnik (1998): "Amnesty yes, amnesia no!" (p. 324). Processes of democratization in transitional societies, which is what almost all European nations were after 1945, probably remain precarious and incomplete if they fail to conduct a critical recapitulation of their own past. The debate on Polish and Hungarian anti-Semitism, the inhumane treatment of the Roma in eastern Europe, and the top-level amnesia in France regarding the Algerian War are no exceptions. Just as European states that have become democracies no longer go to war with one another, so the democratic process is beginning to find legitimacy through a pan-European politics of history in which local grassroots initiatives are as involved as official school textbook commissions and governmental and nongovernmental instances.

It is perfectly possible to capitalize on this progress, both pedagogically and politically. Here I come to the seventh circle of European memory—the undeniable success of western Europe after 1950, which will occupy an important place in the House of European History, due to open in Brussels in 2014. Since the end of World War II, Europe has undergone a development that leads out of the cycle of totalitarianism and the ideological division of East and West. One cannot really contend that the EU's eastern enlargement in 2004 has already mended this rift but neither need one be afraid of building a European museum that addresses this success story.

European integration has indisputably been a success. For most people, economic performance is what counts—one only need compare present levels of development and affluence with those of the 1930s or 1950s to get an idea of the strength of the economic union. For others, what is important is the political dividends of permanent peace between states that were once bitter enemies, a change that affects the communication between states ("Germany is hemmed in by friends," as once put by Volker Rühe, former Defense Minister of Germany) and helps overcome irreconcilable internal political ideologies and lines of fracture. Today's Europe consists exclusively of parliamentary and semipresidential democracies that rate highly on global freedom rankings, and legal and constitutional orders are equally stable. Yet other people emphasize the strengths of European cultures, maintaining that Europe can draw on its heyday in the nineteenth and twentieth centuries. Nowhere else does there exist such a dense network of cultural initiatives; no other place in the world is so inclusive; nowhere else have cultural workers—despite increasing encroachments—attained such a high degree of autonomy. For Europe's present authors, what is most important is the strength of European civil society, which, it might be added, is responsible for many of the merits listed above.

There is no life insurance on any of these things, and in many places economic and cultural globalization and neoliberal policies of social exclusion have already severely clouded the picture. Even more remarkable is the fact that the positive balance of Europe after 1945 has had little impact on European self-confidence, accounting for Europe's relatively limited influence in world politics. In this sense the assertion that Europe is a success story hardly has the character of self-congratulation. Ironically, one aspect of a critical discussion of European history is that too much confidence is placed in the nation-states and that Brussels is notoriously mistrusted.

The above-mentioned House of European History, according to experts, is to remain scientific, draw on the most recent museological and didactic innovations, and bring a wide variety of object, text, and media elements to bear. The museum can draw on the concept of the site of memory, which in this case must a priori be supranationally oriented, that is, recognizeable in many European countries and thus capable of being viewed and categorized in numerous and possibly controversial ways. Controversies will exist within as well as between states, and this book's central idea is that these conflicts, as long as they are waged peacefully and treated at the institutional level, are precisely what can create and strengthen a community of memory.

***

I do not claim that the seven circles of European memory sketched above are exhaustive. Moreover, their mutual overlaps have become apparent. Awareness that this memory is dominated by a history of crime and trauma is common to all Europeans, and it imposes upon them a heavy burden. The historical reports that follow in this volume deal with conflicts of memory and politicohistorical controversies in countries that geographically belong to Europe and aim for EU accession. However, to a great extent because they have "a past yet to be addressed" and because acute conflicts with minorities exist within them, their belonging and their membership are not recognized. They have at least an indirect connection to the pivotal European myth, the Holocaust, which they both associate themselves with and distance themselves from.

Notes

1. The first countries to introduce a Holocaust memorial day were the United Kingdom and Italy, with Germany following in 1996. Public buildings flew flags at half mast, and there were mourning ceremonies, readings, church services, and educational events. In 2010 the president of Israel addressed the German parliament.
2. During a pogrom in July 1946, 42 Jewish Holocaust survivors were killed by a mob and a further 80 wounded.
3. It goes without saying that collaboration does not serve only the exculpation from German crimes.
4. The UNIFIL fleet assumed responsibility for surveillance of the Lebanese borders.
5. The neocommunist revival currently being staged by postcommunist intellectuals like Slavoj Zizek, Antonio Negri, and Alain Badiou also seems bizarrely blind in a historical sense.
6. Naimark characterizes ethnic cleansing as a European phenomenon of the twentieth century, taking the examples of the Armenian genocide, the Holocaust, the Soviet deportations in Caucasus, the expulsion of the Germans after 1945, and the wars in the former Yugoslavia. Sundhaussen (2010) defines ethnic cleansings as "measures initiated and carried out, encouraged or tolerated by a modern state or para-state and its actors, whose aim is to remove a population group that on the basis of its ethnicity is stigmatized as 'foreign', 'threatening', or 'inferior' from a particular territory, as well as all that that could recall its presence" (p. 231).
7. Retrieved November 5, 2010, from http://untreaty.un.org/cod/icc/statute/romefra.htm
8. Retrieved November 5, 2010, from http://www.hrweb.org/legal/genocide.html
9. For the minutes of the full parliamentary debate in the Bundestag, see Deutscher Bundestag (2005, pp. 16127–16132).
10. The term *Holodomor* awakens associations with the Holocaust. The word is formed from the two Ukrainian words *holod* (hunger) and *mor* (death, plague). *Holodomor* (Russian: *golodomor*) literally means "famine." There is no etymological connection with the word *Holocaust*.
11. See also von Trotha's notorious appeal to the Herero people, in Behnen (1977, pp. 291–293); Schaller (2004); Zimmerer and Zeller (2003).

References

Adorno, T. (1971). *Erziehung nach Auschwitz* [Education after Auschwitz]. In T. Adorno (Ed.), *Erziehung zur Mündigkeit. Vorträge und Gespräche mit Hellmut Becker 1959–1969* (pp. 88–104). Frankfurt am Main: Suhrkamp Taschenbuch.

Antrag der Fraktionen SPD, CDU/CSU, Bündnis 90/Die Grünen und FDP. (2005, June 15). Drucksache 15/5689. Retrieved October 29, 2010, from http://dipbt.bundestag.de/doc/btd/15/056/1505689.pdf

Ausstellungen zur Flucht und Vertreibung in Bonn und Berlin [Exhibitions on flight and expulsion in Bonn and Berlin]. (2006, May 18–August 27). Konzept Berlin. Retrieved October 27, 2010, from http://www.dhm.de/ausstellungen/flucht-vertreibung/index.html

Basic, N., & Welzer, H. (Eds.). (2007). *Der Krieg der Erinnerung: Holocaust, Kollaboration und Widerstand im europäischen Gedächtnis* [The war of memory: Holocaust, collaboration, and resistance in the European memory]. Frankfurt am Main: Fischer.

Behnen, M. (Ed.). (1977). *Ausgewählte Quellen zur deutschen Geschichte der Neuzeit: Bd. 26. Quellen zur deutschen Außenpolitik im Zeitalter der Imperialismus 1890–1911* [Selected

sources on modern German history: Sources on German foreign policy in the age of imperialism, 1890–1911]. Darmstadt: Wissenschaftliche Buchgesellschaft.

Bernlocher, L., & Geiss, P. (Eds.). (2006). *L'Europe et le Monde depuis 1945* [Europe and the
world since 1945]. Histoire/Geschichte 1 (Manuel d'histoire franco-allemand). Paris: Nathan.

Brumlik, M. (2010). Neoleninismus in der Postdemokratie [Neo-Leninism in the postdemocratic
era]. *Blätter für deutsche und internationale Politik, 8,* 105–116.

Bundestag, D. (2005, April 21). Stenografischer Bericht der 172 Sitzung: Plenarprotokoll 15/172
[Minutes of the 172nd General Session] (pp. 16127–16136). Retrieved October 29, 2010, from
http://dipbt.bundestag.de/dip21/btp/15/15172.pdf

Council Framework Decision 2008/913/JHA. (2008, November 28) combating certain forms
and expressions of racism and xenophobia by means of criminal law. Official Journal, L
328, December 6, 2008. Retrieved October 8, 2010, from http://eur-lex.europa.eu/LexUriServ/
LexUriServ.do?uri=CELEX:32008F0913:EN:HTML

Drechsel, B. (2010). The Berlin Wall from a visual perspective: Comments on the construction of
a political media icon. *Visual Communication, 1,* 3–24.

Drechsler, H. (1984). *Südwestafrika unter deutscher Kolonialherrschaft. Der Kampf der Herero
und Nama gegen den deutschen Imperialismus (1884–1915)* [Southwest Africa under German
colonial rule: The battle of the Herero and Nama against German imperialism (1884–1915)].
Berlin: Akademische Verlagsgesellschaft.

Greiner, B. (2010). *Verdrängter Terror. Geschichte und Wahrnehmung sowjetischer Speziallager in
Deutschland* [Repressed terror: History and perception of Soviet special camps in Germany].
Hamburg: Hamburger Edition.

Gross, J. (2006). *Fear: Anti-Semitism in Poland after Auschwitz: An essay in historical interpretation.* Princeton, NJ: Princeton University Press.

Gudkov, L. (2005). Die Fesseln des Sieges. Russlands Identität aus der Erinnerung an den Krieg
[The bondage of victory: Russia's identity stemming from the memory of the war]. *Osteuropa,
55*(4–6), 56–73.

Hillenbrand, K. (2010, May 25). Simon Wiesenthal Center: Die Organisation fahndet intensiv nach
noch lebenden Kriegsverbrecher [Simon Wiesenthal Center: The organization is hunting down
war criminals who are still alive]. *Tageszeitung,* Berlin, p. 5.

Kalniete, S. (2004). Old Europe, new Europe: Speech at the opening of the Leipzig Book Fair,
2004. Retrieved March 24, 2004, from http://www.mdr.de/DL/1290734.pdf

Kalniete, S. (2006). *With dance shoes in Siberian snows* (M. Gailītis, Trans.). Riga: The Latvian
Occupation Museum Association. (Original work published 2001)

Leggewie, C. (Ed.). (2004). *Die Türkei und Europa. Die Positionen* [Turkey and Europe: The
positions]. Frankfurt am Main: Suhrkamp.

Le Quintrec, G., Geiss, P., & Bernlocher, L. (Eds.). (2006). *Europa und die Welt seit 1945*
[Europe and the world since 1945]. Histoire/Geschichte 1 (Schülerband), Leipzig: Klett-
Schulbuchverlag.

Levy, D., & Sznaider, N. (2001). *Erinnerung im globalen Zeitalter: Der Holocaust* [Remembering
in the global age: The Holocaust]. Frankfurt am Main: Suhrkamp.

Manutscharjan, A. (2005, April 18). Eine äußerst sperrige Last der Erinnerung. Seit 90
Jahren offiziell tabu: Der Völkermord an den Armeniern in der Türkei [A highly cum-
bersome memory—officially taboo: The Armenien genocide in Turkey]. *Das Parlament,*
No. 16. Retrieved October 27th from http://www.bundestag.de/dasparlament/2005/16/
ThemaderWoche/001.html

MEPs: ban hammer, sickle and swastika. (2005, February 2). *Baltic Times* (Riga), p. 1. Retrieved
October 22, 2010, from http://www.baltictimes.com/news/articles/11860

Michnik, A. (1998). *Letters from freedom: Post-Cold War realities and perspectives.* Berkeley, CA:
University of California Press.

Naimark, N. (2001). *Fires of hatred: Ethnic cleansing in twentieth-century Europe.* Cambridge,
MA: Harvard University Press.

Paletschek, S. (2008). Der Weihnachtsfrieden 1914 und der erste Weltkrieg als neuer (west-)
europäischer Erinnerungsort. Epilog [Epilogue: The Christmas Truce of 1914 and World War

I as a new western European site of memory]. In B. Korte, S. Paletschek, & W. Hochbruck (Eds.), *Der erste Weltkrieg in der populären Erinnerungskultur* (pp. 213–221). Essen: Klartext.

Protokoll der Bundestagsdebatte, Tagesordnungspunkt 6. (2005, April 21). Drucksache 15/4933 [Stenographic record of the Bundestag debate (172nd General Session), Document 15/4933]. Retrieved October 29, 2010, from http://www.bergner.de/files/Antrag%20Armenien%201504933.pdf

Rabinovici, D., Speck, U., & Sznaider, N. (Eds.). (2004). *Neuer Antisemitismus?—Eine globale Debatte* [New anti-Semitism? A global debate]. Frankfurt am Main: Suhrkamp.

Sabrow, M. (Ed.). (2010). *Bewältigte Diktaturvergangenheit? 20 Jahre DDR-Aufarbeitung* [Dictatorial past overcome? Twenty years of research on the GDR]. Leipzig: Universitätsverlag.

Schaller, D. J. (2004). "Ich glaube, dass die Nation als solche vernichtet werden muss": Kolonialkrieg und Völkermord in "Deutsch-Südwestafrika" 1904–1907 ["I believe that the nation as such must be annihilated": Colonial war and genocide in "German Southwest Africa," 1904–1907]. *Journal of Genocide Research, 6,* 395–430.

Schmale, W. (2008). "Osteuropa": Zwischen Ende und Neudefinition? ["Eastern Europe": Between end and new definition?]. In J. M. Faraldo, P. Gulińska-Jurgiel, & C. Domnitz (Eds.), *Europa im Ostblock: Vorstellungen und Diskurse (1945–1991)* (pp. 23–35). Cologne: Böhlau.

Schmid, B. (2008, February 9). Geschichtspolitik: Schlupfloch am andern Ufer. Frankreich: Die jüngsten Polemiken um das Kolonialismusgesetz zeigen, wie die Geschichte zum Spielball der Politik wird [History policy: Loophole on the other bank of the river—France: The recent polemics surrounding the colonial law show how history is becoming a political football]. *Wochenzeitung* (Paris). Retrieved October 21, 2010, from http://www.uni-kassel.de/fb5/frieden/regionen/Frankreich/kolonialismus.html

Schmid, H. (2008). Europäisierung des Auschwitzgedenkens? Zum Aufstieg des 27. Januar 1945 als "Holocaustgedenktag" in Europa [The Europeanization of the commemoration of Auschwitz? On the rise of January 27 as a "Holocaust Remembrance Day" in Europe]. In J. Eckel & C. Moisel (Eds.), *Universalisierung des Holocaust? Erinnerungskultur und Geschichtspolitik in internationaler Perspektive* (pp. 174–202). Göttingen: Wallstein.

Semprún, J. (2005, April 14). Niemand wird mehr sagen können: "ja so war es" [Nobody will be able to say: "Yes, that's how it was"]. *ZEIT-Online, Kultur,* No. 16. Retrieved October 27, 2010, from http://www.zeit.de/2005/16/BefreiungBuchenw_

Sundhaussen, H. (2010). Ethnische Säuberung [Ethnic cleansing]. In D. Brandes, H. Sundhaussen, & S. Troebst (Eds.), *Lexikon der Vertreibungen. Deportation, Zwangsaussiedlung und ethnische Säuberung im Europa des 20. Jahrhunderts* (pp. 229–234). Vienna: Böhlau.

Troebst, S. (2005). Jalta versus Stalingrad, GULag versus Holocaust. Konfligierende Erinnerungskulturen im größeren Europa [Yalta versus Stalingrad, Gulag versus Holocaust: Conflicting cultures of memory in greater Europe]. *Berliner Journal für Soziologie, 3,* 381–400.

Troebst, S. (Ed.). (2010). *Postdiktatorische Geschichtskulturen im Süden und Osten Europas. Bestandsaufnahme und Forschungsperspektiven* [Postdictatorial cultures of history in the south and east of Europe: Inventory and research perspectives]. Göttingen: Wallstein.

Tych, F. (2010). Holocaust muss in ganz Europa aufgearbeitet werden: Interview mit der Zeitung *Das Parlament* [The Holocaust has to be addressed throughout Europe: Interview in *Das Parlament.*]. Retrieved October 9, 2010, from http://www.bundestag.de/presse/pressemitteilungen/2010/pm_1001227.html

Vuckovic, N. (2003). Qui demande des réparations et pour quels crimes? In M. Ferro (Ed.), *Le livre noir du colonialisme* (pp. 1023–1056). Paris: Robert Laffont.

Wegmann, H. (2010, July 13). Unsere Vorfahren ruhen nicht in Frieden. *Tageszeitung* (Berlin), p. 14.

Zeitgeschichte-online. (2004, January). Die Erinnerung an Flucht und Vertreibung [Memory of flight and expulsion]. Retrieved November 15, 2010, from http://www.zeitgeschichte-online.de/md=Vertreibung-Inhalt

Zimmerer, J., & Zeller, J. (Eds.). (2003). *Völkermord in Deutsch-Südwestafrika. Der Kolonialkrieg (1904–1908) in Namibia und seine Folgen* [Genocide in German Southwest Africa: The colonial war (1904–1908) in Namibia and its aftermath]. Berlin: C. Links.

Halecki Revisited: Europe's Conflicting Cultures of Remembrance

Stefan Troebst

Among the most popular metaphors for the profession of the historian are textile ones. "The diachronic thread," thus Carl Schorske in his *Fin-de-siècle Vienna*, "is the warp, the synchronic thread the woof in the fabric of cultural history. The historian is the weaver" (Schorske, 1981, p. xxii). And according to Carlo Levi's famous definition, history is the pattern that is woven into chaos ex post.[1] Sometimes the patterns of rather remote historical subjects resemble each other to such a degree that the question arises as to whether sheer coincidence is at work or whether there is a connection between the two phenomena. This observation is particularly true of Oskar Halecki's still widely read and discussed book, *Limits and Divisions of European History* (1950), and of the various lines dividing the landscape of memory of contemporary (post-1989) Europe.

I bring these two things together for a pragmatic reason. In 2004 I was asked to give a paper on the conflicting cultures of remembrance in post-communist Eastern Europe (Troebst, 2005c; see also Troebst, 2005a, b), and while I tried to group the various societies of the region into analytical categories, Halecki's division of European history into four historical mesoregions occurred to me. The question "coincidence or logic?" thus came up almost automatically. I venture an answer to it at the end of this chapter, but first, I briefly present Halecki's model—a somewhat tedious academic exercise but a worthwhile one. Second, I give an overview of conflicts and dividing lines in Europe's current cultures of remembrance as I see them. Beforehand, however, I should point out the striking fact that the two phenomena called "memory" and "space," or "place," seem to be tightly connected in a way still underexplored. Pierre Nora's term *lieu de mémoire* (realms of memory; see, for example, Nora, 1984) brings the two closely together, as does Aleida Assmann in her term *Erinnerungsraum* (space of remembrance; Assmann, 1999, 2006, pp. 217–234).

S. Troebst (✉)
Geisteswissenschaftliches Zentrum Geschichte und Kultur Ostmitteleuropas,
University of Leipzig, 04177 Leipzig, Germany
e-mail: stefan.troebst@snafu.de

An earlier version is published in Pakier and B. Stråth (2010).

Halecki's Theory

Being a Habsburg Pole born in Vienna, Oskar Ritter von Halecki became the leading historian of interwar Poland (Bömelburg, 2007; Morawiec, 2006). In 1923, his paper at the international historical congress in Brussels—"L'histoire de l'Europe Orientale. Sa divisions en époches, son milieu géographique et ses problèmes fondamentaux" (The history of Eastern Europe: Its divisions in epochs, its geographical milieu, and its fundamental problems)—triggered an intense and long international debate among historians from Czechoslovakia, Poland, and Germany on whether the history of Eastern Europe was different from that of Western Europe (Halecki, 1924; on the debate following Halecki's presentation, see Wandycz, 1992). In his seminal book, The Limits and Divisions of European History Halecki (1950) expanded his frames of analysis in terms of space and time by looking at all of Europe from late antiquity to the Cold War. Drawing on cultural and particularly religious criteria, he divided the historical macroregion of "Europe" into three historical mesoregions, namely, "Western Europe," "Central Europe," and "Eastern Europe." In his view, however, Central Europe consisted of two rather different parts—"West Central Europe" (Germany, and probably Austria) and "East Central Europe" (the lands between Germany and Russia). Not surprisingly, Halecki's East Central Europe historically resembled the Polish-Lithuanian Commonwealth of the early modern period and the group of states that fell under Soviet hegemony as decided in Yalta in 1945 (Troebst, 2003).

Halecki's book became, and still is, influential among historians, not so much because of its sophistication but because for decades after its publication no one dared tackle the subject of introducing an intermediary, transnational level between the various national histories of Europe and European history. Not until the second half of the 1970s did things change. The German historian Klaus Zernack took the divisions identified by his Polish colleague as a starting point for (a) combining Halecki's "Eastern Europe" and "East Central Europe" into one historical region, called again "Eastern Europe," and (b) subdividing this extended Eastern Europe into four parts. They were, first, Southeastern Europe, that is, the Balkan-Danube region; second, a narrower East Central Europe, comprising Hungary, Poland, and the Bohemian Lands; third, Northeastern Europe, with the historical Baltic lands as its core; and fourth, the Eastern Slavic lands, with the various Russian state-formations from the Kievan Rus' via Muscovy to Russia and the Soviet Union (Zernack, 1977, pp. 20–30, 88–92). When in 1981 the Hungarian historian Jenő Szűcs came up with a socioeconomic model of "The Three Historical Regions of Europe," it turned out that it fit Halecki's perfectly well. The only difference was that Szűcs made no distinction between "Western" and "West Central" Europe and spoke instead—terminologically somewhat inconsistent—of "Western," "East Central," and "Eastern Europe" (Szűcs, 1983). In short, the three main dividing lines drawn by Halecki were basically confirmed by later research. They are (a) the one between Germany and Western Europe, (b) the one between East Central Europe and Russia, and (c) the one between Germany and East Central Europe.

Memory Conflicts in Contemporary Europe

In my attempt in 2004 to describe the various postcommunist cultures of remembrance from Tirana to Moscow and from Prague to Kiev, I thought it helpful to try to form groups of the many cases and ultimately identified four categories. In the first category I put societies with a strong anticommunist consensus on recent history, a stance such as the one in the Baltic states. The second category consisted of societies where such a consensus did not exist, where instead fierce public debates on how history should be remembered take place. Hungary, with its antagonistic camps of anticommunist liberals and postcommunist socialists, was included, for instance, but also Poland, and even Ukraine. The third category encompassed cases where ambivalence and apathy dominated, where the urge to come to terms with the past was relatively weak—as in Bulgaria, Romania, Serbia, and Albania. The fourth and last category comprised societies where communism was not delegitimized and where, accordingly, the communist past was hardly discussed. This group had Belarus, Moldova, and, above all, the Russian Federation, where communism is perceived as part of the imperial legacy.

Although I was aware of the fact that the natural frame of any given culture of remembrance—and thus also the adequate unit of analysis—is a national one, the transnational similarities within the four categories struck me as being historically connoted, if not charged. For all the differences between the three Baltic states (my category 1), they had a similar political fate from 1918 on; Poland and Hungary (category 2) shared the same noble and imperial background; and the Balkan states (category 3) had a common Byzantine and Ottoman heritage. In other words, Halecki's dividing line between "Eastern" and "East Central Europe" was there, as were Zernack's distinctions between "Northeastern," "East Central," and "Southeastern Europe."

The Commemoriation of V-E Day

A good occasion to test the hypothesis on historically shaped mesoregional divisions of European cultures of remembrance was provided by the 60th anniversary of the end of World War II in 2005. The European *lieu de mémoire* "1945" can function as the litmus test for the hypothesis. Indeed, with the approach of May 8, 2005, the various transnational categories of national cultures of remembrance appeared on the radar screen of European politics. The Russian invitation to the former Soviet satellites and republics to participate in the Moscow celebrations of what was termed "the victory over Fascism" and "the liberation of Europe" met fierce and unanimous disapproval in Tallinn, Riga, Vilnius, and Warsaw. From the Baltic perspective, 1945 was not a liberation but a mere change from one occupation by an alien dictatorial and genocidal regime to another. In Poland, the invitation triggered a heated debate on whether to accept it or not. Whereas some observers thought *raison d'état* required the presence of Poland as an ally in the wartime alliance against Hitler, others strongly resented the post-Soviet interpretation of history. In the eyes of most Poles, the main component of the *lieu de mémoire* "1945" was not "May 8 (or 9)" but "Yalta" a couple of weeks before. In Southeastern Europe the Russian invitation did not stir much emotion: Hungary, Romania, and Bulgaria had lost World War II on the German side and did not feel like celebrating anything, and the post-Yugoslav states looked upon post-Soviet Russia through the prism of the Tito–Stalin split.

Interestingly enough, the Russian invitation was finally accepted by the Polish President, Aleksander Kwaśniewski, who, like his Russian counterpart President Vladimir Putin, was a postcommunist. Also traveling to Moscow, however—independently of Kwaśniewski, and on Putin's personal invitation—was General Wojciech Jaruzelski, who, as the strong man in communist Poland in 1981, had proclaimed martial law. So on May 9, two Polands were present on Red Square: the democratic republic as well as the Soviet vassal. The conflicting emotions pervading this encounter also characterized the decision of the Latvian president Vaira Vike-Freiberga to accept Putin's invitation instead of declining it, as her Estonian and Lithuanian colleagues did. Vike-Freiberga explained her courageous choice by stating that she was going to Moscow to confront the post-Soviet interpretation of twentieth-century history with the alternative Latvian and Baltic interpretation (Onken, 2007; see also Veser, 2005; von Lucius, 2005a, b). Her move was related to the fact that she had spent most of her life in the United States rather than in her native country, a background typical in Lithuania and Estonia as well as in parts of the Latvian public. Her connection with Washington was excellent, as was proven by the stopover that US President George W. Bush made in Riga on his way to Moscow on May 7, 2005. In the speech he gave in the Latvian capital, he thoroughly subscribed to the Baltic interpretation of twentieth-century history:

> For much of Eastern and Central Europe, victory brought the iron rule of another empire. V-E Day marked the end of fascism, but it did not end oppression.... The captivity of millions in Central and Eastern Europe will be remembered as one of the greatest wrongs of history. (Bush, 2005)

In the eyes of the Latvians, the Balts, and the East Central Europeans in general, Bush thus managed to combine the emphasis on democracy with the memory of the wartime alliance. There were no such signals from the West Europeans to the East Central Europeans, just as there was no German gesture of this kind. In fact, the contrary was demonstrated soon after the May 9 celebrations. When Putin invited the German chancellor Gerhard Schröder and French president Jacques Chirac to celebrate the 750th anniversary of the founding of the former Prussian city of Königsberg, now the Russian enclave of Kaliningrad, neither western statesman protested that the heads of neighboring Lithuania and Poland had deliberately not been invited.

In terms of transnational cultures of remembrance, the 60th anniversary of the end of World War II grouped the national societies of Europe into four camps. They were (a) the Soviet-nostalgic host, Russia; (b) the anti-Soviet camp in East Central Europe; (c) a disoriented Germany, which after decades of being excluded from

Allied celebrations took its participation in the Moscow ceremonies as something like an international rehabilitation; and (d) Western European societies clinging in this instance to a culture of remembrance that was less continental than it was "Atlantic." Seen through the prism of "1945," today's dividing lines perfectly coincide with Halecki's division.

Holocaust Versus Gulag

Yet Halecki's divisions do not fit all levels of European cultures of remembrance. In March 2004, for example, just some weeks before the European Union's major eastward enlargement, a controversy arose in Germany and some other parts of Europe about the relationship between a "Western" Holocaust memory and an "Eastern" Gulag remembrance. In this case, the dividing line between "East" and "West" ran parallel to the Iron Curtain of the Cold War—not to the EU's new eastern border, which, as noted above, is Halecki's line between his "East Central" and "Eastern" Europe. In a public speech entitled with a somewhat provocative reference to Donald Rumsfeld's 2003 remark "Old Europe, New Europe," the former Latvian Minister of Foreign Affairs and, at that time, Latvian EU Commissioner-to-be, Sandra Kalniete, stated in Leipzig (i.e., eastern Germany), "the two totalitarian regimes—Nazism and Communism—were equally criminal" (Kalniete, 2004). Accordingly, Kalniete demanded that the victims of both regimes be remembered equally, too. In Germany, her call prompted a vehement debate in which Kalniete was initially accused of "illegitame comparison," of "downgrading the Holocaust," and ultimately of "anti-Semitism" (Troebst, 2006a).

Whereas a certain rapprochement developed between Kalniete and her opponents in 2005, the debate flared up again in February 2006. In another speech in Germany, this time in Hamburg, Kalniete detailed her view on National Socialism and Stalinism as being "equally criminal." In doing so, she came up with death counts for both regimes—94.5 million for the Soviet variety of totalitarianism and 56 million for the German one (Kalniete, 2006a; see also Bauer, 2006; Jeismann, 2006; Kalniete, 2005, 2006b)—thus implying that communism was the greater evil. Despite the strong reaction from sectors of the German public, Kalniete has managed to put the Gulag on the agenda of the politics of remembrance, at least in Germany. The exclusive focus on the Holocaust as a negative "EU founding myth"—the message of the 2000 Stockholm International Forum on the Holocaust (Jeismann, 2000; see also Kroh, 2005; Levy & Sznaider, 2001, pp. 210–216; Probst, 2002)—is giving way to what is termed "multiperspectivity." At the same time, Kalniete's views nicely fit a political tendency in Germany to move from self-perception as a nation of perpetrators to self-perception as a nation of victims. The Allied bombing of Germany, the expulsion of Germans from East Central Europe, and other "revisionist" topics figure prominently in media and politics. Still, something like a "Kalniete effect" is apparent in other European societies and publics, too, as in France, where the publication of the *Livre noir du communisme* (Courtoise et al., 1997) was of crucial importance. It therefore seems as though the divide running through the EU's cultures of remembrance along the Gulag–Holocaust line is narrowing.

The Central European Culture of Remembrance

My last example again confirms Halecki's perception of one "Central Europe" being subdivided into "West Central" and "East Central Europe." For years now, Germany and, to a lesser degree, Austria on one side and the Visegrád Group of States (Poland, the Czech Republic, Slovakia, and Hungary) on the other have engaged in periodically heated national and transnational debates on ethnic cleansing and processes of forced migration in twentieth-century Central and Eastern Europe, particularly on mass expulsions of Germans from East Central and Southeastern Europe to Germany and of Poles from what had been the eastern part of interwar Poland and what were Soviet territories as of 1944 to the new People's Republic of Poland. Despite the militant overtones heard in relatively large segments of German and Polish society and media, the political elites of the two countries created, in 2005, one of the few institutionalized joint ventures for a common European culture of remembrance focusing on forced migration and ethnic cleansing. This *European Network Remembrance and Solidarity* was initiated by Warsaw and Berlin and is supported by Budapest and Bratislava, probably also by Vienna, but not yet by Prague (Quack, 2006; Troebst, 2007). A similar initiative, again with Germany and Poland as the driving forces, was launched in 2004 in the Parliamentary Assembly of the Council of Europe—under the somewhat clumsy title of *European Remembrance Centre for Victims of Forced Population Movements and Ethnic Cleansing* (see Troebst, 2006b). In terms of politics of history and a culture of remembrance, Germany and her neighbors to the east can obviously be grouped into a common "Central Europe" as Halecki identified it.

The Connection Between Halecki's Theory and Post-1989 European Cultures of Remembrance

So much for empiricism. I return now back to my initial question of whether the resemblance of the patterns of Halecki's division of European history and of post-1989 European cultures of remembrance is just coincidence or whether there is a logical, even causal connection between the two phenomena. Of course, one could argue that what Halecki has analyzed from late antiquity to the mid-twentieth century—the emergence of four historical mesoregions in Europe—is valid for the early twenty-first century, too. That line of reasoning, however, would be something like a truism and would imply that Halecki's *longue-durée* interpretation is correct. I think the explanation for the resemblance of the two patterns is much simpler and more direct. Halecki's division of European history into four distinct mesoregions, despite its underlying long-duration pattern, is very much a product of the Cold War. A closer look at his fourfold regional model reveals it to be binary one. Culturally, Halecki makes a distinction between two parts of Europe: the "West," consisting of Western, West Central, and, notably, East Central Europe; and the "East," consisting of Eastern Europe, that is, Russia, aka the Soviet Union. And the political fact that East Central Europe had been under Soviet hegemony since Yalta was, as Halecki implied, an ahistorical one, a deplorable, yet temporary, political reality to be corrected in order to fit "history" again. This message was the core thesis of Halecki's other book published in the 1950s and somewhat dramatically entitled *Borderlands of Western Civilization: A History of East Central Europe* (Halecki, 1952). So despite Halecki's elaborate historical argumentation, his mesoregionalizing model is basically a child of its time. The 1980s discussion on *Mitteleuropa* can be identified as the missing link to today's actors of the politics of history in East Central Europe. The concept of an *occident kidnappé* (Kundera, 1983), of an East Central Europe highjacked by Stalin, is in fact an unconscious reiteration of Halecki's time-bound world view 30 years earlier.

Towards a Transatlantic Culture of Remembrance

All these considerations bring me to the final question: What does one make of it all? To what degree indeed are European national cultures of remembrance historically shaped, maybe even programmed? And what is their average historical "depth of focus"? 60 years? 100 years? Or, taking the Serbian case, 500 years, even 4,000 years, as historical entrepreneurs in contemporary Greece have been saying since the latest flare-up of the Macedonian controversy in the early 1990s? Again, I think each national case is different, yet national cases tend to form identifiable clusters and categories—as Halecki has helped to explain. He even hints at whether Europe's conflicting national cultures of remembrance will one day merge into one, a European, transcontinental, or even global one. In the last sentence of his *Borderlands of Western Civilization*, he imagines "a new era. . . . for all those who today suffer in East Central Europe, or at least for their descendants, because for the first time in history they would belong to the same great community, not only with Western Europe, but also with America" (Halecki, 1952, pp. 516–517). Halecki thereby takes Nora's dictum—or verdict—"History unites, memory divides" (Nora, 2001, p. 686) and turns it around. In exile in North America during the Cold War, the East Central European historian came to the conclusion that *history* divides while memory *unites*. Seen from this point of view, the emergence of a transatlantic culture of remembrance—out of the many national memories—indeed seems possible.

Note

1. Retrieved July 27, 2010, from http://www.gutzitiert.de/zitat_autor_carlo_levi_thema_geschichte_zitat_9688.html

References

Assmann, A. (1999). *Erinnerungsräume. Formen und Wandlungen des kulturellen Gedächtnisses* [Commemorative spaces: Forms and changes in cultural memory]. Munich: C. H. Beck.

Assmann, A. (2006). *Der lange Schatten der Vergangenheit. Erinnerungskultur und Geschichtspolitik* [The long shadow of the past: Culture of remembrance and the politics of history]. Munich: C. H. Beck.

Bauer, M. (2006, February 18–19). Schlimme Kommunisten. Sandra Kalniete spricht in Hamburg über das halbierte Gewissen [Bad communists: Sandra Kalniete speaks in Hamburg about halved conscience.]. *Süddeutsche Zeitung*, p. 14.

Bush, G. W. (2005, May 7). President discusses freedom and democracy in Latvia, Riga, Latvia. Speech given at The Small Guild Hall, Riga, Latvia. Retrieved May 7, 2005, from http://www. whitehouse.gov.edgesuite.net/news/releases/2005/05/print/20050507-8.html

Bömelburg, H.-J. (2007). Zwischen imperialer Geschichte und Ostmitteleuropa als Geschichtsregion: Oskar Halecki und die polnische "jagiellonische Idee" [Between imperial history and East Central Europe as a region of history: Oskar Halecki and the Polish "Jagielonian idea"]. In F. Hadler & M. Mesenhöller (Eds.), *Vergangene Größe und Ohnmacht in Ostmitteleuropa: Repräsentationen imperialer Erfahrung in der Historiographie seit 1918* (pp. 99–130). Leipzig: Akademische Verlagsanstalt.

Courtoise, S., Werth, N., Panné, J.-L., Paczkowski, A., Bartošek, K., & Margolin, J.-L. (Eds.). (1997). *Livres noir du communisme—Crimes, terreur, répression.* Paris: Editions Robert Laffont.

Halecki, O. (1924). L'histoire de L'Europe Orientale. Sa divisions en époches, son milieu géographique et ses problèmes fondamentaux [The history of Eastern Europe: Its divisions in epochs, its geographical milieu, and its fundamental problems]. In *La Pologne au Ve Congrès International des Sciences Historiques à Bruxelles, 1923* (pp. 73–94). Warsaw: Polska Akademia Nauk.

Halecki, O. (1950). *The limits and divisions of European history.* London: Sheed & Ward.

Halecki, O. (1952). *Borderlands of Western civilization: A history of East Central Europe.* New York: Ronald Press.

Jeismann, M. (2000). Schuld—der neue Gründungsmythos Europas? Die Internationale Holocaust-Konferenz von Stockholm (26–28 Januar 2000) und eine Moral, die nach hinten losgeht [Guilt—Europe's new founding myth? The International Holocaust Conference, Stockholm (26–28 January 2000) and a moral that backfires]. *Historische Anthropologie, 8,* 454–458.

Jeismann, M. (2006, February 18). Zur Zukunft. Erinnerungsanspruch: Sandra Kalnietes Rede über Europa [On the future: Claim to rememberance in Sandra Kalniete's Speech on Europe]. *Frankfurter Allgemeine Zeitung*, p. 40.

Kalniete, S. (2004). Old Europe, new Europe: Speech at the opening of the Leipzig Book Fair, 2004. Retrieved March 24, 2004, from http://www.mdr.de/DL/1290734.pdf

Kalniete, S. (2005, November 13). "Ich werde nie ein ganz freier Mensch sein". Sandra Kalniete über den GULag, das Elend ihrer Familie und die Gleichgültigkeit des Westens ["I will never be a completely free human being": Sandra Kalniete on the Gulag, her family's misery, and the indifference of the West]. *Frankfurter Allgemeinen Sonntagszeitung*, p. 9.

Kalniete, S. (2006a). Europa: Wiedervereinigung der Geschichte [Europe: Reunification of history]. Address delivered at the annual EUSTORY conference, Hamburg, 16 February 2006. (Unpublished manuscript)

Kalniete, S. (2006b, February 16). Verdrängter GULag—Europas gespaltene Erinnerung [Repressed Gulag–Europe's divided memory]. *Die Welt.* Retrieved February 16, 2006, from http://www.welt.de/data/2006/02/16/846362.html

Kroh, J. (2005). Holocaust transnational. Zur Institutionalisierung des Holocaust-Gedenkens [Holocaust transnational: On the institutionalization of Holocaust commemoration]. *Blätter für deutsche und internationale Politik, 50,* 741–750.

Kundera, M. (1983). Un occident kidnappé, ou la tragédie de l'Europe Centrale [A highjacked West: On the tragedy of Central Europe]. *Le Débat, 27*, 2–24.

Levy, D., & Sznaider, N. (2001). *Erinnerung im globalen Zeitalter. Der Holocaust* [Remembering in the global age: The Holocaust]. Frankfurt am Main: Suhrkamp.

Morawiec, M. (2006). Oskar Halecki (1891–1973). In H. Duchhardt, M. Morawiec, W. Schmale, & W. Schulze (Eds.), *Europa-Historiker. Ein biographisches Handbuch* (pp. 215–239). Göttingen: Vandenhoeck & Ruprecht.

Nora, P. (1984–1992). *Les lieux de mémoire* [Realms of memory] (7 vols.). Paris: Gallimard.

Nora, P. (2001). Nachwort [Afterword]. In E. François & H. Schulze (Eds.), *Deutsche Erinnerungsorte III* (pp. 681–686). Munich: C. H. Beck.

Onken, E.-C. (2007). The Baltic States and Moscow's 9 May Commemoration: Analysing memory politics in Europe. *Europe-Asia Studies, 59*, 23–46.

Pakier M., & Stråth B. (Eds.). (2010) *A European memory? Contested histories and politics of remembrance* (pp. 56–63). New York: Berghahn.

Probst, L. (2002). Europäisierung des Holocaust. eine neue Zivilreligion für Europa? [Europeanization of the Holocaust: A new civil religion for Europe?]. *Kommune. Forum für Politik, Ökonomie, Kultur, 20*(7), 42–45.

Quack, S. (2006). Divided history—common memory? A question of the culture of memory in the European Union. Lecture at the European Union Studies Center, CUNY, New York, April 20, 2006. Retrieved September 21, 2010, from http://web.gc.cuny.edu/Eusc/activities/paper/Quack07.htm

Schorske, C. E. (1981). *Fin-de-siècle Vienna: Politics and Culture*. New York: Alfred Knopf.

Szűcs, J. (1983). The three historical regions of Europe: An outline. *Acta Historica. Revue de l'Academie des Sciences de Hongrie, 29*, 131–184.

Troebst, S. (Ed.). (2006b). *Vertreibungsdiskurs und europäische Erinnerungskultur. Deutsch-polnische Initiativen zur Institutionalisierung. Eine Dokumentation* [Discourse on expulsion and European culture of memory: A documentation of German–Polish initiatives for institutionalization]. Osnabrück: fibre Verlag.

Troebst, S. (2003). "Intermarium" and "Wedding to the Sea": Politics of history and mental mapping in East Central Europe. *European Review of History/Revue européenne d'histoire, 10*, 293–321.

Troebst, S. (2005a). Jalta versus Stalingrad, GULag versus Holocaust. Konfligierende Erinnerungskulturen im grösseren Europa [Yalta versus Stalingrad, Gulag versus Holocaust: Conflicting cultures of memory in the greater Europe]. *Berliner Journal für Soziologie, 15*, 381–400.

Troebst, S. (2005b). *Postkommunistische Erinnerungskulturen im östlichen Europa. Bestandsaufnahme, Kategorisierung, Periodisierung*/Postkomunistyczne kultury pamięci w Europie Wschodniej [Postcommunist cultures of memory in Eastern Europe: Inventory, categorization, and periodization]. Stan, kategoryzacja, periodyzacja. Wrocław: Wydawnictwo Uniwersytetu Wrocławskiego. (Berichte des Willy-Brandt-Zentrums für Deutschland- und Europastudien der Universität Wrocław/Raporty Centrum Studiów Niemieckich i Europejskich im. Willy Brandta Uniwersytetu Wrocławskiego, 7)

Troebst, S. (2005c). "Was für ein Teppich?" Postkommunistische Erinnerungskulturen in Ost(mittel)europa ["What kind of carpet?" Postcommunist cultures of memory in East Central Europe]. In V. Knigge & U. Mählert (Eds.), *Der Kommunismus im Museum. Formen der Auseinandersetzung in Deutschland und Ostmitteleuropa* (pp. 31–54). Cologne: Böhlau.

Troebst, S. (2006a). Von Nikita Chruščëv zu Sandra Kalniete. Der lieu de mémoire "1956" und Europas aktuelle Erinnerungskonflikte [From Nikita Khrushchev to Sandra Kalniete: 1956 as a realm of memory and Europa's current conflicts over memory]. *Comparativ, 16*, 150–170.

Troebst, S. (2007). Das Europäische Netzwerk Erinnerung und Solidarität. Eine zentraleuropäische Initiative zur Institutionalisierung des Vertreibungsgedenkens 2002–2006 [The European Network remembrance and solidarity: A Central European initiative on institutionalizing the remembrance of expulsion, 2002–2006]. *Zeitgeschichte, 34*, 43–57.

Veser, R. (2005, March 1). Feindliche Einladung [Hostile invitation]. *Frankfurter Allgemeine Zeitung*, p. 1.

von Lucius, R. (2005a, March 3). "Kriegsende brachte weiteres Morden" [War's end meant continued murder]. *Frankfurter Allgemeine Zeitung*, p. 9.

von Lucius, R. (2005b, February 16). Zwei Geschichtsdeutungen. Die baltischen Länder wollen die EU für ihre Sicht des "9. Mai" gewinnen [Two interpretations of history: The Baltic countries seek to win over the EU for their view of "May 9"]. *Frankfurter Allgemeine Zeitung*, p. 10.

Wandycz, P. S. (1992). East European history and its meaning: The Halecki-Bidlo-Handelsman debate. In P. Jónás (Ed.), *Király Béla emlékkőnyv. Háború és társadalom. War and Society. Guerre et société. Krieg und Gesellschaft* (pp. 308–321). Budapest: Századvég.

Zernack, K. (1977). *Osteuropa. Eine Einführung in seine Geschichte* [An introduction to the history of Eastern Europe]. Munich: C. H. Beck.

Remembering for Whom? Concepts for Memorials in Western Europe

Rainer Eckert

European Remembrance

Every attempt to ascertain what makes up the heart of Europe is always about division and the setting of limits. More important are the things that East and West, North and South have in common. From that perspective the history of the European continent quickly becomes the main focus. It is a basis for a common European identity and future, but it automatically begs the question of which elements of common remembrance should be retained. It is about the essence of the force that binds Europe together at its center and about the realization that, as former Latvian Foreign Minister Sandra Kalniete put it, without a "reunification of history" a political unification of Europe will not be successful (Baumann & Müller, 2006, p. 3). On a global scale Europe is a kind of unified entity—albeit only one among many (Boyer, 2007, p. 9)—but the inside view of Europe's unity raises a number of questions about where the borders of the continent are and what is actually "European" (Muschg, 2005). It quickly becomes obvious when addressing these issues that Europe will never be either an exclusively political or solely European phenomenon. Europe consists of competing nation-states, whose interests and conflicts span the globe.

Given this background, I am essentially of the opinion that Europe should not just be a political, economic. or financial construct (hopefully a prosperous one). It needs a fundamental idea to sustain it, one based foremost on freedom of speech; human rights; the Western (i.e., Judeo-Christian) culture; and the complexity of Europe with its divisions, ambiguities, and doubts. Additional elements that it may incorporate are secularization; Enlightenment; curiosity about others; the notion that humanity lacks a higher purpose; and the tradition of resisting foreign dominion, oppression, and tyranny. Realistically, the fundamental idea of Europe will also bear negative aspects: a legacy of myriad reciprocal wars, intra-European conflicts

R. Eckert (✉)
Stiftung Haus der Geschichte der Bundesrepublik Deutschland, Zeitgeschichtliches Forum
Leipzig, 04109 Leipzig, Germany
e-mail: eckert@hdg.de

P. Meusburger et al. (eds.), *Cultural Memories*, Knowledge and Space 4,
DOI 10.1007/978-90-481-8945-8_10, © Springer Science+Business Media B.V. 2011

(Speth, 1999, p. 169), nationalism, racism, colonialism, and imperialism. Worst of all is the ideological, racist, mass-murder by the National Socialists (Nazis), which has developed into a kind of negative founding myth of Western Europe (Leggewie, 2008), and ideological mass-murder by the Communists.

Europe's coalescence also has a politicohistorical side—the differing historical experiences in the east and west of the continent, a common European identity, and that identity's historical roots (Kraft, 2004, p. 37). As always at the national level, there is the danger of instrumentalizing history and turning it into a political battlefield (Bock & Wolfrum, 1999, p. 7). An example is the dispute between Germany and Poland over the planned "Center against Expulsions" in Berlin (see, for example, Hawley, 2005; Mayfield, 2008) International progress in this area is possible only if an end is put to the ignorance and contempt the West shows for the East, which has its own experience, including the formative ones of the years from 1945 through 1989 or from 1917 through 1989. The fundamental idea of Europe should encompass and integrate the life experiences and national sensibilities of Central Eastern European peoples as well, including, at its extreme, their need to catch up on becoming nations. Turning to their own nations and histories also means acknowledging the emancipation from communist reign and Moscow's hegemony (Faulenbach, 2006, p. 237). The process of reconstructing national memories is fully underway in Eastern Europe and will claim its dues in Europe. World War II will remain the foremost factor of European remembrance, the Holocaust will gain recognition as a European event (Grunenberg, 2001, p. 169), and the crimes the communists committed while eliminating "class enemies and enemies of the people" (Leggewie, 2008) must not be forgotten or downplayed. It is, however, debatable whether there should or can be a binding European standard of memory (Kraft, 2004, p. 38) or whether the collective memory will at its core remain as multifarious as the nations that constitute Europe (Leggewie, 2008; MEMORIAL, 2008). It should be clarified whether the differing memories of individual nations or parts of nations need to be overcome and whether such a goal is something worth aspiring to.

In essence, the future of the European construct will be about the unity of Eastern and Western Europe and will reflect the constituent countries' collective and differing individual experiences far beyond the twentieth century (Schlögel, 2008). In this context the period from November 9, 1989, to October 3, 1990, was the starting point in Central Eastern Europe for the revaluation of the previous 50 years, in some cases of whole national histories. By contrast, Western Europe's break with historical memory came in the 1980s, as marked by the change in dealing with the Holocaust.

In this chapter I look upon World War II in Western Europe (in a political sense) as the formative part of this remembrance, a component that will gain increasing importance in the East as well. It stands to reason to differentiate the various European nations into categories such as fascist states and democratic states, occupied and free countries, or loosely and closely collaborating states, but the problems lie in the details, as the example of Austria makes evident. The simplest approach is to divide Europe into fascist countries (Italy, Spain), occupied countries (Belgium, Denmark, France, Greece, the Netherlands, Norway, and, as part of the Greater German Empire, or *Großdeutsches Reich*, Austria), and unoccupied countries (Finland, Great Britain, Sweden, and Switzerland). Because that classification scheme is of only limited value for recollections after 1945, looking at the development of this memory in each country is indispensible in making generally valid conclusions.

Belgium

After the liberation from German occupation, what many Belgians considered memorable was their suffering under the Germans rather than the active resistance against them (Beyen, 2004, pp. 67–94). Belgians saw themselves as helpless casualties of terror or as people who were fortunate to be liberated by the Allies. The memory of shared war experiences, however, led to a division of the nation into victims and collaborators, the latter group being persecuted soon after the war. Additionally, there were differences in the Flemish and Wallonian recollection of these experiences. In particular, the matter of Flemish collaboration was tabooed early on, and Belgians repressed as far as possible what had happened to their Jewish countrymen.

Many people thought of the resistance as a martyrdom they had suffered through, for most of the population was not involved in it actively and the reprisals caused by the resistance had created a reluctance to act. Almost everyone, though, could regard themselves as victims of the occupation. Hence, Fort Breendonk, a reception camp for political prisoners and Jews, changed into an important national memorial, whereas the resistance fighters never became the center of national commemoration. Remembrance of Jewish victims finally developed in the 1960s, but stemmed primarily from the Jewish community itself. This remembrance has never reached the ritualized form it has acquired in other European states. Anti-German prejudices too, were entailed, albeit less so than in the Netherlands, for example (Verbeeck, 2008, p. 25). Another difference between remembrance in Belgium and that in other Western European countries is that Belgium did not engage in a serious and public discussion of its own history until the 1990s.

In 2001, the then Belgian prime minister, Guy Verhofstadt, seized the initiative by setting up a Holocaust museum in Mechelen to stop the spread of right-wing extremist ideas. His action paved the way for consideration of whether the concept of "a 'museum to commemorate persecution and genocide' should be expanded to break the taboo on the uniqueness of the Holocaust" (Verbeeck, 2008, p. 29). The issue of whether the Holocaust is beyond comprehension is still open in Belgium, however. In the meantime, the decision has been reached to have the planned museum deal with human-rights abuses. The worries of the country's francophone south that the museum will become a Flemish place of remembrance for attempts to institutionally expropriate the French-speaking community have not been assuaged.

Denmark

The occupation is a trauma towering over all other memories in the minds of the Danes who survived it and in the minds of the following generation (Straede, 2004). This burden has to do with the fact that most of the population found ways of getting along with the enemy and did not start supporting the resistance until 1943. A large percentage of high-ranking Danish functionaries saw pragmatic cooperation with the Germans as the best strategy. For most of those who resisted, it was about regaining freedom and reactivating the old political system.

After 1945, however, most Danes saw themselves as fighters in the resistance. They saw the occupation as a national insult and concentrated their hate on the Germans. In the years thereafter, the moral supremacy of the resistance nevertheless declined, and former collaboration attained the status of normal behavior. The memory of the resistance largely crumbled with the end of Central European Communism. Since the beginning of the 1990s, doubts have finally surfaced about the moral integrity of people who helped the Jews. To be more exact, resistance fighters and collaborators have come to be seen as victims in the postwar years. A myth of remembrance became institutionalized in the 1980s and 1990s, and the role of the royal family as a symbol of national continuity grew. The rescue of Jews, far from becoming the point of departure for a broad Danish culture of remembrance, was cast as a unique humanitarian and political action and was thereby shunted to the margins of historical remembrance. Only after the public discussions in the 1970s did the Danish people include the Holocaust in the canon of memories of the occupation. The domestic Danish debate on remembrance is still in progress.

Finland

The Hitler–Stalin Pact of August 23, 1939, placed Finland within Moscow's sphere of influence, and the country had to defend itself against Soviet aggression (Rautkallio, 2004). In July 1941 Finland launched an offensive known as the Continuation War to reclaim lost territories, fighting alongside the Germans. As a result, after World War II there was a debate on the need for the war, and quite a few Finns agreed, for the sake of mutual understanding with their powerful neighbor, that their state could and should have avoided it. Only with the end of Communism in the Soviet Union could the question of responsibility for the war be made a public issue again. The unknown soldier and Finnish hero moved to the center of historic remembrance symbolizing the Finnish fight for survival. Their memory is kept in countless monuments to heroes, memorials, remembrance days, works of art, and memoires. This form of remembrance culminates in the worship of Finnish Field Marshal Mannerheim.

Immediately after World War II, the Finns, who had remained unoccupied, did not deal with the questions about resistance, collaboration, and liberation. Instead, Finland was one of the few countries in which segments of society cultivated the remembrance of the war and the relationship of brothers-in-arms with the Germans. There was no in-depth analysis or criticism of Nazism. Even before the collapse of the Soviet Union, the Finns set out to shed any feelings of guilt related to the war.

Instead of paying reverence to human suffering, the Finns chose to remember a heroic tale. Unsurprisingly, that narrative has drawn little attention to the Nazi genocide. Finnish Holocaust literature in the last few years has not sprung from discussion genuinely anchored in Finland but rather from a sense that it is necessary for keeping in touch with the international discourse on this subject. It was not until the autumn of 2003 that an examination of possible Finnish culpability in terms of collaboration with Nazi Germany began, a debate brought on by the Finnish surrender of Soviet prisoners to the Gestapo.

France

French remembrance has gone through profound changes since World War II. Immediately after the war, the idea was to win back the glory and honor of the nation (Rousso, 2004). To do so, the country mainly invoked the legendary *Résistance*, with monuments and rituals serving chiefly as places and acts of national remembrance in the old monarchic tradition. At the same time, society brutally tried to "cleanse" itself of collaborators.

The country pursued moral and material reconstruction until the early 1970s, at which juncture an exploration of France's complicity in the events of World War II opened. A discussion of complicity in the Holocaust arose only later. Remembrance was at first reserved for the resistance fighters. There was little differentiation between different groups of victims of the occupation, and Jewish victims were not permitted any special status, a denial visibly expressed in the design of memorials.

The conveyance of memories through movies was seminal in the 1980s. Just as French consciousness changed, especially after the end of Communism in Europe, so did the perception of the Holocaust after the broadcast of Claude Lanzmann's film *Shoa*. Thenceforth, the myth of the resistance could be questioned, too. Jewish victims or often rather their families received material compensations. Today, after long years of silence, one cannot imagine France without the discussions about the "black years," which are now recognized in numerous monuments and commemorations. The Shoa and the difficulties of racism and anti-Semitism are attracting particular interest.

Greece

The liberation from German occupation is no longer celebrated in Greece, for the conflict was fought as a civil war and eventually became part of the great controversy between the blocs at the outset of the Cold War (Karakatsane & Berbeniote, 2004). The political character of the argument over Greece's postwar history came through in the very labels that different camps had chosen for it. The Communists called the conflict a civil war, whereas the "national camp" called it a "bandit war." Another facet rather peculiar to Greece is that national remembrance centers on the beginning of World War II rather than on its end. Greek authors stress that their country's forces succeeded in pushing back Mussolini's troops into Albanian territory after Italy attacked Greece through Albania in October 1940.

Over the course of the historical discussion, especially as of the early 1980s, interest in the Greek resistance to German and Italian occupation troops turned to patriots, and the imposition of a "leftist–rightist" scheme ceased. The political situations in the various stages of Greece's postwar history are a major theme in this discourse. Under the dictatorship of the military junta (1967–1974), Greek historical memory primarily underscored the principles of country, patriotism, and military power. The end of the dictatorship was followed by reorientation to a policy of remembrance. The term "bandit war" no doubt supplanted the term "civil war," for this postwar conflict was tagged less and less with a taboo of remembrance. In the 1970s, the emphasis shifted to the fate of Greek Jews, whose persecution and murder increasingly emerged as a topic in the 1990s, though it did not overshadow the civil war in public memory.

Great Britain

Great Britain's historical memory takes a special place among European Allied nations, for the country was not occupied during World War II (Syriatou, 2004). At the end of the conflict many Britons saw themselves as keepers of freedom and liberators of Europe. In the following years, their memory focused on various phases of the war, with the victory over the Third Reich constituting a formative experience rooted in national solidarity, the burden of wartime shortages, and shared sorrows. Today, the self-image of the nation still builds strongly on World War II.

But the recollections of that period faded in the 1960s, and the memory of the Holocaust languished, steadily losing relevance. This trend changed in 1978—as it did in other European countries—with the broadcast of the four-part TV series entitled *The Holocaust*. Even so, broad public interest in that mass murder based on a racial ideology was not abidingly ensured until the Jewish community became involved. The opening of a permanent Holocaust exhibition in London's Imperial War Museum in 2000 has had special, lasting impact.

In the 1970s and 1980s, history in Great Britain had become a commodity of mass consumption. One aspect of this interest in recent years has been the surge in the construction of monuments and memorials. Initially, these structures had military battles and victories as their main point of reference, but they have finally also begun to commemorate the contributions of women, civilians, common workers, and colonial soldiers. World War II itself has been gaining importance in the official portrayal of the British state, especially since 2005, the fiftieth anniversary of the conflict's end. The message underlines the contrast between moral values during the war and those today. The monuments and memorials also make it clear that anti-German sentiment associated with World War II has still not dissipated.

Italy

Barbara Spinelli has conclusively shown that Italy suffers from an unusual affliction: widely agreed amnesia alternating with attacks of vengeful memories (Azzaro, 2004; Spinelli, 2002, p. 177). The reason for this affliction is that the crimes of the fascist regime were not addressed in courts. Moreover, the Communists saw the resistance to fascism as their monopoly, with memories always returning when their recollection was useful. On principle, the Italians have not considered a debate of their recent history to be worthwhile, and the realization that the twentieth century was shaped by two equal horrors has not been wholly convincing to them. Whereas some people have wanted to forget their country's fascist legacy, others have appropriated for themselves the role of the victim and have looked back only at the painful events in their own lives without looking ahead to the future (Spinelli, 2002, p. 238).

In Italy the memory of war, displacement, and genocide is tied to experiences with fascism (Azzaro, 2004, p. 343). Italy's view of itself after 1945 was thus predominantly that the dictatorship, the war, and genocide were fascist or even exclusively German affairs; that Italians had suffered for their misdeeds, had risen, and had finally prevailed; and that fascism therefore did not belong to Italy's historical heritage. This opinion could not be left unchallenged. It was also necessary to counter the attempt to purge the persecution and murder of Jews from Italian consciousness and to evade whenever possible the question of complicity.

Remembrance in Italy split when the neofascists developed an alternate view of history in an attempt to justify the decision to fight alongside the Germans. At that point, the Resistenza became the spearhead of an economic and political renaissance for the whole country, with the Communists seeking to claim the resistance solely for themselves. Only with the end of European Communism did it become possible to interpret the Resistenza, too, as a civil war. Meanwhile, the memory of a "red resistance" faded. The neofascists, who joined the government for the first time in 1996, acknowledged the part played by the Resistenza and no longer defamed it as a "betrayal of the nation." A "Day of Remembrance" recalling the race laws was finally instituted in 2001.

The Netherlands

Memories in the Netherlands after 1945 were strongly influenced by the German occupation during World War II and by the attendant question of people's collaboration or status as a victim (Tops, 2004). With recollections of wartime famine and the liberation gripping Dutch minds, the dominant narrative for 15 years was about a heroic and staunch population confronting an inhumane occupation force. In the weeks before and after the liberation, hundreds of local authorities and committees developed plans for the erection of memorials and other symbols of remembrance (Vree, 2000, p. 28) to honor the people who fell in the struggle against the occupation and to encourage the survivors. Other citizens of the country, however, thought that the money allotted for these symbols would be better spent on social and cultural projects.

Public remembrance was assigned to the Ministry of Education, Science, and Culture, nationalizing it in a sense. This official view was expressed in a stained-glass window of St. Jans Church in Gouda, which commemorated the liberation and embedded the years from 1940 to 1945 in the overall context of national history. By contrast, the monuments reminding people of the fate suffered by specific groups of victims were supposed to be created by representatives of the individual groups themselves. The Jewish community was thereby put at the same level as other groups, such as sports clubs (Vree, 2000, p. 32). In the Netherlands some people felt that it would be basically wrong to pay special remembrance to a group of victims, for such favoritism would eventually mean that those people would be treated differently, as had been the case under the Nazis. This opinion may explain why the persecution and destruction of Jews was long noted by only a single monument in the Netherlands.

Some of the stereotypes that formed in the postwar years still exist, but they have lost much of their importance and cohesive power. In 1945 the Germans were mainly accorded negative qualities, whereas the Dutch were regarded as passive, suffering, and innocent. Memorial ceremonies, schoolbooks, and monuments— and the National Commission on Monuments—stressed effective resistance as a national characteristic (Lieshout, 2001). The question of Dutch responsibility for certain events arose for the first time in the 1960s. Like the question of memorials, it was intertwined with the strong conviction that the Holocaust perpetrated by the Germans had been a capital crime against which the Dutch could hardly have put up effective resistance and that the Jews were, after all, still only one of many persecuted groups. The question of how the Nazis managed to murder a far higher percentage of Dutch Jews than Belgian Jews went unaddressed. The answer was almost inherently linked to the question of why the Dutch were so subservient to authority and why they cooperated so well with the occupiers.

The "old-style" national culture of remembrance peaked between 1960 and 1965 with the broadcast of the television documentary *De Bezetting*. The producers of this film focused on the idea that all Dutch people had a common fate and a common history that climaxed in a dramatic tale of suffering and struggle, loyalty and treachery, humanity and barbarism, and good and bad (Vree, 2000, p. 36). The film conveyed the message that harm had been done to the Dutch people, who, under the leadership of their queen, had withstood that trial through their own mental power and steadfastness. The narrative left no room for conformists, skeptics, or collaborators.

This view of history was already being challenged by the mid-1960s. The Eichmann trial in Jerusalem and the connection between the Cultural Revolution and young people greatly furthered to its erosion. Television generated much discussion of the Dutch people's submissiveness during the war and prompted many young people to reject middle-class rules and morals. Specifically, the Dutch student generation of the 1960s saw the course of the war as convincing proof of the failure of middle-class norms and values.

The demise of the Dutch Jews also became a key issue in the mid-1960s. A breakthrough finally came in 1965 with Jacques Presser's (1965) study entitled *Ondergang*, which detailed the destruction of the Dutch Jews and pinpointed gaps in dealing with this subject. Anne Frank and the dockworkers' strike against the deportation of Jews evolved into national icons. This memory is still important for the Dutch self-image and is constantly invoked by events such as the 1995 massacre in Srebrenica and by the country's solidarity with Israel.

Since the mid-1960s, the Dutch have heightened the attention they direct to the survivors of the camps and prisons, including such groups of victims like Sinti, Roma, and homosexuals. A notion that has recently gained currency is that the mass murder by the Nazis is also a gauge for dealing with the history of the Netherlands (Vree, 2000, pp. 39–41). Today, Auschwitz is taken as a symbol of the failure of traditional nationalism, of belief in linear progress, and of great political ideologies. In the minds of many Dutch people, this failure signals doubt in the vision of the Enlightenment, of progress, and of the superiority of Western civilization. It has changed the culture of thought fundamentally, with public discussion being marked again and again by outrage over how little the Dutch people supported their Jewish neighbors and how well the state apparatus collaborated with the occupiers. Auschwitz is now so dominant as a subject that the originally central points of its discussion—remembering the resistance and solidarity—have been pushed into the background and at times even seem to verge on total eclipse.

Norway

The resistance against the German occupation has a large bearing on the way Norway views itself. The importance of the royal family, too, is strongly accentuated (Bruland, 2004). As in other countries, movies did much to develop myths of resistance. The deportation of Jews, by contrast, was neither seen as a warlike act nor associated with the resistance. The Holocaust thus became almost a suppressed topic in Norway for many years. Later, the Norwegians attributed the fate of the Jews solely to the occupying forces.

The process by which the resistance was turned into a legend had much to do with the Western powers; the communist resistance was forgotten, however. According to the underlying logic, the wartime resistance against the Germans transitioned into a postwar fight against Communism. At the same time, the remembrance of the resistance gradually stabilized Norway's self-image as a country with especially high moral standards and strong rights. Within this framework the fate of the Jews was uninteresting, and the Norwegian part in their deportation was generally described as "carelessness."

Austria

Under the second Austrian republic, established after the country's liberation from
National Socialism, Austria saw itself as the first victim and regarded the years
from 1938 to 1945 as a period of foreign rule (Uhl, 2004). This idea of being a
victim was also expressed in the experience with prisoner-of-war camps and the
austerity of the postwar years. The idea of being a victim and the emphasis on the
Austrian resistance figured greatly in the process of becoming a nation (Perz, 2002,
p. 151). The attempt to saddle Germany alone with the blame and responsibility
for Nazi crimes was officially codified first in Austria's declaration of independence
of April 27, 1945 (Uhl, 2005, p. 185). Austria subsequently cultivated a myth of
its victimization and the memory of its resistance, but it proved to be both consistent and self-contradictory. In 1946 the government in Vienna had demanded in the
Rot-Weiss-Rot-Book[1] that the resistance in Austria be pointed out through hitherto
unpublished pictures that showed people despairing over the *Anschluss*, the union
with Germany in 1938 (Hoppe, 2008).

This tone had already been set by the Allies at the Tehran Conference in 1943,
when they described Austria as Hitler's first victim. The murder of Austrian Jews
found little mention and was a region of silence in the minds of Austrians. Instead,
Austria was presented as a nation of cultured, comfortable, and peaceful people (Uhl, 2005, p. 186). As of 1947, however, there was increased integration of
National Socialists, who were becoming interesting as potential voters. As the Cold
War escalated, antifascism gave way to anti-Communism. The Austrian prisoners-
of-war were presented as the true victims, and the surviving Jews saw themselves
confronted by escalating anti-Semitism. From Austria's assumed posture as a victim, it followed that the country did not want to accept any material or moral
responsibility for Nazism.

Because Austria saw itself as the first victim of the Nazis, the public culture of
commemoration was dominated by monuments to soldiers who served in World War
II. These monuments paid tribute to the duty and courage to protect one's homeland
and emphasized Austria's victimization. The Mauthausen concentration camp was
expanded into a place commemorating the martyrdom of the Austrian fight for freedom (Perz, 2002, p. 155). That portrayal, however, disregarded the fact that only a
minority of the prisoners there had been Austrian and that Austrians had probably
accounted for many of the guards. Not until the 1960s did a burgeoning number
of monuments touch on the *persecution* as well as the resistance. A fundamental
change in perspective had set in.

Concealment and failure to remember was first broken in 1979 by the TV series
entitled *Holocaust*, which ushered in an examination of Austria's role in the "final
solution" (*Endlösung*) for the first time. This opening encouraged exploration of
the country's National Socialist past, including involvement in war crimes that had
been committed in the Balkans. Broad discussion was sparked, for example, by
Kurt Waldheim, a later president of Austria (1986–1992), who had commented
that he had only been doing his duty as a soldier in the *Wehrmacht* (the German
armed forces) during World War II. Slowly, the Austrians became aware of the fact

that their country had ceased being a democracy long before the *Wehrmacht* had crossed the border in 1938 and that the idea of the Anschluss had been a constant in Austrians politics during the interwar period. National Socialism thereby became the normative point of reference in the culture of remembrance in the late 1980s. Austrian complicity in the crimes of the Nazis was admitted by the Austrian government, though it did not completely abandon its image as a victim (Stuhlpfarrer, 2002, p. 233).

In 1997 the Austrian republic finally announced that May 5—the liberation of Mauthausen—would be the day for remembering the victims of the Nazis, and in 1998 it set up an independent commission of historians for the unrestricted investigation of Austria's Nazi past. Work on "dealing" with that part of Austria's past intensified thereafter (Stuhlpfarrer, 2002, p. 244). The deliberation over whether May 8, the end of World War II in Europe, should be a day of "liberation" or of "defeat" was closely bound up with Austria's departure from the myth of Austria as a victim of the Nazis, a renunciation that started at the beginning of the twenty-first century. Austria acknowledged its share of responsibility for the crimes of the Nazis and concentrated, alongside other European nations, on the global memory of the Holocaust as the center of the politics of remembrance. This new outlook was expressed in a broad consensus on Rachel Whiteread's Holocaust memorial erected in 2000, which incorporated the memory of the murdered Jews into the main symbolic space of the capital.

In 2005, however, the fiftieth anniversary of World War II's end was predominantly a celebration of successes. As in 1945, Austria was presented as a victim of Nazism and a bombing war, and the government officially stressed the absence of Austria's fault and share of responsibility. The Holocaust was left unmentioned. The liberation of the Mauthausen concentration camp was commemorated but only because it underlined Austrian sacrifice. On the whole, this regression in the politics of remembrance in the alpine republic gives reason to believe that the fight for remembrance in Austria has not yet been decided. Discrepancies and ambivalence have been preserved, leaving two opposing cultures of history in Austria. It is unlikely, though, that the developments over the last 20 years will be rolled back.

Sweden

After World War II, Sweden saw itself as a great humanitarian power and its policies as far-sighted (Liljefors & Zander, 2004). The whole of Swedish society, as a commune, had given up class conflict in favor of close cooperation with the people in an attempt to decrease the differences between classes. General opinion in Sweden was that concessions to Nazi Germany had been necessary. The only episode to tarnish the picture was the fact that Balts who had fled to Sweden in 1945 and 1946 were handed over by Sweden to the Soviets. No note was taken of Sweden's dubious foreign-trade policies and press censorship during the war.

The portrait of a Sweden marked by humanity and neutrality began to crack in the early 1990s, in textbooks, for example. This disintegration of the Swedish depiction of history progressed as interest in the Holocaust swelled in the 1990s in Europe and the United States. The politics of remembrance finally shifted to a recognition that the integration of Europe must rest on the legacy of World War II and on the remembrance of the victims of Nazism and fascism. There is now an awareness that democracy, tolerance, and human rights need to be understood against the background of the Holocaust, yet the official view of history still emphasizes the correctness of the Sweden's politics of neutrality and still tries to justify it morally.

Switzerland

Switzerland long saw itself as a country that gave merciful support to refugees (Kreis, 2004). The life boat as a metaphor became deeply engrained in the country's historical memory and became a staple in the discussion. "The boat is full" policy, which had been directed mainly at Jewish asylum-seekers, has come to be viewed more and more as an unfortunate cruelty as criticism of it has mounted. But even the confrontation of the Swiss people with their own problematic past has reinforced their positive self-image and has pushed it further than ever into the forefront.

Spain

In the narrative of World War II and the Holocaust, Spain occupies a special position (Brinkmann & Riuz, 2004). It derives from the history of the Spanish Civil War and the fact that the memory of Spain's "official" alliance with the *Wehrmacht* was suppressed after the Allied victory. The only positive memory from World War II was Spain's neutrality. When the last of the country's "Russia fighters" returned to Spain in 1954, the interpretation of their service as a "crusade" against the "steppe" was reevaluated. With postwar discussion of historical events being repressed in Spain, the question of Spanish Holocaust victims could not become publicly relevant.

After Franco's death in 1975, Spain underwent a peaceful transition from dictatorship to democracy, a shift shaped by "collective amnesia" and an absence of political reckoning ("Ich bleibe ein Roter", 2008). Most Spanish people thought that this process would be the "high road" to dealing with the past, for it avoided a self-torturing search of conscience (Perger, 2006). Today, many Spanish observers see this as bad judgment and in recent years, especially since the discovery of mass graves from the Franco era, the wish to recover some degree of historic remembrance has grown. The current generation in particular is intensifying its search for the past, engaging in a Spanish culture of remembrance and pushing for the dismantlement of numerous monuments to the dictator. This effort reflects a typical split in society: Whereas the political right refuses to engage seriously in the political debate on remembrance, private organizations and the political left are increasingly concentrating on it. Such divergence clearly shows how missing an opportunity to challenge a dictatorial past in an enlightening way can eventually provoke social division. The politicohistorical fronts are entrenched by the fact that the conflict is occurring between the center and autonomous groups, especially in Catalonia and the Basque country (Säez-Arance, 2004, p. 272), with Madrid having ever less success with pushing through national ideas on which a consensus seems possible. It remains to be seen whether the situation will be fundamentally changed by the "Law on Historical Remembrance" of 2008, which enhances the pensions to the victims of the dictatorship, improves the accessibility of archives, and facilitates the opening of mass graves. The emblems of the Falange are already disappearing from public spaces, Franco monuments are being dismantled, and public remembrance of the dictator is illegal.

Western European Types of Remembrance

Comparisons between "Western" countries in Europe reveal a group whose historical remembrance after 1945 concentrates primarily on the members' own suffering under the German terror during World War II. This set includes Belgium and Austria. Other cultures of remembrance, such as those in Denmark, France, the Netherlands, and Norway, are rooted more strongly in a tradition of resistance. In almost all countries, however, the conflict over collaboration was late to ignite. A self-image as keepers of freedom and humanity or as winners in the fight for national identity was initially dominant in those countries that were not occupied. Gaps are apparent in the memories of Germany's wartime allies, but those countries also remember the "heroic fight" of their own soldiers while generally distancing themselves from the Germans and their way of running the war.

Surprisingly, the Holocaust figured little in Western memory for many years after 1945. The veil over the topic began to lift in the 1960s (Belgium). The oblivion dissipated further partially through the *Holocaust* TV series and other films of the late 1970s. In some places, the story did not emerge until after the end of European Communism. In all of these countries today, the memory of the Holocaust is internationally connected, anchored in their educational systems, and promoted by their governments (Reichel, 1996, p. 9). The mass murder of Jews by the Nazis has evolved into the measure of their respective histories. This change owes much to the Stockholm declaration of January 2000, with its call to governments worldwide to emphasize the infamy of the genocide. This criterion should be used for Central Eastern European memories as well. It is about synchronizing memories of the Holocaust across national borders while respecting national traditions (Uhl, 2005, pp. 196–197).

Remembering the racially and ideologically motivated mass murders committed by the National Socialists is only one side of the coin, however. The other side is about the need to remember the crimes of Stalinism. Only when both legacies become components of remembrance can the public embark on the journey to a European consciousness of history and overcome narrow national boundaries

(Thamer, 2007, p. 175). Three prerequisites for taking the first step are to inculcate the civic duty that each people has for its own history (MEMORIAL, 2008), to instill an interest in the history of others, and to create common institutions and forums that can make it possible to achieve both aims.

Note

1. This publication, commissioned by the Austrian foreign ministry in 1946, was a collection of documents dating from 1933 to 1945. The book's account of the role played by the Austrian state before its union with Germany in 1938 and of what happened during World War II was intended to support the position of the postwar Austrian government in relation to the Allied occupation powers.

References

Azzaro, P. (2004). Italien: Kampf der Erinnerungen [Italy: The battle of memories]. In M. Flacke (Ed.), *Mythen der Nationen: 1945 Arena der Erinnerungen* (Vol. 1, pp. 343–372). Berlin: Deutsches Historisches Museum.

Baumann, G., & Müller, N. (2006). Vergangenheitsbewältigung und Erinnerungskultur in den Ländern Mittelost- und Südosteuropas [Dealing with the past and the culture of remembrance in the countries of Central Eastern and Southeastern Europe]. Berlin: Konrad-Adenauer-Stiftung.

Beyen, M. (2004). Belgien: Der Kampf um das Leid [Belgium: The battle about misery]. In M. Flacke (Ed.), *Mythen der Nationen: 1945 Arena der Erinnerungen* (Vol. 1, pp. 67–94). Berlin: Deutsches Historisches Museum.

Bock, P., & Wolfrum, E. (Eds.). (1999). *Umkämpfte Vergangenheit: Geschichtsbilder, Erinnerung und Vergangenheitspolitik im internationalen Vergleich* [The embattled past: International comparison of historical perceptions, memory, and the politics of the past]. Göttingen: Vandenhoeck & Ruprecht.

Boyer, C. (2007). Perspektiven einer europäischen Zeitgeschichtsschreibung [Perspectives on contemporary European historiography]. *ZeitRäume: Potsdamer Almanach für Zeithistorische Forschung*, pp. 9–20.

Brinkmann, S., & Riuz, V. P. (2004). Spanien: Weder Opfer noch Täter [Spain: Neither victim nor culprit]. In M. Flacke (Ed.), *Mythen der Nationen: 1945 Arena der Erinnerungen* (Vol. 2, pp. 757–772). Berlin: Deutsches Historisches Museum.

Bruland, B. (2004). Norwegen: Wie sich erinnern? Norwegen und der Krieg [Norway: How should we remember? Norway and the war]. In M. Flacke (Ed.), *Mythen der Nationen: 1945 Arena der Erinnerungen* (Vol. 1, pp. 453–480). Berlin: Deutsches Historisches Museum.

Faulenbach, B. (2006). Öffentliches Erinnern im vereinten Deutschland und in Osteuropa seit dem 1990er Jahren [Public remembrance in a united Germany and in Eastern Europe since the 1990s]. In P. Haustein (Ed.), *Instrumentalisierung, Verdrängung, Aufarbeitung: Die sowjetischen Speziallager in der gesellschaftlichen Wahrnehmung 1945 bis heute* (pp. 233–249). Berlin: Wallstein.

Grunenberg, A. (2001). *Die Lust an der Schuld: Von der Macht der Vergangenheit über die Gegenwart* [The pleasure of guilt: The power of the past over the present]. Berlin: Rowohlt.

Hawley, C. (2005, April 11). *Is the world ready for German victimhood?* Retrieved November 9, 2010, from http://www.spiegel.de/international/0,1518,383263,00.html

Hoppe, B. (2008, March 13). Das erste Opfer? Vor 75 Jahre wurde Österreich an Deutschland "angeschlossen" [The first victim? Austria's "Anschluss" 75 years ago]. *Berliner Zeitung*, p. 33.

"Ich bleibe ein Roter" (2008, February 25). Die Schrifstellerlegende Jorge Semprún über Demokratie, Erinnerung und die Wahlen in Spanien ["I'll stay a Red": Legendary author Jorge Semprún on democracy, memory, and the elections in Spain]. *Der Tagesspiegel* (Berlin), p. 17.

Karakatsane, D., & Berbeniote, T. (2004). Griechenland: Doppelter Diskurs und gespaltene Erinnerung [Greece: Dual discourse and divided memories]. In M. Flacke (Ed.), *Mythen der Nationen: 1945 Arena der Erinnerungen* (Vol. 1, pp. 257–284). Berlin: Deutsches Historisches Museum.

Kraft, C. (2004). Diktaturbewältigung und Geschichtskultur in Polen und Spanien im Vergleich [A comparison of overcoming dictatorship and dealing with historical culture in Poland and Spain]. In K. Ruchniewicz & S. Troebst (Eds.), *Diktaturbewältigung und nationale Selbstvergewisserung in Polen und Spanien im Vergleich* (pp. 37–42). Wroclaw: Wydawnistwo Uniwersytetu Wroclawskiego.

Kreis, G. (2004). Schweiz: Das Bild der Schweiz und die Bilder von der Schweiz zur Zeit des Zweiten Weltkrieges [Switzerland: Switzerland's self-image and images of Switzerland during World War II]. In M. Flacke (Ed.), *Mythen der Nationen: 1945 Arena der Erinnerungen* (Vol. 2, pp. 593–617). Berlin: Deutsches Historisches Museum.

Leggewie, C. (2008, April 24). Die Grenzen der Nationalkultur. Kann Europa, das größte Noch-nicht-Volk der Erde, eine Identität entwickeln? In Brüssel sucht eine Ausstellung nach der Antwort [The limits of national culture: Can Europe, the largest nonnation on Earth develop an identity? An exhibit in Brussels seeks answers]. *Die Zeit* (Hamburg), p. 28.

Lieshout, J. W. V. van (2001). *Der Stammbaum eines Museums: Vol. 2. Vom Schlachtfeld zum Friedenszeichen* [The bloodline of a museum: Vol. 2. From the battlefield to the sign of peace]. Overloon: Nationaal Oorlogs- en Verzetsmuseum.

Liljefors, M., & Zander, U. (2004). Schweden: Der Zweite Weltkrieg und die schwedische Utopie [Sweden: World War II and the Swedish vision]. In M. Flacke (Ed.), *Mythen der Nationen: 1945 Arena der Erinnerungen* (Vol. 2, pp. 569–592). Berlin: Deutsches Historisches Museum.

Mayfield, J. (2008). *The post-WWII expulsion of over 10,000,000 ethnic German civilians from Eastern Europe as the Allies look on.* Retrieved November 9, 2010, from http://eurohieritage. net/germanexpellees.shtml

MEMORIAL. (2008). Nationale Geschichtsbilder: Das 20. Jahrhundert und der "Krieg der Erinnerungen." Ein Aufruf der Internationalen Gesellschaft [National images of history. The twentieth century and the "war of memories": An appeal by international society]. In M. Sapper & V. Weichsal (Eds.), *Geschichtspolitik und Gegenerinnerung: Krieg, Gewalt und Trauma im Osten Europas* (pp. 67–76). Berlin: Berliner Wissenschafts-Verlag.

Muschg, A. (2005). Was ist europäisch? Reden für einen gastlichen Erdteil [What is European? Speeches for a hospitable continent]. Bonn: Bundeszentrale für politische Bildung.

Perger, W. A. (2006, June 18). 1936—Spaniens Trauma: Vor 70 Jahren begann der spanische Bürgerkrieg: Heute erlebt das Land einen erbitterten "Kampf der Erinnerungen" [Spain's dream: The Spanish Civil War began 70 years ago: Today the country is seeing a grim "battle of memories"]. *Die Zeit* (Hamburg). Retrieved November 9, 2010, from http://www.zeit.de/ online/2006/29/Spanien-Buergerkrieg

Perz, B. (2002). Österreich [Austria]. In V. Knigge & N. Frei (Eds.), *Verbrechen erinnern: Die Auseinandersetzung mit Holocaust und Völkermord* (pp. 150–162). Munich: Beck.

Presser, J. (1965). *Ondergang. De vervolging en verdelging van het Nederlandse Jodendom, 1940–1945* [Doom: Persecution and annihilation of the Netherlands' Jews, 1940–1945] (2 vols.). Gravenhage: Staatsuitgeverij.

Rautkallio, H. (2004). Finnland: Politik und Volk—die zwei Seiten Finnlands [Politics and the people—The two sides of Finland]. In M. Flacke (Ed.), *Mythen der Nationen: 1945 Arena der Erinnerungen* (Vol. 1, pp. 203–226). Berlin: Deutsches Historisches Museum.

Reichel, P. (1996). *Politik mit der Erinnerung: Gedächtnisorte im Streit um die nationalsozialistische Vergangenheit* [Politics of memory: Places of remembrance in the discussion on National Socialist history]. Munich: Hauser.

Rousso, H. (2004). Frankreich: Vom nationalen Vergessen zur kollektiven Wiedergutmachung [France: From national denial to collective repentance]. In M. Flacke (Ed.), *Mythen der Nationen: 1945 Arena der Erinnerungen* (Vol. 1, pp. 227–256). Berlin: Deutsches Historisches Museum.

Säez-Arance, A. (2004). Auf der Suche nach einem "demokratischen Zentralismus"? Nationalkonservativer Geschichtsrevisionismus im Spanien der Jahrtausendwende [Searching for a "democratic centralism"? National conservative historical revisionism in Spain at the turn of the millennium]. In K. Ruchniewicz & S. Troebst (Eds.), *Diktaturbewältigung und nationale Selbstvergewisserung in Polen und Spanien im Vergleich* (pp. 267–273). Wroclaw: Wydawnistwo Uniwersytetu Wrociawskiego.

Schlögel, K. (2008, February 22). Generation Marienborn: Mauer, Geisterbahnhöfe, entwürdigende Grenzkontrollen—das alles ist lange her und doch so nah; Die Wende von 1989 hat ein neues Europa geschaffen; Es muss nur noch zusammenwachsen [The Marienborn generation: The wall, deserted train stations, degrading border controls—All that is so long ago and yet still so recent; The fall of Communism in 1989 has created a new Europe; it only needs to grow together]. *Die Welt* (Berlin), p. 11.

Speth, R. (1999). Europäische Geschichtsbilder heute [European perceptions of history today]. In P. Bock & E. Wolfrum (Eds.), *Umkämpfte Vergangenheit: Geschichtsbilder, Erinnerung und Vergangenheitspolitik im internationalen Vergleich* (pp. 159–175). Göttingen: Vandenhoeck & Ruprecht.

Spinelli, B. (2002). *Der Gebrauch der Erinnerung: Europa und das Ende des Totalitarismus* [The utilization of remembrance: Europe and the end of totalitarianism]. Munich: Kunstmann.

Straede, T. (2004). Dänemark: Die schwierige Erinnerung an Kollaboration und Widerstand [Denmark: The difficult memory of collaboration and resistance]. In M. Flacke (Ed.), *Mythen der Nationen: 1945 Arena der Erinnerungen* (Vol. 1, pp. 123–150). Berlin: Deutsches Historisches Museum.

Stuhlpfarrer, K. (2002). Österreich [Austria]. In V. Knigge & N. Frei (Eds.), *Verbrechen erinnern: Die Auseinandersetzung mit Holocaust und Völkermord* (pp. 233–252). Munich: Beck.

Syriatou, A. (2004). Großbritannien: "Der Krieg wird uns zusammenhalten" [Great Britain: "The war will keep us together"]. In M. Flacke (Ed.), *Mythen der Nationen: 1945 Arena der Erinnerungen* (Vol. 1, pp. 285–313). Berlin: Deutsches Historisches Museum.

Thamer, H.-U. (2007). Sonderfall Zeitgeschichte? Die Geschichte des 20. Jahrhunderts in historischen Ausstellungen und Museen [The special case of contemporary history? The history of the twentieth century in historical exhibitions and museums]. *Zeithistorische Forschungen, 4*(1–2), 167–176.

Tops, E. (2004). Niederlande: Lebendige Vergangenheit [The Netherlands: A living past]. In M. Flacke (Ed.), *Mythen der Nationen: 1945 Arena der Erinnerungen* (Vol. 1, pp. 427–452). Berlin: Deutsches Historisches Museum.

Uhl, H. (2004). Österreich: Vom Opfermythos zur Mitverantwortungsthese: Die Transformation des österreichischen Gedächtnisses [Austria: From the myth of the victim to the theory of complicity—The transformation of the Austrian memory]. In M. Flacke (Ed.), *Mythen der Nationen: 1945 Arena der Erinnerungen* (Vol. 2, pp. 481–508). Berlin: Deutsches Historisches Museum.

Uhl, H. (2005). Vergessen und Erinnern der NS-Vergangenheit in der Zweiten Republik [Forgetting and remembering the Nazi past in the Second Republic]. In Stiftung Haus der Geschichte der Bundesrepublik Deutschland (Ed.), *Deutschland-Österreich: Verfreundete Nachbarn* (pp. 184–197). Bonn: Stiftung Haus der Geschichte der Bundesrepublik Deutschland.

Verbeeck, G. (2008). Erinnerungspolitik in Belgien [The politics of remembrance in Belgium]. *Aus Politik und Zeitgeschichte, 8*, 25–32.

Vree, R. van (2000). Gedenken an den Zweiten Weltkrieg in den Niederlanden [Remembering World War II in the Netherlands]. In Stiftung Haus der Geschichte der Bundesrepublik Deutschland (Ed.), *Heiter bis wolkig* (pp. 28–41). Bonn: Stiftung Haus der Geschichte der Bundesrepublik Deutschland.

Family Memories of World War II and the Holocaust in Europe, or Is There a European Memory?

Harald Welzer

Grandpa Wasn't a Nazi

In Germany, Holocaust education, teaching through memorials, and school lessons about Nazism and the *Shoah* have become very popular and successful. The survey data show that young Germans are generally quite well informed about the historical events and can associate correctly with key words such as "Auschwitz" and "SS" (*Schutzstaffel*, or elitist guard). Thus, education on the history of the "Third Reich" (1933–1945) might be considered a successfully completed project—but only if one does not ask what use the young recipients of this instruction actually make of it. Knowledge and the assimilation of knowledge on a personal basis are two very different things.

For too long the tacit assumption was that one needed only to say the right things for the right things to be understood and assimilated. There was too little appreciation that the transmission of history is accompanied by a range of subtexts—fascinating, daunting, anesthetizing—and that information is interpreted within a framework of social mechanisms that exist outside of school. As reflected by the studies discussed in this chapter, the apparent result has been that young people in Germany acquire knowledge of history in general, and of Nazism and the Holocaust in particular, in a way very different from what their educators have intended.

A person's awareness of history and his or her concepts about the past come from many sources of which history lessons are only one, others being films, television, novels, comics, computer games, and family histories. The aim of formal lessons is to pass on knowledge, but they cannot compete with the emotional wallop of images from the past offered by most other sources. Cognitive knowledge

H. Welzer (✉)
Kulturwissenschaftliches Institut, 45128 Essen, Germany
e-mail: herald.welzer@kwi-nrw.de

The studies on which this chapter is based were published in German by Welzer, Moller, and Tschuggnall (2002) and Welzer (2007). Parts of the text have been translated by Belinda Cooper and Lesley Anne Bleakney.

of history differs from the emotional relationship to history that arises when one's own grandparents talk about the time before one was born. Surprisingly, however, research on historical consciousness has only recently delved into these other sources (see, for example, Seixas, 2001; Wineburg, 2001, 2002). Research on the effects of Holocaust educational efforts has been slow to broaden. Until just the last few years, the research field was characterized by quantitative studies on historical awareness (especially Angvik & von Borries, 2000) and by qualitative studies on the ways in which young Germans deal with the history of an unparalleled crime whose occurrence overlapped with the lifetimes of their grandparents and great-grandparents (see Georgi, 2003; Gudehus, 2006; Radtke, Hollstein, Meseth, Müller-Mahnkopp, & Proske, 2002; Wineburg, 2001). The questions being asked are not about knowledge of history alone but also about the use of such knowledge. For example, the researchers focus on how history lessons on Nazism inform the students' interpretation and acquisition process mainly in terms of the politically correct way of talking about the Third Reich. They study how immigrant children absorb history lessons that have little relevance for their group of origin. Or they analyze tours of historical sites and the messages they impart.

This new work, though exploratory and limited in scope, points to conclusions that are distressing. In the multigenerational study presented in this chapter, my colleagues and I observe the direct communication of concepts about the past in German families and find a pronounced discrepancy between the official and the private cultures of remembrance in Germany. It documents a clear tendency on the part of grandchildren to rewrite their grandparents' histories into tales of anti-Nazi heroism and resistance. The pilot study that Radtke et al. (2002) conducted on history teaching suggests that students learn one primary thing in classes on the Third Reich: how to talk in a politically correct way about the problematic past.

The investigation by Gudehus (2006) implies similar results, and Georgi's (2003) study comes to the remarkable finding that immigrant children use their sometimes intensive study of the Nazi past as a ticket to seeing themselves as "true Germans."[1] All in all, people on the receiving end of educational efforts in history have proven to be stubborn and unpredictable, a response that reveals why further research on the results of history teaching appears to be so necessary and promising.

Design of the Study

The research project, entitled "Transmitting Historical Awareness," dealt with family communication about the Nazi period in the Federal Republic of Germany. For this study, forty western and eastern German families were interviewed within the context of one-family discussions and separate interviews with at least one member from each of three generations within the family: eyewitnesses, children, and grandchildren.[2] The design of the study was quite simple: The members of the eyewitness generation were asked about their biographical experience during the period after 1933; then their children and grandchildren were asked what they had heard from their parents and grandparents about the years after 1933. A family discussion was introduced by a brief video consisting of amateur films from the period of the Third Reich.

A total of 182 interviews and family discussions were conducted. The material was transcribed and evaluated through a combination of hermeneutic analysis of individual cases and computer-aided qualitative content analysis.

The following excerpts illustrate how history is formed and transmitted through conversations among the generations, how anti-Jewish stereotypes are similarly passed down, and how Germans interpret the roles of their parents or grandparents in the Third Reich. The final section examines how the study has been publicly discussed in Germany.

Making Sense of History: How Histories Change in Transmission Through the Generations

Johanna Kurz (all names are pseudonyms) was born in 1927. Her father had been in the SA (*Sturmabteiling*, the storm troopers) and the SS; her mother had been in the Nazi women's organization for a short time but had quit "after two or three years." The following exchange from the oral interview with Ms. Kurz refers to *Kristallnacht* (Night of Broken Glass), the anti-Jewish pogroms in Nazi Germany and Austria on the night of November 9–10, 1938.

> *Johanna Kurz*: I only know that we stared at those smoking ruins. . ... The synagogue wasn't destroyed; it was just burned out. Everything was smoldering, and my mother almost went crazy. She said, "How can they do that?" It was like a church for her. But it wasn't just in Hanover; on the contrary, it was everywhere, you know. And I remember that my mother said to my father, "I know you were involved; don't talk to me ever again!"
> *Interviewer*: But he wasn't involved, or was he?
> *Johanna Kurz*: I don't know. I don't think so, but I don't know. I'd like—I can't say, I don't know.
> *Interviewer*: So it was just an expressed threat?
> *Johanna Kurz*: The two of them never came together again, so, and then the war broke out, and the marriage just went on the side, nothing violent. When he came home in 1947, he came back from prison, and in 1948 they divorced.

Ms. Kurz had already given the information about her father's membership in the SA and SS in the interview when she began talking about the burning synagogue. Nevertheless, the interviewer, born in 1971, could not believe that Ms. Kurz's father was "involved." Her leading question considerably shook Ms. Kurz's confidence, and this uncertainty seems to have strengthened the interviewer in her views. As she put it, "That was just... a threat," an interpretation that caused Ms. Kurz to answer, yet also not answer, by reporting the result. It had not been just a threat, for the conflict was so serious that her parents "never came together again."

The interviewer, who reported in her protocol of the interview that she had found the eyewitness, Ms. Kurz, extremely nice, plainly could not accept the possibility that Johanna's father had been an actor in *Kristallnacht*. Despite having detailed knowledge of the history of the Third Reich, the interviewer resisted the possibility that even a relative of the old lady she was interviewing could have been a fellow traveler or a perpetrator in the persecution of Jews.

This example indicates how quickly loyalty relationships become generalized within the social situation of a conversation. The interviewer, with her hopeful follow-up question, was not only trying to free her conversation partner from any suspicion of complicity in criminal activity but was also extending this need to that person's close relatives, whom the interviewer neither knew nor could have known. It was as though she had not registered anything of what Ms. Kurz had just said about her father's history. This phenomenon often occurred in the family discussions conducted in our study—even, or maybe especially—when the explicit theme was murders committed by the storyteller.

Rainer Hofer, born in 1925, was a NAPOLA (National Socialist elite school) student and a member of the Waffen SS (the armed, military wing of the SS) and of the SS unit "Leibstandarte Adolf Hitler" (named after Hitler's personal bodyguard unit). He presented himself, both in the individual interview and the family discussion, as a reformed Nazi. Although he wrote in his diary, at the news of the Führer's death, "My best comrade has fallen," he was, in his retrospective telling, soon appalled by the crimes of the Nazis. Mr. Hofer, well read and well educated, made a career in postwar Germany as a manager and, in his own way, contributed to the reconstruction. He spoke unself-consciously about joining the Waffen SS, entering the Leibstandarte, participating in the Russian campaign, and, in 1943, being deployed as an SS man in the Ukraine. In this connection, the interview proceeded as follows:

> *Interviewer*: Are there any stories that you wouldn't tell your daughter or your grandchildren?
>
> *Rainer Hofer*: No, I would be completely open. I don't need to tell them that I shot Jews [he bangs on the table] or that sort of thing; even if I had done it, I would tell about it. Why? It's my daughter, and I lived my life. I can't let any of it somehow sink into the Hades of the past. I can't do that. There's nothing I'd say I wouldn't tell her, even if it touched on the honor of German soldiers. I remember once that we rode to an attack, and when we came back, attached to infantry, a couple of Russian soldiers were idiotic enough to surrender. Of course, they didn't live a moment longer [knocks on the table]. But that, of course, was one of those things: Where were they supposed to ride with us? In the tank? They could have had a hand grenade hidden somewhere [laughs]. ... If they had just laid low, nothing would have happened. But I'd tell my daughter that, although it actually touched the honor of German soldiers. I can't say there was anything that I wouldn't tell her, or my granddaughter, either. No. Why should I?

As though to prove his supposed openness, Mr. Hofer described to the interviewer a crime that might be enough to sully "the honor of German soldiers." There was no questioning of this crime whatsoever from today's perspective. On the contrary, Mr. Hofer provided a goal-oriented justification for the murder of the Russian prisoners, obviously assuming that his calculus would be apparent, even to the interviewer. And anyway, this was all part of his life as he lived it—so why, asked Mr. Hofer rhetorically, should not he tell about it?

As further evidence of his openness, Mr. Hofer even divulged that the Hofer family archive contained letters he sent home from the eastern front, one of which he alluded to in the interview:

> *Rainer Hofer*: I'm horrified today about what I wrote then. What [laughs] I can't understand today. ... We, of course, saw Russian women on the opposite side, in uniform, with weapons, and armed. And, imagine this, at [he knocks on the table] eighteen years old, I shot one down with my machine gun and wrote very proudly that "the head and the breast were just a bloody mess," or something like that. Today you wonder how you could have written something like that.

Note that the question is not how he could *do* it, but how he could write about it—a reference to the subjective assessment of the act. It should be pointed out that it is not usual for such documents to be kept in family archives and known to the children. Generally, a rather nebulous formulation is used—such as "something happened"— leaving listeners the possibility of drawing from vaguely recounted events a story that best allows them to live with the central conflict of German family history a half century after the Third Reich. It is, namely, the conflict in which the children's and grandchildren's awareness of the criminal nature of Nazism and the Holocaust is pitted against the need to see their parents or grandparents as being untouched by the horror.

This positioning is not easy to achieve, especially when the crimes were written down, as in the case of Mr. Hofer. Regina Seiler, his daughter, knew the letters but, surprisingly, emphasized repeatedly in both the family discussion and her separate interview how important it was for her to "figure out what people were thinking back then." At another point in the interviews, she stated, "I can't imagine that the German people, even my father, ... I really think they couldn't imagine that something like that could happen."

In the interview Ms. Seiler referred to her father's letter quoted from above: "[A]nd in the war he wrote to his parents that they had just attacked a Russian village; he was 16 or 18 years old, I don't remember exactly, and I was so upset by how euphorically he talked about it." But she wondered during the entire interview whether the Germans could have "imagined" that something like a war of extermination and a Holocaust could happen.

What motivated this question, which obviously ignored that Ms. Seiler's father did not need to "imagine" crimes that he himself committed? The question of whether the father could have imagined such things functioned to maneuver him out of the perpetrator group into the much less suspect group of accidental witnesses or at least fellow travelers, for one imagines only those things of which one has no personal knowledge. Second, Ms. Seiler argued, much as her father did, within a dual framework—a structure of knowledge and ignorance. The crimes undoubtedly occurred, but no one could imagine them. Her own father took part in them, but the daughter did not register this complicity.

How this dual structure functioned in discussions about the past came out in the family interview. Astonishingly, one finds—and by no means only in the Hofer family—that these encounters contain a whole range of stories that seem completely paradoxical to a detached reader but appear to be experienced by participants as a coherent picture of the past. Mr. Hofer recalled that in 1944, after his deployment to the Ukraine, he had been in a tank division in France and had heard from an SS major (*Sturmbannführer*) "that in the East, in Russia, partisans in any case, but also other people, were killed by a shot to the neck and so forth. I remember [laughs] that we talked about this later among the comrades, and we thought, 'He's crazy!'".

This was what Mr. Hofer thought after he had done exactly same thing half a year earlier, an act that he now could not believe others were committing. To say that Hofer was lying would underestimate the effect of this dual structure. The fact that he told about both his own deeds and his disbelief at the deeds of others demonstrates that he can integrate his own deeds subjectively into a meaningful context of a particular rationality and morality, excluding them from the overall accusation of criminality.

Thus, perpetrators such as Mr. Hofer do not reckon their actions as part of the Holocaust—and this very self-perception and self-portrayal provides an interpretative option readily embraced by the following generations. In the group discussion Ms. Seiler posed quite penetrating questions as she concentrated on finding out from her father why no one could "imagine" what was happening—thereby protecting him from the knowledge that he and she actually share. In the Hofer family interaction, what was transmitted was not knowledge of the crimes but rather how one could simultaneously know and not know.

Contrary to the widespread notion that grandparents and parents do not tell their children and grandchildren problematic wartime stories—especially ones that highlight their participation in Nazi crimes—some of the interviewees did divulge their experiences during the war in ways that cast them as perpetrators. But these revelations did not lead to dismay in their listeners, to conflicts, or even to embarrassing situations. They led to nothing at all. It was as though such tales were not heard by the family members present. It seems that ties of family loyalty did not permit a father or grandfather to come across as someone who killed people a few decades earlier. The images formed about the beloved relative through socialization and time spent together was retroactively also applied to the period of that person's life before the births of his offspring, who are now listening and who later will themselves pass on the wartime stories. This tendency to ignore perpetrator stories occurs accidentally, as though automatically. The tape recorder records the stories, but the family's memory does not. In other words, wartime memories are preserved in the family's lore as stories that can be reshaped according to the idealized vision that succeeding generations have of the eyewitness who is telling them. And so they are remembered and retold.

Moving through the generations, stories can become so altered that their meaning changes completely. This reconfiguration generally functions to turn grandparents into people who always possessed moral integrity by today's standards and normative appraisal. This reformulation of stories is undertaken precisely because, in interviews, most members of the children's and grandchildren's generations exhibit no doubt at all that Nazism was a criminal system and the Holocaust an unparalleled crime. This assessment of the Nazi past—the standard fare of history lessons, the media, and the official German culture of commemoration—breaks down under the resulting questions about the role played by one's own grandparents during the period. It even evokes the subjective need to assign one's grandfather or grandmother the role of the "good" German in everyday life under the Nazis. Thus emerges the paradoxical outcome of successful education about the Nazi past: The more comprehensive the knowledge is about war crimes, persecution, and extermination, the stronger the need is to develop stories to reconcile the crimes of "the Nazis" or "the Germans" and the moral integrity of parents or grandparents.

This dual function is performable only through stories that depict one's relatives as human beings who perhaps cautiously, but also courageously, defied contemporary norms and worked against the system in their practical behavior, even though their party membership and functions reveal that they were anything but opponents of the system. The eyewitnesses appeared, in the retellings by their descendants, to be inconspicuous resistance fighters—smart enough to blend in as seen from the outside but, when push came to shove, ready to help victims of persecution, hide Jews, or carry out small acts of opposition.

These stories and episodes of "being against" were embedded in the idea that any nonconformist behavior, from "opening one's mouth" to "protecting Jews," from continuing to "buy from Jews" to showing opposition to superiors and "150 percent" Nazis, could have brought the harshest consequences. The grandparents who acted courageously, from the perspective of their progeny, found themselves chronically in danger of career setbacks, family conflicts, the concentration camp, or even death sentences as a result of their views and behavior. Lars Groothe, the 17-year-old grandson of the Groothe family, therefore defended his forebears:

> But I think in any case that most people thought that, for example, Jews... are people and so forth. But, as one person you couldn't defend yourself. As one person you couldn't do anything. You could say, I think it's bad, you'd be locked up and probably shot.

This interpretation not only allows a synthesis of the image of a totalitarian system, its methods of coercion, and the reinterpretation of the grandparents' roles. It is also a product of an intergenerational chain whereby, in many stories told by the eyewitness generation, their parents are described as people who were "against" the system. The stylization of the great-grandparents' generation as anti-Nazi can go so far that even an "old fighter" who was already a "staunch," middle-ranking Nazi (*Ortsgruppenleiter*) in 1931 can be portrayed as someone who was always ready to oppose the norms of Nazi society; who, for example, continued to shop "from Jews," "did business with the Jewish cattle trader," and finally, according to his great-grandson, "hid" Jews.

Cumulative Heroization

The term *cumulative heroization* is used to refer to the phenomenon that figures in the previous section, that of history becoming "better and better" from generation to generation. It was observed in 26 of the 40 families in the study. Heroization of forebears characterized roughly 15% of all stories told in the interviews and family discussions; victimization, around 50%. In other words, two thirds of all the stories were about family members from the eyewitness generation or their relatives who were victims of the Nazi past, heroes of everyday resistance, or both.

Like her 65-year-old son Bernd Hoffmann, 91-year-old Elli Krug insisted in the individual interview and in the family discussion that she did not know what a concentration camp was until the end of the war, though she lived close to the Bergen-Belsen camp. Later, however, former inmates of the camp passed through her village, and Mrs. Krug was forced by the British occupiers to make her home available to them—an arrangement that clearly displeased her.

> *Elli Krug*: The Jews were the worst afterwards. They really harassed us. ... They sat there and made us serve them, and then they didn't want, we had this big hayloft, they slept there, overnight. ... The Jews and Russians, I always made sure that I didn't get them. They were really disgusting, you know? And then I always stood down in the street, in front of the gate, and when they said "Quarters," I said, "No, everything's full!" If the Jews... came, I said, "It's all full of Russians, you can come in with me!"... And when the Russians came, then I said the same thing, that there were Jews here or something like that.

Mrs. Krug still told how she was able to avoid giving quarters to "Jews" and "Russians" through a trick, while the attributes she used ("the worst," "disgusting") signal a clear anti-Semitic or racist attitude even today. The fact that she was speaking about accommodating prisoners who had survived the nearby Bergen-Belsen concentration camp was not an issue to her at all. The main theme of her story was the burden that she had taken upon herself by providing accommodation and her clever technique for keeping the "Jews" and the "Russians" out of her yard.

Mrs. Krug's son, too, said that people did not know about the camps until the end of the war. But he told a story that he had heard from his wife, who has meanwhile died. She had worked on an estate near Bergen-Belsen and had heard there that the owner had hidden escapees from the camp. Bernd Hoffmann called this person "the grandma."

Bernd Hoffmann: She [his wife] was on a farm in Belsen for a year. They came right by there. The grandma hid some of them, and then they sat in a wooden box. And then they [the SS men] got around, searching everywhere: "He must be here." They would have shot the grandma immediately. She put a hot pot on top of it, with boiling potatoes, on the wooden box, so they wouldn't get them.

The 26-year-old granddaughter, Silvia Hoffmann, then told her version of what her own grandmother did:

Silvia Hoffmann: Once she told some story I thought was really interesting, that our village was on the road to Bergen-Belsen, and that she hid someone who escaped from one of those transports, and in a really interesting way in some grain box with straws sticking out, and she really hid them. And then people came and looked in her farmyard and she kept quiet, and I think, that's a little thing that I really give her a lot of credit for.

This story pieces together elements previously mentioned in her grandmother's and father's separate stories: The "road to Bergen-Belsen," a stout-hearted woman, the box, even the haystack has left a mark on the granddaughter's story, in the form of straw. But the narrative matrix in which the actors appear points to a new message: The strange grandmother is appropriated, wooden boxes and all, and the hay becomes a dramatic element in a tale of how her own grandmother tricked the persecutors. In this way, the granddaughter creates her own image of a good grandmother, which was present in neither her grandmother's nor her father's stories.

Cumulative heroization happens rapidly and simply. The generalized image of a respected grandmother or grandfather seems to provide the framework in which any point of reference suggested by stories can be expanded into a "good story." As with Silvia Hoffmann, the results can be a stripping away of the problematic implications of the true tale. Plots are rearranged so as to reduce the nuanced, ambivalent, often troubling tales by the eyewitnesses to a morally clear attitude on the part of the protagonists—an obviously positive one. The tendency to heroize the grandparents' generation illustrates the strong effects, never to be underestimated, that ties of loyalty to loved ones have on historical awareness and the retrospective construction of the past.

What conclusions can be drawn from the tendency toward cumulative heroization? One finding, not unimportant to the pedagogy of history, is that education that instills comprehensive historical knowledge of Nazi crimes paradoxically evokes a need to remove one's relatives from this knowledge. Yet this need not to be assessed only negatively. From the revised history of heroism, resistance, and civil courage on the part of the grandparents, one can derive a practical view that resistance by an individual is possible and sensible even in a totalitarian context—that it is, emphatically, a question of individual responsibility. To this extent, the stories of oppositional grandparents and great-grandparents, whether or not they are true, can be examples motivating people to act courageously when others around them are threatened or persecuted. In addition, it is clear that the majority of grandchildren favor the example of the anti-Nazis—only four of the forty-four grandchildren interviewed indicated any admiration for or affirmation of "the Nazis."

Cumulative heroization, however, has very different significance for the historical image of Nazism and the Holocaust. It represents a restoration of the theory, thought to be long superseded, that "the Nazis" and "the Germans" were two different groups—that "the Germans" can be seen to have been seduced, abused, and robbed of their youth, that they were themselves victims of Nazism. The fact that this historical model apparently holds a secure place in the cultural memory of the Federal Republic is demonstrated by the renaissance of historical documentaries based on the home-front perspective, such as *Hitler's Helpers* and *Hitler's Children*, two series broadcast on the German public television channel ZDF in 1998. Although the Holocaust has been commemorated in the framework of international conferences like the 2000 Stockholm Holocaust Conference, and although anniversaries of liberation have established a liturgical rhetoric of confession and responsibility, the historical and political elements are disappearing from German historical awareness of Nazism.

What is being lost is the awareness that it was possible, in a civilized twentieth-century society and with the active participation of the overwhelming majority of a well-educated population, to exclude a part of this same population from the universe of obligations (Fein, 1993, p. 14), to see its members as harmful and "worthless," to look on as they were deported, and to accept their extermination. What is also vanishing is awareness of the actual perpetrators, some of whom appear in the interviews—their willingness to murder and their largely unproblematic reintegration into postwar West German society.

Our material signals that an increasing dehistoricization of both Nazism and a crime against humanity is threatening to obscure the process governing the social production of a genocidal development—despite all the factual historical knowledge successfully imparted by history lessons, political education, and memorial work over the past decades. The phenomenon of cumulative heroization shows how deeply an individual's awareness of history is affected by emotional views of the roles played by close relatives and how detached cognitive knowledge of history can be. The subjective synthesis consists of removing one's own ancestors from one's knowledge of history by heroizing them—thus bringing the "evil" of Nazi rule and the "good" of one's own grandparents and great-grandparents into peaceful coexistence.

It appears as though the use of historical knowledge is determined by its frame of reference, which has developed beyond intentional history education. Or as one of the interviewees from the grandchild generation frankly put it, "We get all the normal stuff at school, and the examples for it we get to hear from grandma."

The results of this project have created considerable alarmism in Germany. That response has been inappropriate in my view, however, for Nazis are not regarded as role models. Quite the opposite is true: those who were in opposition to National Socialism and resisted the regime are considered role models. If this does not apply to one's own grandfather, his stories are reinterpreted in a way that ultimately presents him as an everyday hero resisting the Nazi regime. These results have generated a new set of questions: Is the gap between official and private memory a specifically German trait? Can this imbalance between public and private interpretation of the past be found in other countries? Is this tendency to set the grandparents in a positive light a specific trait of dealing with the problematic German past? Or do the research results indicate universal psychological attributes within generational relationships?

Is There a "European Memory?"

To address these questions, my research team and I set up a comparative project modeled on the design of the research in Germany (family interviews and one-on-one interviews with the family members of the different generations).[3] Special comparative attention was drawn to the meanings associated with times of war and of occupation within historiography and memory culture in the respective countries. Unlike the study conducted in Germany, the international comparative one accounted for generational specificity of historical interpretation by including the evaluation of an age-differentiated sample of group discussions in addition to family samples.

The aim of this second project was to identify various historical references to World War II and German occupation and to ascertain the influences such references have on the perception of current social and political problems and debates. (For example, what is the reference frame for interpreting the Iraq war?) Not only can the space between emotive and cognitive dimensions of historical consciousness be measured by our research, the collected data also enable us to speculate about what may promote or hinder creation of a "European memory."

One cannot analyze individual remembrance and family-transmitted memories without considering a society's official and, as it were, authoritative historiography, the basic narrative of a nation. The term *basic narrative* was coined by Norwegian ethnologist Anne Eriksen and the Danish historians Claus Bryld and Annette Warring. Bryld and Warring (1998) describe the central characteristic of a nation's basic narrative as a unifying and harmonizing effect on "cultural and political production of meaning" (p. 55). This narrative "has served as a classic example insofar as contradictory narratives have had to orient themselves to it just to become visible" (p. 55). In this case memories, as individual ways of processing experience and development, are set in a mutually influencing relation to canonized depictions and interactions of war and occupation periods. The basic narrative "functions as a guiding framework for the interpretation of individual memories" and as guiding conceptions and interpretations of those people "who were not involved" (p. 55). In this respect the basic narrative is an intermediary matrix for generationally differentiated interpretations. This authoritative version of the German occupation's official and public remembrance also takes on almost time-transcending and even mythical qualities. Norwegians, Danes, Dutch, Serbs, and Swiss are seen as having specific characteristics of "the way they always were." Consequently, certain narratives and interpretations of the past are excluded from spheres of communication, just as certain groups, their history, and their narratives are excluded.

However, public memory cultures do not offer only static inventories of basic narratives but rather a field of constant negotiation and conflict. The dialogue between generations testifies to the influence that political debates, historical events, and political transformation processes have on historiography and on private memory cultures. At the same time, emotional ties and family loyalties work in the opposite direction, meaning that aspects of family history are not always interpreted or reinterpreted in accordance with historical facts.

On the other hand, even within dominating versions of history there is interpretational leeway that permits detailed delineations of hegemonic narratives without completely invalidating them. In Norway, Denmark, and the Netherlands the black-and-white nature of the basic narratives painted each of those nations as being unified in resistance against its internal and external enemies. This image dominated historiography and memory cultures in those countries for decades. National memory and remembrance of the occupation was a component of national memory politics with which national values were evaluated and political positions could be authorized. Public debates have led to changes within Swiss memory culture, leaving imprints on Swiss narratives not least because of questions about economic linkage, the role of banks (*Raubgold*) or political decisions within refugee politics. The examination of these issues has shattered the national narrative in which a heroic resistance helped spare the country from war.

But critical questioning of resistance myths since the 1980s and 1990s and an expansion of historical perceptions (e.g., aspects of collaboration and reactions of the non-Jewish population to Jewish deportations) run parallel only in western countries. Countries of southeastern Europe have undergone a real change of historical space through civil war and the dissolution of Yugoslavia, experiences that have resulted in strongly revised national perceptions of history during postwar times. The remembrance of the victorious fight of the partisans against fascism disappeared from the public memory agenda as the whole idea a multiethnic Yugoslavia became fragile.

The following overview presents results from our second study.

Norway, Denmark, and the Netherlands

Despite the critical expansion and questioning of national basic narratives mostly on the part of younger generations, the study of Norwegian, Danish, and Dutch families indicated that these dominating perceptions and images of history continue to serve as a matrix for private memories in their countries. In this respect Norway, Denmark, and the Netherlands clearly differed from Germany, whose memory culture lacks precisely that kind of basic narrative. Its absence leads third- and fourth-generation family members to invent a positive family past. The reason for this invention is explicit: Holocaust narratives do not offer the stuff for positive identifications, and it seems that individual identity cannot build without positive references to the group one belongs to. In other western European countries the national basic narratives coin and structure familial "consensus narratives" in a way that enable family members to appear as "good," meaning that they chose the "right" side. Differences lay merely in the specific form these narratives have been given in the different countries. Taking ordinary stories about everyday life in times of war and imbuing them with meanings of "resistance" has been an overall phenomenon and a recurring motif in these three countries.

The national basic narrative remains valid when new generations of family members integrate critical aspects of relatively recent historical accounts into their version of their family history. Norwegian, Danish, and Dutch grandchildren portray their grandparents in a positive way, just as German grandchildren do. The only difference is that most members of the former three groups do not need to avoid the difficult aspects of national history and can inscribe their family history into the basic narrative. But the war experienced by the grandparents does not always fit into the basic narrative's black-and-white pattern. It is striking that narratives from "the other side," those of collaboration, are also preserved in private memory. They are merely interpreted in a way that either diminishes their relevance ("grandfather was already senile") or denies any connection to the family.

In that context family memory is reconcilable with publicly transmitted norms and values, and this affinity allows younger generations a critical dissociation from myths of national memory without questioning their normative content and their orienting function. Indeed, narratives of heroes and ceremonial commemoration of veterans are often not taken seriously. Nevertheless, the *values* communicated in public memory and in education about the occupation are not devaluated; they are *updated* through universalization, as in the framework of Holocaust memory.

This process is, of course, especially apparent in the topic of Jewish persecution. In Norway the subject remained a blank within national memory; in the Netherlands it was an element difficult to integrate. By contrast, the rescue of Danish Jews matched Denmark's self-image as a nation with moral integrity. Grandchildren in particular had intimate knowledge of National Socialist policies on annihilation, especially of a medially transported iconography of the Holocaust. However, this statement does not imply that they possessed substantiated knowledge about historic events in their own country; nor does it imply that they had such knowledge about the destiny of the Jewish population in Denmark.

Switzerland

Debates on transnational memory have had an impact on perceptions of the past in Switzerland. They have universalized the country's perspective on World War II and National Socialism, especially among younger participants in group discussions.

The group interviews in the Swiss project suggest that younger participants see the Holocaust as an event from which universally valid humanitarian lessons can be drawn. In this case it is remarkable that the Holocaust serves as a reference point for evaluating and comparing current events more than traditional heroic elements of a national narrative. The Swiss results also imply that these shifts within perception and interpretation of the past point to a conflicting phenomenon. It is not just that younger family members replace national narratives with universal narratives but that national narratives and nationalized values are actually *updated*. New motives are integrated into more traditional structures, and universalized perspectives can be combined with national perspectives. This combination is accomplished by shifting the center of narratives from heroes to victims, referring particularly to *national* victims, not primarily to European Jews. Near the end of the Swiss group discussions, it seemed as though *everyone* was victimized, even Germans. Switzerland's former policy on refugees can thus be interpreted as a deviation from a universal humanitarian attitude.

Because of their different historical positions, these countries still allow members of their third generation to refer positively to first-generation formative narratives and historical perceptions. Social continuity and social stability also play an important role in these countries, offering references to democracy, tolerance, and human rights as a continuous source for updating national self-images. These varying propositions for a historic formation of meaning can be negotiated or selectively used without national historical narratives and interpretations eventually disintegrating.

Serbia and Croatia

Wartime experiences in Serbia and Croatia in the 1990s have contributed to fundamental political and economic changes, creating a vacuum in orientation and perspective when the populations of these countries deal with the past. This void is conspicuous in views on World War II and the way family members talk about them. Contemporary witnesses offer almost no narratives to which younger generations can connect.

In discussions about Serbia and Croatia, it is important to realize that speaking of *one* memory culture is inaccurate. Aside from differing and competing historical narratives about World War II, civil war and the subsequent formation of societies seem to have made transgenerational communication about the past far more difficult than in western European countries. In fact, it is almost impossible. A national formative narrative on which younger generations can take positions in a skeptical, but loyal, way no longer exists. A factually changed history has rendered the experiences and interpretations of contemporary witnesses useless for meeting the identification and orientation needs of younger generations.

Comparing the intergenerationally negotiated war stories from the western European countries studied in this chapter, one finds the most striking difference to be that grandchildren align stories of their grandparents with *their own war experiences*. From an intergenerational perspective, this phenomenon results in a distinct and decisive variation. Instead of a socialist hero, there is another character: someone who knows how to stay alive, a political opportunist who has no heroic characteristics but who is clever and devious. In these reversed interpretations partisans are sometimes even described as brutal criminals, and the ability to trick the partisans is associated with admiration. Collaboration can be interpreted as a sharp survival strategy that is in no way morally questionable. Vice versa, the image of the German soldier of World War II has detached itself from old depictions of the enemy. Memories of German acts of violence seem to have lost their efficacy, explaining the polarization into collaboration and resistance.

Universalism and Identity

In western European interviews and especially in group discussions, many of the younger interviewees connect their perspective on the past to reflections on antiracism, tolerance, human rights, and current mass violence and genocides. These perceptions often go hand in hand with anthropological considerations on war and violence ("people have always been that way"). *Universalizing* and *anthropologizing* are two observable interpretation patterns, with nationally specific behavior patterns and attitudes being inscribed into a universal narrative in such a way that it can be both a universal and nationalistic perception of history.

Another key observation is the transnational importance of media and memory. Movies and books that may be referred to as globalized, or at least Europeanized, memory media influence knowledge and interpretation patterns mainly with respect to World War II, especially the Holocaust. Examples are *The Diary of Anne Frank* and the movie *Schindler's List*. These media were referred to and cited by most of the western European interviewees, who also linked them with similar interpretation patterns, such as the mentioned victimization discourse and Oskar Schindler's belief that there had been numerous German saviors. This image countered the concept of "the bad Germans," which had been seminal in national formative narratives after 1945, and was crucial in the forging of close political, economic, and military relations with Germany within the European Community (EC) and NATO.

Today, the same media constitute elements of a developing field named "Holocaust Education," whose main goal is to establish a European "Humanitarian Education."[4] It is evident that medially transmitted images of history and historical knowledge are sources of meaning that are adaptable to varying sociocultural and political contexts. These processes of negotiating and transforming historical meaning are constantly at work within family and private life. They offer options for communication in which nonfitting and formerly excluded narratives and interpretations can be fostered.

    In one respect the national comparison that my research team and I have drawn
in this chapter makes for a fairly consistent conclusion: that anti-Semitic interpretation patterns have not disappeared but arise more often within dialogues than in
regular surveys, which consistently indicate anti-Semitic attitudes at a distribution
level of 20%. The material on which our two studies rest shows no appreciable anti-
Semitism but an obvious transmission of anti-Semitic perspectives on the past, an
example being a Swiss group discussion in which neither Germans nor the Swiss
were ever said to have done anything condemnable but in which Jews were chronically made out to be a problem. The German study suggests a latency of anti-Semitic
stereotypes, expressed through depictions of Jews as "rich" and "cunning." In the
comparative study negative descriptions of Jews appeared especially when strong
disapproval of Israeli behavior in the Middle East conflict was expressed. Israelis
were compared with Nazis, the sole difference being that the Israelis were expected
to know better because of their own past.

    This type of secondary anti-Semitism is found not only at the private level of
family discussions but also at a public level. In Norway, for instance, philosopher
and best-seller author Jostein Gaarder has commented that Israel lost its "right to
exist" after war with the Hezbollah (Gaarder, 2006), and on July 10, 2006, a cartoon
published in the left-liberal *Dagbladet* in Oslo showed the then-Israeli prime minister Ehud Olmert dressed in an SS uniform and standing in front of a wall bearing the
inscription "*Arbeit macht frei.*" The dispersion of latent and apparent anti-Semitic
orientations surprised us and will be the object of further analysis. It seems to be the
most alarming and discomforting aspect of our research project.

    Because the universalization of meaning can correspond to a change of national
self-conceptions and self-positioning in a globalized world, one needs to ask if shifts
of meaning that bear on occupation are phenomena of de- or renationalization processes. A political orientation incorporating acknowledgment of human rights has
long been part of the rhetoric of national foreign policy, a commitment that third-
generation members often refer to as "lessons" learned from history. Thus, national
traits are not dissolving or becoming obsolete; instead, they are being paraphrased
in interaction with universal perspectives. From the viewpoint of subsequent generations, "good" Swiss, Danish, Norwegian, and Dutch people had to model themselves
on ideals of equality, tolerance, and human dignity in times of war. For children
and grandchildren it is not hard to associate with family narratives presenting their
grandparents in such a modern light.

    This finding does not apply to research results from Serbia and Croatia. The
most blatant difference between these two southeastern European countries on the
one hand and western European countries on the other seems to be that standing
and challenged national formative narratives do not coexist in Serbia and Croatia
and that the younger generations there do not engage in extensive reinterpretations.
War and social collapse after delegitimation of the formative socialist narrative have
entailed a loss of interconnected normative orientations and a devaluation of memories and historical interpretations of contemporary witnesses. This difference is
significant not just when Serbia and Croatia are compared with Norway, Denmark,
the Netherlands, and Switzerland but with Germany as well. It seems as though

transmitted interpretation frameworks have become obsolete in Serbia and Croatia and that propositions for new collective interpretations do not exist. Whereas reinterpretation and renegotiation in public memory culture and family narratives are precisely what bear witness to a stable normative background in western European countries, history seems to have become useless for the orientation of younger generations in Serbia and Croatia.

These results illustrate how closely public and private references to respective pasts are linked to their corresponding presents. In states still lacking a firm foundation for civil society—those in which democratization is a recent process and in which short- and middle-term needs for economic consolidation are uppermost in mind—a history that ended in destruction offers some kind of future, but it is bleak.

The research presented in this chapter can provide indicators for the stability of the identifications that individuals have with their societies—a surprising result. Whereas German grandchildren invent good grandmas and grandpas to avoid negative identity ascriptions, young Serbs and Croatians have problems making use of the past as an identity resource. The young and confident Swiss, Norwegians, Danish, and Dutch interviewees can easily integrate problematic aspects of their national history because history poses no harsh questions about collective identity formation. References to the past stem from needs associated with identity development. Individuals must become aware of their specific generational identity needs in a social arena defined by family members, groups, diverse memory communities, the media, and the official memory culture of the society they are part of. It appears that these identity needs are easier to satisfy on some occasions than on others, depending on the problems a society faces with its history.

Notes

1. In Georgi (2003), for example, a 16-year-old Turkish interviewee who had been born in Germany and who was very interested in history, felt "like a German" (p. 301) for the first time during an excursion to Theresienstadt. "I forgot the Turk in me," he stated, because the Czechs in his student group saw him as part of the German collective subject. Thus, paradoxically, identification with the most negative part of German history led to an emphatic feeling of being "pure German" (p. 301), of feeling fully integrated.
2. Many students took part in the collection and analysis of this study, including Erika Rothärmel, Jenna Voss, and Angelika Kompmann. Olaf Jensen, Torsten Koch, Sabine Moller, and Karoline Tschuggnall assisted in writing the report.
3. The following passage was written together with Dr. Claudia Lenz of the Center for Studies of Holocaust and Religious Minorities in Oslo, Norway.
4. This aim is manifest in the explanation by the Stockholm International Forum on the Holocaust, which stated in 2000 that "humanity [is] still scared by genocide, ethnic cleansing, racism, Anti-Semitism and xenophobia, the international community shares a solemn responsibility to fight those evils. . . .. We must strengthen the moral commitment of our peoples, and the political commitment of our governments, to ensure that future generations can understand the causes of the Holocaust and reflect upon its consequences." See the Stockholm International Forum on the Holocaust. Retrieved July 30, 2010, from http://www.holocaustforum.gov.se/pdfandforms/deklarat.

References

Angvik, M., & von Borries, B. (2000). *Youth and history: A comparative European survey on historical consciousness and political attitudes among adolescents: Vol. A. Description; Vol. B. Documentation.* Hamburg: Körber-Stiftung.

Bryld, C., & Warring, A. (1998). *Besættelsestiden som kollektiv erindring. Historie og traditions-forvaltning af krig og besættelse 1945–1997* [Occupation as collective memory. History and coping techniques of war and occupation]. Copenhagen: Roskilde.

Fein, H. (1993). *Genocide: A sociological perspective.* London: Sage.

Gaarder, J. (2006, August 5). *Guds utvalgte folk* [God's chosen people]. Retrieved July 30, 2010, from http://www.aftenposten.no/meninger/kronikker/article1411153.ece

Georgi, V. (2003). *Entliehene Erinnerung. Geschichtsbilder junger Migranten in Deutschland* [Borrowed memory: Historical perceptions among young migrants in Germany]. Hamburg: Hamburger Edition.

Gudehus, C. (2006). *Dem Gedächtnis zuhören* [Listen to memory]. Essen: Klartext.

Radtke, F.-O., Hollstein, O., Meseth, W., Müller-Mahnkopp, C., & Proske, M. (Eds.). (2002). *Nationalsozialismus im Geschichtsunterricht: Beobachtungen unterrichtlicher Kommunikation* [National Socialism in the history class: Observations on instructional communication]. Frankfurt am Main: University of Frankfurt, Frankfurter Beiträge zur Erziehungswissenschaft.

Seixas, P. (2001). Geschichte und Schule [History and school]. In H. Welzer (Ed.), *Das soziale Gedächtnis* (pp. 205–218). Hamburg: Hamburger Edition.

Welzer, H. (Ed.). (2007). *Der Krieg der Erinnerung* [The war of memory]. Stuttgart: S. Fischer.

Welzer, H., Moller, S., & Tschuggnall, K. (2002). *Opa war kein Nazi* [Grandpa wasn't a Nazi]. Stuttgart: S. Fischer.

Wineburg, S. (2001). Sinn machen. Wie Geschichte zwischen den Generationen gebildet wird [Making sense: How history is created between the generations]. In H. Welzer (Ed.), *Das soziale Gedächtnis* (pp. 179–204). Hamburg: Hamburger Edition.

Wineburg, S. (2002). *Teaching history and other unnatural acts.* Philadelphia: Temple University Press.

Annihilating—Preserving—Remembering: The "Aryanization" of Jewish History and Memory During the Holocaust

Dirk Rupnow

Discourses on memory in cultural studies since the late 1980s have often raised the suspicion that the National Socialists not only planned the physical annihilation of the Jews but also wanted to erase them from history and memory (Freed, 1994; Hoffmann, 1998; Lyotard, 1988; Young, 1997). After all, that additional aim would not have been unprecedented. One might see it as having been modeled on the Roman practice of *damnatio memoriae*, whereby statues of a person found to be an enemy of the state were destroyed and his name removed from inscriptions and coins. Moreover, the stereotypical, albeit understandable, characterization of Jews as the people of history with privileged access to memory seems to increase the plausibility of the putative Nazi intention to inflict total destruction that transcends the physical one. Thus, terms such as *Gedächtnozid* (Münz, 1994), *Mnemozid* (Assmann, 1999), and *Gedächtnismord* and *Memorizid* (Weinrich, 1997) have been coined to modify and strengthen the notion of genocide.

The allegation of memorycide reflects the current significance of the memory paradigm in the humanities and social sciences. If the aim is to preserve the special status of the Holocaust, it seems that one must focus on those measures that go even beyond the total physical annihilation of the Jews. In times when identity is determined by one's status as victim, the concept of a victimized memory, of a memory that has itself become a victim, is the best legitimization for the new central concept in cultural studies.

The assumed project of memorycide also offers a negative foil for the duty to remember and for the establishment of museums, memorials, and monuments in the countries of the perpetrators. The duty to remember is derived not only from the mass murder committed by the National Socialists but, above all, from its particular character as a double homicide, as a lethal act that was directed both at the people and the memory of them. By mirroring it, the allegation of memorycide justifies the statement that remembering the crimes is necessary to prevent comparable ones.

D. Rupnow (✉)
Institut für Zeitgeschichte, University of Innsbruck, 6020 Innsbruck, Austria
e-mail: dirk.rupnow@uibk.ac.at

P. Meusburger et al. (eds.), *Cultural Memories*, Knowledge and Space 4,
DOI 10.1007/978-90-481-8945-8_12, © Springer Science+Business Media B.V. 2011

The ritualized commemoration of the persecution and mass murder of the Jews, the rhetoric of not-forgetting in the countries of the perpetrators, is ultimately based on the assumption that the committed crimes cannot be repeated as long as they are remembered. Destruction and forgetting on the one hand and remembrance and justice on the other are apparently seen not simply as arbitrarily linked but as inherently inseparable.

The deliberate actions to erase the evidence of mass murder at the end of the Third Reich offer factual points of reference and models for the claim of memorycide. They include the exhumations at the main sites of murders carried out as of 1942 by *Aktion 1005* under SS Standartenführer Paul Blobel and the destruction of documents by German authorities following an order of the Reich's interior ministry at the end of the war (Brather, 1958; Spector, 1990). The incriminating nature of the racist policies of extermination meant that no traces of them could be allowed to fall into Allied hands. Heinrich Himmler's so-called *Posen speech*, which the SS chief delivered in the presence of SS Gruppenführer (lieutenant generals) on October 4, 1943, has often been cited as a proof of the intent to commit memorycide. Particular attention has been given to a passage about the mass murder of Jews and the SS men's "propriety" (*Anständigkeit*),[1] which according to Himmler remained untarnished after the murders: "This is a glorious chapter in our history that has never been written and that never will be" (International Military Tribunal, 1948, Dok. PS-1919, p. 64).

What frequently goes unmentioned is another speech Himmler gave only two days later at the same place, this time before high-ranking officials of the Nazi party—Reichsleiter and Gauleiter. This document explicitly but even more undecidedly addresses the problems of secrecy and historical transmission with regard to the "Final Solution of the Jewish question":

> The hard decision had to be made to let this people [the Jews] disappear from this earth. . .. One can consider at a much later time whether the German people should be told more about this. I think it is better that we—we as a whole—have carried this for our people, have carried the responsibility (the responsibility for a deed not just for an idea); and then we will carry this secret to our graves. (Smith & Peterson, 1974, pp. 170–172)

Of course, the question of remembrance or forgetting became more and more acute as the mass murder progressed. Kurt Gerstein, a Waffen SS hygiene expert who eyewitnessed gassings at Belzec and Treblinka and who was complicit in providing Zyklon B for mass murder, reported that an exchange is said to have taken place in Lublin in August 1942 between Hitler, Himmler, Odilo Globocnik (Himmler's friend and confidant, who was the SS and Police Leader in the Lublin district and the head of *Aktion Reinhard*[2]), and Dr. Herbert Linden of the interior ministry (who was involved in conducting the "Euthanasia" program):

> *Ministerialrat* Dr. Herbert Linden then asked: "Mr. Globocnik, do you consider it right and fair to bury the corpses instead of burning them? A generation could follow us that does not understand this!" Globocnik replies: "Sirs, if we are ever succeeded by a generation that is so weak and lily-livered as to fail to understand our great task, then, admittedly, National Socialism has existed entirely in vain. On the contrary, I am of the opinion that

we should install bronze plates documenting that we had the courage to carry out this big
and necessary project." The *Führer* answers: "Right, Globocnik, I indeed share your view."
(Rothfels, 1953, p. 189)

Even if this suggestion was only a fleeting idea, a boast by Globocnik (who is said
to be the one to have recounted the exchange to Gerstein only a few days later),
or an imprecise recollection or invention of Gerstein's (Hitler never visited a concentration or extermination camp), the ambivalence of the perpetrators is clear. For
Himmler, who vacillates between secrecy and self-glorification of the perpetrators,
the need for secrecy wins out, an outcome that only confirms and underlines the elite
character of the SS. By contrast, Globocnik calls for a calculated way of remembering an act that is understood to be heroic. Only deferred covert commemoration is
possible, for the criminal character of the actions seems to be obvious even to the
perpetrators. For reasons of secrecy, however, an open and direct representation is
only postponed, not entirely avoided. In Himmler's and Globocnik's commentaries,
the victims do not play any visible role at first, but one has to assume that it is necessary and virtually decisive to have them in the picture in order to reinterpret the
crime as a historical necessity.

During the war, legal scholar and political scientist Franz Neumann (1942–
1944/1984) assumed in his work about the structure and the practice of National
Socialism that the value of antisemitism[3] for domestic policies would never allow
a "complete annihilation of the Jews" (p. 163): "The enemy cannot and may not
disappear; he constantly has to be available as the scapegoat for all the ills that the
sociopolitical system produces" (p. 163). At about the same time as Neumann's
study, historian Emanuel Ringelblum (1958) wrote down the same idea in the
Warsaw Ghetto.

The existence of two conflicting sets of ideological requisites also comes out
in Broszat's (1969/2000) description of Hitler's Germany. On the one hand, the
Nazi worldview relied on the propagandistic psychological necessity of stereotypical enemies. On the other hand, the original discrimination against the Jews had
to climax in systematic mass murder if the Nazi ideology were to be applied consistently. To Broszat this contradiction demonstrates the inevitably self-destructive
and pathological nature of the Nazi state—a very common interpretation in early
German research on the Third Reich. Erich Goldhagen (1976) came to a similar
conclusion: "By murdering the Jews, the National Socialists destroyed their instrument for power (*Herrschaftsinstrument*). Instead of preserving the scapegoat, they
slaughtered it" (p. 93).

Preserving "the Other" in Nazi Germany

Obviously, the mass murder of Jews became fact. One also knows of the meaning
and importance of antisemitism for the National Socialist system. If one assumes
that images of "the Other" are essential for the construction of a "we," then how
could the National Socialists have done without "the Jew"? This problem was
ostensibly apparent even to ordinary Germans in the Third Reich. In October 1942,

a pharmacist from Frankfurt wrote under the heading "A Suggestion" to the editors of *Der Stürmer*, a blatantly antisemitic weekly Nazi tabloid published from 1923 to 1945:

> The number of people on our streets with the yellow star of David and with the imprint *Jew* are decreasing in quite a pleasing manner. But what is entirely lost through this uplifting occurrence, especially for the younger generation, is the repellent impression that the Jew gives in everyday life. I suggest, therefore, constructing a roomy cage next to the monkey cages at the zoo. In one part of this cage, a Jewish family will be displayed with the typical Jewish attributes: flat feet, crooked nose, curly black hair, hunchback posture, thick lips, half-closed eyes, heavy eye lids; in the other part of the cage, there will be a family whose appearance will not appear Jewish. (Stadtarchiv Nürnberg: E39, 2326/1)

This suggestion of preserving Jews alive was offered as the only way to compensate for the explicitly approved policy of deportation. But there were other means that made it possible actually to murder the supposed enemy and conserve him for future representation.

The only high-ranking National Socialist to refer clearly to the antagonism between implementing the "Final Solution" and persistently needing a counterimage was Alfred Rosenberg. In a speech on March 16, 1941, at the opening of the Institut zur Erforschung der Judenfrage (Institute for Research on the Jewish Question) in Frankfurt am Main, the first branch of his alternative university, the Hohe Schule, he stated:

> When the Jewish question in Germany—and at some point in all of Europe—is resolved, there could be a generation after us that could not render account of *what* really happened in these decades. Our grandchildren, freed from the Jewish influence, could perhaps again fall victim to fanciful ideas and no longer judge the effect of the Jewish people among the Europeans the way we have to do it today. People's memory is very short. Often 30 or 50 years are enough to no longer even remember the greatest destinies in the *volkish* consciousness. This is why we cannot be content with the results of the past decades, not only with the books and speeches that emerged from the immediate fight, but we have to substitute our lived knowledge, which to a certain degree was already founded on deep insights, with extensive research. (Rosenberg, 1941, p. 5)

Parallel to the anti-Jewish policy of the National Socialists, the so-called "research on the Jewish question," or *Judenforschung* (literally, research on Jews), was able to establish itself as an independent field of study, beyond the boundaries of traditional disciplines, with specific institutions, publications, and events. However, this kind of anti-Jewish scholarship was never identical with racial biology or anthropology. Instead, the field was occupied by historians, theologians, specialists in German studies, orientalists, classical philologists, jurists, and sociologists. Research on the East (*Ostforschung*) and volkish history (*Volksgeschichte*) obviously had antisemitic components but were by no means centered on Judaism or the "Jewish question." In Nazi *Judenforschung,* antisemitism was the leading principle, with the antisemitically constructed Jewish question being the point of departure for scholarly interest and the focus of research activity. In the thinking and planning of research on the East and volkish history, Jewish populations were always just a negative element that had to be removed. But during the Third Reich—contrary to the tradition of

German historiography still practiced after World War II—themes of Jewish history were in themselves respectable subjects of research (Rupnow, 2006; Steinweis, 2006; Weinreich, 1999).

In Germany scholarly interest in Jewish history did not begin with Nazi anti-Jewish research, but it was never clearly institutionalized and widely acknowledged by non-Jewish academics until Jewish history was forcibly integrated into German history by the actors who were simultaneously legitimizing and conducting anti-Jewish policies. The institutionalization of Jewish studies in Germany paralleled and complemented the expulsion and murder of German and European Jewry. History became the leading discipline in the interdisciplinary field of anti-Jewish research because, with the "Final Solution" on the Nazi agenda, a "final" historicization of the Jewish question had become possible and necessary. Studies on the history of antisemitism served the Nazi anti-Jewish policies by reconstructing a tradition. The analysis of historical attempts to solve the Jewish question could help develop and provide the rationale for the Nazi initiative by constructing supposedly aporetic situations that justified ever more radical strategies as a way out of them. But even beyond that purpose, history was used as an argument. In cases of doubt, discrimination and persecution in history furnished a criterion for the classification as "Jewish" according to Nazi racial policy. Persecution was the best argument for continuing persecution. In Nazi *Judenforschung*, the concept of race, oscillating between spirit and nature, ended in a circular historical argument (Rupnow, 2004, 2008).

The main function of anti-Jewish research did not lie in the propagandistic facilitation of the Nazi deportation and extermination policies or potentially in their planning and scientific endorsement. Learned analysis was intended to replace propaganda *after* Auschwitz and had to preserve an image of the alleged enemy. The academics involved in that kind of research repeatedly tried to distinguish their work from both anti-Jewish propaganda and practical anti-Jewish policy and sought thereby to define their position as "scholarly." But they also profited from and took part directly in the plundering and mass murder, as with the looting of libraries throughout Europe and the definition of certain groups in occupied countries as "Jewish."

Preservation was similarly intertwined with mass murder. Fritz Hippler, the *Reichsfilmintendant* (who was in charge of film department in the propaganda ministry) reports that Goebbels gave him the following order after the German troops had marched into Poland in September 1939:

> Go to Litzmannstadt (Lodz) tomorrow with a few cameramen and have them film everything that comes across their path. The life and business on the street, the trading and bartering, the ritual in the synagogue, don't forget the kosher butchering (*schächten*). We have to record all of this at these original places because soon there will be no Jews here. The *Führer* wants to deport all of them, to Madagascar or to other areas. Therefore we need these film documents for our archive. (Hippler, 1981, p. 187)

This footage was turned into what was probably the most brutal and obvious propaganda film of National Socialist antisemitism, *Der ewige Jude* (The Eternal Jew), which was used chiefly to prepare the public for the deportations in Germany, its occupied territories and countries, and its allies and for a radical solution of the

"Jewish question". It was also specifically screened for police, *Wehrmacht* (the German armed forces), and *Einsatzgruppen* (SS death squads). The filming was driven by the need to document in the nick of time what the film-makers themselves were about to destroy. Hence, the material was used in the very process of mass murder but was also destined for "the archive" of the perpetrators—for the time afterwards.

Also directly connected to the politics of extermination and the practice of deportations, and, more specifically, the politics and practice of looting was another project to preserve and present an image of the victims. Under the aegis of the *Jüdisches Zentralmuseum* (Jewish Central Museum), systematic collection and storage of ritual objects from the Protectorate of Bohemia and Moravia was begun in Prague by Jewish scholars in the spring of 1942. Some of these materials were exhibited in synagogues in the old Jewish ghetto of Prague. This work was ordered, supervised, and directed by the Security Service (SD) of the SS, specifically, the *Zentralstelle für jüdische Auswanderung* (Central Office for Jewish Emigration; later known as the *Zentralamt zur Regelung der Judenfrage in Böhmen und Mähren*, or the Central Office for the Regulation of the Jewish Question in Bohemia and Moravia), which was the Prague outpost of Adolf Eichmann's Jewish Affairs section in the Reich Main Security Office (Potthast, 2002; Rupnow, 2000, 2002, 2005).

The Jewish Central Museum appears to have been the result of compatibility between SD and Jewish interests within the framework of the Nazi politics of "Aryanization" and destruction. In the process of collecting—which oscillated between looting and preservation—Jewish and German interests seemed to converge. The museum, whose exhibits were not known and not accessible to the public until the end of the war, was first developed as a depot. The question of how to deal with religious objects necessarily arose from the highly methodical collection activities of the *Treuhandstelle* (Trust Agency) in Prague, which seized the movable goods and nonreligious belongings of Czech Jews and was, just like the museum, a department under the leadership of the Jewish Authority (*Jüdische Kultusgemeinde*), which was itself controlled by the Central Office.

Ritual objects were, of course, left behind in massive numbers as well—as a result of the deportations to the ghettos and death camps. The Central Museum, therefore, became a repository for those items that were exploitable and usable neither in the plain economic sense nor for purposes of racial policies. Unlike the objects of everyday Jewish life that were collected at the Trust Agency, those held by the Central Museum could not be passed on to non-Jews (i.e., they could not be "Aryanized"), and they no longer had any value for the racial identification of individuals. The Central Office had decided early on that only objects of genuinely museological value should be included in the collection, not those documents that could be considered for genealogy. Those were organized separately, into the *Zentralmatrik* (registry of births, marriages, and deaths). Whereas these archives were important during the preparation of the deportations—they functioned as its organizational basis—the museum, like the Trust Agency, was the vehicle for exploiting and utilizing the deportations afterwards. The Jewish Central Museum in Prague was thus in no way what it is often portrayed to have been: the absurd or, in

light of its location, Kafkaesque satyr play as a contrast to the tragedy of the extermination of the Jews. The museum was in fact a component of the "Final Solution"
and is explicable through the specific logic behind the Nazi politics of looting and
extermination.

To be sure, it was no normal musealization movement that was underway in
Prague in the early to mid-1940s; it was imposed. Religious ritual objects were
torn from their everyday uses, just as the people who used them were torn from
their lives. If there has always been an alliance between museums and death, it
was closer and more immediate in Prague: Musealization facilitates murder. The
expansion of the Prague museum's collections—from about 1,000 objects in 1941
to 200,000 in eight buildings and fifty warehouses by the end of the war—directly
reflected the deportation of the Jewish communities from the Protectorate. The relationship between deportation and this museum work was not only a metaphor but
also a reality: Objects accumulated at the Prague museum, such as the eyeglasses
and suitcases on display in Auschwitz today.

The final depository (*Endlager*) museum made further use of the stored objects
in order to represent what had been destroyed. Even in Prague, propaganda in the
usual sense was not the intention. The existing photographs of the displays show
the concept of a Jewish museum that might exist nowadays. They bear no resemblance to the infamous propaganda exhibit *Der ewige Jude*. Naturally, though, the
transitions are flowing, and different intents, such as conservation, exhibition, and
propaganda are virtually impossible to separate. But the character of anti-Jewish
propaganda after a completed "Final Solution" would not necessarily have been the
same as during that solution's preparation and implementation.

The Nazi Politics of Memory

The murder of millions of people leaves not only traces but also a blank spot that
is hard to ignore. Such a crime is impossible to forget by decree. It can, of course,
go unexplained, but no art of forgetting can guarantee oblivion for either the deed
itself or the victims. The alternative, the attempt to seize control of remembrance,
thus appears to be more effective as well as more perfidious. The "Final Solution"
would not have been accomplished until even the memory of the victims had been
hegemonically defined by the perpetrators. Musealization and museums, scholarship
and research, and visual media such as photographs and film made possible both the
annihilation of the alleged enemy and his conservation.

One might therefore be apt to suppose that the National Socialists had a
concept of a calculated, coordinated, and centrally planned politics of memory
(*Gedächtnispolitik*). That assumption is just as impossible to prove as the assumption that there was a planned memorycide and is just as misleading as the assumption
that a monolithic "Hitler state" existed. It underestimates the initiative of single
agencies and agents within the Third Reich, the competition within the system, and
the momentum within the entire process of expulsion, deportation, looting, and mass
murder. A close look at the museum project in Prague reveals that pragmatic and

situational considerations and specific conditions were locally more important than directives, that the periphery decided and acted without instructions from the center, and that the project was limited to a certain, local level. Moreover, Prague was not the only site of Jewish musealization under Nazi auspices. It also happened at other places and in local, not necessarily Jewish, history museums. But all the competition and initiatives were unified and guided by an antisemitic intent shared by all the protagonists.

According to Assmann (1996), "if Hitler had succeeded, the memorial landscape would look different today—the Gestapo headquarters would still be standing, and there would no longer be any traces of the extermination camps" (p. 24). As obvious as his comment seems to be, it cannot be readily confirmed. One can only speculate about the appearance of the memorial landscape that would have emerged had Germany been victorious and able to carry out its extermination plans unimpeded. For all the popularity that this hypothetical issue is gaining among historians, it can only be entertained very cautiously and tentatively. The analysis is impeded by the very intolerability of thinking about what would have been had Germany finally prevailed.

Historians usually direct their attention to the last phase of the war—to the perpetrators who had already realized that they were going to lose the war. The approaching Allied armies were, understandably, not supposed to find any evidence of the mass crimes. Accordingly, the works on history and memory, including the research on genocide, have dealt mostly with the traumatic consequences of mass murder and the process of coming to terms with them. Aside from the hypothesis of memorycide, the function of memory in the context of the genocide has received little notice. Incomplete documentation of the events in question has left only fragments and traces for reconstructing a National Socialist politics of memory parallel to the politics of extermination.

Even those pieces partly conflict with each other. One finds no coordinated goal and cannot always distinguish between preserving an image of the crime and preserving an image of the victims. Participants acted independently, and the standpoints of some protagonists could vary depending on the circumstances. Himmler wanted to preserve the process of extermination at most as esoteric secret knowledge of the SS, yet he supported the anatomist August Hirt at the Reichsuniversität Strassburg in establishing a collection of Jewish skulls for scientific examinations of "lesser humans" (*Untermenschentum*). This extreme example of a trophy collection helped conserve the putative enemy beyond his physical destruction, so even in the event of a German victory it would have pointed at least indirectly to mass murder, contradicting the attempts at secrecy (Klee, 1997).

The term *politics of memory* is thus intended to refer to the proleptic construction of memory, that is, the anticipatory formation and structuring of remembrance. It refers to how memory was constructed not in a distant or recent past but rather in a past present—or to how it even might have facilitated or prevented memory. The politics of memory, therefore, occurs in a time frame to which politics of the past and politics of history refer only after the fact. The politics of memory parallels and complements the politics of extermination. It connotes an attempt to influence contemporary and later images in order to imbue cultural memory with specific content. It thus constitutes a condition that the politics of the past and the politics of history have to grapple with and react to. The Nazi perpetrators tried to establish their own structure of memory that would have determined today's present—their future—and that in fact reaches into and effects today's present even though they could not complete their objective of completely annihilating the Jewish people. Within this framework, remembrance and memory must be understood not only as strategies for managing the past but also as plans for designing the future.

The National Socialist politics of memory cannot be seen as a marginal area. It leads directly into the vortex of expulsion, deportation, looting, and mass murder—the dynamic of the "Final Solution" as well as the intentions and self-images of the perpetrators. Expropriation of the memory of the victims would have been their ultimate humiliation and annihilation. The phenomenon complementing physical annihilation does not have to be the act of forgetting; it can be the act of remembering.

Although the Jews were denounced as superfluous and useless, killed at the execution sites, and murdered in the camps, they had to be preserved as the Others in museums, scholarship, and images. Even though they were removed from everyday reality, they had to remain visible within Nazi ideology, as made clear by the word *judenfrei* (free of Jews), the Nazi term designating the completion of the "Final Solution" in a given area. It communicates the absence that is described and thereby kept present; the erasure, the murder, remains visible. A German Reich and a Europe free of Jews under National Socialist rule would have meant an ever-present absence of the Jews, a condition described in a key novel whose author had worked at the Jewish museum in Prague for a time after the war. Capturing wartime Prague and the events at the museum, the book includes a figure—an SS officer overseeing the work at the museum, who summarizes the situation: "You have to be, even when you don't exist anymore" (Ihr müßt sein, auch wenn ihr nicht mehr seid) (Adler, 1989, p. 413).

A final German victory, contrary to the common assumption that it would have led to memorycide, could have resulted in Jewish museums and research about the victims (still understood as enemies) and memorials to the German crimes (perceived as heroic deeds), just as they appeared bearing the diametrical message after the defeat of Nazi regime. The outcome, unlike that today, would have been a dead memory without any living and dissenting counterpart, without competition. The people depicted would not have had any part in it. In any case, the allegedly essential connection between annihilation and forgetting on the one hand and between memory (or remembrance) and justice (or compensation) on the other hand—a link that seems to be one of the fundamental principles of postwar memorial culture—is unmasked as a short-circuit.

Referring to projects like the Prague museum, some scholars have spoken of a "Final Solution of remembrance" (e.g., Potthast, 2002, pp. 424, 427–428). Instead, one must speak of the attempt at an "Aryanization" of memory, a further conservation and instrumentalization for the purposes of the National Socialist ideology. From the start, "Aryanization" meant both the appropriation and expropriation of

Jewish property: its transfer into non-Jewish hands and the exclusion of Jews from business and public life. This double strategy was consistently pursued until the end of the Nazi regime. Not only did the perpetrators appropriate the material assets of their victims but they tried to appropriate the memory of the victims for further use and their own advantage. The goal was the appropriation of Jewish history for their own purposes, together with their objects, while murdering the bearers of this history and the owner of the objects at the same time.

The crimes of the perpetrators and their projects for preserving an image of their victims affect the culture of remembrance in the postwar era, where, too often, memory alone counts as a satisfactory response to the Holocaust. But there can be no discussion of a postwar culture of remembrance without a look at the crimes, their conceptualization, and the construction of the Jews as enemies by the perpetrators. Neither does it make sense to examine the crimes but then discontinue their examination and that of their representation after 1945, as often happened in earlier scholarship and sometimes still does. One cannot be understood without the other. Representation was part of the crime—and a crime in itself. The crime consequently remains part of the representation.

Not only are the politics and the culture of remembrance, today's images and knowledge of the past, reciprocal references significant for today's social and political interests. They also point back to the conscious or unconscious handling of the generation of perpetrators and their tradition, their representation of their present, and their politics of memory. The perpetrators—but also the victims—have left their traces in that field of memory. They had their intentions and pursued them. Hence, memory does not have an incidental or random relationship to the crimes that are their focus. Today's landscape of memory necessarily mirrors the perpetrators' politics of memory and must thus grapple with its framework, whether transparently and consciously or not. The postwar history of coming to terms with the mass crimes of National Socialism is therefore not merely "the second history" of National Socialism (Reichel, 2001, p. 199). Rather, it is its own second history—the second history of the representation of the crimes.

Notes

1. Unless otherwise indicated, all translations in this chapter are my own.
2. *Aktion Reinhard* was the code name of the Nazi plan by which more than one million Polish Jews were murdered in a part of German-occupied Poland that was known as the General Government.
3. Scholars are divided over the question of whether the appropriate spelling is *anti-Semitism* (and *anti-Semitic*) or rather *antisemitism* (and *antisemitic*). I avoid the variant with the hyphen because it misleadingly suggests the existence of Semitism.

References

Adler, H. G. (1989). *Die unsichtbare Wand* [The invisible wall]. Vienna: Zsolnay.
Assmann, A. (1996). Erinnerungsorte und Gedächtnislandschaften [Commemorative places and landscapes of memory]. In H. Loewy & B. Moltmann (Vol. Eds.), *Wissenschaftliche Reihe*

des Fritz Bauer Instituts: Vol. 3. Erlebnis, Gedächtnis, Sinn: Authentische und konstruierte Erinnerung (pp. 13–29). Frankfurt am Main and New York: Campus.

Assmann, A. (1999). *Erinnerungsräume: Formen und Wandlungen des kulturellen Gedächtnisses* [Commemorative spaces: Forms and changes of cultural memory]. Munich: C. H. Beck.

Brather, H.-S. (1958). Aktenvernichtung durch deutsche Dienststellen beim Zusammenbruch des Faschismus [The destruction of files by German authorities during the collapse of fascism]. *Archivmitteilungen, 8*(4), 115–117.

Broszat, M. (1969/2000). *Der Staat Hitlers: Grundlegung und Entwicklung seiner inneren Verfassung* [Hitler's state: Foundation and development of its internal structure]. Munich: dtv.

Freed, J. I. (1994). Das United States Holocaust Memorial Museum [The United States Holocaust Memorial Museum]. In J. E. Young (Ed.), *Mahnmale des Holocaust: Motive, Rituale und Stätten des Gedenkens* (pp. 63–77). Munich: Prestel.

Goldhagen, E. (1976). Weltanschauung und Endlösung: Zum Antisemitismus der nationalsozialistischen Führungsschicht [Worldview and final solution: On the antisemitism of the Nazi elite]. *Vierteljahreshefte für Zeitgeschichte, 24*(4), 379–405.

Hippler, F. (1981). *Die Verstrickung. Auch ein Filmbuch...* [The involvement: Another film book...]. Düsseldorf: Mehr Wissen.

Hoffmann, D. (1998). Das Gedächtnis der Dinge [The memory of things]. In D. Hoffman (Vol. Ed.), *Wissenschaftliche Reihe des Fritz Bauer Instituts: Vol. 4. Das Gedächtnis der Dinge: KZ-Relikte und KZ-Denkmäler 1945–1995* (pp. 6–35). Frankfurt am Main and New York: Campus.

International Military Tribunal. (1948). [Heinrich Himmler:] Rede vor SS-Gruppenführern in Posen, 4.10.1943 [Speech before SS Lieutenant Generals in Posen, 4 October 1943]. In *Trial of the Major War Criminals before the International Military Tribunal, 14 November 1945—1 October 1948* (Vol. XXIX, p. 145, Dok. PS-1919, p. 64). Nuremberg: n.p.

Klee, E. (1997). *Auschwitz, die NS-Medizin und ihre Opfer* [Auschwitz, Nazi medicine, and its victims]. Frankfurt am Main: S. Fischer.

Lyotard, J.-F. (1988). *Heidegger und "die Juden"* [Heidegger and "the Jews"]. Vienna: Passagen.

Münz, C. (1994). *Geschichtstheologie und jüdisches Gedächtnis nach Auschwitz: Über den Versuch, den Schrecken der Geschichte zu bannen* [Theology of history and Jewish memory after Auschwitz: On the attempt to ban the horror of history]. Frankfurt am Main: Fritz Bauer Institut.

Neumann, F. (1984). *Behemoth: Struktur und Praxis des Nationalsozialismus 1933–1944* [Behemoth: Structure and practice of National socialism, 1933–1944]. Frankfurt am Main: Fischer. (Original work published 1942–1944)

Potthast, J. B. (2002). *Das Jüdische Zentralmuseum der SS in Prag. Gegnerforschung und Völkermord im Nationalsozialismus* [The Jewish Central Museum of the SS in Prague. Research on enemies and genocide during National Socialism]. Frankfurt am Main and New York: Campus.

Reichel, P. (2001). *Vergangenheitsbewältigung in Deutschland. Die Auseinandersetzung mit der NS-Diktatur von 1945 bis heute* [Coming to terms with the past in Germany: The examination of the Nazi dictatorship from 1945 to the present]. Munich: C. H. Beck.

Ringelblum, E. (1958). *Notes from the Warsaw ghetto* (J. Sloan, Ed.). New York: McGraw-Hill.

Rosenberg, A. (1941). Nationalsozialismus und Wissenschaft [National socialism and science]. *Weltkampf: Die Judenfrage in Geschichte und Gegenwart, 1*(2), 3–6.

Rothfels, H. (Ed.). (1953). Augenzeugenbericht zu den Massenvergasungen (Dokumentation) [Eyewitness report on the mass gassings]. *Vierteljahreshefte für Zeitgeschichte, 1*(2), 177–194.

Rupnow, D. (2000). *Täter—Gedächtnis—Opfer. Das "Jüdische Zentralmuseum" in Prag 1942–1945* [Perpetrators—memory—victims: The "Jewish central museum" in Prague, 1942–1945]. Vienna: Picus.

Rupnow, D. (2002). "Ihr müßt sein, auch wenn ihr nicht mehr seid." The Jewish Central Museum in Prague and historical memory in the Third Reich. *Holocaust and Genocide Studies, 16*(1), 23–53.

Rupnow, D. (2004). "Arisierung" jüdischer Geschichte. Zur nationalsozialistischen "Judenforschung" ["Aryanization" of Jewish history: On national socialist research on Jews]. *Leipziger Beiträge zur jüdischen Geschichte und Kultur, 2*, 349–367.

Rupnow, D. (2005). *Vernichten und Erinnern. Spuren nationalsozialistischer Gedächtnispolitik* [Annihilate and remember: Traces of national socialist policy on memory]. Göttingen: Wallstein.

Rupnow, D. (2006). Antijüdische Wissenschaft im "Dritten Reich". Wege, Probleme und Perspektiven der Forschung [Anti-Jewish scholarship in the "Third Reich": Paths, problems, and perspectives of research]. *Jahrbuch des Simon-Dubnow-Instituts/Simon Dubnow Institute Yearbook, 5*, 539–598.

Rupnow, D. (2008). Racializing historiography: Anti-Jewish scholarship in the Third Reich. *Patterns of Prejudice, 42*(1), 27–59.

Smith, B. F., & Peterson, A. F. (Eds.). (1974). *Heinrich Himmler: Geheimreden 1933 bis 1945 und andere Ansprachen* [Heinrich Himmler: Secret speeches, 1933–1945, and other addresses]. Frankfurt am Main: Propyläen.

Spector, S. (1990). Aktion 1005—Effacing the Murder of Millions. *Holocaust and Genocide Studies, 5*(2), 157–173.

Steinweis, A. (2006). *Studying the Jew: Scholarly antisemitism in Nazi Germany*. Cambridge, MA: Harvard University Press.

Weinreich, M. (1999). *Hitler's professors: The part of scholarship in Germany's crimes against the Jewish people*. New Haven, CN: Yale University Press.

Weinrich, H. (1997). *Lethe. Kunst und Kritik des Vergessens* [Lethe: Art and critique of forgetting]. Munich: C. H. Beck.

Young, J. E. (1997). *Beschreiben des Holocaust: Darstellung und Folgen der Interpretation* [Describing the Holocaust: Representation and consequences of interpretation]. Frankfurt am Main: Suhrkamp.

History/Archive/Memory: A Historical Geography of the US Naval Memorial in Brest, France

Michael Heffernan

Il pleut sans cesse sur Brest
Comme il pleuvait avant
Mais ce n'est plus pareil et tout est abîmé
C'est une pluie de deuil terrible et désolée
Ce n'est même plus l'orage
De fer d'acier de sang
Tout simplement des nuages
Qui crèvent comme des chiens
Des chiens qui disparaissent
Au fil de l'eau sur Brest
Et vont pourrir au loin
Au loin très loin de Brest
Dont il ne reste rien.[1]

So ends Jacques Prévert's poem "Barbara," a haunting evocation of love, loss, and memory set against the destruction of the city of Brest in northwest France during World War II. The poem, first published in 1946, tells the story of a passionate love affair, tragically cut short by the outbreak of war. The eponymous Barbara is repeatedly urged to remember her joyful life before the war, how once she ran to her lover's arms amid Atlantic squalls that washed over her city, bringing only "Cette pluie sage et heureuse; Sur ton visage heureux; Sur cette ville heureuse."[2] The war swept away Barbara's lover, his fate agonizingly uncertain ("Est-il mort disparu ou bien encore vivant?"[3]), and reduced her once happy city to a landscape of shattered rubble, destroyed beneath "cette pluie de fer; De feu d'acier de sang."[4]

Prévert's poem provides an appropriate starting point for this chapter, the themes of which are also memory and the wartime destruction of Brest. Three of the poem's central concerns have a direct bearing on what follows. Like the poem, my essay examines how cherished urban environments give meaning to, and are themselves shaped by, the lives and loves of their citizens, a relationship so intimate that the destruction of the former inevitably entails the wholesale disruption of the latter. The essay also considers how memories of traumatic events become

M. Heffernan (✉)
School of Geography, University of Nottingham, Nottingham NG7 2RD, UK
e-mail: mike.heffernan@nottingham.ac.uk

P. Meusburger et al. (eds.), *Cultural Memories*, Knowledge and Space 4,
DOI 10.1007/978-90-481-8945-8_13, © Springer Science+Business Media B.V. 2011

urgent moral and even political imperatives, the theme invoked by Prévert's repeated poetic inducement not only to remember, but never to forget: "Rapelle-toi Barbara; N'oublie pas."[5] And finally, the essay examines how conflicts between differing memories are facilitated by uncertainty, suggested in the poem by the unresolved fate of Barbara's lover.

The specific geographical focus is one of Brest's most prominent memorials, a 50 meter tower that rises from the city's massive defensive walls, designed in the seventeenth century by the military architect Vauban (Gallo, 1992; Fig. 1). The tower was constructed in the early 1930s by an official agency of the US federal government, the American Battle Monuments Commission (ABMC). It was designed to commemorate the US contribution to World War I and specifically to mark the principal landing place of the troops and materiel that comprised the American Expeditionary Force (AEF). The US Naval Memorial in Brest, to use its official title, was inaugurated in 1937 and is one of several military cemeteries and memorials created at great expense in France, Belgium, and Britain between the wars, the oldest elements in a much larger, and still expanding, global network of American commemorative sites maintained by the ABMC.

Fig. 1 The US Naval Memorial in Brest, France. Source: Author's photograph

The Brest memorial's "biography," to borrow a word from Young (1993, pp. 155), is more complex and contested than other ABMC sites in Europe, some of which lend credence to Robert Musil's (1932/1987, pp. 64–68) observation that monuments tend to mellow into the landscape to the point where they become almost invisible, sites of amnesia rather than memory. In the case of the Brest memorial, the process of "memorial fade" was dramatically arrested during the German occupation of the city in World War II when the tower was destroyed in circumstances that remain less than entirely clear even now. The memorial that looms above the city's docks today is a replica of the original structure, rebuilt in the 1950s and different only to the extent that it bears a short inscription about the wartime destruction and the second inauguration ceremony.

During research into this curious story, several different, often mutually exclusive versions of the memorial's tangled history emerged from official accounts published by the AMBC; from unpublished documents in archives in Washington, DC, and Brest; and from the personal recollections of some of the city's inhabitants. These alternative narratives of the Brest memorial's rise, fall, and rise again reveal how the process of commemoration involved multiple contestations, symbolic acts of creation and destruction, and public debates that were often shockingly devoid of reverence.

There are three reasons why these stories are worth reconsidering. First, they demonstrate how commemorative sites can cease to function as memorials to the events they were originally designed to recall, and become associated instead with new memory battles arising from their construction, destruction, or reconstruction. Second, as these narratives relate to an American memorial in France, they complicate the existing research on the politics of World War I commemoration, hitherto framed largely in European terms (Winter, 1995; though see Budreau, 2010). They likewise complicate existing literature on the politics of American commemoration, previously dominated by sites constructed on American territory (Glassberg & Moore, 1996) and by other conflicts, particularly the Civil War (Savage, 1997), World War II, and Vietnam (Bodnar, 1992). The stories about the Brest memorial involve four nation-states, the United States, France, Germany, and the United Kingdom, and reveal how the commemorative process involved struggles about the most appropriate scale at which memory should operate—the local, the regional, the national, and the international.

Third, and perhaps most important, the stories about the Brest memorial pivot on a singular event involving a mysterious act of destruction during World War II. They therefore provide an opportunity to develop a historical and cultural geography informed by the arguments of anthropologist Marshall Sahlins (2000, pp. 239–252) and political sociologist Rogers Brubaker (1996, pp. 13–22) about the transformative potential of unique, often unexpected events. The idea of an "eventful temporality," one that recognizes both the significance of deeper structural forces and the importance of singular events, has been championed by historical sociologist William H. Sewell, Jr. (2005, pp. 81–124) to develop a "theory of the event" (pp. 197–225), a way of thinking about specific occurrences as something other than mere epiphenomena, an approach echoed in the intriguing writings of cultural theorist Paul Virilio (2000, 2007) on the "landscape of the event" and the concept of the accident.

The renewed interest in the constitutive power of events, and the relationship between events and deeper structural change, lies at the heart of several recent trends in historical inquiry, including the rapid rise of environmental history. It also corresponds with, and has been partly inspired by, the expanding academic and popular interest in memory as an identity-shaping social and political force, a truly international phenomenon of the last fin-de-siècle (Huyssen, 2003).

It is significant, in this respect, that the French cultural historian Pierre Nora, one of the principal guiding spirits behind much of the work in memory studies since the 1980s (Nora, 1984), was also one of the earliest advocates of an event-based history (Nora, 1974). Nora's challenge to previously hegemonic structural forms of historical inquiry, whether Marxist, Annaliste, Braudelian, or otherwise, recognized that memory exerts a complex, unpredictable, and potentially subversive social and political role partly because it is inherently "eventful," or at least "event-focused." Whereas historical explanations rely on temporal narratives, on deep-seated social and economic forces, and on historical records readily manipulated by those in authority, memory is created and recreated within civil society and is therefore free-floating, partial, complex, and contested.

Memory is also, and for these same reasons, inescapably spatial in ways that history, in its more conventional register, is not. The term *lieux de mémoire* implies that memory is place-bound and place-specific, requiring geographical as well as historical interrogation. As Maurice Halbwachs (1950/1980), the pioneer theorist in this field, observed: "[M]emory unfolds within a spatial framework... [and] we can understand how we recapture the past only by understanding how it is... preserved in our physical surroundings" (p. 140). An insistence on the integrity of "events," therefore, not only challenges structural forms of historical inquiry and legitimizes the study of memory as a kind of unruly alternative to conventional history; it also foregrounds geography as an important explanatory arena wherein memory is created. Insofar as memory tends to relate to unique events, it follows that the geographical study of memory requires a willingness to recognize the ideographic specificity of location. By highlighting the importance of a specific event and a particular location, I seek in this chapter to explore the possibilities of an "eventful" historical geography.

Smoothing the Surface: The Official Story

The official story of the Brest memorial, as recounted by documents published by the American Battle Monuments Commission, forms part of a wider narrative about the necessary and positive international interventions of the United States, beginning with World War I. The US declaration of war against the Central Powers on April 6, 1917, two months after the German High Command announced unrestricted submarine warfare against all shipping supplying Allied countries, presaged what

Henry F. May called, in homage to Edith Wharton, "the end of American innocence" (May, 1960). American involvement in an international war fought mainly in Europe was a momentous, nation- and century-defining event, both for United States itself and for the wider world. It was the most important departure from the self-imposed geopolitical constraints that had previously limited American overseas engagements to Central America, the Caribbean, and the Pacific (Bristow, 1996; Farwell, 1999; Keene, 2001; Kennedy, 1980; Schaffer, 1991; Wynn, 1986).

Conscription, introduced on May 18, 1917, produced an army of over 10 million Americans within a month, broadly representative of the country's ethnic composition. First- and second-generation European immigrants formed the overwhelming majority of the AEF, though significant numbers of African-Americans also rallied to the flag, encouraged by prominent black leaders such as W. E. B. Dubois (Ellis, 2001; Slotkin, 2005). The first contingent of American troops, under the command of General John J. Pershing, landed at St. Nazaire on June 26, 1917. By the end that year, a quarter of a million American soldiers were passing through the French Atlantic ports every month. When the German army launched its make-or-break spring offensive on the Western Front in 1918, there were two million Americans in the field, more than the British deployment at that time. By the end of the war, 3.7 million Americans had crossed the Atlantic, and the AEF, an army that had remained entirely independent of Allied command throughout the final phase of the war, held over 20% of the front-line trenches on the Western Front (Winter, 1988, p. 156).

Almost 120,000 American soldiers perished in Europe during and immediately after the war, the majority succumbing to disease rather than the conflict itself. A further 204,000 were left permanently wounded. The Vietnam War produced less than half these numbers of dead and wounded (ABMC, 1995c). For the Progressive, internationally minded political elites who had supported and funded America's war effort, these terrible losses reinforced the idea that World War I was a national rite of passage separating a nineteenth-century America, shaped by the quest to create a continental-scale nation, from a twentieth-century United States, a new world power whose arena would be truly global.

Many Americans believed that the dreadful experience of industrialized, twentieth-century warfare demanded an entirely new form of commemoration, comparable in taste and sophistication to that being formulated by European nations. Unlike memorials constructed on American soil to recall the more numerous casualties of the Civil War, memorials to honor Americans who died in World War I would need to be built on European battlefields alongside those of other nations. Whereas Civil War memorials had been designed to bring about reconciliation between opposing sides in a domestic quarrel and bolster a still fragile unity, even to the extent of air-brushing out the contentious and divisive issue of slavery (Blight, 2001, 2002; O'Leary, 1999; Sandage, 1993; Savage, 1997), the new American memorials in Europe needed to communicate an entirely different message, one that heralded the arrival on the world stage of an ardent, vigorous, and united young nation, a great power ready to assume its full international responsibilities.

The decision of the postwar US Congress to reject membership of the League of Nations and retreat into a more traditional isolationism seriously compromised these ambitions, but even the most die-hard isolationists could not ignore the sacrifices made by so many of their fellow Americans in 1917 and 1918. The establishment of the ABMC as an executive branch of the federal government in March 1923, with Pershing as its first chairman and Major Xenophon H. Price as permanent secretary, reflected the determination, shared by a wide spectrum of American political opinion, to construct seemly and fitting landscapes of commemoration for America's war dead in Europe (ABMC, 1995c; www.abmc.gov/home). In carrying out this mission, the ABMC was assisted by the National Committee of Fine Arts (NCFA), established in 1910 under the direction of Chicago architect Daniel H. Burnham, the official agency responsible for ensuring the aesthetic quality of federal architecture within and beyond the United States (Kohler, 1996).

The ABMC's attempt to coordinate and centralize the commemorative process generated widespread resentment. There were challenges to its authority throughout the 1920s from families desperate to reclaim the bodies of their loved ones; from elements within the US military that hoped to build their own memorials to honor particular divisions or battalions; and from private and public agencies that harbored similar ambitions in towns, cities, and states across the United States (Budreau, 2010; Robin, 1992, pp. 30–62). The ABMC was never able replicate the control exerted by the Imperial (now Commonwealth) War Graves Commission over British commemoration (Heffernan, 1995). Nevertheless, it did oversee the construction of a network of sublimely beautiful American cemeteries and memorials in France, Belgium, and the United Kingdom through the interwar years on land granted in perpetuity to the United States by the governments of these countries, including the stunning monuments at Montfaucon, Château-Thierry, and Montsec (see also Grossman, 1984; Pershing, 1934). These and other American memorials to World War I reflect the neoclassical, beaux-arts style favored by the NCFA at the time and exemplified by the small group of American architects who won most of the ABMC commissions, including John Russell Pope (Bedford, 1998), who designed the Montfaucon tower, and the French-born Paul Philippe Cret, architect of the monument at Château-Thierry (Eltin, 1994, pp. 55–85; Grossman, 1996). These and the similarly inclined architects regularly used by the ABMC were responsible for many of the more prominent buildings and monuments erected at the same time in and around the Federal Triangle in Washington, DC.

The Brest naval memorial was an important ABMC project. The idea of a tower rising from the city's defensive walls was proposed by Cret, the ABMC's principal architectural adviser, who toured his native country in 1925 and 1926 searching for suitable locations. Brest seemed an obvious site, for almost one million American troops had passed through the harbor in the last year of the war, many of them billeted for extended periods at the nearby US military camp at Pontanézen. President Woodrow Wilson had also been triumphantly received when he arrived in Brest aboard the USS *George Washington* on December 13, 1918, for the Peace Conferences. Cret also reasoned that a prominent US memorial located above a busy port would be seen by more people than any other American monument.

The preliminary version of the winning design was submitted in the spring of 1926 by the Chicago architect Howard Van Doren Shaw (Greene, 1998), who died before his proposal was accepted. A revised version was proposed by Ralph Milman, one of Shaw's associates, with the assistance of John Storrs, an American modernist sculptor and student of Auguste Rodin who had lived and worked in France since before the war (Frackman, 1986), and the Parisian "art deco" interior designers Pierre Lahalle and Georges Levard. Storrs was responsible for the exterior sculptural details, with Lahalle and Levard designing the inner spiral staircase, windows, fittings, and doorways (ABMC, 1926, p. 21).

The memorial was completed in late 1931 at a cost $172,000, substantially more than the $100,000 original estimate. It was inaugurated on August 12, 1937, the twentieth anniversary of the US intervention (ABMC, 1938, pp. 21–25). According to ABMC reports, the Brest memorial stood as a popular and distinctive landmark until the German occupation of the city in the summer of 1940 (Fig. 2). A year later, some six months before the United States entered World War II, the memorial was apparently destroyed by the German military authorities on July 4, 1941, American Independence Day, in a shocking act of provocation motivated by anger at American support for the British war effort (e.g., ABMC, 1995a, p. 23, 1995b, p. 11). The ABMC website states unequivocally that "[t]he original monument built on this site to commemorate the achievements of the United States Navy during World War I, was destroyed by the Germans on July 4, 1941, prior to the United States entry into World War II" (www.abme.gov/memorials/memorials/bt.php).

Three years later, on August 6, 1944, the VIIIth US Army Corps, under the command of General Troy Middleton, reached the outskirts of Brest after a rapid advance along the northern coast of Brittany. Hitler had decreed that the French

Fig. 2 The US Naval Memorial in Brest in the early 1930s. Source: Photograph by W. Robert Moore to accompany an article, Our National War Memorials in Europe, by John J. Pershing (1934) (Plate VI, p. 22). Reproduced with permission of the National Geographical Society

Channel and Atlantic ports—Le Havre, St. Malo, Brest, Lorient, and Nantes—were to be defended to the last man, and most German forces in the peninsula had retreated before the advancing US troops to one or other of these "fortresses." Up to 20,000 German troops parachuted into Brest after the arrival of the Americans, reinforcing the 10,000 already stationed there.

For the next 40 days, one of the more savage battles of the liberation took place within the city, involving an unrelenting US bombardment and hand-to-hand street fighting. There were many thousands of military and civilian casualties, though the precise number remains uncertain, and fully half the city's buildings were destroyed (Clout, 2000, pp. 172–174). On September 19, 1944, the German commander, General Hermann-Bernhard Ramcke, surrendered, and American troops were able to stand once more on the small patch of battered parkland adjacent to where the memorial had once stood, land that was still, officially at least, American soil. The ferocity of the battle for Brest persuaded the Allied commanders to besiege the other Atlantic French ports rather than risk further devastation, and some remained in German hands until the end of the war (Gawne, 2002).

The ABMC and the US Navy decided in 1946 that an exact replica of the original memorial should be built in the same location to reaffirm America's commitment to the ideals of peace and democracy in Europe, the values that American soldiers had now fought two costly wars to uphold and that the new, postwar Atlantic alliance would hopefully forever preserve. This decision was enthusiastically endorsed by the Brest City Council and the French government. The new tower, completed in 1958 (at five times the original cost), used the same pink Breton granite. It is in all respects identical to the original structure except for an additional pediment on which the following inscription appears, in English and French, on either side of a metal plate bearing the great seal of the United States:

THE MONUMENT
BUILT ON THIS SITE IN 1932
WAS DESTROYED BY ENEMY ACTION ON 4 JULY 1941
THIS REPLICA OF THE ORIGINAL STRUCTURE
WAS ERECTED BY
THE UNITED STATES OF AMERICA
*** 1958 ***

The new memorial tower was inaugurated for a second time before a large, appreciative audience on July 16, 1960, in the presence of Prime Minister Michel Debré, US Ambassador Amory Houghton, and the city's mayor, Georges Lombard (ABMC, 1960, pp. 22–25).

Cracks Appear: From History to the Archive

Insofar as memorials are intended to create memories, and ultimately histories, the official account of the Brest memorial's construction, destruction, and reconstruction outlined above sits neatly within a larger narrative about the relationship between the United States and Europe. Within this narrative, the memorial symbolizes the close historical and ideological bond between the "sister" republics of the United States and France; its construction and destruction reveals the continuity of American support for a liberal, democratic Europe, threatened in World War I by German militarism and in World War II by international fascism; and its reconstruction highlights America's steadfast commitment to the post-1945 Atlantic alliance. Unfortunately, unpublished archival records in the United States and France cast doubt on this account and suggest that each phase of the memorial's history was controversial and deeply contested.

Cret's idea of an imposing tower rising from the city's defensive walls on the Cours Dajot (usually spelled d'Ajot at the time), an impressive cliff-top promenade and public park overlooking the harbor close to the ancient château, was formulated after his visit in the summer of 1925.[6] His proposal was agreed to in principle by the ABMC and later by the city's socialist mayor, Louis Léon Nardon. The French naval authorities in the city, and the Prefect of the Finistère, the administrative district surrounding Brest, also concurred.[7] On October 15, 1926, a patch of 4,300 m^2 (slightly more than 1 acre) of the Cours Dajot was formally presented, in the name of the French government, to the ABMC. This land would henceforth be regarded as US territory.[8]

When news of the ABMC plan filtered out the following spring, a dispute broke out in which the prospective memorial became embroiled in the city's fractious local politics. Nardon's main political rival in the city was the center-right leader of the local Radical party, Victor le Gorgeu, a respected physician and owner-editor of the major local newspaper, *La Dépêche de Brest* (Galliou, 2007, pp. 95–105). Anything Nardon supported, Le Gorgeu tended to oppose almost as a matter of principle, and he initially lent support to a growing campaign against the memorial from an unlikely alliance of conservationists, architects, engineers, and assorted anti-Americans who argued variously that a tower would be an act of vandalism against a historically significant site; that the Council had bowed to American and French government pressure without public consultation; that the rightful place for large war memorials was on the battlefield, close to where soldiers had died, rather than the cities through which they passed; that the use of an American sculptor, albeit one domiciled in France, was an insult to better qualified French artists; and that a structure of this size would be inherently unstable without hugely expensive and unsightly foundations.[9]

The local branch of the Touring Club de France (TCF), directed by a retired naval commander, Admiral Motet, also campaigned vigorously against the memorial (P. Young, 2002, 2007, 2009). The TCF, one of several French organizations seeking to preserve and enhance the nation's architectural heritage and cultural landscape on behalf of the tourist industry, was strongly associated with the commemoration of World War I, particularly the project to demarcate the trench lines of the Western Front with "bornes Vauthier," the familiar marker statues designed by the sculptor Paul Moreau-Vauthier. In an attempt to halt the ABMC project, the TCF sought in July 1927 to persuade officials in the Commission des Monuments Historiques (CMH), part of the Ministry of Public Instruction, to reclassify Vauban's defensive wall as a site of special historic significance, only to discover that the

CMH had already agreed to the proposal, as would three other national ministries—War, Navy, and Foreign Affairs—over the next few weeks. On August 13, Gaston Doumergue, the conservative President of the Republic, formally agreed to the ABMC proposal.[10]

Before the construction work began, however, the 1929 elections swept Nardon and the socialists from power, with the still dominant left-wing vote splitting between the SFIO (the official socialist party) and the increasingly powerful Communist Party, the latter in uneasy alliance with a small but influential anarcho-syndicalist movement active among the city's dockworkers (Baal, 1973). The City Council now had a Radical majority and a new mayor—Victor Le Gorgeu. When the Council was informed on May 23, 1929, that work on the memorial would begin within days, Le Gorgeu demanded time to consider the ABMC's plans in more detail.[11] Although the Council ratified the earlier decision by a small majority on July 22, 1929, Le Gorgeu specified several new conditions, including a requirement that construction work should be carried out wherever possible by local firms, a stipulation previously proposed by Louis Moret, Secretary of the Syndicat des Artisans Français de la Statuaire, in a letter to the ABMC pressing them to use unemployed French stonemasons, particularly veterans.[12]

A few days later, the TCF presented Le Gorgeu with a strongly worded petition, signed by 300 of the city's more prominent citizens and businesses, protesting the construction of a "disgraceful skyscraper" and calling once again for Vauban's for-tifications to be designated as a site of special historic significance. According to the TCF, the original agreement had been taken without appropriate consultation with any of the relevant conservationist and business agencies, and its ratification by the new Council compounded this initial oversight. The TCF's concerns were supported by the Syndicat d'Initiative (the city's tourist office), the Comité des Sites et Monuments du Finistère, and the local Société des Amis des Arts and the Société pour la Protection des Paysages de la France. According to the director of the Syndicat d'Initiative (who wrote independently to Le Gorgeu, the TCF, and the Ministry of Public Instruction in Paris), the ABMC's plan for a "flamboyant tower" looming over the city's port was an especially egregious example of the "destructive demons that threaten our ancient monuments."[13]

Marcel Rondeleux, one of the leading opponents of the memorial, persuaded the hugely popular national weekly magazine L'Illustration to publish an article criticizing the ABMC scheme, including a map of the proposed memorial site and two photographs of the Cour Dajot with a dotted outline of the tower superimposed. The Cours Dajot offered the best views of "the most beautiful harbor in France and perhaps Europe," claimed Rondeleux, and the construction of "an enormous tower resembling a factory chimney, twice the height of the walls, will destroy the surrounding landscape and reduce the line of the ramparts to that of a supporting foundation. . ... People with taste will wish to oppose this mutilation of a beautiful site admired by all travelers arriving at Brest from the sea."[14]

Recognizing the powerful interests supporting the ABMC's proposal, Motet sug-gested a compromise alternative location, beneath the city walls adjacent to the harbor itself. This proposal was presented to the Council on August 17, 1929, and promptly accepted. A delighted Le Gorgeu immediately cabled the ABMC, the local Prefect, and the Ministry of Public Instruction, informing them that the memorial could not be constructed on the Cours Dajot after all, but in the vicinity of the harbor, a statement that elicited instant responses from bewildered state officials reiterating the government's support for the original ABMC proposal.[15]

On September 9, Xenophon Price, based at the time in the ABMC's European headquarters in Paris, wrote to Le Gorgeu, expressing amazement at the Council's change of heart. It was too late for any modifications to the original proposal, Price insisted, as the national authorities had agreed to it and binding contracts worth F300,000 had already been signed with the suppliers and the main construction company, which, to Le Gorgeu's irritation, turned out to be the Paris-based Le Bomin et Cie. The tower would enhance rather than detract from Vauban's fortifications, Price continued, and make the location more attractive to tourists, especially Americans:

> The monument has been designed for the Cours d'Ajot, as an integral part of the ramparts. From an artistic point of view, a monument without the ramparts would be a monstrosity. The whole project would have to be completely reconsidered. The artistic and historic values of the fortifications have been taken fully into account by the Commission's architects and, far from diminishing the views of the harbor from the sea, and the sea from the harbor, the tower, which will be built of local Breton granite, will enhance both aspects.[16]

Tempers frayed as each side accused the other of insensitivity and philistinism. Le Gorgeu, fearing he had overstepped his authority, thrashed about in search of a compromise, eventually agreeing to have his newspaper print an open letter from Price making the case for the memorial.[17] Motet (to whom Le Gorgeu sent a draft copy of Price's letter in advance) duly responded, making the usual contrary arguments, adding ruefully that the whole episode was yet another unfortunate legacy of Nardon's tenure as mayor. The endorsement of national ministries was not legally binding, Motet insisted, particularly as the relevant agency, the Commission des Monuments Historiques, had yet to visit the site.[18]

The arguments against the memorial were eloquently expressed by the Comtesse de Rodellec du Portzic, one of Brest's grandest inhabitants, in a letter to the new US Ambassador in Paris, Walter Evans Edge.[19] The United States should tread carefully, cautioned the Comtesse, for there was a danger of causing serious offence by appearing to celebrate, in an inappropriately triumphant manner, the American contribution to the war effort in ways that contrasted dramatically with the more restrained and muted commemorative tone adopted by European countries that had experienced vastly greater losses. France's war dead outnumbered those from the AEF by ten to one, noted the Comtesse, and Brittany alone had lost twice as many young men as the whole of the United States. The AEF had been crucial to the Allied victory, the Comtesse acknowledged, but the United States government should commemorate its war dead in Europe in a manner consistent with the somber and reflective mood of a war-ravaged continent. In her view, the construction of a giant tower built on the ancient fortifications around the harbor in Brest was a disproportionate response to the arrival of American troops on French soil and the scarcely unprecedented achievement of the US navy in transporting these men and their equipment in 1917 and 1918.

These were powerful words but the ABMC was in no mood to alter plans that Price believed had been devised to communicate precisely the sentiments advocated by the Comtesse. In a carefully worded response, written at the behest of the US Embassy, Price stoutly defended the Brest memorial and other ABMC plans. The Brest memorial had only become a matter of controversy, Price insisted, because anti-American elements within and beyond the city had spread falsehoods and lies about the ABMC's plans. The ABMC had received several anonymous letters, Price continued, that could only be described as "fanatical, ignorant, and ungrateful."[20] Unlike the Comtesse's wholly legitimate concerns, these anonymous correspondents seemed convinced that the United States, having benefited financially from a war that had crippled France, was seeking to rewrite history by using its vastly superior wealth to create a network of grandiose war memorials on French soil, more costly than anything the French government could afford to honor its own war dead. There was more than a hint of racism in these criticisms, Price implied, pointedly remarking that a significant proportion of the troops who had worked as stevedores in the port unloading equipment had been "Negroes" (nègres).[21]

There was also an irony to these criticisms. The Brest memorial, a legacy of the Progressive American internationalism rejected by a majority of Americans after 1918, had evidently been enveloped by a tide of French anti-Americanism, motivated paradoxically by the economic consequences of the isolationist stance adopted by the postwar US administration. Several factors had combined to intensify French hostility to the United States in this period, including the introduction of prohibition in 1920, a reform that removed the enormous and growing American market for French wine. Another irritant consisted of the economic plans devised by Charles G. Dawes in 1924 and Owen D. Young in 1929, both of whom mobilized American capital to help Germany meet its reparation payments to France while insisting that France must pay its wartime debts to the United States. The financial crash of 1929 and the subsequent decision to close the US market to foreign imports under the 1930 Smoot-Hawley tariff was the final straw, provoking an upsurge of French anti-American journalism denouncing the United States as the epicenter of consumerism, materialism, and rampant capitalism, the primary causes of the cultural, spiritual, and moral crises of twentieth-century modernity. French anti-Americanism, like the anti-Semitism with which it was so often associated, could be detected on the far right, the far left, and in most ideological positions in between (e.g., Aron & Dandieu, 1931a, 1931b; Duhamel, 1930; Morand, 1930; Pomaret, 1931; see also Roger, 2005; Weber, 1995, pp. 94–102).

Work began on the memorial in early 1930, despite continuing local resistance, much of it directed at the unfortunate workmen, who complained of threats and intimidation from local residents. On August 18, 1930, leaflets were discovered on park benches and adjacent walls, the work of far-right, royalist sympathizers, proclaiming,

America is our master! Despite the protests of the people of Brest, the Americans are irredeemably destroying the beauty of the Cours d'Ajot by erecting a monstrous pylon. Defend the independence of France. Down with the Republic! Long live the King![22]

Le Gorgeu, who had risen to national prominence as a Senator, condemned these actions from his position as the city's mayor but seemed determined to disrupt the construction process in his own way, initially chastising the construction company for the slow pace of progress, then insisting that work be postponed during the summer so that tourists could enjoy what was left of the promenade. Articles attacking the memorial continued to appear in *La Dépêche de Brest*, some with accusatory photographs showing a half-built tower and the surrounding building site.[23] Even a short visit by Pershing in late May 1931 did not placate the memorial's opponents, Le Gorgeu pointedly observing in an otherwise celebratory editorial in *La Dépêche de Brest* that the city's exalted visitor had failed to specify when the memorial would be inaugurated.[24]

This was a sensitive point, as Le Gorgeu knew well, for Price made no secret of his fear that memorial dedication ceremonies could easily be hijacked by anti-American demonstrations, a view he communicated in forthright terms to the ABMC in Washington, DC. In Price's view, dedications should be postponed until French political opinion was less antagonistic toward the United States.[25] When the last stone was put in place on the exterior structure of the Brest memorial on November 22, 1931, no inauguration date had been specified. Le Gorgeu, by now reconciled to the memorial, was anxious that the dedication ceremony should take place as soon as possible, sensing an opportunity to promote both the city and his own position as mayor. The ABMC was in no rush, however, and either rejected or ignored the various dates Le Gorgeu suggested, from July 4, 1932, through the remainder of that summer. Price eventually wrote to the Chamber of Commerce in the city announcing that due to "circumstances of an exceptional character," all ABMC dedication ceremonies would take place in the summer of 1933.[26] Le Gorgeu lamented the delay in *La Dépêche de Brest*,[27] prompting further anonymous letters from members of the public speculating whether the ABMC would ever be able to ensure the memorial's maintenance and safety.[28] A nameless correspondent later suggested the ABMC would be wise to postpone the inauguration indefinitely given the strength of feeling against the United States in the city,[29] though the eloquent defense of the memorial from a self-styled "student of the SFIO" (the French Socialist Party), who nevertheless attacked American policy toward France, probably expressed the majority view.[30]

The summer of 1933 passed without an inauguration, and the relationship between the City Council and the ABMC deteriorated still further when the harbor authorities broke ranks with other French ports and imposed duty on imported ABMC material for American war memorials, including the furnishings and additional ironwork destined for the interior of the naval memorial. Le Gorgeu insisted that he could do nothing about this, nor would the Council reimburse the unforeseen F28,500 being requested from a French company hired by the ABMC. Frosty exchanges ensued between Price, Le Gorgeu, and government officials in Paris, the necessary cash eventually being raised jointly by the ABMC and the French government.[31]

The political situation grew worse over the next two years, exacerbated by economic collapse, further delaying the dedication ceremony. The depression came late to France but lingered longer than elsewhere in Europe, precipitating an era of virtual civil war between right and left in the mid-1930s (Jackson, 1985). Violence was never far from the surface, especially in Paris, and 2 days of rioting between communists and supporters of the far right in Brest on August 6–7, 1935, left three dead and 200 injured.[32] The ABMC waited a further two years before organizing the memorial dedications in the summer of 1937, in the middle of the socialist experiment of the Popular Front (Jackson, 1988). The delay was justified on the rather tenuous grounds that the summer of 1937 marked the twentieth anniversary of the arrival of American troops, though there was a measure of surprise among the Brest public when it was announced that the by now familiar memorial (which needed to be cleaned of its accumulated grime in preparation for the event) was to be "inaugurated" six years after it was completed.

The dedication ceremony passed off without incident and was reported in detail in *La Dépêche de Brest* and in some national newspapers, though it was a rather subdued event with no national political or diplomatic representation. Pershing, who was to have presided over the ceremony, withdrew at the last minute because of illness, leaving Le Gorgeu and Josephus Daniels, the US Ambassador to Mexico, who had been Secretary of the Navy during the war, to deliver the main speeches. Le Gorgeu waxed lyrical in his address about the memorial as a symbol of the historic bond between two great democracies animated by the same ideals "despite their occasional differences," though he could not resist adding, rather pointedly, that this was a view shared only by "a majority of my fellow citizens."[33]

If the long-forgotten bitterness generated by the construction of the Brest memorial becomes manifest only when the researcher moves from the published historical record to the unpublished archival evidence, the stories generated by the memorial's destruction during the wartime German occupation of the city add further, even murkier layers of complexity and contradiction and require yet another research maneuver, from the archives to the realm of personal memory.

The Politics of Destruction: From the Archive to Memory

The official story that the German occupying forces were solely responsible for the Brest memorial's destruction on American Independence Day 1941, a claim stated on the rebuilt monument and repeated in numerous ABMC publications, is almost certainly false, and the archival records suggest that the ABMC knew this from the outset. Until Germany declared war in December 1941, the United States was a neutral power in the European conflict and retained a significant diplomatic presence in Vichy, the new capital of the unoccupied French zone, until France severed diplomatic relations in November 1942. Large numbers of US citizens also lived in German-occupied French towns and cities, particularly Paris, where at least 5,000 Americans remained throughout the war and where the ABMC maintained its small office (Glass, 2009).

The ABMC received regular reports from US citizens and representatives in France about war damage to its memorials from 1940 to 1942 and would certainly have known that the Brest memorial was in serious danger from Allied bombing. Early in 1941, a brief report reached the ABMC that the tower had been damaged during a British bombing raid on the night of January 4, 1941. The American Consul in Nantes, H. H. Dick, contacted the local administration (délégation speciale) in Brest requesting further information and was sent a detailed report on January 27 stating that the damage was superficial and that repairs could be arranged if the ABMC wished, an offer declined on April 28 "in view of the current circumstances."[34]

Le Gorgeu, still clinging on as mayor, had no direct involvement in these exchanges. His attention was no doubt focused on the more urgent task of holding on to some semblance of political authority after his brave decision to vote, alongside 79 others, in the new National Assembly in Vichy (the joint body of the Senate and the Chamber of Deputies) against the armistice with Germany and the transfer of absolute power to the collaborationist regime led by the then premier Marshal Philippe Pétain on July 10, 1940 (on this vote, see Wieviorka, 2009). He lost this struggle the following December when his position as mayor was revoked following his refusal to swear the oath of loyalty to Pétain. He was required to hand over control of *La Dépêche de Brest*, henceforth a compliant pro-Vichy newspaper under the direction of a rival proprietor, the Breton nationalist Yann Fouéré. The "retired" Le Gorgeu subsequently went on to become an important figure in the Breton Resistance movement, fleeing to safe houses in Paris in early 1944 to escape arrest by the Gestapo, before returning triumphantly as regional commissioner in Rennes to oversee the reestablishment of civilian rule the following August (Bougeard, 1992, 2005).

In June and July 1941, the Royal Air Force (RAF) launched a more sustained aerial bombardment of Brest, part of an ultimately fruitless attempt to destroy a key strategic naval base that included one of the largest radio masts in France, a U-boat harbor, and the dockyards within which the German battleships *Scharnhorst*, *Gneisenau*, and *Prinz Eugen* were being repaired after causing enormous damage to Allied shipping earlier that year (see, more generally, Dodd & Knapp, 2008; Knapp, 2007; Konvitz, 1989, 1992). The RAF's attempt to destroy these battleships by massive aerial bombardment was reported in detail by *The Times*, one article noting with satisfaction that "great damage was done to the Brest dockyard" on July 24, 1941, in "the most extensive and elaborate operation yet undertaken by the Royal Air Force in their daylight offensive over occupied territory."[35] According to the memoires of an RAF pilot involved in over 30 raids against Brest in 1941, however, the German defenses, which included mobile anti-aircraft guns, search lights, decoys, and camouflaging smoke, greatly diminished the impact of British attacks, most of which caused more damage to surrounding built-up areas than to the docks themselves. The three German battleships survived the onslaught unscathed and were later able escape from the port and run the gauntlet of an equally ineffective British blockade in the Channel to rejoin the German North Sea fleet in February 1942 (O'Brien, 1990; see also Gibson, 1946, p. 170).

It is highly likely that one of the early RAF raids seriously damaged the Brest memorial. A letter from Henry R. Brown, the ABMC official in Paris, to the City Engineer in Brest on July 1 asking the authorities to take possession of the memorial's valuable stone and make the area safe indicates that the ABMC knew what had happened. The official's response, noting that the German authorities had the matter in hand, confirms that lines of communication between Brest and the ABMC were

Fig. 3 (**a–c**) The memorial and its surroundings in ruins, autumn 1944. Source: Photographs in USNA/ABMC/RG117/11/2

Fig. 3 (continued)

functioning perfectly well.[36] The following spring, shortly after the German battleships had escaped from the Brest harbor, German military engineers laid small
controlled explosions at the foot of the destroyed memorial to bring down the
remaining parts of the structure, from which chunks of masonry had been falling.[37]

A year later, Pierre Rod, a representative of a French veterans' association that had taken over the work of the ABMC in Paris after December 1941, was informed that a gardener still tended the surrounding area, paid by the civil authorities.[38]

Although the ABMC had a fairly clear idea what had happened to the Brest memorial, the US army organized an inquiry shortly after taking control of the city in September 1944 and photographed the site from every conceivable angle (Fig. 3a–c). Twenty-five local residents and an unspecified number of German prisoners of war, including three officers, were interviewed over a 3-week period. Their accounts were bewilderingly inconsistent. None of the German soldiers interviewed had been stationed in the city in 1941, and though some local residents claimed that the tower had been partially destroyed by Allied air raids and the remnants later removed by the Germans, there was no consistency about the timing of these events. Some mentioned early 1941, others specified the summer of that year, and still others insisted the monument was intact in late 1942 and even early 1943. One interviewee claimed to have seen an open-top German staff car from which soldiers had unloaded boxes on the evening of July 4–5, 1941, the group "bursting out laughing" as they departed minutes before a massive explosion destroyed the memorial. Another "witness," a dockworker, claimed an explosion brought down the monument in the spring of 1942. Shortly before the blast, he had apparently encountered a mysterious man in civilian clothing who shouted out a warning "in a broad Italian accent."[39]

Despite these unconvincing accounts, the ABMC's Brigadier General Thomas Bentley Mott concluded on April 2, 1945, that "it is evident that the monument was wantonly destroyed by the German military authorities while the country was at peace with the United States i.e. on the night of July 4th, 1941."[40] He further surmised that occupying German forces had then compounded their initial crime by using some of the memorial stones to construct a machine gun encasement nearby. In his view, the ABMC should seek $170,000 in reparation costs from the new German government.

Bentley Mott did not explicitly recommend rebuilding the memorial, though his ABMC colleague Major Charles B. Shaw had already canvassed opinion on this matter from advisers, including Cret, who were sent a provisional report of the damage in March 1945. In Cret's view, rebuilding the memorial would be most ill-advised, and the French authorities should be encouraged to recreate the park and walls as they had existed in the 1920s when he had first visited the area.[41] As Cret correctly inferred, the reconstruction of monuments destroyed during the war was a delicate problem in France. The wartime Vichy authorities had gone to considerable lengths to remove French statues and memorials deemed inappropriate to the new order, and the postwar officials now struggling to re-establish a semblance of normality in a war-damaged country were understandably reluctant to re-visit such contentious matters, not least because many of these men had worked for the Vichy regime (Freeman, 2009, 2010).

Not everyone in the ABMC shared Cret's analysis. Brigadier General Thomas North, one of the ABMC's most senior military officials, firmly believed that the memorial should be rebuilt immediately to symbolize America's defiance of Nazi aggression and signify renewed US commitment to the Atlantic alliance. On

September 20, 1946, North wrote to Secretary of State James F. Byrnes, in Paris for the 1946 reparations conference, asking whether a claim might be made against Germany for funds to rebuild the memorial. In his letter North described a recent visit to the site, where he claimed to have learned from local witnesses, including the new mayor, Jules Lullien, that the memorial had been "demolished by German forces on July 4, 1941," who had also "deliberately obliterated" the inscription on the rock face below, "an act of vandalism [carried out] many months before the United States entered the war."[42] Although Byrnes politely declined to raise the matter at the reparations conference,[43] the story that the memorial had been deliberately destroyed by the Germans on American Independence Day 1941 would henceforth become the officially accepted version of events.

Nothing came of North's suggestion, and after gentle pressure from local politicians in Brest and the US State Department, the ABMC voted unanimously on May 15, 1947, to defer the question of rebuilding the memorial, recognizing that spending up to $500,000 on what one commissioner called "a stone shaft in a devastated region which would stand out amongst the ruins of this area"[44] was not a priority task (on the re-building of the city, see Dieudonné, 1994; Le Goïc, 2001). To mark what was still officially US territory, however, a part-time gardener was employed by the ABMC to maintain the grounds, and two flag poles were erected on which the Stars and Stripes and French tricolor could be flown when required.[45]

The ABMC discreetly monitored public opinion in Brest over the next few years. On August 23, 1950, the ABMC's Colonel A. T. W. Moore visited the city and reported there would be no "unfavorable reaction from the populace" if the memorial were to be rebuilt, though the sample of four shopkeepers with whom he spoke had confirmed that "the communists in Brest would object to anything we did."[46] The ABMC remained cautious, however, largely because it was focused on building new memorials elsewhere in Europe and the Pacific to commemorate the events of World War II.[47]

On May 6, 1952, the US Consul in Cherbourg visited Brest at the invitation of city's mayor, Alfred Chupin, and was formally invited to establish whether the ABMC would be willing and able to rebuild the memorial, now deemed appropriate given "the rapidly progressing reconstruction of the center portion of Brest."[48] North responded positively and set about the long and at times difficult task of raising the necessary funds and beginning the reconstruction.[49] Chupin's assurances that the public mood in the city was now solidly pro-American were occasionally compromised by actions suggesting otherwise, notably the arrest of three activists from the Union des Femmes Françaises, a Communist Party organization, who broke into the park on May 30, 1952, and replaced the American flag with the French tricolor, a small act of defiance for which they were given two-week prison sentences, prompting demonstrations outside the court. Two male comrades repeated the action the following evening, this time evading capture.[50]

The new memorial was completed with minimal fuss in 1958 and inaugurated on July 16, 1960. Compared to the restrained 1937 inauguration, the second dedication ceremony was an altogether more celebratory and high-profile occasion, informed by the very different spirit of liberation and optimism (Fig. 4). A large,

Fig. 4 Press coverage of the second inauguration ceremony for the Naval War Memorial in Brest, July 16, 1960. Source: AMB M174/2 Monuments brestois: Monument Américain, deuxième monument—press clipping from *Le Télégramme de Brest* (July 18, 1960), p. 14

flag-waving crowd assembled on the promenade, decked out for the occasion in red, white, and blue bunting, and sang along with a noisy brass band playing French and American popular tunes while a full-scale naval review took place in the harbor. US Ambassador Amory Houghton's speech included a message from President Eisenhower, once again blaming the Germans for the destruction of the original tower. The Gaullist Prime Minister Michel Debré, the first person to occupy that position under the constitution of the new Fifth Republic (though he had also served as an official under the Vichy regime), made an important and widely quoted speech championing the need for closer Atlantic unity, that "ever strengthening force in the service of civilization, patriotism, and humanity."[51]

The Brest naval memorial remains a prominent and visible feature of the city's cultural landscape, though it scarcely ranks as a significant tourist attraction. On the fiftieth anniversary of the first dedication, the city's main newspaper printed a two-page article about the memorial, noting that while most residents would recognize it, few would know what it represented, or its complex history. The familiar official account described above, complete with the story of wartime destruction and German culpability, was obligingly repeated, and readers were encouraged to climb the memorial's elegant interior staircase to enjoy the views over the city, the harbor, and the sea.[52]

To test how residents in today's city interpret this familiar tower within their midst, I spent two summer weekend evenings in 2004 chatting—in an informal and entirely unscientific manner—to people taking early evening strolls along the Cours Dajot, asking whether those who passed the memorial knew anything about its history and, if so, whether their information was based on personal memories. I recorded about 20 conversations, some lasting no more than a minute, others continuing for much longer in a nearby café. Most people knew only the official story that the memorial itself communicates through the inscription it carries, but five people—two women and three men whom I will call Jeanne, Jean-Paul, Marie-Claire, Maurice, and Xavier—claimed a more intimate personal knowledge of the memorial's history. Three of these individuals had personal memories that add further complications to the accounts discussed above.

Jeanne and Jean-Paul, a married couple in their 70s, had lived in the city all their lives, and both remembered the first dedication ceremony in 1937, though neither could recall the Cours Dajot before the memorial was constructed. Both knew the official story of the memorial's destruction at the hands of the German army, but insisted that the memorial had been destroyed during the RAF bombing raids of 1941 and left in ruins for several months. Though pointing out that the entire area had been out-of-bounds to French citizens throughout most of the war, Jeanne and Jean-Paul were nevertheless adamant that their account was common knowledge in the city, and neither expressed surprise that it was endorsed by the archival evidence. They seemed even less concerned that the blame for the memorial's destruction had subsequently shifted entirely onto the German army.

Marie-Claire and Maurice, another married couple, had lived in various French cities and overseas (Marie-Claire in Italy, Maurice serving briefly in the French navy), but both remembered the war years when they were young teenagers, Maurice living in the city itself, Marie-Claire in the nearby countryside. Their account of the memorial's destruction was entirely different and had, they claimed, been deliberately suppressed by the French and American authorities after the war. The initial explosion that brought down the memorial had taken place on the evening of July 4, 1941, Maurice asserted. It was caused by neither the RAF nor the occupying Germans, however, but by the local French Resistance, whose motives were fantastically complex. Maurice, who did most of the talking during a long interview, proudly mentioning his background as a trade unionist and member of the French Communist Party, insisted that most of the résistants in Brest were communists or "fellow travelers," including several former dockworkers previously active in anarcho-syndicalist politics. Especially significant, in his view, were the members of an anarchist youth movement established before World War I by two charismatic labor organizers and dedicated pacifists, Victor Pengam and Jules Le Gall (Baal, 1973). My own research confirms that Pengam and Le Gall had struggled for years against the militarization of the city's docks, notably during World War I, enduring regular periods of imprisonment for encouraging soldiers and sailors to desert and for inciting dockworkers to commit acts of sabotage. Pengam, who established a school and cooperative restaurant for workers in the docks, died of tuberculosis in 1920, but Le Gall continued his campaigns during the interwar years, notably through another anarchist organization he had cofounded with Pengam, Les Temps Nouveaux (see, more generally, Berry, 2002).

In Maurice's story, a group of former dockworkers in the Resistance broke into the park on the Cours Dajot under cover of darkness on July 4, 1941, taking advantage of damage caused to the perimeter fence by the British bombardment, and managed partially to destroy the memorial, which the Germans had been using as a tower for a search light. Their objective was to cause disruption to the German defenses, to be sure, but Maurice claimed that the timing was deliberate and multiply symbolic. The Resistance recognized that the still neutral Americans would realize that their memorial had been destroyed on an evening of great significance to Americans when no RAF bombing raids had taken place, and would assume a deliberate act of provocation by the Germans. But the attack served a double purpose, insisted Maurice, particularly for those résistants formerly involved in the anarcho-syndicalist movement in the docks. To these men, the memorial had no obvious connection with America's war dead but had served merely to celebrate American naval prowess. It was an unwanted symbol of international military and political power in an arena that should rightfully be fashioned in the image of honest proletarian labor. Their attack on the memorial was therefore part of a much longer struggle to liberate the city's docks from the grip of military-industrial capital, the corrupting force they believed had generated both twentieth-century wars and claimed so many lives. The fact that July 4 was also the first anniversary of the British destruction of France's Mediterranean fleet at Mers-el-Kébir in Algeria, an event that cost the lives of 1,267 French sailors, sacrificed so their ships would not fall into German hands, added further symbolic significance in a naval city such as Brest. The attack on the memorial on July 4 was designed to communicate to those able to interpret such events as evidence that organized labor within the Resistance movement was capable of continuing the struggle to demilitarize their former workplace, even in the midst of its occupation by an enemy power. It is most unlikely that Le Gall, who would have been 60 in 1941, could have taken part in this action, reasoned Maurice, but the fact that he was arrested by the Gestapo ten days later (a fact I have subsequently confirmed) was no coincidence. Le Gall was never released from detention and died three years later in Buchenwald.

The story told by Xavier, the oldest interviewee, was even more surprising. He had also lived in Brest for most of his long life and remembered the memorial's original dedication. Xavier also claimed the tower had been destroyed on July 4, 1941, though in quite different circumstances and by an entirely different organization. In his account, the action had been carried out by a shadowy group of militant Breton nationalists, Gwenn ha du. Xavier, who expressed utter contempt for all forms of Breton separatism, revealed nevertheless a quite remarkable knowledge of the movement's history and its many often warring factions, most of which has been subsequently corroborated by further research (Ford, 1993; Gemie, 2007; Reece, 1977).

Gwenn ha du was founded in 1930 in Paris by Célestin Lainé and for a while included Yann Goulet, the charismatic artist and sculptor who fled France in 1944 to settle (along with several of his fellow Breton nationalists) in Dublin. Like much of the Breton nationalist movement between the wars, Gwenn ha du espoused an ultramontane Catholicism and was anti-republican, anti-urban, anti-Semitic, and, above all, anti-French, though willing to collaborate with other far-right and even fascist groups within and beyond France. Gwenn-ha-du carried out a sporadic bombing campaign in the 1930s, beginning with several high-profile attacks in 1932, the four-hundredth anniversary of the union of France and Brittany, including an attack on the Paris–Brest railway line moments before the arrival of a train carrying President Édouard Herriot on an official visit to the region. The group was also responsible for an explosion that destroyed a statue in the center of Rennes depicting Anne, the Duchess of Brittany, kneeling in supplication before Louis XII, the French king she married in 1499, paving the way to the union of the previously independent duchy with France (Déniel, 1976, p. 149; Gildea, 1994, pp. 199–208).

Many Breton nationalists, including Lainé and Goulet, welcomed the German occupation as an opportunity to advance the cause of an autonomous, even independent Brittany within a new European order, and some of them collaborated enthusiastically with the Nazis. Operating within the German occupying army, Lainé became a member of a special unit entitled Bezen Perrot in honor of a collaborating Breton Catholic priest killed by the Communist Resistance in the early days of the war (Leach, 2008). According to Xavier, Gwenn ha du's attack on the American memorial, which failed to bring the structure down, was inspired by hatred of the United States, France, and the city of Brest itself, which was viewed as an immoral communist outpost in the midst of traditional, rural, and Catholic Brittany. The group's action had received tacit support, Xavier claimed, from the SS, eager to exploit the propaganda value of a Breton paramilitary unit helping to police the region, though most German officers in the city had no knowledge of the operation and were dismayed by it, not least because they were obliged to deliver the coup de grace to the tottering memorial to make the area safe.

Maurice, Marie-Claire, and Xavier all claimed to have first heard their versions of the memorial's destruction shortly after the war, each insisting that their account had been widely accepted within the city. They freely acknowledged that corroborating evidence was unlikely to exist, though reasoned correctly that the same could be said of the scarcely more substantiated official narrative. For my purposes, the question here is not which of these accounts is true but rather why so many conflicting stories should exist and how an investigation that moves from the accepted historical record to the archival sources and from there to the realms of personal memory generates an accumulating series of competing and complicated narratives, each apparently shaped by divergent ideological perspectives.

Concluding Remarks

The stories that swirl around the construction, destruction, and reconstruction of the US naval memorial in Brest underline how World War II and the German occupation have become the ultimate French battleground of memory and forgetting

(Barcellini & Wieviorka, 1995; Farmer, 1999; Gildea, 2002, pp. 377–413; Jackson, 2001, pp. 601–632; Lorcin, 2009; Namer, 1987; Rousso & Conan, 1998; Rousso, 1991). If the official version of events conforms to a comforting narrative of Allied virtue and German vice, the alternative accounts have a darker and more disturbing quality, occasionally veering toward the tragicomic and the absurd, and often shockingly at odds with the sense of propriety and reverence that—one hopes and assumes—inform any attempt to commemorate victims of war. The very idea that a war memorial might be destroyed, either willfully or as collateral damage in a less-than-precise air raid, is rather distressing. Such havoc is emphatically not what is supposed to happen, though it is perhaps a more frequent occurrence than one might wish to admit (see Gildea, 2002, pp. 50–51, on the destruction in 1940 of a French war memorial in Nantes).

The alternative versions of the Brest memorial return to the themes identified in the introduction and force one to confront, once again, the bleak and genuinely tragic conclusion that attempts to commemorate victims of twentieth-century warfare, though invariably motivated by noble ambitions, rarely transcend the grim social and political realities that generate violent conflict in the first place. Those who die in one conflict are almost always, in one way or another, manipulated by those who survive, usually for narrow political advantage. In this sense, there is only one convincing answer to the question that lies at the core of this chapter: Who was responsible for the destruction of the US Naval Memorial in Brest? Sadly, everyone was; there were no victims, and no obviously culpable perpetrators. The actors and agencies involved in these stories were all simultaneously both.

This conclusion has significant political as well as intellectual ramifications, for it further destabilizes the dubious moral distinctions between "just" and "unjust" warfare that still shape people's thinking about the nature of violence in the twentieth century, a distinction that is as philosophically problematic as it is psychologically disabling (Grayling, 2006). As Sebald (1999/2003) observes in his brilliant discussion of the aerial bombardment of German cities during World War II, and as Gregory argues elsewhere in this volume, the idea that Allied aerial attacks on Germany were morally defensible whereas the comparable German attacks on Britain and occupied Europe were not relies on official histories that suppress and distort, deliberately or otherwise, a more complex historical reality (see also Barnouw, 2005; Biddle, 2002). In the case of Brest, the alternative stories, myths, and countermyths have coexisted with the official version of events—a consequence of the complex international nature of the commemorative process within the city prior to 1940, the equally complex international violence that reduced the city to rubble between 1940 and 1944, and the no less elaborate politics of remembrance and forgetting since 1945 (see also Calder, 1992).

The histories and memories of the Brest memorial also highlight how dramatic events generate multiple narratives that continuously evolve to create a sense of place and that demand the simultaneous analysis of written historical accounts, archival sources, and popular memories, though with an appropriate measure of skepticism in each arena. In this instance, the bitterness and rivalries that shaped the memorial's creation and the strange stories associated with its destruction in the midst of a much wider process of urban devastation, one that truly deserves the recently coined label "urbicide" (Coward, 2009), all point to a different reading of the prewar and wartime city from that invoked by Prévert's powerfully nostalgic poem at the outset of this chapter. In this case, urbicide did not efface memory, even when it removed a site specially designed to create memory (Bevan, 2006; Hewitt, 1983). Rather, destruction created a new and entirely different set of contested memories. Whereas Prévert's lyrical vision of a happy, innocent prewar city destroyed by total war set the scene for this chapter, the disturbing complexity of the Brest memorial suggests that Jean Genet's (1953) much darker and more disturbing vision of the same time and place in *Querelle de Brest*, though in its own way an equally nostalgic account of the rough and violent amorality of the prewar docks, provides a more fitting contextual note on which to end this essay (White, 1994).

It might reasonably be countered, of course, that none of these stories really matters anymore, for the controversies and disputes surrounding the Brest memorial are no more than rapidly dimming memories, recalled only by the elderly, and no doubt very imperfectly at that. Once that generation has passed, perhaps Robert Musil's aforementioned observation may, in the end, be proved right as even the Brest memorial fades into that curious state of visible invisibility and familiar obscurity. And yet the commemorative impulse remains as powerful today as it has ever been; it is certainly no less contentious. Despite the very different nature of recent globalized warfare, for the most part conducted in places far beyond Europe and North America, new memorials and commemorative practices are still being created to recall victims of today's wars. These memorials may well slide quickly and smoothly into the gentle obscurity noted by Musil, but I would not bank on it.

Notes

1. It's rained all day on Brest today/As it was raining before/But it isn't the same anymore/And everything is wrecked/It's a rain of mourning terrible and desolate/Nor is it still a storm/Of iron and steel and blood/But simply clouds/That die like dogs/Dogs that disappear/In the downpour drowning Brest/And float away to rot/A long way off/A long way from Brest/Of which there's nothing left.

   The French original is widely available, though the classic edition is Prévert (1949, p. 237). This translation is by American poet Lawrence Ferlinghetti (1958, p. 32). All other translations from French sources cited below are my own.
2. This wise and happy rain/On your happy face/On that happy town
3. Is he dead and gone or still so much alive?
4. this rain of iron/Of fire of steel of blood
5. Remember Barbara/Don't forget
6. US National Archives, ABMC Records, Record Group 117, Box 1A [hereafter USNA/ABMC/RG117/1A]: Proceedings of the ABMC, 12th meeting, March 17, 1925, pp. 32, 33, 37; 14th meeting, November 4, 1925, p. 44; 15th meeting, November 16, 1925, p. 45.
7. Archives Municipales de Brest [hereafter AMB] M174/1/1: Monuments Brestois—Monument Américain (Construction—Inauguration, 1926–1945) Lieutenant Thomas North (ABMC representative in Paris) to Nardon, February 23, 1926; North to Nardon, February 27,

1926; Nardon to North, March 23, 1926; Nardon to Commandant Perroud (Chef du Génie, Brest), March 23, 1926; North to M. Milineau (Architecte de la Ville de Brest), February 23, 1926.

8. AMB M174/1/1: Monuments Brestois—Monument Américain (Construction—Inauguration, 1926–1945) North to Nardon, September 8, 1926; Extrait du registre des délibérations du Conseil Municipal, October 15, 1926.

9. AMB M174/1/2: Presse, especially Encore le monument commémoratif américain [The American memorial monument again], La Dépêche de Brest, July 11, 1927, p. 3.

10. AMB M174/1/1 Motet to Ministry of Public Instruction, July 12, 1927; USNA/ABMC/ RG117/11/3: Brest Naval Memorial—Presidential decree authorizing the ABMC to construct the memorial, August 13, 1927.

11. AMB M174/1/1 Xenophon Price (ABMC) to Victor Le Gorgeu, May 23, 1929; Le Gorgeu to Price, June 12, 1929.

12. AMB M174/1/1 Extraits du registre des délibérations du Conseil Municipal, July 22, 1929; Le Gorgeu to Price, July 26, 1929; AMB M174/1/1 Moret to Price, April 28, 1928.

13. AMB M174/1/1 Motet to Le Gorgeu, July 29, 1929; M. Thiebault (Syndicat d'Initiative du Nord Finistère) to Le Gorgeu, TCF, and Ministry of Public Instruction, August 16, 1929; Senateur Cornudet (President of the SPPF) to Price, September 26, and December 5, 1929.

14. Marcel Rondeleux, Un chef d'oeuvre de Vauban menacé [A Vauban masterpiece threatened], L'Illustration (August 24, 1929), p. 4.

15. AMB M174/1/1 Le Gorgeu to Price, Prefect of Finistère, and Ministry of Public Instruction, August 17, 1929 (telegrams); Ministry of Public Instruction to Le Gorgeu, August 17, 1929 (telegram); Prefect of Finistère to Le Gorgeu, August 20, 1929.

16. AMB M174/1/1/ Price to Le Gorgeu, September 9, 1929. (Original in French)

17. AMB M174/1/1 Le Gorgeu to Price, September 17, 1929; Xenophon H. Price, Le "memorial" du l'US Navy [The US navy "memorial"], La Dépêche de Brest, September 24, 1929, p. 1.

18. AMB M174/1/1 Le Gorgeu to Motet, September 2, 1929; Motet to Le Gorgeu, September 27, 1929; Amiral Motet, Le mémorial américain [The American memorial], La Dépêche de Brest, September 29, 1929, p. 1.

19. AMB M174/1/1 Comtesse de Rodellec du Portzic to Edge, October 12, 1929.

20. AMB M174/1/1 AMB M174/1/1 Price to Comtesse de Rodellec du Portzic, October 29, 1929. (Original in French)

21. On the tension between American troops and the local population in Brest during the war, see the police reports in Archives Départementales du Finistère, 1M267. It is worth noting that there are no anonymous letters criticizing the Brest memorial in the ABMC archives.

22. AMB M174/1/1 Bomin to Le Gorgeu, August 18, 1930.

23. AMB M174/1/1 Le Gorgeu to Bomin, February 24, 1930, March 10, 1930; Thiebault to Le Gorgeu, March 7, 1930; Thiebault to Bomin, March 26, 1930; Bomin to Thiebault, April 15, 1930; La Dépêche de Brest, February 22, 1930, p. 2; March 21, 1930, p. 2; December 14, 1930, p. 3; January 18, 1931, p. 2; February 27, 1931, p. 3; March 18, 1931, p. 4; March 27, 1931, p. 3; August 27, 1931, p. 2.

24. AMB M174/1/1 V. Le Gorgeu, La visite du Général Pershing [General Pershing's visit], La Dépêche de Brest, May 20, 1931, p. 1. Further articles on Pershing's visit appeared in the same newspaper on May 21, 1931, pp. 1–3.

25. USNA/ABMC/RG117/1A Proceedings of the AMBC, monthly meetings.

26. AMB M 174/1/1 Le Gorgeu to Price, December 7, 1931; Edge to Georges Lombard (President of the Comité Génerale des Fêtes Brestois), December 18, 1931; Price to Le Gorgeu, January 12, 1932; Price to Lombard, March 9, 1932.

27. AMB M174/1/1 Victor Le Gorgeu, L'inauguration du mémorial américain [The inauguration of the American memorial], La Dépêche de Brest, March 13, 1932, p. 2.

28. AMB M174/1/1 Le mémorial américain [The American memorial], La Dépêche de Brest, March 15, 1932, p. 2.

29. AMB M174/1/1 Le monument américain [The American memorial], La Dépêche de Brest, December 9, 1932, p. 4.

30. AMB M174/1/1 La politique américain [American policy], *La Dépêche de Brest*, December 14, 1932, p. 2.
31. AMB M174/1/1/ Price to Ministry of Public Instruction, October 17, 1933; Ministry of Public Instruction to Prefect of Finistère, December 1, 1933; Le Gorgeu to Ministry of Public Instruction, January 4, 1934; Ministry of Public Instruction to Le Gorgeu, January 27, 1934.
32. Police reports on the Brest riots can be found in Archives Nationales F7 13305.
33. USNA/ABMC/RG117/11/5: Press cuttings: dedication, Brest Naval Memorial 1937. The speeches were reproduced in full, alongside photographs, in *La Dépêche de Brest*. See AMB M174/1/1 P. Nicolas, Brest, base no. 5 des forces expéditionnaires Américains (1917–18–19) [Brest, base no. 5 of the American Expeditionary Force (1917–1919)], *La Dépêche de Brest*, August 12, 1937, p. 5; and L'inauguration officielle du monument américain du Cours Dajot [The official inauguration of the American monument on Cours Dajot], *La Dépêche de Brest*, August 13, 1937, p. 3.
34. AMB M174/1/1 Colonel Thomas Bentley Mott (ABMC) to Délégation Spéciale, January 25, 1941; Bentley Mott to Brest Architect's Office, January 27, 1941; Dick to Délégation Spéciale, January 21, 1941; Bentley Mott to Délégation Spéciale, April 28, 1941.
35. *The Times* (London) reported bombing raids against Brest on the following dates in 1941: June 26 (p. 4, col. d), June 29 (3d), July 3 (4 g), July 8 (4d), July 25 (4d), July 26 (4d, 5c), August 18 (4 g), September 1 (4e), September 5 (4 g), September 15 (4 g), October 4 (4f), October 6 (4 g), October 23 (4f), October 24 (4f), October 25 (4 g), October 27 (4f), and October 31 (4 g).
36. AMB M174/1/1 Brown to City Engineer, July 1, 1941; Brown to City Engineer, July 9, 1941; City Engineer to ABMC, July 15, 1941; Délégation Spéciale to ABMC, October 28, 1941; German Commandant to Délégation Spéciale, October 14, 1941.
37. AMB M174/1/1/ Extraits des rapports journalières de police, March 30–31 and April 2–3, 1942.
38. AMB M174/1/1 Rod to Prefect of Finistère, April 22, 1943; Prefect of Finistère to Rod, May 11, 1943.
39. USNA/ABMC/RG117/12/1–3.
40. USNA/ABMC/RG117/12/1 Bentley Mott to Major Charles B. Shaw (ABMC), May 2, 1945.
41. USNA/ABMC/RG117/12/1 Cret to Shaw, March 7, 1945.
42. USNA/ABMC/RG117/12/1 North to Byrnes, September 20, 1946.
43. USNA/ABMC/RG117/12/1 Byrnes to North, September 26, 1946.
44. USNA/ABMC/RG117/12/1 ABMC, Extract of minutes of 50th Meeting, May 15, 1947; D. John Markey to North, September 30, 1947.
45. AMB M174/2 Le Cours Dajot [The Cours Dajot], *Le Télégramme de Brest*, August 3, 1949, p. 4.
46. USNA/ABMC/RG117/12/1 Moore to North, August 23, 1950.
47. USNA/ABMC/RG117/12/1 North to Shaw, August 9, 1951.
48. USNA/ABMC/RG117/12/1 American Consul (Cherbourg) to US Embassy, Paris, May 6, 1952.
49. USNA/ABMC/RG117/12/1 North to US Embassy, Paris, May 12, 1952. Materials, including press cuttings, on the reconstruction phase are available in USNA/ABMC/RG117/12/2-3.
50. USNA/ABMC/RG117/12/1 A Brest—trois manifestants condamnés [Three demonstrators convicted in Brest], *France-Soir* (Paris), June 6, 1952, p. 2.
51. AMB M174/2 Monuments brestois: Monument Américain, deuxième monument, Le mémorial américaine a été inauguré samedi à Brest en présence de M. Michel Debré [American memorial inaugurated Saturday in Brest in the presence of M. Michel Debré], *Le Télégramme de Brest*, July 18, 1960, p. 14.
52. AMB M174/2 Le monument américain du Cours Dajot—une propriété de l'Oncle Sam à visiter [The American monument on Cours Dajot—Property of Uncle Sam to visit], *Le Télégramme de Brest*, August 6, 1987, pp. 3–4.

References

ABMC. (1926). *Annual report of the American Battle Monuments Commission to the President of the United States.* Washington, DC: Government Printing Office.

ABMC. (1938). *Annual report of the American Battle Monuments Commission to the President of the United States.* Washington, DC: Government Printing Office.

ABMC. (1960). *Annual report of the American Battle Monuments Commission to the President of the United States.* Washington, DC: Government Printing Office.

ABMC. (1995a). *American armies and battlefields in Europe.* Washington, DC: Government Printing Office.

ABMC. (1995b). *American memorials and overseas military cemeteries.* Washington, DC: Government Printing Office.

ABMC. (1995c). *Fact sheet and newsletter: Vol. 1. Organization and functions manual, 1/1/1995.* Washington, DC. Unpublished report, no pagination

Aron, R., & Dandieu, A. (1931a). *Le cancer américain* [The American cancer]. Paris: Éditions Rieder.

Aron, R., & Dandieu, A. (1931b). *Décadence de la nation française* [Decadence of the French Nation]. Paris: Éditions Rieder.

Baal, G. (1973). Victor Pengam et l'évolution du syndicalisme révolutionnaire à Brest (1904–1914) [Victor Pengam and the evolution of revolutionary syndicalism in Brest (1904–1914)]. *Le Mouvement Social, 82,* 55–82.

Barcellini, S., & Wieviorka, A. (1995). *Passant, souviens-toi! Les lieux de souvenir de la Seconde Guerre Mondiale en France* [Passerby, remember! World War II places of remembrance in France]. Paris: Plon.

Barnouw, D. (2005). *The war in the empty air: Victims, perpetrators, and postwar Germans.* Bloomington, IN: Indiana University Press.

Bedford, S. M. (1998). *John Russell Pope: Architect of empire.* New York: Rizzoli.

Berry, D. (2002). *A history of the French anarchist movement, 1917–1945.* Westport, CT: Greenwood Press.

Bevan, R. (2006). *The destruction of memory: Architecture at war.* London: Reaktion.

Biddle, T. D. (2002). *Rhetoric and reality in air warfare: The evolution of British and American ideas about strategic bombing, 1914–1954.* Princeton, NJ: Princeton University Press.

Blight, D. W. (2001). *Race and reunion: The Civil War in American memory.* Cambridge, MA: Harvard University Press.

Blight, D. W. (2002). *Beyond the battlefield: Race, memory, and the American Civil War.* Amherst, MA: University of Massachusetts Press.

Bodnar, J. (1992). *Remaking America: Public memory, commemoration, and patriotism in the twentieth century.* Princeton, NJ: Princeton University Press.

Bougeard, C. (1992). *Histoire de la Résistance en Bretagne* [History of the Resistance in Brittany]. Paris: Éditions Jean-Paul Gisserot.

Bougeard, C. (2005). *Occupation, Résistance et libération en Bretagne en 30 questions* [Occupation, Resistance, and liberation in Brittany in 30 questions]. La Crèche: Geste Éditions.

Bristow, N. (1996). *Making men moral: Social engineering during the Great War.* New York: New York University Press.

Brubaker, R. (1996). *Nationalism reframed: Nationhood and the national question in the New Europe.* Cambridge, UK: Cambridge University Press.

Budreau, L. (2010). *Bodies of war: World War I and the politics of commemoration in America, 1919–1933.* New York: New York University Press.

Calder, A. (1992). *The myth of the Blitz.* London: Pimlico.

Clout, H. (2000). Place annihilation and urban reconstruction: The experience of four towns in Brittany, 1940 to 1960. *Geografiska Annaler, 82B,* 165–180.

Coward, M. (2009). *Urbicide: The politics of urban destruction.* London: Routledge.

Déniel, A. (1976). *Le mouvement breton de 1919 à 1945* [The Breton movement from 1919 to 1945]. Paris: Maspéro.

Dieudonné, P. (1994). *Villes reconstruites du dessin au destin* [Towns rebuilt from design to destiny] (2 vols.). Paris: L'Harmattan.

Dodd, L., & Knapp, A. (2008). "How many Frenchmen did you kill?": British bombing policy towards France (1940–1945). *French History, 22*, 469–498.

Duhamel, G. (1930). *Scènes de la vie future* [Scenes of future life]. Paris: Mercure de France.

Ellis, M. (2001). *Race, war, and surveillance: African Americans and the United States government during World War I*. Bloomington: Indiana University Press.

Eltin, R. A. (1994). *Symbolic space: French Enlightenment architecture and its legacy*. Chicago: University of Chicago Press.

Farmer, S. (1999). *Martyred village: Commemorating the 1944 massacre at Oradour-sur-Glane*. Berkeley and Los Angeles, CA: University of California Press.

Farwell, B. (1999). *Over there: The United States and the Great War, 1917–1918*. New York: W. W. Norton.

Ferlinghetti, L. (1958). *Selections from "Paroles."* San Francisco, CA: City Lights Books.

Ford, C. (1993). *Creating the nation in provincial France: Religion and popular identity in Brittany*. Princeton, NJ: Princeton University Press.

Frackman, N. (1986). *John Storrs*. New York: Whitney Museum of American Art.

Freeman, K. (2009). *Bronze to bullets: Vichy and the destruction of French public statuary, 1941–1944*. Stanford, CA: Stanford University Press.

Freeman, K. (2010). "Filling the void": Absence, memory and politics in Place Clichy. *Modern and Contemporary France, 18*, 51–65.

Galliou, P. (2007). *Histoire de Brest* [History of Brest]. Paris: Éditions Jean-Paul Gisserot.

Gallo, Y. (Ed.). (1992). *Brest alias Brest: trois siècles d'urbanisme* [Brest alias Brest: Three centuries of urbanism]. Liège: Mardaga.

Gawne, J. (2002). *Americans in Brittany, 1944: The battle for Brest*. Paris: Histoires et Collections.

Gemie, S. (2007). *Brittany, 1750–1950: The invisible nation*. Cardiff, Wales: University of Wales Press.

Genet, J. (1953). *Querelle de Brest* [The Querelle de Brest]. Paris: Gallimard.

Gibson, G. (1946). *Enemy coast ahead*. London: Michael Joseph.

Gildea, R. (1994). *The past in French history*. New Haven, CT: Yale University Press.

Gildea, R. (2002). *Marianne in chains: In search of the German occupation, 1940–1945*. London: Macmillan.

Glass, C. (2009). *Americans in Paris: Life and death under Nazi occupation*. London: Harper Press.

Glassberg, D., & Moore, J. M. (1996). Patriotism in Orange: The memory of World War I in a Massachusetts town. In J. Bodnar (Ed.), *Bonds of affection: Americans define their patriotism* (pp. 160–190). Princeton, NJ: Princeton University Press.

Grayling, A. C. (2006). *Among the dead cities: The history and moral legacy of the WWII bombing of civilians in Germany and Japan*. London: Bloomsbury.

Greene, V. A. (1998). *The architecture of Howard Van Doren Shaw*. Chicago: Chicago Review Press.

Grossman, E. G. (1984). Architecture for a public client: The monuments and chapels of the American Battle Monuments Commission. *Journal of the Society of Architectural Historians, 43*, 119–143.

Grossman, E. G. (1996). *The civic architecture of Paul Cret*. Cambridge, UK: Cambridge University Press.

Halbwachs, M. (1980). *The collective memory* (F. J. Didder Jr. & V. Yazdi Ditter, Trans., with an introduction by M. Douglas). New York: Harper & Row. (Original work published 1950)

Heffernan, M. (1995). For ever England: The Western Front and the politics of remembrance in Britain. *Ecumene, 2*, 293–324.

Hewitt, K. (1983). Place annihilation: Area bombing and the fate of urban places. *Annals of the Association of American Geographers, 73*, 257–284.

Huyssen, A. (2003). *Present pasts: Urban palimpsests and the politics of memory*. Stanford, CA: Stanford University Press.

Jackson, J. (1985). *The politics of depression in France, 1932–1936*. Cambridge, UK: Cambridge University Press.

Jackson, J. (1988). *The Popular Front in France: Defending democracy, 1934–38*. Cambridge, UK: Cambridge University Press.

Jackson, J. (2001). *France: The dark years 1940–1944*. Oxford, UK: Oxford University Press.

Keene, J. D. (2001). *Doughboys, the Great War, and the remaking of America*. Baltimore, MD: Johns Hopkins University Press.

Kennedy, D. M. (1980). *Over here: The First World War and American society*. Oxford, UK: Oxford University Press.

Knapp, A. (2007). The destruction and liberation of Le Havre in modern memory. *War in History, 14*, 476–498.

Kohler, S. (1996). *The commission of fine arts: A brief history, 1910–1995*. Washington, DC: Commission of Fine Arts.

Konvitz, J. (1989). Répresentations urbaines et bombardements stratégiques, 1914–1945 [Urban representations and strategic bombing, 1914–1945]. *Annales. Économies. Sociétés. Civilisations. 44*, 823–847.

Konvitz, J. (1992). Bombs, cities and submarines: Allied bombing of the French ports, 1942–1943. *International History Review, 14*, 28–36.

Le Goïc, P. (2001). *Brest en reconstruction: antimémoires d'une ville* [Brest under reconstruction: Countermemories of a city]. Rennes: Presses Universitaires de Rennes.

Leach, D. (2008). Bezen Perrot: The Breton nationalist unit in the SS, 1943–5. *E-Keltoi: Journal of Interdisciplinary Celtic Studies, 4*, 1–38.

Lorcin, P. (Ed.). (2009). *France and its spaces of war: Experience, memory, image*. London: Palgrave.

May, H. F. (1960). *The end of American innocence: A study of the first years of our own time, 1912–1917*. London: Jonathan Cape.

Morand, P. (1930). *Champions du monde* [Champions of the world]. Paris: B. Grasset.

Musil, R. (1987). *Posthumous papers of a living author*. New York: Marsilio. (Original work published 1932)

Namer, G. (1987). *La commémoration en France de 1945 à nos jours* [Commemoration in France from 1945 to the present]. Paris: L'Harmattan.

Nora, P. (1974). Le retour de l'événement [The return of the event]. In J. Legoff & P. Nora (Eds.), *Faire de l'histoire: Vol. 1. Nouveaux problèmes* (pp. 285–308). Paris: Gallimard.

Nora, P. (Ed.). (1984–1992). *Les lieux de mémoire* [Realms of memory] (7 vols.). Paris: Gallimard.

O'Brien, T. (1990). *Chasing after danger: A combat pilot's war over Europe and the Far East, 1939–42*. London: Arrow Books.

O'Leary, C. E. (1999). *To die for: The paradox of American patriotism*. Princeton, NJ: Princeton University Press.

Pershing, J. (1934). Our national war memorials in Europe. *National Geographic Magazine, 65*, 1–36.

Pomaret, C. (1931). *L'Amérique à la conquête de l'Europe* [America and the conquest of Europe]. Paris: Armand Colin.

Prévert, J. (1949). *Paroles*. Paris: Gallimard. (Original work published 1946 by Les Éditions du Point du Jour)

Reece, J. E. (1977). *The Bretons against France: Ethnic minority nationalism in twentieth-century Brittany*. Chapel Hill, NC: University of North Carolina Press.

Robin, R. (1992). *Enclaves of America: The rhetoric of American political architecture abroad, 1900–1965*. Princeton, NJ: Princeton University Press.

Roger, P. (2005). *The American enemy: The history of French anti-Americanism* (S. Bowman, Trans.). Chicago: University of Chicago Press.

Rousso, H. (1991). *The Vichy syndrome: History and memory in France since 1944*. Cambridge, MA: Harvard University Press.

Rousso, H., & Conan, E. (1998). *Vichy: An ever present past*. Lebanon, NH: University Press of New England.

Sahlins, M. (2000). *Culture in practice: Selected essays*. New York: Zone Books.

Sandage, S. (1993). "A marble house divided": The Lincoln Memorial, the Civil Rights movement, and the politics of memory, 1939–1963. *Journal of American History, 80*, 135–167.

Savage, K. (1997). *Standing soldiers, kneeling slaves: Race, war, and monument in nineteenth-century America*. Princeton, NJ: Princeton University Press.

Schaffer, R. (1991). *America in the Great War: The rise of the war welfare state*. Oxford, UK: Oxford University Press.

Sebald, W. G. (2003). *On the natural history of destruction* (A. Bell, Trans.). London: Hamish Hamilton. (Original work published in German 1999)

Sewell, W. H., Jr. (2005). *Logics of history: Social theory and social transformation*. Chicago: University of Chicago Press.

Slotkin, R. (2005). *Lost battalions: The Great War and the crisis of American nationality*. New York: Henry Holt and Company.

Virilio, P. (2000). *A landscape of events*. Cambridge, MA: MIT Press.

Virilio, P. (2007). *The original accident*. Cambridge, UK: Polity Press.

Weber, E. (1995). *The hollow years: France in the 1930s*. London: Sinclair Stevenson.

White, E. (1994). *Genet*. London: Picador.

Wieviorka, O. (2009). *Orphans of the Republic: The nation's legislators in Vichy France*. Cambridge, MA: Harvard University Press.

Winter, J. M. (1988). *The experience of World War I*. London: Guild Publications.

Winter, J. M. (1995). *Sites of memory, sites of mourning: The Great War and the European cultural heritage*. Cambridge, UK: Cambridge University Press.

Wynn, N. A. (1986). *From progressivism to prosperity: World War I and American society*. New York: Holmes and Meier.

Young, J. (1993). *The texture of memory: Holocaust memorials and meaning*. New Haven, CT: Yale University Press.

Young, P. (2002). La vieille France as object of bourgeois desire: The Touring Club de France and the French regions. In R. Koshar (Ed.), *Histories of leisure* (pp. 169–191). Oxford, UK: Berg.

Young, P. (2007). Of pardons, loss and longing: The tourist's pursuit of originality in Brittany, 1890–1935. *French Historical Studies, 30*, 269–304.

Young, P. (2009). Fashioning heritage: Regional costume and tourism in Brittany, 1890–1937. *Journal of Social History, 42*, 631–656.

Places and Spaces: The Remembrance of D-Day 1944 in Normandy

Sandra Petermann

The Allied landing in Normandy, carried out under the code name "Operation Overlord" on June 6, 1944, 16 months after Germany's defeat in Stalingrad, was crucial for liberating Europe from the dictatorship of National Socialism. To this day the section of coast that served as the site of the largest amphibious assault in military history is still scarred by the war and marked by scores of memorials in the French *département* of Lower Normandy. Since 1945, rituals have been organized every year to honor the dead and commemorate the historic events of the Allied landing there. I begin my examination of such remembrance with a theoretical discussion of how rituals create different places and spaces. I then take the Allied landing in Normandy as an empirical illustration of how the ceremonies have contributed to a continual interpretation of the operation's significance to Europe over the years.

Current Status of Research and Terminology Pertaining to the Interrelation Between Space and Rituals

Little has been written about the interrelation between space and rituals. This gap is especially surprising in the discipline of geography, and that for two reasons. First, spaces are a key epistemic interest of geographers. Second, spatial concepts derived from action theory are prevalent in the field of human geography. The positions taken in literature on space and ritual diverge, however, producing a host of differing definitions and approaches. It therefore makes sense to define the terms that are relevant to this topic.

S. Petermann (✉)
Department of Geography, University of Mainz, 55128 Mainz, Germany
e-mail: S.Petermann@uni-mainz.de

P. Meusburger et al. (eds.), *Cultural Memories*, Knowledge and Space 4,
DOI 10.1007/978-90-481-8945-8_14, © Springer Science+Business Media B.V. 2011

Rituals—Ceremonies

According to Soeffner (1992, p. 107), rituals are conventionalized and symbolically formed boundary-crossing actions that are frequently associated with religious acts and aspects in religious studies and social anthropology (see also Moore & Myerhoff, 1977). Rituals are characterized by the existence of a transitional phase (V. Turner, 1989). This threshold phase is marked by liminality, a phenomenon referring to infrequent and somewhat paradoxical parts of a ritual, that is, to an alternative order for the "normal" social structure (the so-called antistructure) and the participant's state of being betwixt and between (V. Turner, 1974, p. 202). By contrast, ceremonies are frequently regarded as secular, formalized, and emblematic actions (Dörrich, 2002, p. 34). In the eyes of Gebauer and Wulf (1998, p. 136), ceremonies serve as an expression of power and involve many participants "who assume a role subordinate to a common goal and stand up for a common issue."[1] All these authors' understanding of the different terms, based as it is on the assumption that there is a clearly recognizable line between secular and religious realms, is suspect. Durkheim (1912/1976), for example, asserts that human behavior can create sacrality such that ceremonies may become rituals as part of their implementation. The transitions between "ritual" and "ceremony" can be considered blurred, so the two terms may be used synonymously.

To improve the ability to isolate rituals as phenomena, it is necessary to highlight their chief characteristics. In the words of Moore and Myerhoff (1977) and Michaels (1999),

> [r]ituals are celebrated and implemented with an explicit intention after people have experienced a change. They are expressly enacted and characterized by formality, repetition, openness, and liminality. Rituals are mediums of implicit, unexpressed meanings as well as explicit statements and symbols and effect a transformation of participants. (Petermann, 2007, pp. 70–71)

Spaces—Places

"Though the concepts of space and place may appear self-explanatory, they have been (and remain) two of the most diffuse, ill-defined and inchoate concepts in the social sciences and humanities" (Hubbard, 2005, p. 41). Clearly, there are very different views of "space." They run the gamut from space in the Kantian sense as a pre-category of the cognitive subject to space as landscape and space as a section of the earth's surface.

Despite the many definitions of space, some dating back to ancient times, this chapter concentrates on an understanding of space based on action theory, by which space is assigned to the mental world. Cassirer (1929/1997) holds that space is to be understood as a schema by which reality is structured. "What we call 'the' space. . . is not an independent object that reveals itself to us directly or allows us to identify it by any 'signs'. Instead, it is its own medium—a particular schematism of representation itself" (p. 174). The action-theory approach addresses questions such as "who communicates under which conditions and for what purpose about certain spaces, and [who] produces and reproduces [those spaces] continuously by every-day actions" (Wardenga, 2002, p. 8). Even the term *place* is subject to a wide variety of attempts at definition. To Bédard (2002), place, unlike space, is not a nonmaterial or idealistic construct: "It is a precisely and clearly defined support, a material arrangement that can be located at the intersection of the geodetic axes of abscissas and ordinates" (p. 51).[2] Thus, each place exists only once on the earth's surface and thereby helps people identify with it.

The notion of space that I use in this chapter can be summarized in three points (Petermann, 2007, p. 71):

1. As objects of fundamental significance, places are part of the construction of spaces and thus an integral element of constructing space.
2. Spaces are created by people's actions. Actions are understood to be any activities performed by human beings and regarded as "reasonable," extending from one-time actions and routines to rituals.
3. Rituals produce spaces that have special significance. This effect can be attributed to the aforementioned characteristics, which delineate rituals from everyday actions.

Collective Memory—Private Memory—Remembrance

There is no unified approach to differentiating *Erinnerung* (private memory) from *Gedächtnis* (collective memory) (Patzel-Mattern, 2002, p. 23). According to Wischermann (1996, p. 15) and his understanding in relation to historical sciences, collective memory comes to bear in the context of associations that are not specific to an individual, whereas private memory entails personal perspectives and experiences. Halbwachs's (1925/1966) concept of collective memory rests on the assumption that individual perception and actions are influenced primarily by a supraindividually organized, social "reality." To Halbwachs, collective memory is therefore a construct that evolves from current social frames of reference. A third view on the distinction between the two types of memory comes from Winter and Sivan (1999), who coined their expression "collective remembrance" (p. 9) while studying war-related events of the twentieth century. To them, remembrance is a connection between extreme positions of personal memories and socially deter-mined memory. Thus, remembrance constitutes a deliberate action, whereas the past is envisioned as a reflection of personal memories and is influenced by aspects of collective memory.

Theoretical Concepts: Rituals Make Spaces

People as creators of space develop ritually occupied spaces at places of remembrances while participating in annually recurring rituals. Selecting individual places, artifacts, or both for rituals establishes social relevance as well as individual

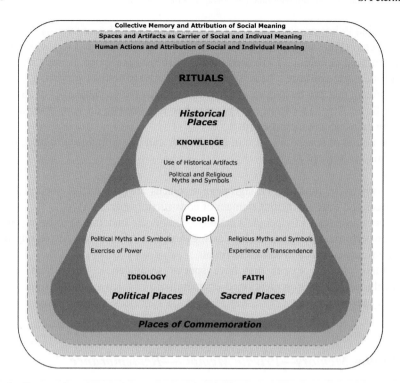

Fig. 1 Construction of spaces by commemorative rituals

perceptions; neglecting to select many other potential places and artifacts leads one to forget or suppress the memory of other incidents. Rituals are implemented in order to commemorate past events. They create spaces of particular significance by intensively integrating symbols and referring to myths, that is, to "narrative symbolic figures having a collective potential effect relating to the underlying classification problem of social associations" (Dörner, 1996, p. 43). The special nature of space also evolves from the fact that public rituals represent actions that have taken place collectively, not individually. Besides the explicit remembrance of the dead and of battles, they also comprise many political, religious, and historical rites[3] that are connected with implicit messages and senses of perception. Participants in rituals therefore create commemorative spaces as well as constructions of political, sacred, and historical space that are rooted in the spheres of ideology, faith, and knowledge (Fig. 1).

Commemorative Spaces

Commemoration as a research topic has boomed over the last 2 decades or more. Lepeltier (2004), for instance, speaks of "enthusiasm for the past" (p. 46); Leclant

(1999), of the "era of remembrance" (p. 185). In so doing, both researchers verify the still earlier observation by Antze and Lambek (1996):

> We live in a time when memory has entered public discourse to an unprecedented degree. Memory is invoked to heal, to blame, to legitimate. It has become a major idiom in the construction of identity, both individual and collective, and a site of struggle as well as identification. (p. vii)

Two popular publications on memory and commemorative spaces are relevant in this context. Nora (1984–1992) may be called a pioneer in the discourse on *lieux de mémoire* (literally, places of memory). In that publication, he inquired into the material and immaterial components of commemorative sites of the French nation, including memorials, commemorative services, rituals, museums, and texts (Nora, 1997). The well-received publication did meet with criticism, however. For example, he listed only memorials that had a positive connotation and ignored the locations of national neglect or oblivion (Lepeltier, 2004, p. 48). Another widely taken approach to viewing commemorative spaces was introduced by Assmann (1999), who defined various media of cultural memory (oral and written forms of language, photos, bodies, and places). Because locations especially embody continuity and serve to trigger memories, they are, in Assmann's opinion, critical to the construction of commemorative spaces (p. 299).

For both Nora and Assmann, rituals are vital either as memorials themselves or as media of memory. Commemorative rituals form a framework and thereby "enhance the recall of memories at given moments and places" (Winter & Sivan, 1999, p. 15). Public days of remembrance effect the synchronization of subjects and, hence, have predominantly social and order-creating functions. "Through it, the group periodically renews the sentiment which it has of itself and of its unity" (Durkheim, 1912/1976, p. 375).

Places and artifacts, too, serve as a means of memory. After all, without reification of "the living and spoken word, the conceived notion would disappear without a trace" (Arendt, 1960, pp. 87–88). Experience with world war is no exception: "[E]vents and actions of a great and yet dark past, require verification through locations and objects" (Assmann, 1999, p. 55).

Political Spaces

In Anglo-Saxon approaches particularly (e.g., Agnew, 1987), political actions have great bearing on the construction of political spaces. Such actions include the politics of remembrance. In this regard Larat (2000, p. 187) talks about "instrumentalization of collective memory," in other words, situations in which "the probability of a political decision's acceptance is to be increased by the medium of private memory, with existing political authority making itself invisible by invoking the past" (Hahn, 2001, p. 447).

Political rituals occupy their own position as well. Their functions can be divided into two areas: (a) they create a consensus among the participants and have an integrating effect (Kertzer, 1992, p. 80), and (b) they can manipulate and legitimate, providing a basis for exercising authority (Lukes, 1975). Large presentations of political ritual "are created by myths, whereas myths cannot exist for long without liturgies [i.e., rituals]" (Bizeul, 2000, p. 19). Political rituals thus gain credibility through myths that they both reproduce and update (Rivière, 1988, p. 13). In addition to drawing on myths, rituals also make use of symbols. Sarcinelli (1989, p. 296) states that the functions of political symbols fall into three areas. First, they simplify complex information and thus serve as a guide (Kertzer, 1998, p. 367). Second, they compensate for the dissatisfaction and indifference displayed by people who are partly overextended in their everyday lives (Meyer, 1992, p. 66). Third, they mainly trigger emotions and associations in viewers instead of inviting a rational approach to the relevant content (Harrison, 1995, p. 270).

Places are just as central to the construction of political spaces as myths and symbols are. All places where or with which "politics are made" are of consequence, including locations at which existing perceptions as to importance increase the impact of political statements. For instance, monuments, memorials, and museums—whose very structure and administration constitute a political issue (Till, 2003, p. 297)—may become political sites, as may former battlefields.

Sacred Spaces

Since time immemorial, people have discussed the existence of spiritual forces and transcendental experiences. There are two fundamental lines of argumentation in questions concerning saints and ecclesiastical matters. First, the ontological-essentialist opinion holds that sacrality comes from God and that it manifests itself at certain locations in one's world (Eliade, 1956/1987; Otto, 1917). Second, there is the opinion that sacrality is not a spiritual reality but rather a construct that results from human actions (Durkheim, 1912/1976; Lévi-Strauss, 1989). Durkheim (1912/1976) emphasizes that "society [is] constantly creating sacred things out of ordinary ones" (p. 212).

In this chapter rituals, symbols, and locations are paramount in the construction of sacred spaces. Rituals can lead to sacred spaces; they are a characteristic element of religious practices, the core of religious experience. This attribute is especially apparent in liturgical rituals such as Eucharist mass and funeral liturgies (e.g., Nölle, 1997) and pilgrimages (e.g., Coleman & Elsner, 1995). According to V. Turner and E. Turner (1978), the pilgrimage represents a way "to a liminal world where the ideal is felt to be real, where the tainted social persona may be cleansed and renewed" (p. 30). Even religious symbols such as thresholds, crosses, relics, and towers can have the effect that people perceive a location as sacred (Eliade, 1987, p. 25). From a constructivist perspective a place is accepted as holy "if other believers acknowledge it and gather there for sacred rituals" (Baudy, 2000, p. 1552). For this purpose any location may be sacralized by collectively arranged rituals (see Petermann, 2007, pp. 62–65).

Historical Spaces

Knowledge forms the basis for creating historical spaces. It is acquired and imparted through historical rituals such as reenactments intended to replicate life on the front or individual battles as "authentically" and with as much detail as possible (Allred, 1996; Cullen, 1995; Hall, 1994). Many historical sites in former theaters of war lend themselves to this purpose. Rather than being transformed into memorials, certain former battlefields have been maintained to preserve authenticity and now serve also as stages for reenacted battles.

There are many different reasons for a person's participation in reenactments. For instance, reenactment participants are interested in history. Allred (1996, p. 7) supposes that reenactments help one come to terms with history and promote the healing process of collective guilt. A different motive for taking part in reenactments is the desire to experience war romanticism, strong community spirit, and fellowship; to escape their everyday life; and to take the opportunity to travel back in time (Cullen, 1995, pp. 176–197). In this vein participation in reenactments may be viewed as a response to a world that is perhaps increasingly perceived as socially isolated (Hall, 1994, p. 8), a world from which the actors feel liberated during the staging and presentation.

Knowledge-based development of historically staged spaces is also promoted by visits to history museums and museums for peace. Like reenactments, museums entail a wide variety of political and religious symbols associated with myths. However, the purpose is completely different in museums, where it is essential to present and explain as many artifacts and facets of war-related events as possible.

The Allied Landing: Rituals Make Spaces of Remembrance

Few areas have been marked by World War II as much as Normandy has, a reality due especially to the many memorials that have been set up in the British-Canadian and America sectors (Fig. 2). The first national ceremonies in both sectors were held on June 6, 1945, and were organized by the landing committee officially appointed to govern the planning and execution of commemorative ceremonies. About 10 years later, the length of the landing beaches, which stretch approximately 120 km (74½ miles), led to the introduction of a rotation system to alternate the annual remembrance ceremonies between the two sectors. Because great distances must nevertheless be traveled within the sectors, a procession of cars is formed to transport participants in the ritual, guests of honor, and public officials responsible for the different memorials on the landing beaches. It is necessary to distinguish between two groups. The first one comprises the members of the landing committee, guests of honor, and veterans, who form a part of the procession and take part in all commemorative ceremonies as a whole. The second group includes local actors (military, veterans and their families, residents, and tourists) who wait at the various memorials for the arrival of the convoy.

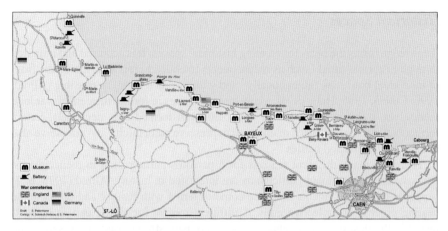

Fig. 2 The beaches of the Allied landing in Normandy—museums, military cemeteries, and fortifications

The procession usually begins in Bayeux, the seat of the landing committee. After the opening service in the cathedral in Bayeux, the procession continues either to the American or the British-Canadian sector, the first station being a cemetery where public officials and veterans collectively lay wreaths. This act is followed by a moment of silence and the tolling of bells. In the American sector the procession leads to Omaha Beach, where the wreath-laying ceremony takes place close to the beach. The next stop is a wreath-laying ceremony at Pointe du Hoc, another place where heavy fighting had occurred. Afterward, the convoy travels to the American monument at Utah Beach, where the closing ceremony takes place in the afternoon with official speeches, wreath-laying ceremonies, the hoisting of national flags, and a solemn parade of the troops. When the itinerary leads to the British-Canadian sector, there is no "standard" route as in the American sector. Basically, the landing committee usually schedules wreath-laying ceremonies at three different locations or beaches after the visit to the cemetery. The closing ceremony, however, likewise includes speeches, the hoisting of national flags, and a military parade.

The pentennial and decennial anniversaries of the Allied landing are marked by commemorative activities in both sectors on June 5 and 6. The ceremonies of the pentennial cycle are characterized by the presence of French ministers, who welcome the heads of state of the Allied nations, their ambassadors, or military attachés as official guests. The ceremonies of the decennial cycle are distinguished above all by the attendance of France's president (except in 1964 and 1974).

Political Spaces of Ideology

The political dimension of the ritual commemoration of D-Day is expressed primarily through speeches by participating politicians and through reference to political symbols and myths. Over the years, the speeches have encompassed a relatively

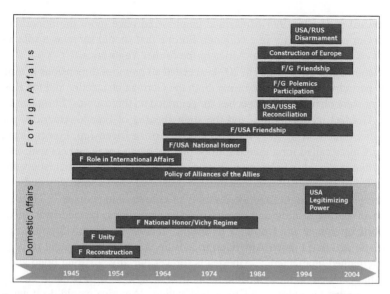

Fig. 3 Themes of domestic and foreign affairs in the speeches commemorating the Allied landing

constant historic part honoring the courage and selflessness of the Allied and French soldiers, yet also a shifting political aspect relating to the internal and foreign policies of France and the other Allies (Fig. 3).[4]

Immediately after World War II, the speeches emphasized the major part the Allies had in D-Day and underlined the courage of France's resistance fighters. The physical and economic rebuilding of France, the re-formation of a national entity, and the construction of a victorious France through the so-called "Thirty Years' War"[5] were also prominent postwar topics. In 1964, however, the Franco-American friendship became a topic of discussion when French President Charles de Gaulle refrained from participating in the ceremonies. Because of Washington's distrust of France's official diplomatic recognition of China in that year (Pottier, 2004, p. 62), de Gaulle felt compelled to express his resentment over America's supremacy and to emphasize France's independence with his absence (Grosser, 1984, p. 1).

It was not until 1984 that a French president—by that time François Mitterrand— was once again present at the ceremonies along with the presidents of the other Allies. In his address Mitterrand referred to the friendship that had come to exist between the former hereditary enemies, France and Germany: "Yesterday's combatants have reconciled themselves and are now jointly building a Europe of freedom."[6] US President Ronald Reagan, one year after Pershing missiles were installed in Europe in response to the Russian SS20 missiles aimed at Western Europe, indicated his willingness to bring about reconciliation between the United States and the Soviet Union: "In truth, there is no reconciliation we would welcome more than a reconciliation with the Soviet Union."[7] America, Reagan continued, was waiting for the Soviet Union to express its willingness to work together and pave a joint path toward peace. In 1994 Mitterrand emphasized once more the importance of Franco-German friendship in a common Europe that should serve as a role model for today's feuding countries in Africa or the former Yugoslavia.

The commemorative rituals in 2004 exceeded all previous dimensions in terms of official participants. For the first time, both the German chancellor and the Russian president were on hand. The speeches concentrated on three topics: European Unity, Franco-German reconciliation, and the strengthening of Franco-American friendship. After underscoring the value of Franco-German friendship, French President Jacques Chirac called for a united Europe that is able to speak and act with a single voice, "that is capable of placing its historical experiences and humanistic values in the service of an international, fair-minded order that shows solidarity and is more respectful of human rights and the diversity of cultures and peoples."[8] The demonstration of Europe's unity and emphasis on human rights, he said, was linked to the efforts by France and Germany to distance themselves from US policy in Iraq. Chirac stressed that Franco-American friendship was based on mutual respect and that it remained unaffected[9]: "America is forever our ally, a strong bond and solidarity that is based on these terrible hours [of D-Day]."[10] US President George W. Bush responded by addressing Chirac and saying, "America would do it again for our friends."[11]

Political spaces are constructed during these ceremonies not only by the speeches but also by political symbols (e.g., national flags and national anthems) that are integrated into the commemorative ceremonies and political myths. After World War II, the French myth of the "grande nation" paled more and more because the country had been quick cooperate with the National Socialists and had needed Allied help to defeat Hitler (Agulhon, 1995, pp. 60–61). Nonetheless, it seems that a new political myth is evolving at a supranational level—a seminal development for European identity and integration. It is the interpretation of D-Day as the beginning, as the founding myth for the European Union. Bayeux, as the center of France's resistance during World War II, is just as decisive for legitimating the political statements of French politicians as Omaha Beach, the nearby American Cemetery of Colleville, Pointe du Hoc, and references to "Bloody Omaha" are for the statements by US politicians.

Sacred Spaces of Faith

In addition to the political instrumentalization of commemorative rituals that are anchored in the context of a secular ideology, one finds a sacralization of battlefields and remembrance ceremonies on the basis of faith. This sacralization utilizes religious symbols and myths and Christian liturgy. For thousands of years, wars, battles, and concomitant military operations have been legitimated and based on religion. D-Day, for example, has been interpreted in the United States as a battle to protect religion, as evident from the prayer spoken by President Franklin D. Roosevelt in 1944 to mark the Allied landing in Normandy: "Almighty God: Our sons, pride of our Nation, this day have set upon a mighty endeavor, a struggle to preserve our

Republic, our religion, and our civilization, and to set free a suffering humanity" (as quoted in Rosenman, 1950, p. 152). For this reason alone, it is hardly surprising that commemoration frequently resembles religion (Cohen, 2004, p. 61) and that processions similar to religious rites such as remembrance masses and funeral liturgies are integrated from place to place.

Additional evidence of sacralization of military conflict and remembrance ceremonies is the fact that participants in rituals undertake regular pilgrimages to hallowed battlefields. Similarly commemorative rituals are dominated by Christian symbols. The cross is almost ubiquitous on the battlefields of World War II, but thresholds and towers, too, point to a world on the other side.

In addition to cemeteries, which frequently have a sacred character due to their function as burial sites, the sacralization of D-Day extends especially to Omaha Beach, the crucial and symbolically charged place of the Allied landing. The town of Sainte-Mère-Eglise, where US paratroopers landed, is also sacred to many people, as is the entire region. One US veteran sums up this opinion very clearly: "And for paratroopers not just Sainte-Mère-Eglise, we say Normandy, the soil, is sacred. It is sacred territory, sacred land."

Historical Spaces of Knowledge

Remembrance and the landing beaches are historicized mainly through reenactment rituals in which diverse artifacts, symbols, and knowledge about historical events are pivotal. The reenactments began several decades ago, but the first time a noteworthy number of reenactments were organized was 1984 to mark the 40th anniversary in Normandy. Not integrated in the official commemorative rituals, most reenactment participants are include collectors of military objects. They converge from all over Europe to live on site in almost completely authentic military camps for the duration of the D-Day celebrations, to travel through the region in military convoys with period vehicles, and to reenact battles and combat operations. Even visits to the many museums in the region have become a ritual trip through history for many history fans and military enthusiasts (regarding the museum visit as a ritual, see Duncan, 1991; Grimes, 1992). The artifacts on display may be political and religious symbols (e.g., old national flags and Bibles from the front) and communicate the past and present.

Reenactments of D-Day differ from the official commemorative rituals mostly by taking place on the beaches and at the bunkers of the Atlantic Wall rather than at the official memorials. The more "authentic" the location is, the more complete the historicization of the commemoration or battlefield.

A Place Holds Many Spaces

Theoretically, it is possible to differentiate three types of space—political, sacred, and historical—which are constructed as part of the actualization of commemorative rituals. Whereas the sacred-space construction remains relatively constant, historical attributions continue to gain significance based on the most precise "factual knowledge" available, and political-space constructions are subject to a continual transformation process that reflects current political conditions. Although many people engage in creating spaces, making a wide variety of different perceptions likely, the participants largely share the space constructions and schemas for interpreting the past as conveyed in rituals. This circumstance is attributable principally to the fact that rituals rest fundamentally on myths and integrate different symbols, providing for high emotional involvement in conjunction with collectively executed gestures. This emotional collectivization shared by many people in the liminal phase allows for both a successful scrutiny of the past and a relatively easy manipulation of a ritual's participants by means of the messages conveyed during the ritual.

So where does this chapter's analysis of how rituals create different places and spaces leave the discussion about tribute to the D-Day invasion in June 1944? My empirical observation of the rituals commemorating the Allied landing in Normandy reveals two phases in the remembrance of battles and of the dead since the end of World War II. The first phase, which lasted mainly until the 1980s, was patriotic remembrance focused on the heroic acts of individual countries. It has gradually given way to remembrance based on reconciliation and unification, culminating in 2004 in the attendance of the former enemies from the National Socialist and Cold War eras. D-Day increasingly seems to be regarded not only as a celebration of victory but as a founding myth of the European Union.

Notes

1. I thank Anthony Frey for the English translations in this chapter.
2. Il est un support précis et délimité, un instituant matériel spatialisé qui se situe à un croisement d'abscisses et d'ordonnées géodésiques.
3. A rite is understood as a subunit of a ritual (Escher & Weick, 2004).
4. The more recent speeches given by France's president and the presidents of the other Allied countries are available on the web pages of the respective speakers. Unless otherwise noted, the French speeches are found in the archives of the "Documentation Française" in Paris or partly online (http://www.discours.vie-public.fr).
5. This "Thirty Years' War" begins with the First Battle of the Marne (September 1914) and ends with D-Day (June 1944). The interpretation of events marks the attempt to revise the story of the Vichy regime, which is viewed as ignominious, and of France's cooperation with the National Socialists (Barcellini, 1999).
6. "Les adversaires d'hier se sont réconciliés et bâtissent ensemble l'Europe de la liberté." Retrieved 08/02/2010, from http://discours.vie-publique.fr/notices/847104700.html
7. Retrieved 08/02/2010, http://www.historyplace.com/speeches/reagan-d-day.htm
8. "Capable de mettre son expérience historique et ses valeurs humanistes au service d'un ordre international, plus juste, plus solidaire, plus respectueux de la dignité de l'homme, de la diversité des cultures et des peuples." Retrieved 08/02/2010, from https://pastel.diplomatie.gouv.fr/editorial/actual/ael2/bulletin.asp?liste=20040607.html&submit.x=9&submit.y=7
9. Prior to the commemorative ceremonies, this friendship became shaky when the US president attempted to legitimate the Iraq war with an analogy to D-Day and the experience acquired from that event. During a visit to the 101st Airborne Division, Bush emphasized, for instance,

that the soldiers had brought the spirit of 1944 to Iraq in order to liberate a country from tyranny (Gibbs, 2004, p. 38). On both sides this statement led to irritation, culminating when the *New York Post* accused France of having forgotten the sacrifice of American soldiers on D-Day ("Sacrifice," 2003, p. 1). These feelings of resentment should be eliminated in the course of the commemorative ceremonies, especially by the tone in the following speech by Chirac.

10. "L'Amérique est notre alliée de toujours, une alliance, une solidarité d'autant plus fortes qu'elles se sont forgées durant ces heures terribles." Retrieved February 8, 2010, from http://discours.vie-publique.fr/notices/047000094.html

11. Retrieved February 8, 2010, from http://georgewbush-whitehouse.archives.gov/news/releases/2004/06/20040606.html

References

Agnew, J. A. (1987). *Place and politics: The geographical mediation of state and society.* Boston: Allen & Unwin.

Agulhon, M. (1995). Die nationale Frage in Frankreich: Geschichte und Anthropologie [The national issue in France: History and anthropology]. In E. François, H. Siegrist, & J. Vogel (Eds.), *Nation und Emotion. Deutschland und Frankreich im Vergleich. 19. und 20. Jahrhundert* (pp. 56–65). Göttingen: Vandenhoeck & Ruprecht.

Allred, R. (1996). Catharsis, revision, and re-enactment: Negotiating the meaning of the American Civil War. *Journal of American Culture, 19*(4), 1–13.

Antze, P., & Lambek, M. (1996). Preface. In P. Antze & M. Lambek (Eds.), *Tense past: Cultural essays in trauma and memory* (pp. vii–ix). New York: Routledge.

Arendt, H. (1960). *Vita Activa—oder Vom tätigen Leben* [Vita Activa—The human condition]. Stuttgart: W. Kohlhammer.

Assmann, A. (1999). *Erinnerungsräume. Formen und Wandlungen des kulturellen Gedächtnisses* [Commemorative spaces: Forms and changes of cultural memory]. Munich: C. H. Beck.

Barcellini, S. (1999). *Deux mémoires en parallèle* [Two parallel memories]. Retrieved August 10, 2003, from www.stratisc.org/partenaires/ihcc/ihcc_44prov_Barcelli.html.

Baudy, D. (2000). Heilige Stätten—Religionswissenschaftlich [Sanctuaries—Theological]. In H. D. Betz (Ed.), *Religion in Geschichte und Gegenwart: Handwörterbuch für Theologie und Religionswissenschaft* (Vol. 3, F–H, pp. 1551–1552). Tübingen: Mohr Siebeck.

Bédard, M. (2002). Une typologie du haut-lieu, ou la quadrature d'un géosymbole [A typology of stronghold, or the quadrature of a geographical symbol]. *Cahiers de Géographie du Québec, 46*(127), 49–74.

Bizeul, Y. (2000). Theorien der politischen Mythen und Rituale [Theories on political myths and rituals]. In Y. Bizeul (Ed.), *Politische Mythen und Rituale in Deutschland, Frankreich und Polen* (pp. 15–39). Berlin: Duncker & Humblot.

Cassirer, E. (1997). *Philosophie der symbolischen Formen. Bd. 3: Phänomenologie der Erkenntnis* [The philosophy of symbolic forms: Vol. 3. The phenomenology of cognition] (10th ed.). Darmstadt: Wissenschaftliche Buchgesellschaft. (Original work published 1929)

Cohen, O.-J. (2004). La mémoire [Remembrance]. *Armées d'aujourd'hui, 291*, 54–61.

Coleman, S., & Elsner, J. (1995). *Pilgrimage—past and present: Sacred travel and sacred space in the world religions.* London: British Museum Press.

Cullen, J. (1995). *The civil war in popular culture: A reusable past.* Washington, DC: Smithsonian Institution Press.

Duncan, C. (1991). Art museums and the ritual of citizenship. In I. Karp & S. D. Lavine (Eds.), *Exhibiting cultures: The poetics and politics of museum display* (pp. 88–103). Washington, DC: Smithsonian Institution Press.

Durkheim, E. (1976). *The elementary forms of the religious life* (J. W. Swain, Trans.) (2nd ed.). London: Allen & Unwin. (Original work published 1912)

Dörner, A. (1996). *Politischer Mythos und symbolische Politik. Der Hermannmythos: zur Entstehung des Nationalbewußtseins der Deutschen* [Political mythos and symbolic politics: The Hermann myth and the evolution of German national consciousness]. Reinbek bei Hamburg: Rowohlt-Taschenbuch-Verlag.

Dörrich, C. (2002). *Poetik des Rituals. Konstruktion und Funktion politischen Handelns in mittelalterlicher Literatur* [Poetics of rituals: Construction and function of political action in medieval literature]. Darmstadt: Wissenschaftliche Buchgesellschaft.

Eliade, M. (1987). *The sacred and the profane: The nature of religion* (W. R. Trask, Trans.). San Diego: Harcourt. (Original work published 1956)

Escher, A., & Weick, C. (2004). "Raum und Ritual" im Kontext von Karten kultureller Ordnung ["Space and ritual" within the context of maps of cultural order]. *Berichte zur deutschen Landeskunde, 78*, 251–268.

Gebauer, G., & Wulf, C. (1998). *Spiel—Ritual—Geste. Mimetisches Handeln in der sozialen Welt* [Play—Ritual—Gestures: Mimesis in a social world]. Reinbek: Rowohlt.

Gibbs, N. (2004, May 31). The greatest day. *Time*, pp. 38–42.

Grimes, R. L. (1992). Sacred objects in museum space. *Studies in Religion/Sciences Religieuses, 21*, 419–430.

Grosser, A. (1984, June 4). Liberté venue de l'ouest [Freedom came from the west]. *Ouest-France*, pp. 1, 4.

Hahn, T. (2001). Politik [Politics]. In N. Pethes & J. Ruchatz (Eds.), *Gedächtnis und Erinnerung. Ein interdisziplinäres Lexikon* (pp. 447–448). Reinbek: Rowohlt.

Halbwachs, M. (1966). *Das Gedächtnis und seine sozialen Bedingungen* [The social frameworks of memory]. Berlin: Luchterhand. (Original work published 1925)

Hall, D. (1994). Civil War reenactors and the postmodern sense of history. *Journal of American Culture, 17*(3), 7–11.

Harrison, S. (1995). Four types of symbolic conflict. *The Journal of the Royal Anthropological Institute, 1*, 255–272.

Hubbard, P. (2005). Space/place. In D. Atkinson, P. Jackson, D. Sibley, & N. Washbourne (Eds.), *Cultural geography: A critical dictionary of key concepts* (pp. 41–48). London: I. B. Tauris.

Kertzer, D. I. (1992). Rituel et symbolisme politiques des sociétés occidentales [Ritual and political symbolism in western societies]. *L'Homme XXXII, 121*, 79–90.

Kertzer, D. I. (1998). Ritual, Politik und Macht [Ritual, politics, and power]. In A. Belliger & D. J. Krieger (Eds.), *Ritualtheorien. Ein einführendes Handbuch* (pp. 365–390). Wiesbaden: Westdeutscher Verlag.

Larat, F. (2000). Instrumentalisierung des kollektiven Gedächtnisses und europäische Integration [Instrumentalization of collective memory and European integration]. In Deutsch-Französisches Institut (Ed.), *Frankreich-Jahrbuch 2000: Politik, Wirtschaft, Gesellschaft, Geschichte, Kultur* (pp. 186–201). Opladen: Leske + Budrich.

Leclant, J. (1999). Les célébrations nationales. Une institution culturelle [The national celebrations. A cultural institution]. *Le débat, 105*, 185–187.

Lepeltier, T. (2004). Nora, Pierre. De l'histoire nationale aux lieux de mémoire [Pierre Nora: From national history to realms of memory]. *Sciences Humaines, 152*, 46–48.

Lukes, S. (1975). Political ritual and social integration. *Sociology, 9*, 289–308.

Lévi-Strauss, C. (1989). Einleitung in das Werk von Marcel Mauss [Introduction to the works of Marcel Mauss]. In M. Mauss (Ed.), *Soziologie und Anthropologie: Vol. 1. Theorie der Magie, soziale Morphologie* (pp. 7–41). Frankfurt: Fischer.

Meyer, T. (1992). *Die Inszenierung des Scheins. Voraussetzungen und Folgen symbolischer Politik. Essay-Montage* [The presentation of appearance: Requirements and consequences of symbolic politics]. Frankfurt: Suhrkamp.

Michaels, A. (Ed.). (1999). *"Le rituel pour le rituel" oder wie sinnlos sind Rituale?* ["Le rituel pour le rituel" or how useless are rituals?]. Berlin: Reimer.

Moore, S. F., & Myerhoff, B. G. (1977). Secular ritual: Forms and meanings. In S. F. Moore & B. G. Myerhoff (Eds.), *Secular ritual* (pp. 3–24). Amsterdam: Van Gorcum.

Nora, P. (Ed.). (1984–1992). *Les lieux de mémoire* [Realms of memory] (7 vols.). Paris: Gallimard.

Nora, P. (1997). Entre Mémoire et Histoire. La problématique des lieux [Between memory and history: The difficulty of places]. In P. Nora (Ed.), *Les Lieux de Mémoire* (Vol. 1, pp. 22–43). Paris: Gallimard. (Original work published 1984).

Nölle, V. (1997). *Vom Umgang mit Verstorbenen. Eine mikrosoziologische Erklärung des Bestattungsverhaltens* [About relations with the deceased: A microsociological interpretation of funeral behavior]. Frankfurt: Peter Lang.

Otto, R. (1917). *Das Heilige. Über das Irrationale in der Idee des Göttlichen und sein Verhältnis zum Rationalen* [The sacred: On the irrational in the idea of the divine and its relation to the rational]. Breslau: Trewendt & Granier.

Patzel-Mattern, K. (2002). *Geschichte im Zeichen der Erinnerung: Subjektivität und kulturwissenschaftliche Theorienbildung* [History in the shadow of memory: Subjectivity and production of cultural theory]. Stuttgart: Steiner.

Petermann, S. (2007). *Rituale machen Räume: zum kollektiven Gedenken der Schlacht von Verdun und der Landung in der Normandie* [Rituals make spaces: On the collective memory of the Battle of Verdun and the Normandy landing]. Bielefeld: Transcript.

Pottier, O. (2004). Les malentendus transatlantiques [The transatlantic disagreement]. *L'Histoire, 287*, 60–64.

Rivière, C. (1988). *Les liturgies politiques* [The political liturgy]. Paris: Presses universitaires de France.

Rosenman, S. I. (Ed.). (1950). *The public papers and addresses of Franklin D. Roosevelt. 1944–45: Vol. 13. Victory and the threshold of peace.* New York: Harper & Brothers Publishers.

Sacrifice: They died for France, but France has forgotten. (2003, February 10). *New York Post*, p. 1.

Sarcinelli, U. (1989). Symbolische Politik und politische Kultur. Das Kommunikationsritual als politische Wirklichkeit [Symbolic politics and political culture: The ritual of communication as political reality]. *Politische Vierteljahresschrift, 30*, 292–309.

Soeffner, H.-G. (1992). *Die Auslegung des Alltags. 2. Die Ordnung der Rituale* [Interpretation of everyday life: Vol. 2. The order of rituals]. Frankfurt: Suhrkamp.

Till, K. E. (2003). Places of memory. In J. Agnew, K. Mitchell, & G. Toal (Eds.), *A companion to political geography* (pp. 289–301). Oxford: Blackwell Publishers.

Turner, V. (1974). *Dramas, fields, and metaphors: Symbolic action in human society.* London: Cornell University Press.

Turner, V. (1989). *Vom Ritual zum Theater. Der Ernst des menschlichen Spiels* [From ritual to theater: The human seriousness of play]. Frankfurt am Main: Ed. Qumran im Campus-Verlag.

Turner, V., & Turner, E. (1978). *Image and pilgrimage in Christian culture: Anthropological perspectives.* New York: Columbia University Press.

Wardenga, U. (2002). Alte und neue Raumkonzepte für den Geographieunterricht [Old and new spatial concepts for teaching geography]. *Geographie heute, 23*(200), 8–11.

Winter, J., & Sivan, E. (1999). Setting the framework. In J. Winter & E. Sivan (Eds.), *War and remembrance in the twentieth century* (pp. 6–39). Cambridge, UK: Cambridge University Press.

Wischermann, C. (1996). Kollektive versus "eigene" Vergangenheit [Collective versus "private" past]. In C. Wischermann (Ed.), *Die Legitimität der Erinnerung und die Geschichtswissenschaft* (pp. 9–17). Stuttgart: Steiner.

"Doors into Nowhere": Dead Cities and the Natural History of Destruction

Derek Gregory

> *Memory is not an instrument for exploring the past but its*
> *theater. It is the medium of past experience, as the ground is the*
> *medium in which dead cities lie interred.*
> Walter Benjamin, "Excavation and memory" (1932, p. 611)

The Dark Side of the Moon

When 28-year-old Heinrich Böll saw his "first undestroyed city" (Böll, 1994, p. 25) at the end of World War II, he broke out in a cold sweat. It was Heidelberg. Böll was a native of Cologne, which had been bombed time and time again by the Royal Air Force (RAF) and the US Eighth Air Force of the United States Army Air Force (USAAF),[1] and he was haunted by the suspicion that Heidelberg had been spared the same fate as other major German towns and cities for purely aesthetic reasons. In postwar Germany "dead cities" were normal cities, so much so that W. G. Sebald, who was born just one year before the war ended, did not attribute the ruins to the bombing and shelling at all. Almost every week on newsreels "we saw the mountains of rubble in places like Berlin and Hamburg," he wrote, yet for the longest time he "did not associate [them] with the destruction wrought in the closing years of the war"—he knew "nothing of it"—but "considered them a natural condition of all larger cities" (Sebald, 1990/2001, p. 187).[2]

The British and American air war against Nazi Germany from 1940 to 1945 was brutal by any measure: necessarily so according to its protagonists, needlessly so according to its critics. Hitler and his ministers condemned the strategic bombing offensive, now usually described as the *Luftkrieg* (air war) or *Bombenkrieg* (bombing war), as a *Terrorkrieg:* a war of terror.[3] Such denunciations must seem hideously ironic, but the descriptions were more than products of the Nazi propaganda machine. The Luftwaffe (German air force) perfected the art of the *Blitzkrieg*, or lightning war, which involved providing tactical air support to the rapid advance of

D. Gregory (✉)
Department of Geography, University of British Columbia, Vancouver, BC, Canada V6T 1Z2
e-mail: derek.gregory@geog.ubc.ca

armored brigades. In September 1939, as German armies poured into Poland, the Luftwaffe flew 1,150 sorties against Warsaw and dropped 500 tons of high explosive bombs and 72 tons of incendiaries on the Polish capital. By the time the city capitulated, 40,000 civilians had been killed. In May 1940, as the Wehrmacht (the German army) swept west, the Luftwaffe bombed Rotterdam, killing 800–900 people and making 80,000 homeless. From September 1940 to May 1941, the Luftwaffe launched a series of attacks against London and provincial cities—the *Blitz*—that killed 43,000 people; during the war as a whole, German bombing killed a total of 60,595 British civilians. But, as Moeller (2006) emphasizes, these air raids were not in support of any ground offensive: "the *Blitz* was the exception; the *Blitzkrieg* the rule" (p. 107). The Luftwaffe recognized the importance of strategic bombing, but its mainstay was the deployment of dive- and medium-bombers to tactical effect, and it did not develop a heavy, long-range bombing capability. In fact, German air raids on Britain dropped only 3% of the total tonnage of bombs dropped on Germany by Britain and the United States, and the Allied bombing campaign over Germany killed as many as ten times the number of civilians killed in Luftwaffe raids on Britain: 350,000–600,000 (Grayling, 2006, p. 104; Overy, 1978, 1981, pp. 35–36, 103).[4] The imbalance is startling and leaves no doubt about the exemplary and extraordinary intensity of the Allied bombing campaign. In two recent studies Canadian political scientist Randall Hansen (2008) claims that "no country had been bombed on the scale Germany was being bombed" (p. 151), while German historian Jörg Friedrich (2002/2006) argues that "Germany was the first country in which the fury of war from the sky was comprehensively and consistently taken to the point of devastation" (p. 62).

The offensive had a defined shape in time and space. First, as Table 1 shows, bombing was concentrated in the last stage of the war, when the tide was running against Germany, and reached its peak during the final six months, when most commentators had concluded that victory was assured. This pattern does not mean that the strategic bombing offensive made a decisive contribution to the Allied victory, however, and arguments continue to rage over its role in the defeat of the Reich. It may even have prolonged the war because the end stage was dominated by what Hohn (1994) describes as an "inconceivable escalation" (p. 222) in the area bombing of towns and cities rather than precision raids on strategic targets like ball-bearing factories, oil plants and refineries, and marshaling yards.

Table 1 Tons of bombs dropped on Germany (compiled from monthly tabulations in Webster and Frankland, 1961, Appendix 44)

	RAF bomber command	US eighth air force
1939	31	
1940	13,033	
1941	31,504	
1942	45,561	1,561
1943	157,457	44,165
1944	525,518	389,119
1945	181,540	188,573

The distinction between the two strategies stemmed from both a difference of opinion and a division of labor. First, as Biddle (2002, p. 245) shows, battles over targeting took place at every level of the Allied wartime hierarchy and raged within the British and American commands as well as between them. The result was that the two air forces waged what Hansen (2008) describes as "parallel but separate" (p. 48) air wars. The RAF preferred the area bombing of towns and cities by night, whereas the USAAF preferred the precision bombing of military and industrial targets by day. That said, the differences between the two were clearer in theory than in practice—Davis (1993) claims that Americans "judged themselves by their motives rather than their results" (p. 435)[5]—since precision bombing often turned out to be remarkably *im*precise. Each American squadron, bomb group, and lead crew was graded for its success in hitting its assigned target, but these priorities were constantly confounded by what Childers (2005) calls "bitter operational realities" (p. 90). From November 1943 on, the USAAF was authorized to attack targets through cloud, but such "blind," or nonvisual (H2X-guided), bombing met with mixed success. In the last three months of 1943, in the best conditions, the USAAF estimated that only 27% of its bombs fell within one thousand feet of the aiming point and 48% within 2,000 ft (Childers, 2005, p. 89). But weather conditions were frequently far from ideal, and during the winter of 1944–1945 42% of bombs fell more than 5 miles from the target (Biddle, 2002, pp. 243–244). Over the same period, the USAAF increased the proportion of incendiaries in the bomb mix so as to start fires in densely built-up areas of towns and cities "to serve as beacons for the RAF to exploit at night" and, "when the occasion warrant[ed]," to raze those areas "by day attack alone" (Biddle, 2002, p. 229). Biddle concludes that the practical effects of these tactics were identical to area bombing. Davis (2006) agrees. The USAAF returned to precision bombing whenever weather conditions permitted and in this sense operated with a model of air power different from that of the RAF, but his detailed analysis of its targeting and operations confirms that the USAAF "engaged in the deliberate bombing of German population centers" (p. 549; see also Sherry, 1987). If the contrast between the two air forces has been overdrawn, and both caused what Overy (2005) identifies as "widespread and random urban destruction and loss of civilian life" (pp. 292–293), the RAF was nevertheless clearly responsible for the lion's share. According to Hansen (2008, p. 273), one study estimated that 75% of German casualties were inflicted by the RAF, 25% by the USAAF, with another estimating that the RAF killed hundreds of thousands, the USAAF tens of thousands.

Second, and following directly from these considerations, the priority of RAF Bomber Command was to attack German towns and cities. The strategy had two main sources. During World War I Germany had carried out air raids by Zeppelins and then by Gotha and Giant bombers over London and the east coast of England, and Britain had responded with the sporadic bombing of cities in the west of Germany. Both sides had been convinced that limited resources and technical limitations would ensure that the "material effect" of bombing would be far outweighed by what was called its "moral [morale] effect": the intimidation of the civilian population through terror. German air raids over Britain were indeed terrifying and caused widespread panic and intense anger, but the total of 836 civilians killed was, as Hanson (2008) remarks, "comfortably exceeded by a single day's losses on the Western Front" (p. 341), and after the war the German high command decided that its strategy had been unsuccessful.[6] But Britain's Chief of Air Staff, Hugh Trenchard, drew the opposite conclusion in his final dispatch. He declared that "the moral effect of bombing stands undoubtedly in a proportion of 20 to 1" (Biddle, 2002, p. 48)—a claim that had no basis either in theory or in fact—and insisted that it was imperative "to create the greatest moral effect possible" (pp. 76–81). Unlike Germany, therefore, Britain intensified its commitment to "moral bombing" and, the second source of its subsequent strategy, developed a specifically colonial doctrine of air control in the 1920s and 1930s that entailed bombing tribal peoples in a terrifying demonstration of its unassailable power. The policy was believed to be peculiarly appropriate to the vast spaces of "Arabia"; its main theater was Mesopotamia, which Britain had occupied in the last stages of World War I and which, as Satia (2008) notes, provided "the only significant British experience of bombing before World War Two" (p. 253). Winston Churchill, who was Minister for Air and War at the time, was an ardent supporter of terror through bombing, and although the original policy was racially inflected, it is not altogether surprising that by June 1940 he could be found vowing to "make Germany a desert, yes a desert" (Friedrich, 2002/2006, p. 61). Churchill was not the only architect of the bombing offensive to cut his teeth in Mesopotamia. When the Kurds rebelled against the British occupation, the RAF launched a series of punitive air raids. As one senior officer reported with evident satisfaction, "[T]hey now know what real bombing means, in casualties and damage: they now know that within 45 min a full-sized village can be practically wiped out and a third of its inhabitants killed or injured[.]" That officer was Squadron Leader Arthur Harris, who became Commander-in-Chief of Bomber Command in February 1942.[7] "In the ruins of this dying village," Omissi (1990) suggests, "one can dimly perceive the horrific firestorms of Hamburg and Dresden" (p. 154).

On February 14, 1942, in preparation for Harris's assumption of command, the Air Staff issued a directive authorizing Bomber Command "to employ your effort without restriction" (Webster & Frankland, 1961b) and requiring "the primary object of your operations" to be "focused on the morale of the enemy civil population" (pp. 143–148). An annex was included stipulating four primary targets (Essen, Duisburg, Dusseldorf, and Cologne) and three alternatives (Bremen, Wilhelmshaven, and Emden), all within Gee radio-navigation range, and a series of more distant alternatives to be bombed if conditions were particularly favorable. This information was followed by a list of "precise"—military and industrial—targets, but the next day a memorandum from the Chief of the Air Staff clarified these instructions: "I suppose it is clear that the aiming-points are to be the built-up areas, *not,* for instance, the dockyards or aircraft facilities. . .. This must be made quite clear, if it is not already understood" (Hansen, 2008, p. 31). Part of the reason for preferring area bombing was pragmatic. The capacity for precision bombing was still limited and, as Strachan (2006) tartly observes, the RAF "hit cities because they were big targets" (p. 13), whereas it was much harder to hit factories distributed around their peripheries. But it was also a matter of conviction, and Strachan emphasizes that the key component of the bomb mix was not high explosives, which precision targeting would have implied, but incendiaries and, hence, fire: "a destructive agent which can feed on itself sucking in oxygen to create firestorms and having effects that are indiscriminate" (p. 13). Harris needed no telling; he pursued the policy with a determination and an enthusiasm that became an obsession. For him, Hansen (2008) writes, "the whole point of bombing was to destroy cities" (p. 273). In a memorandum written two days before Christmas 1943, Harris made it plain that "cities, including everything and everybody in them which is a help to the German war effort, are the objectives which Bomber Command in accordance with its directives is aiming to destroy," the overall objective, he repeated, being to "wipe out" or "eliminate entire German cities" (Biddle, 2002, pp. 220–221; Hansen, 2008, p. 159).

As Harris pursued his vision of urban cataclysm, a series of memoranda from the Air Ministry sought to establish a more nuanced policy that would accommodate the importance of economic targets. Fortnightly Industrial Target Reports had been issued since 1940, later called Industrial Damage Reports, but by November 1941, with some 2,400 targets listed in the target books at Bomber Command stations, the Air Ministry solicited guidance on "what specific industries were the best targets as well as what towns should be the primary objects of area bombing" (Webster & Frankland, 1961a, p. 460). Targets were assigned a key point rating (a measure of industrial importance) and a key point factor (based on the proportion of the urban population engaged in or dependent on industrial production). These measures were tabulated in a comprehensive survey ("the Bomber's Baedeker") that was published in January 1943 and extended in August 1944 (Hohn, 1994). But Harris would not be deflected. He had no time for the Ministry of Economic Warfare and its targeting priorities, which he repeatedly dismissed as a "panacea." He kept careful score and, by the summer of 1943, "wanted everyone to see for themselves what the bomber offensive was doing to Germany" (Harris, 1947/1990, p. 149). He ordered the preparation of a large book (which eventually extended to several volumes), the so-called Blue Book, which would show the "spectacular" results of the bomber offensive. "After each attack on a German city," he explained, "the area of devastation was progressively marked with blue paint over a mosaic of air photographs of the city as a whole" (p. 149). Harris was immensely proud of this "inventory of destruction," as Biddle (2002, p. 218) calls it, and showed it to all his prominent visitors.[8] But he was even more proud of the destruction itself, and the language used in internal memoranda made no secret of the fact that moral bombing had become "terror bombing." After the air raids on Dresden and Pforzheim in February 1945, Harris noted that Bomber Command had "now destroyed 63 German towns" in what was "popularly known as a deliberate terror attack" (Hansen, 2008, p. 246).[9]

By the end of the following month, even Churchill had become alarmed and wondered whether "the moment has come when the question of bombing of German cities simply for the sake of increasing the terror, *though under other pretexts*, should be reviewed. Otherwise we shall come into control of an utterly ruined land" (Hansen, 2008, p. 260). He called for "more precise" concentration on

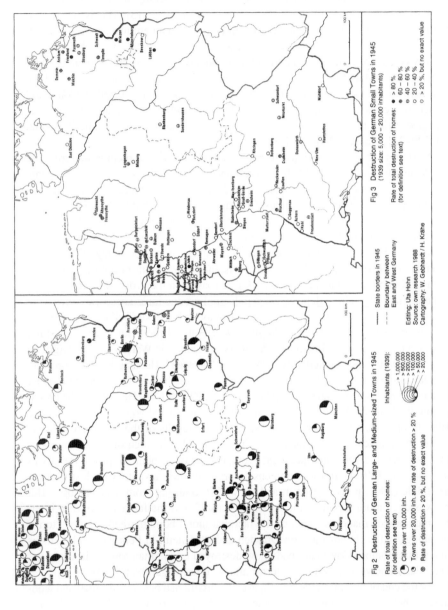

Fig. 1 The Allied bombing of Germany. Source: Hohn 1994

military objectives rather than "mere acts of terror and wanton destruction, however impressive" (p. 260). This was private talk rather than public discussion; there had been condemnation of the bombing offensive by some politicians, commentators, and clerics, but Churchill's self-serving minute offended many of those involved in the conduct of the campaign. The Chief of Air Staff demanded that the Prime Minister withdraw it, and the revised version noted only that "We must see to it that our attacks do not do more harm to ourselves in the long run than they do to the enemy's immediate war effort" (Biddle, 2002, p. 260). But changing the words could not alter the consequences. By the end of the war, 131 German towns and cities had been bombed, and 80% of those with populations of more than 100,000 had been seriously damaged or devastated (Fig. 1; for a detailed discussion, see Hohn, 1994).

W. G. Sebald and the Air War

In the late autumn of 1997 W. G. Sebald delivered a short series of lectures in Zurich on the Allied bombing campaign. They were published in the *Neuer Zürcher Zeitung*, revised as *Luftkrieg und Literatur* and published in Germany in 1999, and translated into English in a slightly different form as *On the natural history of destruction* in 2003. Sebald acknowledged that World War II had raised acute questions about German complicity and guilt that had animated scholarly and public debate for decades, yet in his view this interrogation had produced an astonishingly partial process of accounting. "In spite of strenuous efforts to come to terms with the past," he argued, "it seems to me that we Germans today are a nation strikingly blind to history." For "when we turn to take a retrospective view, particularly of the years 1930–1950, we are always looking and looking away at the same time" (Sebald, 1999/2003, p. ix). The focus had been on Germans as perpetrators of war crimes and on the profound problems—philosophical, existential, and historiographical—involved in representing and, hence, accounting for the Holocaust. Much of Sebald's own fictional work had been preoccupied with the same issues. His purpose in Zurich was not to revive the historians' debate of the 1980s, however, but to explore the sense in which Germans were *also* the victims of an air war whose fury was immensely difficult to recover. And in both cases, it was impossible to find the terms for analysis and atonement—and, crucially, prevention—without representation.

> The destruction, on a scale without precedent, entered the annals of the nation as it set about rebuilding itself, only in the form of vague generalizations. It seems to have left scarcely a trace of pain behind in the collective consciousness, it has been largely obliterated from the retrospective understanding of those affected, and it never played any appreciable part in the discussion of the internal constitution of our country. As Alexander Kluge later confirmed, it never became an experience capable of public decipherment. (Sebald, 1999/2003, p. 4)[10]

Sebald was not equating the Holocaust with the air war, but even with that allowance several critics were skeptical of his claim. Childers (2005, p. 78), invoking a familiar calculus, insisted that the scale of destruction was nothing compared to the deaths of Polish or Soviet citizens at the hands of the Nazis. Others doubted that the silence was as total as Sebald imagined. According to Hage (2005, see also 2003, 2006), the issue was less one of production than of reception. "Many novels and stories about the bombing were published," he argued, but "they were quickly and completely forgotten" (2005, p. 266).[11] Yet that collective amnesia was precisely Sebald's point, which he sharpened through a discussion of memory that spiraled through his exploration of a "natural history of destruction."

Sebald found the phrase in an essay that had been proposed by British government scientist Solly Zuckerman—but which, significantly, remained unwritten. Trained in zoology and anatomy, Zuckerman joined the Ministry of Home Security's Research and Experiments Department early in the war to study the effects of blast on the human body. His expertise rapidly widened to include a systematic study of the statistics and logistics of bombing as part of the fledgling science of operations research, and he became Scientific Director of the RAF's Bombing Analysis Unit. In 1943 he was appointed to Combined Operations Headquarters and in January 1944 joined the Allied Expeditionary Air Force's planning team for D-Day. He was a fierce opponent of area bombing, and in March 1944 his dogged attempts to persuade military planners to switch to strategic attacks on the rail network in occupied Europe were dismissed by Harris as "a panacea" devised "by a civilian professor whose peacetime forte is the study of the sexual aberrations of the higher apes" (Biddle, 2002, p. 235; Hansen, 2008, pp. 171–173). The jibe combined arrogance and ignorance in equal measure. Zuckerman (1978) described himself as a "professional student of destruction" who had learned "not be over-impressed" (p. 218) by photographs of it. At their very first meeting Harris had invited him "to admire aerial photographs of destroyed German cities" (p. 218) in his Blue Book, but Zuckerman had seen many of them before and remained unconvinced. Later, "once the noise of exploding bombs had died away, and the sense of fear that went with it," he wrote, "I always wanted to get as quickly as possible to the places that suffered" (p. 324). He was not alone. "Almost everyone who had played any part in the arguments about the air-war," he said, "wanted to see the rubble of Germany with their own eyes" (p. 324). But none of his calculations and analyses prepared him for what he eventually saw when, in December 1944, he visited Aachen. Close to Germany's border with Belgium and the Netherlands, the city had been subjected to a devastating air raid in the summer of 1943, and then, on the night of April 11–12, 1944, most of what was left had been destroyed in a raid that Friedrich (2002/2006) reports "churned up the ground in an unparalleled concentration" (p. 246). Over 60% of the remaining buildings were destroyed and more than 1,500 people killed. There were two more raids the following month, and then, just before ground troops occupied the city, artillery flattened what was left. The American officer who directed the barrage described the destruction as "the worst I've ever seen. Nobody will ever know what this has been like up here" (p. 119). Zuckerman was no less affected; the devastation was "greater in extent than anything I had ever seen," he wrote (Zuckerman, 1978, p. 309). Later that month he returned to Britain and dined with Cyril Connolly, editor of the literary periodical *Horizon*. "I had been so moved by the devastation I had seen in Aachen, which I described to him," he recalled, "that he eagerly agreed to my suggestion that I should write for him a piece to the title 'The Natural History of Destruction'" (p. 322).[12]

Zuckerman returned to Germany the following spring and, following the Allied advance, arrived in Cologne in early April. This city had been the target of the first "Thousand Bomber raid" on the night of May 30–31, 1942, which one pilot compared to "rush-hour in a three-dimensional circus": 1,455 tons of bombs (high explosive and incendiaries) were dropped on the city in just 90 min, creating raging infernos that devastated 600 acres (E. Taylor, 2004).[13] It was bombed repeatedly thereafter, including large raids on October 15–16, 1942; February 26–27, 1943; June 16–17, 1943; June 28–29, 1943; July 4–5, 1943; and July 8–9, 1943. Finally, on March 2, 1945, four days before the city fell to ground troops, 858 aircraft sealed "the end of Cologne" (Friedrich, 2002/2006, pp. 222–225; Hansen, 2008, pp. 69, 148).[14] American war correspondents got there before Zuckerman. Sidney Olson cabled *TIME* and *LIFE* magazines:

> The first impression was that of silence and emptiness. When we stopped the jeep you heard nothing, you saw no movement down the great deserted avenues lined with empty white boxes. We looked vainly for people. In a city of 700,000 none now seemed alive. But there were people, perhaps some 120,000 of them. They had gone underground. They live and work in a long series of cellars, "mouseholes," cut from one house to the next. (Olson, 1945, p. 28)

In her "Letter from Cologne," published in the *New Yorker* on 19 March 1945, Janet Flanner (as cited in Wilms, 2006, p. 189) described the city as "a model of destruction" so comprehensively destroyed that maps were no longer needed because the streets, squares, and parks had ceased to exist. Although these writers found what Wilms calls a "usable language of destruction" (p. 189), Zuckerman simply could not.[15] His first view of the devastated city, and particularly of the area around the cathedral—"to this day I incorrectly visualize that great church standing in some vast square" (Fig. 2)—made it impossible for him to complete his report for Connolly, saying that it cried out for more eloquence than he could muster (Zuckerman, 1978, p. 322).[16] Sebald notes that Zuckerman was so "overwhelmed by what he had seen" that he found it impossible to convey the enormity of the destruction. Years later, when Sebald asked him about it, all Zuckerman could remember was a surreal still life, "the image of the blackened cathedral rising from the stony desert around it, and the memory of a severed finger that he had found on a heap of rubble." It is immediately after this passage that Sebald asks: "How ought such a natural history of destruction to begin?" (Sebald, 1999/2003, pp. 31–33).[17]

Sebald's recovery of Zuckerman's "natural history" raises two important questions. The first, naturally enough, is how Zuckerman understood the phrase. Because his report was never written, it is impossible know for sure; but given Zuckerman's training, it is not surprising that his interventions over the direction of the bombing campaign should have had recourse to biological-physiological metaphors that conjured up a natural history of sorts. Zuckerman intended these metaphors to convey the effects of bombing not on the human body, however, but on the body politic. He made it clear that he was interested in "the functional inferences" that could be drawn "from aerial photographs of devastated towns" (Zuckerman,

Fig. 2 Cologne, 1945 (permission to reprint by abracus Gmbh)

1978, p. 218), "translating areas of physical destruction into a functional assessment" (p. 242), and when he attempted to persuade his opponents of the need to target transportation nodes, he said he "constantly resorted to biological analogies" like arteries, circulation, and paralysis to show that the first priority ought to be "to disrupt a system" (p. 240). This usage was not unprecedented. Similar metaphors could be found in the RAF's *War Manual* in 1935, and Overy (2005) notes that "biological metaphors were commonly used in describing targets" while "paradoxically ignoring the many thousands of real bodies that bombing would destroy" (p. 284).[18] There was nothing paradoxical about it, of course: It was a studied exercise in abstraction. Sebald's (1999/2003) enumeration of possible prefaces to a "natural history of destruction" identifies other strategies that work to the same end: "a summary of the technical, organizational and political prerequisites for carrying out large-scale air-raids"; "a scientific account of the previously unknown phenomenon of the firestorms"; "a pathographical record of typical modes of death" (p. 33). But in each case, significantly, these possibilities are followed by a question mark.

Sebald's rhetorical hesitation is significant, I suggest, because what he understood by a "natural history of destruction" was something different. This is the second question, needless to say, and the most common answer to it has attracted the fiercest criticism. Many commentators have focused on a series of images that Sebald deploys in his description of the air raids on Hamburg between July 24 and

August 2, 1943—"Operation Gomorrah"—which killed 45,000 people in a single week. Sebald (1999/2003) writes of "the whole airspace [as] a sea of flames" (p. 26), a firestorm on the ground "of hurricane force" whose flames "rolled like a tidal wave" through the streets, and smoke rising high in the air to form "a vast, anvil-shaped cumulonimbus cloud" (p. 27). He then describes "horribly disfigured corpses," flames still flickering around them, "doubled up in pools of their own melted fat," and "clumps of flesh and bone" and bodies reduced so completely to ash so that the remains of whole families "could be carried away in a single laundry basket" (p. 28).

Sebald's critics object that the opening images reduce the air war to a natural disaster "for which no ordinary person was responsible but from which everyone eventually suffered" (Crew, 2007, p. 132), that a "natural history" of destruction conceived in such terms "assimilates a human-induced and -produced cataclysm into an event of nature" so that it "ontologizes and neutralizes a human product, an historical event" (Mendieta, 2007, note 14). Others conclude that Sebald's morbid anatomy of grotesquely deformed bodies shows that he has no interest in excavating the cultural landscape of terror, pain, and suffering: that, in effect, he multiplies Zuckerman's abstracted image of the cathedral and the finger. Thus Barnouw (2005) pointedly subtitles her counternarrative of the air war "a *moral* history of destruction" and objects:

> Sebald is not interested in the people who experienced these horrors and have had to live with the trauma they left behind. He is interested in the hyper-physical effects of this kind of destruction: the ruins of the Cathedral and the severed finger, the shrunk purpled corpses, the congealed fat of the bodies cured by fire; the surreally clear, incomprehensible mass transformations. (p. 115)

I think this criticism is unfair, not least (but not only) because it ignores the testimony of those who survived. The extraordinary firestorms produced by the raids *were* acutely physical in their causes and effects, and survivors repeatedly used the same images to describe them: a "sea of flames," "a hurricane," and even "a volcanic eruption." "The word *Flammenmeer*—'sea of flames'—comes up again and again in accounts of the firestorm," one historian notes, and is "a literal description of what those people saw: a vast sea of fire in the grip of a hurricane" (Lowe, 2007, p. 213). But I think the characterization is unfair for another reason too. Sebald only raises his question about how a natural history of destruction might begin after describing the raids on Hamburg; whatever one might make of these paragraphs, they surely cannot be read as an answer to a question that had not yet been asked.

On these readings, however, a truly critical and *non*natural history of destruction must necessarily recoil from physical and physiological images to recover the experience of survivors-as-victims. In his own account of the raids on Hamburg, Lowe (2007) endorses Sebald's claim that "Germans have collectively avoided looking at the ordeal they experienced" (p. xiv). But he adds an arresting coda: the British and Americans have also looked away. "After the bombs have been dropped, and the surviving bombers have returned home," he continues, "the story tends to end.

What happened on the ground, to the cities full of people beneath the bombs, is rarely talked about" (p. xv).[19]

Beneath the Bombs

This silence is the starting point of the most controversial post-Sebald history of the air war, Jörg Friedrich's *Der Brand*, which was first serialized in the tabloid *Bild-Zeitung*, then published as a book in 2002 and translated into English as *The Fire* in 2006.[20] Because "the air war didn't happen in the air, as most of the British and American literature has it," Friedrich (2007) explains that he begins his narrative "at the moment the Anglo-American literature stops, when the bomb hits the ground" (p. 12).[21] Even his opponents concede that his representation of the experience of those crouching beneath the bombs is consummately powerful. For Childers (2005), for example, Friedrich provides "descriptions of the devastation and carnage so vivid, so achingly painful, that they are almost unbearable to read" (p. 77). They deliver "one visceral emotional shock after another" because they are not couched in "antiseptic military language" that would "numb the senses and rob the experience of its barbaric reality" (p. 77). Yet those shocks affronted many of Friedrich's readers, who interpreted his consciously creative, literary prose as symptomatic of a failure of *moral* imagination. Film critic Andreas Kilb dismissed it as "an act of hysterical expressivity" (Friedrich, 2007). Friedrich received an equally cool reception from reviewers in Britain and America who privileged the objectivist language of Science—like the air power theory in which Zuckerman had been immersed and which had left him so bereft in Cologne—and the objectivist canons of a History aimed at a singular Truth. From the US Air War College at Maxwell Air Force Base, Friedrich was accused of writing "in terms of images, experience and emotion" and "providing graphic descriptions of human suffering at the expense of a careful, chronological reconstruction of the air war against Germany" (Peifer, 2004, p. 123).[22] The charge was a common one; Childers (2005) was only one of many to object that Friedrich "decouples the air assault on Hitler's Germany from its proper historical framework" (p. 78).[23] Comments like these not only assume that affect has no place in historical inquiry; they also assume that there is a single—"careful," "proper"—historical framework whose propriety is to be measured by its capacity to vindicate those who orchestrated the bombing campaign.

In a parallel indictment, Friedrich is said to describe the bombing war in language that had been reserved for the Holocaust. This claim is more complicated than it appears. Although the English-language edition of Sebald's Zurich lectures has "destruction" in its new title, the word used in the body of the original text is *Vernichtung,* which is usually translated as "annihilation" or "extermination," vocubulary which makes Sebald vulnerable to the same accusation.[24] But it is an absolutist one that ignores the fact that this rebarbative language ran like a red thread throughout contemporary British discussions of the bomber offensive. I have already noted Harris's explicit determination to 'eliminate entire

German cities', and Sebald cities a memorandum written by Churchill in June 1940 to Lord Beaverbrook, Minister for Aircraft Production to the same effect: "There is only one thing that will bring ... [Hitler] down, and that is an absolutely devastating, exterminating attack by very heavy bombers" (see also Biddle, 2002, p. 188; Overy, 2005, p. 288).[25] After the war the American critic Lewis Mumford revised his seminal account of *The Culture of Cities* (1938) under the title *The City in History* and made a direct comparison: "Besides the millions of people—six million Jews alone—killed by Germans in their suburban extermination camps[,]... whole cities were turned into extermination camps by the demoralized strategists of democracy" (Mumford, 1961/1987, p. 634). Friedrich's (2002/2006) use of this language is more elaborate and systematic than any of these writers—air-raid shelters and cellars as ovens and crematoria (pp. 93, 167, 340) and "execution sites" (p. 313); the RAF's No. 5 Bomber Group as "No. 5 Mass Destruction Group" (p. 306)—but I do not believe that it is intended to assimilate the air war to the Holocaust, still less to affirm some moral calculus in which the deaths of as many as 600,000 German civilians are to be weighed against the murder of six million Jews.[26] The two are incommensurable, but it is more than magnitude that holds them apart. For the air war was not conducted in order to bring the Holocaust to an end, and so the enormity of the one cannot eclipse the horror of the other—unless the fury of the bombing campaign is seen as retribution and the postwar silence over its victims as atonement. Friedrich refuses this reading and instead brings the two together in a different, profoundly nonsacralized register. His language is calculated to deliver not only an emotional shock, as Childers (2005) says, but also an ethical one. Friedrich aims to provoke an otherwise mute sensibility into acknowledging that both the Holocaust and the air war were systematic, concerted campaigns of the mass killing of noncombatants that combined a thoroughly modern, scientific-technological apparatus with an atavistic dehumanization and, at the limit, a nullification of the enemy other. There are crucial differences, to be sure, and the realization of the Holocaust relied on the production of a serial spatiality that cannot be assimilated to that of the bombing campaign (Clarke, Doel, & McDonough, 1996; Doel & Clarke, 1998).[27] But Friedrich shows the language of the bomber offensive, indeed its very *grammar* (Friedrich, 2002/2006, p. 169), was also articulated through a spatiality that produced its own distinctive necropolitics. After pathfinders and bombers began to divide up the work, the grammar of targeting changed:

> The pathfinder no longer indicated a point but outlined an area. It was then not a matter of "hitting" discrete objects within the area—instead, the demarcated area comprised all that was to be removed from the world. Annihilation is the spatial extension of death. The victim does not die his death, because he does not have one. He finds himself in a sphere in which life has ceased. (Friedrich, 2002/2006, p. 69)

From the beginning of 1942, Friedrich continues, "Bomber Command had not only the will but also the basic technology to create an annihilation zone. This zone was the sector of a city. An act of war was the process by which the sector was brought into a state of annihilation" (p. 69).

I attribute the critical force of Friedrich's project to the way in which his rendering of the processes through which these spaces were performed disrupts the objectivist language of Science with the force-field of affect and unbuttons the framework of History through the irruptions of memory. The memoir of an Australian navigator in Bomber Command captures something of what I mean. Returning from a mission over Germany, he recalled that he "would try to tell myself then that this was a city, a place inhabited by beings such as ourselves, a place with the familiar sights of civilization" (Charlwood, 1956/2000, p. 131). But "the thought would carry little conviction":

> A German city was always this, this hellish picture of flame, gunfire and searchlights, an unreal picture because we could not hear it or feel its breath. Sometimes when the smoke rolled back and we saw streets and buildings I felt startled. Perhaps if we had seen the white, upturned faces of people, as over England we sometimes did, our hearts would have rebelled. (p. 131)

Friedrich's achievement is to recover those spectral faces in the spaces in which *and through which* they were erased.

The affective force of Friedrich's account and the extraordinary public attention it commanded (including special issues of *Der Spiegel* and *GEO*) help explain why, only months after *Der Brand* was published in the fall of 2002, many Germans invoked the Allied air war in their protests against the impending US-led invasion of Iraq. Those who did so were arguing "less from the moral certainty of having been victims than from the fear of becoming perpetrators again" (Grossman as cited in Nolan, 2005, p. 26). Granted, there was a well-founded conviction that the invasion would violate international law. But Grossman's reading arguably provides a better explanation of German *support* for Luftwaffe participation in the NATO bombing of the former Yugoslavia in 1999—when "the threat of genocide hung in the air" (Huyssen, 2003b, p. 165)—than of German *opposition* to the bombing of Iraq four years later.[28] As it happens, Friedrich supported the invasion, but he also affirmed that "the stance of the Germans and their spiritual place is since 1945 beneath the bombs and never in the bombers" (Moeller, 2006, p. 113), a claim that implies not a "moral certainty" but certainly a post-*Brand* affinity with the victims of bombing. In that respect the question of memory is crucial. When the US offensive opened in March 2003 with the spectacular bombing of Baghdad, *Der Spiegel* reported that "[m]any observers were reminded of Dresden as the pictures of unbridled explosive power and merciless destruction were broadcast around the world. Just as in 1945, new bombing terror was being unleashed on the banks of the Tigris for freedom" ("Höllenfeuer", 2003, p. 13).

Huyssen had no quarrel with a critique of the doctrine of preemptive war, but he wholly rejected these parallels as a "self-serving" invocation of German suffering during the air war. While he accepted that Friedrich was not the Nolte of a second historians' debate—the right-wing historian had insisted that the Holocaust was a defensive reaction to Soviet aggression and claimed a moral equivalence between it and the air war—Huyssen (2003b) argued that *Der Brand* had "expanded the present backwards, offering the growing opposition to the Iraq war a decontextualized and experiential take on German history that made Baghdad look like Dresden, the firestorms of the 1940s like the 'shock and awe' campaign of the allies, and the Germans into the arbiters of history" (p. 168). This passage is a theoretically inflected restatement of the previous objections. Huyssen summons the same two bogey words—*Der Brand* as "decontextualized" and "experiential"—to claim that Friedrich's artful combination of text and photographs traps his readers "in an imaginary in which the firestorms of Hamburg and Dresden are immediately present, ready to be linked to other sets of images soon to explode on television screens once the bombing of Baghdad began" (p. 10).

In this context, too, it seems, memory is to be disciplined by History.[29] Indeed, the Bush administration invoked World War II as a memory model for its "liberation" of Iraq (Saddam as Hitler, the delusions of appeasement, the reunion of the Allies). Although it may well be true, as Schama (2004) observed, that "memory craves the reassurance of the Good War in the middle of a bad one" (n.p.), I think Zehfuss (2007) was much closer to the mark when she insisted that the countermemory invoked by those protesting against the invasion of Iraq did not entail conflating the two. It was about empathy, not identity. *"At issue is not an analogy between the bombing of German cities during the Second World War and the Iraq war but the impact which the memories of the former may have on our political imagination in relation to the latter"* (Zehfuss, 2007, pp. 119–120; my emphasis). Through this collective, intrinsically cultural memory, she continued, "the Other may be recognized as Self: we are able to empathise" (p. 120). And our ability to do so is crucially dependent on affect because "memory cannot be grasped within the context of a narrowly conceived rationality; it is in part significant because of the emotions attached and aroused by it" (Zehfuss, 2007, pp. 225–226).

But Zehfuss (2007) added a significant rider. "There is a quality to memory beyond what may be simply described," she argued, so that "the memory—be it of an unspeakable horror of something else—may never entirely be grasped by language" (p. 226). As I now want to show, this elusiveness returns us to the dilemma posed by a natural history of destruction. I have shown that Sebald was criticized for using a language that supposedly disabled the ascription of responsibility for the air war and was indifferent to the human suffering caused by it, whereas Friedrich, who sought to recover the experience of its victims, was accused of resorting to a language that issued in a naïve emotionalism or, worse, an apologetics. It is high time to see if Sebald's "natural history of destruction" might mean something different.

The Natural History of Destruction

In my view, most of the critical responses to the idea of a natural history of destruction have failed to take seriously Zuckerman's inability to convey what he had seen. His attempt to render the devastation of Cologne in "natural" or "physiological" terms (which is what I suggested *his* sense of natural history required) was overwhelmed by an inability to make the ruined landscape meaningful. This failure of ordinary language is central to Sebald's account. The survivors, even more than Zuckerman, confronted "a world that could no longer be presented in comprehensible terms," and like them (though also, of course, unlike them), Sebald (1999/2003) is struck by the incapacity of ordinary language to convey the extraordinary; it was simply inadequate to the task of rendering "the reality of total destruction" (p. 10).[30] More than this, there is an intimate connection between the destruction of a city and the ruin of language, which novelist Peter Ho Davies (2007) conveys through an arresting image of bomb-damaged Liverpool:

> Esther stares out at the ruins around her. . . . A single gutted house still stands at the end of one flattened terrace like an exclamation mark, and she suddenly sees the streets as sentences in a vast book, sentences that have had their nouns and verbs scored through, rubbed out, until they no longer make any sense. (p. 282)[31]

Ward (2006a, 2006b) suggests that "ruin" in Sebald's oeuvre more generally marks a site of broken narration. These ruins are dispersed, and they mark traumas that rupture language and leave visible, often photographic traces that evade or confound linguistic expression. This is the very ground of a natural history of destruction, which, in turn, implies that most of the critical responses to such a project have also failed to take Sebald seriously. In one of the most overreaching commentaries on Sebald, Mendieta (2007) objects that the reference to a "natural history" in the title of the posthumous English translation of the Zurich lectures is misleading and asserts—on what basis I don't know—that it is "not one that Sebald would have chosen" (p. 14). Yet, as I have shown, Sebald clearly regarded the possibility of a natural history of destruction as a crucial question. In fact, he had explored the idea in relation to the air war in an earlier essay where he noted Zuckerman's abandoned project and discussed a radically different concept of natural history to the one vilified by his critics (Sebald, 1982, pp. 365–366).[32] For the concept of natural history—and it is a concept, not a wish image—derives from Adorno and Benjamin (it is also found in Arendt), and it marks both the difficulty that Zuckerman faced—the resistance of a ruined, reified world to interpretation—and the ground of Sebald's own inquiry: the site at which memory falters.

"Natural history" conceived in these terms is located at the dialectical intersection of Nature and History or, as Pensky (2004) has it, of "physical matter and the production of meaning" (p. 233) It brings into view a reified, obdurately physical world—for Adorno and Benjamin, the commodity landscape of capitalist modernity; for Sebald, the moonscape of modern war—that has been hollowed out and emptied of human meaning. These landscapes thus appear to be "artificially natural" (p. 232). Pensky's is an intricate discussion, and it is impossible to convey its subtleties here. But the crux of the matter is captured in a remarkable image in A. L. Kennedy's novel *Day* (2007), where Allied aircrew are being flown back to Britain after the liberation of their prisoner of war camps:

> [T]hey flew low and level above the bombed thing that was Germany, above their work. As if the cities had been eaten, as if something unnatural had fed on them until they were gashes and shells and staring spaces, as if it was still down there like a plague in the dust. (p. 271)

There is a hideous literalness to this image, and Sebald (1999/2003) describes a "striking change in the natural order of the cities" (p. 34) in the weeks after the air raids: a "sudden and alarming increase in the parasitical creatures thriving on the unburied bodies" (p. 34); a "multiplication of species that are usually suppressed in every possible way" (p. 35); in short, the burgeoning populations of rats and flies, the "repulsive fauna of the rubble" (p. 35)—as if the cities were being ravaged all over again. These are extraordinary passages, in which Sebald documents sensation without feeling, morphology without meaning, and records life reasserting itself without language (Nossack, 1948/2004, identified rats and flies as "the new lords of the city" [p. 46]). In doing so, his descriptions of a mutely physical geography evoke an altogether different plane that is also conveyed through Kennedy's image: the existential difficulty of recognizing the ruined landscape as the product of human action. Indeed, to recognize it *as* a human creation would be so unbearably traumatic that language would be replaced by silence. As you approached the center of Cologne, the New Statesman reported in July 1945, you saw only "a white sea of rubble, faceless and featureless in the bright sunlight," like "the sprawling skeleton of a giant animal" (as quoted in Wyman, 1998, p. 16).[33] Such a "charnel house of rotted interiorities," as Lukàcs described the fetishized landscape of capitalism, cannot be recovered through memory (quoted in Adorno, 1984, p. 118). Pensky (2004) insists that natural history is directed *against* the claim of memory as recuperation or recollection and that it works instead to recover "only concrete, singular and utterly empirical facts and bodies, each 'transient,' which is to say incapable of being incorporated into a meaning-giving conception of historical continuity and historical experience" (pp. 233–234). Pensky's reading also explains Sebald's (1999/2003) repeated insistence on a "concrete and documentary" approach (p. 58). And against those who propose a counternatural or "moral" history of destruction to Sebald's, it is necessary to insist that "transience" here *is* a moral term, a mark of what Pensky (2004) calls "the forgetting of the bodily suffering that constitutes the materiality of historical time" (p. 243). In short, there is, in the production of this reified, ruined world, "a functional equivalence between 'that which suffers' and 'that which cannot (must not) be remembered'" (p. 243).

These are significant elaborations, but Pensky (2004, p. 232; see also Buck-Morss, 1989) also shows that natural history operates through a particular "way of seeing" or a scopic regime. This observation speaks directly to Sebald's project, too: not only to the optical anxiety to which he draws attention—"we are always looking and looking away at the same time (1999/2003, p. ix)"—but also to the visual register that enframes his own account. Sebald's use of photographs in his work has attracted considerable critical commentary, but Duttlinger (2007) has argued that their incorporation in *Luftkrieg und Literatur* (the same images reappear in the English translation) departs from the photographic strategies that inform his literary texts. She is concerned that the totalizing aerial views of destroyed cities (an unsourced photograph of Frankfurt and a photograph of Halberstadt borrowed from Kluge) are not subjected to interrogation. They invite the viewer "to adopt a detached stance" by staging "an abstract geometrical survey which gives the viewer a sense of mastery in the face of chaos," she contends (p. 166), and in doing so "starkly parallel the perspective of the Allied planes during the attacks"

Fig. 3 Lancaster bomber over Hamburg. The photograph was taken on the night of January 30–31, 1943, which was the first raid in which H2S was used by Pathfinder aircraft to navigate the bomber stream to the target. This raid was thus *not* the one described by W. G. Sebald

(p. 172) (as shown in the image Sebald reproduces of a bomber over Hamburg; see Fig. 3).[34]

This optical detachment animates Sebald's narrative of the bombing of Hamburg, which is punctuated by a series of aerial perspectives, opening with what Presner (2004) calls "a high-angle establishing shot" (p. 354) from the viewpoint of the bombers, and then "a kind of cinematic logic" (p. 355) that swoops down to the ground only to return to the air. Duttlinger (2007) glimpses a critical potentiality in this movement, but it is at best a fleeting one: "What starts out as a position of mastery, an ordered overview, can suddenly tip over into a state of vertiginous disorientation at the sight of destruction" (p. 177).

But I think there is another critical potentiality to be seen in Sebald's account. For these shifts between the air and the ground are mirrored in a stream of measurements: 10,000 tons of bombs, a target area of 20 km^2, flames rising 2,000 m, fire advancing at over 150 km/h, smoke rising to a height of 8,000 m. The result is, as Presner shows, a modernist montage that multiplies different perspectives; it furnishes what Sebald (1999/2003) himself saw as "a synoptic and artificial view" (p. 26), which, so Hell (2004) argues, "positions us between the illusion of immediate visual access and the consciousness that our 'seeing' is highly mediated" (p. 370). That critical awareness of mediation, which is what Duttlinger (2007) believes Sebald to marginalize, depends on the "establishing shot" and the return to the enframing of the city-as-target. As I want to show, however, it also depends on a matrix of measurements, a lethal calculus that abstracted, ensnared, and transformed living cities into dead ones.

This calculus took the form of a progressively developing chain—described today as the "kill-chain"—that extended from the identification of targets to their destruction. It included the collection and analysis of aerial reconnaissance photographs and the collation of target books and target folders. From January 1943 on, it also encompassed the assignment of numerical and graphical key point ratings and key point factors to establish a hierarchy of targets, as I noted in the first section of this chapter. By the end of that year it also involved the production of zone maps of target cities, based on the work of geographer R. E. Dickinson, showing population and building densities that were essential for calibrating and setting firestorms (Fig. 4) (Hohn, 1994). The chain also included the production of stylized target maps, which were limited to outlined shapes in grey, purple, black, and white—further detail would have been superfluous because the RAF conducted area

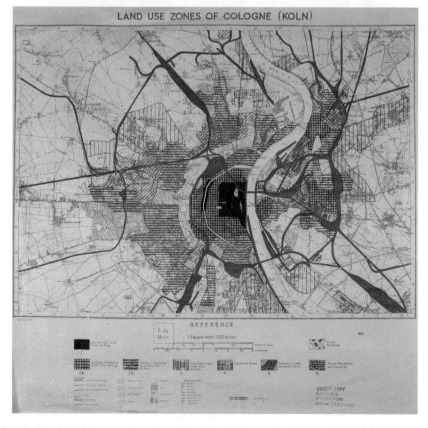

Fig. 4 Royal Air Force zone map of Cologne (permission to reprint, British Library)

bombing at night—together with the position of antiaircraft batteries, Luftwaffe air-
fields, and decoy fires. Concentric circles radiated out from the target at 1 mile
intervals (Fig. 5).[35] From January 1943 ground-scanning H2S radar allowed these
maps to be supplemented by crude real-time images of the outline of the target on
the aircraft's Plan Position Indicator screen (Fig. 6).[36] Finally, there was the intricate choreography of the raid itself, which from December 1942 was orchestrated
by a "Master Bomber," a Pathfinder circling above the target to direct the bombers
through a shifting grid of flares and red and green markers dropped to outline the target area and, to correct for creep-back, to recenter the force over the aiming point(s).
The aerial photographs taken during each raid fed back to start the next cycle, and

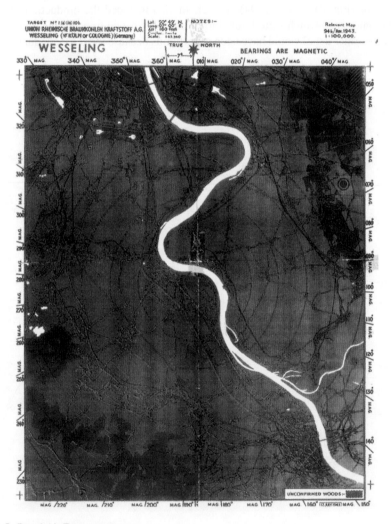

Fig. 5 Royal Air Force target map

Fig. 6 H2S ground-scanning radar image of the type that enabled Royal Air Force bombers to have an outline of their targets (as of 1943)

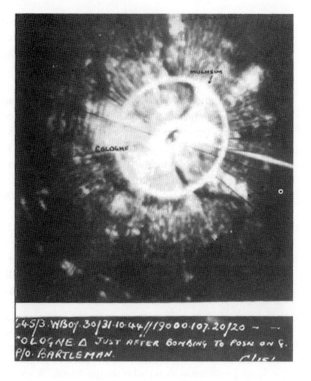

when on February 28, 1944, LIFE published Bob Landry's photographs of Harris poring over the views of destruction in his Blue Book, the headline read: "The brain behind the death of Berlin looks at his work from afar" (p. 38). As that caption implied, the kill-chain was thus a concatenation of aerial views produced through a process of calculation that was also a process of abstraction.

Sebald's stream of measurements mimics this process, although he does not refer to it. But drawing out the chain, even in this incomplete form, makes it clear that the mediations involved in enframing the city as a target were by no means secure. None of the images was stable, including the maps that were nominally fixed. Far from being "immutable mobiles," as Latour (1987, p. 227) would have it, they were all subject to constant revision, annotation, and interpretation at each of the points through which the chain extended.[37] And their tacit promise to produce the effects they named—the reduction of a city to a target and thence to rubble—was always conditional. The bomber did not always get through, as Stanley Baldwin had predicted in 1932, and mortality rates in the air were extremely high because there was an elaborate German counterimaginary, a parallel system that tracked and enframed the bomber as the target. The system was revised after the attacks on Hamburg in 1943. This counterchain extended from ground observers, listening posts, and radar stations, which were grouped into sectors to plot an "air picture" (*Luftlage*) that was transmitted to the Luftwaffe's divisional fighter command centers or "opera houses," where a consolidated air picture (*Hauptluftlage*) was projected onto giant 1:50,000 maps on vertical frosted glass screens using colored beams of light. Intercept information was then transmitted to Luftwaffe Headquarters in Berlin, to other divisional fighter command centers, and out to searchlight batteries, flak batteries, and night-fighter squadrons across occupied Europe.

The two systems moved in counterpoint, and each rationalized its own kill-chain by subdividing its production and regulating its practices through standard operating procedures. This rationalization entailed not only an abstraction of the target *but also an abstraction of the process through which the target was produced,* which was made to appear inevitable—target as telos—and its destruction the terminus of a more or less "natural" history. It is in this sense, I think, that Sebald "regards the events of war precisely as a kind of condition that captures participants in its logic whatever their intentions" (Osborne, 2005, p. 111). In other words, the chain enframes the target *and entrains its operators.* The execution of an air raid was animated by a volatile mix of emotions—anger and fear, rivalry and comradeship, excitement and exultation among them—but they were filtered to leave what Alexander Kluge (1978), in his montage of the Allied bombing of Halberstadt, called the *Angriffsmethode*: the pure method of the strike.

> In the flight and the bombing, in the gradual purification from the troublesome ballast of reality, such as personal motivation, moral condemnation of what is to be bombed (moral-bombing), in the calculated know-how, the looking which is replaced by radar control, etc., there is a formalism. It is not aeroplanes. . . that are flying here; instead, a conceptual system is flying, a structure of ideas clad in tin. (pp. 65–66, 76; see also Bowie, 1982)

This effect was produced not only for those in the chain, enveloped in the conceptual system and the practices through which it was performed—the manuals and the maps, the drills and the procedures—but also for a watching public. In July 1941 the Crown Film Unit released Harry Watt's *Target for Tonight,* a dramatized documentary of the bombing of a military-industrial target in Germany, which had been made with the cooperation of Bomber Command using RAF personnel instead of actors. Early in the film the objective is described as "a peach of a target," and its plucking, mediated by a series of aerial photographs and maps meticulously followed by the camera, becomes purely axiomatic and perfectly natural. Indeed, this effect was so powerful that Graham Greene, writing in the *Spectator*, praised the film—and by implication the process that it represented—because everyone in the operation had carried out "their difficult and dangerous job in daily routine just like shop or office workers" so that "what we see is no more than a technical exercise" (Short, 1997, p. 195).[38]

If the visualizations that produced the target had performative force, however, then it is not only the sight of destruction on the ground that has the power to call the aerial mastery of this "technical exercise" into question. That critical response is common and, as Duttlinger (2007) suggests, depends on memory work that deliberately abandons detachment: hence Kluge's (1978) distinction between "the strategy from above" and "the strategy from below."[39] But in an illuminating discussion of the crisis of representation and modern war, Hüppauf (1993) argues that "an iconography based on an opposition between the human face and inhuman technology oversimplifies complex structures" (p. 46), and this opposition reappears in the usual separations between above and below, air and ground, bomber and bombed. I understand the gesture of imaginatively crouching beneath the bombs and establishing an affinity with their victims, but I also believe that by the time we do so it is too late. Another critical response is necessary to precede, supplement, and reinforce this act of empathy and its mobilization of memory: one that has the power to reveal and denaturalize the conceptual system through which the world is reduced to a target (Chow, 2006). This parallel response is the task of a truly critical natural history of destruction capable of addressing the present and future as well as the past.

Doors into Nowhere

Such a project can take many forms, but here I continue to focus on the explicitly visual register through a remarkable series of more than 60 images by American artist and scholar elin o'Hara slavick. I only have space for two of them: *Dresden* (Fig. 7) and *Baghdad* (Fig. 8). Although the sources for slavick's work are the media of modern war—the aerial photographs, surveillance imagery, and maps I have been discussing—and there is a photographic quality to her images, she works by hand rather than, say, video in the hope that her viewers will, like her, "take their time" (2006, p. 249) with them and "work to understand them on a deeper and more

Fig. 7 Dresden. From the series *Protesting cartography: Places the US has bombed* (mixed media on paper) (elin o'Hara slavick)

Fig. 8 Baghdad. From the
series *Protesting
cartography: Places the US
has bombed* (mixed media on
paper) (elin o'Hara slavick)

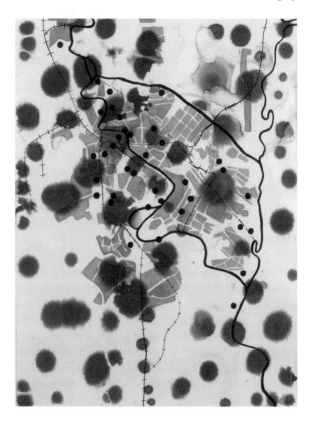

complicated level than they might when seeing a photograph" (2007, p. 98). She
begins by dropping ink or watercolor onto wet paper and uses "this common ground
of abstract swirling or bleeding" to suggest "the manner in which bombs do not
stay within their intended borders" (2006, p. 247). In doing so, she adopts an aerial
view—the position of the bombers—in order to stage *and to subvert* the power of
aerial mastery. The drawings are made beautiful "to seduce the viewer," she says
(2007, p. 97), to draw them into the deadly embrace of the image only to have their
pleasure disrupted when they take a closer look. "Like an Impressionist or Pointillist
painting," slavick explains, "I wish for the viewer to be captured by the colors and
lost in the patterns and then to have their optical pleasure interrupted by the very real
dots or bombs that make up the painting" (http://www.unc.edu/~eoslavic/projects/
bombsites/index.html).[40] Her strategy is thus one of deliberate abstraction, but slavick is uncomfortable at its implications. She confesses that Sebald's criticism of
the production of aesthetic effects from the ruins of an annihilated world "both
challenges and paralyzes" her (2007, p. 98):

> What then is an artist to do? Should I put these drawings away? Should I display images of
> shrivelled and burnt corpses, photographs of the guilty military generals, pictures of ruins
> next to the drawings? I am troubled by these very serious questions, but I think I have

reached many people who may have otherwise walked away from realistic descriptions of war. As Sebald also writes, "The issue, then, is not to resolve, but to reveal the conflict." (p. 98)

That final remark comes not from Sebald's discussion of the air war, however, but from an essay on Jean Améry that he added to the English edition of the Zurich lectures. Améry was an Austrian-Jewish victim of the Gestapo and the camps, and he had no truck with either forgetting or forgiving the Holocaust. His watchword was not reconciliation but rather resentment—which he insisted had a moral charge. The "conflict" that haunted his work was thus, as Sebald (1999/2003) puts it, "the conflict between the overpowered and those who overpowered them" (p. 158). This antipathy makes it difficult to invoke Améry's writings in a discussion of the Allied bombing of Germany, but Améry made two demands that speak directly to Sebald's critical sense of a natural history of destruction. First, he required a public recognition of the immensity of the injury so that it cannot be denied. It is in this spirit that I hear Sebald echoing Kluge's puzzlement that the air war "never became an experience capable of public decipherment" (Sebald, 1999/2003, p. 4), but it is in this spirit, too, that "revealing the conflict" (p. 158) making political violence public, must also reveal the complicity of the public in the destruction. Second, Améry set so much store on the moral force of resentment because, as he put it himself, "absurdly, it demands that the irreversible be turned around, that the event be undone" (Sebald, 1999/2003, p. 156). He thus expressed a desire for those responsible "to join the victim in being affected by or bound by the wish to undo what had happened" (Brudholm, 2006, p. 21; see also Vetlesen, 2006).[41]

With those twin observations in mind, here is American historian Howard Zinn, who served as a bombardier with the 490th Bomb Group during World War II:

> As I look at [slavick's] drawings, I become painfully aware of how ignorant I was, when I dropped those bombs on France and on cities in Germany, Hungary, Czechoslovakia, of the effects of these bombings on human beings. Not because she shows us bloody corpses... She does not do that. But her drawings, in ways that I cannot comprehend, compel me to envision such scenes. (Zinn, 2007, p. 9)

That compulsion arises, I suggest, because slavick makes visible a temporality that is contained within the logic of targeting and even invites its desperate, because agonizingly impossible, reversal. In layering the ghosts of maps and air photographs over the bomb bursts on the ground, and composing beneath and around them a spectral, almost subliminal cellular imagery that, in slavick's own words (2007, p. 93), "conjures up the buried dead" ("replicated stains in the background, connected tissue in the foreground, concentric targets like microscopic views of damaged cells"), these drawings produce precisely that dizzying, vertiginous glissade that Duttlinger (2007) wants to topple the assumption of aerial mastery: but they do so by setting it in motion *from within the aerial view itself*.[42] The bomb-aimer asks the pilot to hold the aircraft steady, and as the bomb doors open, the viewer is precipitated into the dying city. Kennedy (2007) achieves a similar effect in reverse:

> Walk anywhere and you'll catch yourself calculating out from where the first cookie [block-buster bomb] would fall and blast the buildings open, let the incendiaries in to lodge and play.... And so you see targets beside targets: nothing but targets and ghost craters looping up from the earth, shock waves of dust and smoke ringing, crossing. *You feel the aerial photograph staring down at you where you stand, waiting to wipe you away.* (pp. 202–203; my emphasis)

That extraordinary last sentence breaches the separation between above and below and captures the percussive force of targeting that is also shown in slavick's drawings. For these cities had been reduced to rubble—they were already dead cities—*before any bombs were dropped.* This was so not only because the violence of representation ("the target") is a necessary condition for the violence on the ground, which ought to be obvious, but also because the one *precipitates* the other: as Kluge (1978) puts it in a fictionalized interview with a USAAF brigadier general, "The town was erased *as soon as the plans were made*" (my emphasis) (p. 80).[43] Similarly, in commentary on *Target for Tonight*, Stewart (n.d.) explains that "the logic of the film is that, from the moment the intelligence photographs land safely at Bomber Command, the fate of Freihausen is sealed." The momentum of this logic can be traced back beyond the plans and the photographs, however, into the public sphere itself. Perhaps the most striking example was the "Wings for Victory" campaign of 1943, when newspapers published photographs of school children sticking National Savings stamps onto a thousand-pound bomb in front of a Lancaster in Trafalgar Square: surely the apotheosis of a "natural" history of destruction.[44]

Friedrich (2002/2006) elects to begin his account of the air war on the ground in Germany, but I hope these last pages have shown that it is also necessary to take the measure of the ground in Britain—in its conventional, geographical sense and in the sense of a conceptual order—where German cities were busily being transformed into targets. The bomber stream was the advancing edge of a process of abstraction that reached right back to that exhibition of a Lancaster and its payload in Trafalgar Square, which represented bombing as a domain of pure objects (aircraft and bombs). In some degree, those objects could be personalized, even domesticated—the names and artwork on the bombers, the messages on the bombs—but that humanizing conceit was not extended to the objects of the targeting process. The visualizations within the kill-chain converted cities into numbers, coordinates, shapes, and images, so that eventually the bombers simply "dropped their load into this abstraction" (Friedrich, 2002/2006, p. 25). As a navigator in one bomber crew wrote in a letter to his wife in the summer of 1943: "Were it more personal, I should be more regretting I suppose. But I sit up there with my charts and my pencils and I don't see a thing. I never look out" (quoted in Bishop, 2008, p. 155). A natural history of destruction conceived in the terms I have been describing would force us to look out—to see our "not-seeing"—and to understand how what Zinn (1997) calls "that infinite chain of causes" is so grievously linked to an "infinite dispersion of responsibility" (p. 279). Kennedy (2007) captures all this, and so much else, when Alfred Day, a tail gunner in a Lancaster, looks back at the bombing war:

My, but wasn't it all just a big, free university—the university of war—with H[igh] E[xplosive] and armour piercing and incendiaries, just for a lark. And so much to find out: the far edges of people and the bloody big doors into nowhere that you don't want to know about. (p. 16)

Acknowledgement I am immensely grateful to Peter Meusburger for his invitation to take part in the symposium from which this chapter derives, and to Trevor Barnes, Anthea Bell, Felix Driver, Jessica Dubow, Stuart Elden, Mike Heffernan, Sara Koopman, Stephen Legg, John Morrissey, Simon Ward, Elvin Wyly, Marilyn Young, Maja Zehfuss, and Howard Zinn for their comments on an earlier version. I am also grateful to elin o'Hara slavick for permission to reproduce two of her drawings.

Notes

1. The USAAF included 16 "air forces" by the end of the war; the Eighth Air Force was formed in January 1942, and its strategic bombing operations in Europe were conducted by its VIII Bomber Command escorted by aircraft from its VIII Fighter Command.
2. I have taken the phrase "dead cities" from the Benjamin epigraph that prefaces this essay, but it is also used by Grayling (2006, p. 12), who derived it from an Allied report on possible sites for the trial of Nazi leaders for war crimes. Nuremberg was chosen not only because it had been the scene of spectacular Nazi rallies but also because its location "among the dead cities of Germany" would provide a vivid illustration of Allied retribution.
3. Luftwaffe air strikes were described as "retaliatory measures" undertaken against a "criminal" enemy (Friedrich, 2002, p. 422).
4. Civilian casualties on both sides included high proportions of women and (despite evacuation) children. Nolan (2005) notes that "total war had feminized German cities" (p. 8) because so many men were involved in military offensives and military occupation elsewhere in Europe.
5. Cf. Crane (1993), who registers "a large difference between the RAF and the [US]AAF both in intent and in effort as to the number of civilians killed" (pp. 75–76). Similarly, Miller (2006) claims that "the Eighth Air Force engaged in terror bombing for 4 weeks. The RAF conducted terror raids for 3 years" (p. 481).
6. Strachan (2006) points out that historians still have "no secure grasp" (p. 5) of the numbers of noncombatants killed during World War I—one estimate suggests six million civilians, compared to ten million combatants—and argues that it was, in part, this "comparative neglect of the civilian casualties of 1914–1918 [that] made more possible the targeting of civilians in 1939–1945" (p. 5).
7. Harris's words appeared in early drafts of an Air Staff report but were excised from the final version.
8. Biddle notes that Harris's Blue Books also included diagrammatic representations of each town's key point rating and key point factor.
9. After the bombing of Dresden, an Associated Press correspondent reported that "Allied air commanders have made the long-awaited decision" to "adopt deliberate terror bombing" of German cities; the phrase was excised by the censor in Britain but blazoned across front pages in the United States (Biddle, 2006, p. 106). In response, the USAAF insisted this was a misrepresentation and that "there has been no change in policy. There has only been a change of emphasis in locale" (Crane, 1987, p. 32).
10. Sebald (1995/1998) had previously advanced the same claim when William Hazel recalls watching bombers taking off from air fields in East Anglia: "I even learnt German, after a fashion, so that I could read what the Germans themselves had said about the bombings and their lives in the ruined cities. To my astonishment, however, I soon found the search for such

accounts invariably proved fruitless. No one at the time seemed to have written about their experiences or afterwards recorded their memories" (p. 39).

11. Similarly, Huyssen (2003a) insists that although there were few literary renderings, "there was always a lot of *talk*" (p. 147). But he also agrees that the air war was "'publicly forgotten' for several decades" (Huyssen, 2003b, p. 166).

12. *Horizon*'s subtitle read "a periodical of literature and art," but the content ranged far and wide and included essays on the war and geopolitics as well as contributions from W. H. Auden, John Betjeman, T. S. Eliot, George Orwell, J. B. Priestley, Stephen Spender, Dylan Thomas, and a host of others. It became one of two prominent reviews during the war (the other was *New Writing*), and Connolly regarded it as his "war work"; see (Shelden, 1989).

13. Hamburg was the original target, but weather conditions forced Bomber Command to switch the attack to Cologne.

14. Friedrich (2006) calculates that 20,000 people were killed in air raids on Cologne. In total the RAF dropped 23,249 tons of bombs on the city; the US Eighth Air Force, 15,165 tons.

15. Wilms argues that Flanner effectively implies that "the cities are not in ruins because British air forces had, since 1942, dropped onto them, according to scientific calculations, the perfect combination of incendiary and high explosive bombs" but rather because "Germany is densely populated" (p. 190).

16. There was in fact a square in front of the cathedral, which was the aiming point for the raid, a decision that ensured that the bomb load, fanning out in a triangle, would fall on the most densely populated area of the city (Bishop, 2008, p. 99). When Zuckerman eventually reached Berlin, he said that the sight of its devastation "made me wish again that I had written that article for Cyril Connolly" (Zuckerman, 1978, p. 328).

17. Their paths crossed at the University of East Anglia (UEA). When Zuckerman retired from Birmingham University in 1969, he was appointed Professor at Large at UEA, and Sebald taught there after he moved permanently to Britain in 1970.

18. In his view "the willingness to detach the language of air power theory from the reality of bomb attack by deliberate abstraction, to render it in some sense metaphorically, is one explanation for the almost complete absence of any discussion about civilian casualties in the theoretical writing of the 1930s" (Overy, 2005, p. 284).

19. The exception, he points out, is always Dresden, but, as he also notes, "this does not excuse our forgetfulness about other cities in Germany" (Lowe, 2007, p. xv; see also F. Taylor, 2004).

20. The English translation incorporates some of the images that were published in a separate book of photographs (Friedrich, 2003).

21. In a postscript to his Zurich lectures (Sebald, 1993/2003) praised Friedrich's earlier (1993) discussion of the air war as the only discussion of "the evolution and consequences of the Allied strategy of destruction" (p. 70) by a German historian to date. He then added: "Characteristically, however, his remarks have not aroused anything like the interest they deserve" (p. 70).

22. Peifer concluded that, "given these flaws, the prospect of *Der Brand*'s being translated into English appear dim" (p. 124).

23. This charge prompted Arnold (2003) to redirect the "natural history" critique from Sebald to Friedrich, whom he accused of reproducing a postwar mythology of the "local memory cultures" of the 1950s: "In this discourse the air war is depicted as a natural disaster that suddenly entraps a peaceable and peace-loving local community between the two evils of allied bombing and persecution by the N[ational]-S[ocialist] regime" (n.p.).

24. See, for example, Annette Seidel Arpaci, 'Lost in translation? The discovery of "German suffering" in W.G. Sebald's Luftkrieg und Literatur', in Helmut Schmitz, ed., A nation of victims? Representation of German wartime suffering from 1945 to the present (Amsterdam and New York: Rodolpi, 2007) pp. 161–180: 164–165.

25. Sebald, Natural history, p. 16; for a fuller discussion, see Overy, 'Allied bombing', p. 288; Biddle, Rhetoric and reality, p. 188.

26. Cf. Heer (2005), who accuses Friedrich of using such inflammatory language that he becomes an "arsonist" (p. 296) who equates the air war with the Holocaust. To take the most unsettling example (Friedrich, 2002/2006) draws attention to the large numbers of air raid victims who were killed by gas in the cellars—70 to 80% in Hamburg (p. 313). But he is also adamant that "there was no correlation between the annihilation of the Jews and the annihilation by bombs. And no analogy. And death by gas will not create one" (p. 296).

27. Cf. Robbins (2007, p. 147), who follows Lindqvist (2000, p. 97) to emphasize differences in magnitude between the Holocaust and the bombing war but also notes that most German cities defended themselves energetically, whereas the victims of the Holocaust were largely defenseless, and that the bombing offensive was not about killing in order to secure *Lebensraum*. These qualifications are important, but they do not erase the parallels (on which see also Markusen & Kopf, 1995).

28. It was during that crisis that Balkan scholars spoke of "urbicide" (see Coward, 2009, pp. 35–38): the deliberate and systematic destruction by Serbian forces of those towns and cities that were most visibly identified with a history of religious, ethnic, and national pluralism. The literal meaning of the term—"killing of cities"—was applied to the Allied bombing of Germany by Mendieta (2007).

29. "There can be no history perhaps without memory, but neither can there be a history that does not discipline memory" (Maier, 2005, p. 439, note 13).

30. The rupture of ordinary language explains his skepticism about eye-witness reports. "The apparently unimpaired ability—shown in most of the eyewitness reports—of everyday language to go on functioning as usual raises doubts of the authenticity of the experiences they record" (Sebald, 1999/2003, p. 25).

31. It is precisely this ruin of language that another novelist, Helen Humphreys (2008), ignores in a passage that I assume was influenced by a different reading of Sebald: "The bombs falling on the city are an unnatural phenomenon, and yet they have to be thought through past experience.... When something is unnatural, there is no new language for it. The words to describe it must be borrowed words, from the old language of natural things." (Humphreys, 2008, p. 112)

32. Sebald's translator, Anthea Bell, confirms that the English-language title was his own:

> The title was Max's idea [Sebald was known to his friends and colleagues as Max]. I would never have made such a sweeping change of title on my own initiative. In the early stages of the translation project, Max was still referring to it as "Air War and Literature," but he soon decided that it would not cover all the material in the book, which in the English-language version includes not just his essay on Alfred Andersch but the essays on Peter Weiss and Jean Améry as well. His rationale for the wording is in fact present in his reference to the account of bombed-out [Cologne] that Solly Zuckerman planned to write, but never did, for *Horizon*. (A. Bell, personal communication, March 27, 2009)

> She also suggests that, when he gave "Zwischen Geschichte und Naturgeschichte" its title, "Max would recently have spoken to Solly Zuckerman, see the end of the first Zurich lecture. So the wording of the never-written *Horizon* title will have been in his mind in the early eighties."

33. These images mirror a persistent feature of the postwar *Trümmerfilm* (rubble film). In an important qualification to Sebald's original thesis, Fisher (2005, p. 474) argues that they "are not silent, but rather *depict* silence: they represent the very process of silently staring at the widespread destruction" (my emphasis).

34. The same rotated and cropped image is used as a cover illustration for some English-language editions of *Natural History*.

35. The daylight "precision" raids conducted by the USAAF required more detail than RAF nighttime attacks did, so a series of perspective target maps ("Geerlings maps") were

produced and eventually distributed to all stations in Bomber Command, too. They included drawings of the target from six different approaches at a height of 26,000 ft. For each approach the target was shown in an outer drawing from 15 miles out (for the navigator) and an inner drawing from 7 miles out (for the bombardier).

36. H2S had influential critics within the RAF. For 3 months before Operation Gomorrah, Bomber Command had concentrated its attacks on the Ruhr, where the targets were within the range of Oboe (a radio-ranging system) and had been marked with "high accuracy." But Hamburg was out of signal range, and by July 1943 the Pathfinders and a large number of bombers had been equipped with H2S. The system was used "to identify the coast... as it unfolded itself on the screen as far as Hamburg and finally as it revealed the bright fingers of light of the dock area" (Lovell, 1991, pp. 175–176). But Hamburg was a relatively easy "read" compared to most inland targets, and the USAAF developed the shorter band H2X system, which provided a sharper image. It was first used in November 1943 and came into widespread use in mid-1944, but the interpretation of its images was still extremely difficult and often intuitive, and accuracy continued to be measured in miles (Brown, 1999).

37. In the British case a minimum mapping would include the (Allied) Central Interpretation Unit at Medmenham, near Marlow (responsible for the analysis of aerial photographs); the Ministry of Economic Warfare and the Air Ministry in London (which identified potential targets); the Air Ministry's Air Intelligence section AI 3 (c) at Hughenden Manor ("Hillside"), near High Wycombe (responsible for producing descriptions of targets for operational planners, and target maps, illustrations, and files for briefing officers and aircrew); Bomber Command Headquarters at High Wycombe: six to eight Bomber Command Groups and their bases; and individual flight crews. The chain is a different version of the registers through which Latour (1995) tracks the appearance of the Amazon rainforest on the pages of a scientific journal in Paris, and in this sense it, too, marks the passage of a parallel "natural history."

38. The effect of a "technical exercise" was compounded because the target was a military-industrial one. Although the film begins with plans for a raid on "Town 434," subsequently identified as Kiel, the assigned targets there were naval docks and barracks, and the film then follows the fortunes of a squadron diverted from the main force to attack oil storage and tankers at "Freihausen." The film was a considerable success in the UK, the United States, and the Commonwealth, but it had no sequel: As Mackenzie (2001) remarks, "a feature film in which area bombing was featured was a nonstarter" (p. 549).

39. This distinction takes other forms, too, like Hewitt's (1994) view from the war room as counterposed to the "civilian view" from underneath the bombs, or Ó'Tuathail's (1996) distinction between a high-level, distanced, and dispassionate geopolitical eye and a grounded, embodied, antigeopolitical eye.

40. I suspect that at least for some of those involved in producing the kill-chain, "optical pleasure" is one of the emotions embedded in the targeting process, too.

41. I am reminded of the scene in *Slaughterhouse Five*, Kurt Vonnegut's 1969 novel of the firebombing of Dresden, where Billy becomes "unstuck in time" (p. 93) and watches the late movie backwards: "The formation flew backwards over a German city that was in flames. The bombers opened their doors, exerted a miraculous magnetism which shrunk the fires, gathered them into cylindrical steel containers, and lifted the containers into the bellies of the planes. . . . . When the bombers got back to their base, the steel cylinders were taken from the racks and shipped back to the United States of America, where factories were operating night and day, dismantling the cylinders." (Vonnegut, 1969/2005, p. 94).

42. See also Mavor (2007), who describes slavick's drawings as "scratched, smudged, layered like the residue of toppled buildings after an airstrike" (p. 15).

43. Sebald (1999/2003) mistakes this interview for fact, but draws a similar conclusion from Kluge's montage. "So much intelligence, capital and labour went into the planning of destruction that, under the pressure of all the accumulated potential, it had to happen in the end" (p. 65).

44. More generally, see Connelly (2002). One of the bombs was delivered to 15 Squadron. "A Wings for Victory week had been held in London's Trafalgar Square," wrote Pilot Officer I. W. Renner, "during which three large bombs had been plastered inches thick with Savings Stamps by the British public on the promise that they would be duly delivered with the bomb. At the end of the week two of the bombs were hurried to our Station and one found its way into our aircraft which we had named Te Kooti, after the famous Maori chief. Three times the raid was postponed. We became quite attached to our bomb and each day the bomb-aimer would go round to make sure it was still loaded on Te Kooti.... The next night, amid rain and sleet, we got off... and we were able to reach Berlin at a reasonable height to deliver our bomb" (Thompson, 1956, p. 58).

References

Adorno, T. (1984). The idea of natural history (R. Hullot-Kentor, Trans.). *Telos, 60*, 111–124.

Arnold, J. (2003, November 3). *Review of Jörg Friedrich, Der Brand. H-German Forum, H-Net: Humanities and social sciences online*. Retrieved August 24, 2010, from http://www.h-net.msu.edu

Arpaci, A. S. (2007). Lost in translation? The discovery of "German suffering" in W. G. Sebald's Luftkrieg und Literatur. In H. Schmitz (Ed.), *A nation of victims? Representation of German wartime suffering from 1945 to the present* (pp. 161–180). Amsterdam: Rodolpi.

Barnouw, D. (2005). *The war in the empty air: Victims, perpetrators, and postwar Germans*. Bloomington, IN: Indiana University Press.

Battle of Berlin: Latest reconnaisance views of a dying city. (1944, February 28). *LIFE*, pp. 38–40.

Benjamin, W. (1932). Berlin Chronicle (E. Jephcott, Trans.). In M. W. Jennings, H. Eiland, G. Smith, & R. Livingstone (Eds.), *Selected writings of Walter Benjamin: Vol. 2. 1927–1934* (pp. 595–637). Cambridge, MA: Harvard University Press.

Biddle, T. D. (2002). *Rhetoric and reality in air warfare: The evolution of British and American ideas about strategic bombing, 1914–1945*. Princeton, NJ: Princeton University Press.

Biddle, T. D. (2006). Wartime reactions. In P. Addison & J. Crang (Eds.), *Firestorm: The bombing of Dresden, 1945* (pp. 96–122). Chicago: Ivan R. Dee.

Bishop, P. (2008). *Bomber boys*. London: Harper.

Böll, H. (1994). Which cologne? In H. Böll (Ed.), *Missing persons and other essays* (pp. 22–27). Evanston, IL: Northwestern University Press.

Bowie, A. (1982). New histories: Aspects of the prose of Alexander Kluge. *Journal of European Studies, 12*, 180–208.

Brown, L. (1999). *A radar history of World War II: Technical and military imperatives*. London: Taylor & Francis.

Brudholm, T. (2006). Revisiting resentments: Jean Améry and the dark side of forgiveness and reconciliation. *Journal of Human Rights, 5*, 7–26.

Buck-Morss, S. (1989). *The dialectics of seeing: Walter Benjamin and the Arcades Project*. Cambridge, MA: MIT Press.

Charlwood, D. (2000). *No moon tonight*. Manchester: Crécy. (Original work published in 1956)

Childers, T. (2005). *"Facilis descensus averni est"*: The Allied bombing of Germany and the issue of German suffering. *Central European History, 38*, 75–105.

Chow, R. (2006). *The age of the world target*. Durham, NC: Duke University Press.

Clarke, D. B., Doel, M. A., & McDonough, F. X. (1996). Holocaust topologies: Singularity, politics, space. *Political Geography, 15*, 457–489.

Connely, M. (2002). The British people, the press and the strategic air campaign against Germany, 1939–1945. *Contemporary British History, 16*, 39–58.

Coward, M. (2009). *Urbicide: The politics of urban destruction*. London: Routledge.

Crane, C. (1987). Evolution of US strategic bombing of urban areas. *The Historian, 50*, 14–39.

Crane, C. (1993). *Bombs, cities and civilians: American airpower strategy in World War II*. Lawrence, KS: University of Kansas Press.

Crew, D. (2007). Sleeping with the enemy. *Central European History, 40*, 117–132.

Davies, P. H. (2007). *The Welsh girl*. New York: Houghton Mifflin.

Davis, R. G. (1993). *Carl A. Spaatz and the air war in Europe*. Washington, DC: Smithsonian Institute Press.

Davis, R. G. (2006). *Bombing the European Axis powers: A historical digest of the combined bomber offensive, 1939–1945*. Maxwell Air Force Base, AL: Air University Press.

Doel, M. A., & Clarke, D. B. (1998). Figuring the Holocaust: Singularity and the purification of space. In S. Dalby & G. Ó'Tuathail (Eds.), *Rethinking geopolitics* (pp. 39–61). London: Routledge.

Duttlinger, C. (2007). A lineage of destruction? Rethinking photography in Luftkrieg und Literatur. In A. Fuchs & J. J. Long (Eds.), *W. G. Sebald and the writing of history* (pp. 163–177). Würzburg: Königshausen & Neumann.

Fisher, J. (2005). Wandering in/to the rubble-film: Filmic *flânerie* and the exploded panorama after 1945. *German Quarterly, 78*, 461–480.

Friedrich, J. (1993). *Das Gesetz des Krieges* [The law of war]. Munich: Piper Verlag.

Friedrich, J. (2002). *Der Brand: Deutschland im Bombenkrieg 1940–1945* [The fire: bombing of Germany, 1940–1945]. Berlin: Propyläen.

Friedrich, J. (2003). *Brandstätten: Der Anblick des Bombenkriegs [Conflagrations: Images of the bombing war]*. Berlin: Propyläen.

Friedrich, J. (2006). *The fire: The bombing of Germany, 1940–1945* (A. Brown, Trans.). New York: Columbia University Press. (Original work published 2002)

Friedrich, J. (2007). *"Bombs away," interview with Noah Isenberg, BookForum, 14/1*, n.p. Retrieved September 27, 2010, http://www.bookforum.com/inprint/014_01/228

Grayling, A. C. (2006). *Among the dead cities: The history and moral legacy of the WWII bombing of civilians in Germany and Japan*. New York: Walker Books.

Hage, V. (2005). Verschüttete Gefühle: Wie die deutschen Schriftsteller den Bombenkrieg bewältigten [Buried feelings: How German writers came to terms with the bombing of Germany]. *Osteuropa, 55*(4–6), 265–268.

Hage, V. (2006). To write or remain silent? The portrayal of the air war in German literature. In L. Cohen-Pfister & D. Wienroder-Skinner (Eds.), *Victims and perpetrators: 1933–1945* (pp. 91–113). Berlin: Walter de Gruyter.

Hage, V. (Ed.). (2003). *Zeugen der Zerstörung: Die Literaten und der Luftkrieg*. Frankfurt am Main: Fischer.

Hansen, R. (2008). *Fire and fury: The Allied bombing of Germany, 1942–1945*. Toronto: Doubleday.

Hanson, N. (2008). *First Blitz*. London: Doubleday.

Harris, A. (1990). *Bomber offensive*. Toronto: Stoddart. (Original work published 1947)

Heer, H. (2005). *Vom Verschwinden der Täter: Der Vernichtungskrieg fand statt, aber keiner war dabei* [The disappearance of the culprits: The war of annihilation took place, but no one was around]. Berlin: Aufbau Verlag.

Hell, J. (2004). The Angel's enigmatic eyes, or the Gothic beauty of catastrophic history in W. G. Sebald's "Air War and Literature". *Criticism, 46*, 361–392.

Hewitt, K. (1994). When the great planes came and made ashes of our city....: Towards an oral geography of the disasters of war. *Antipode, 26*, 1–34.

Hohn, U. (1994). The Bomber's Baedeker: Target book for strategic bombing in the economic warfare against German towns, 1943–1945. *GeoJournal, 34*, 213–230.

Höllenfeuer in Bagdad. (2003, March 24). *Der Spiegel*, p. 13.

Humphreys, H. (2008). *Coventry*. Toronto: HarperCollins.

Hüppauf, B. (1993). Experiences of western warfare and the crisis of representation. *New German Critique, 59*, 41–76.

Huyssen, A. (2003a). Rewritings and new beginnings: W. G. Sebald and the literature on the air war. In A. Huyssen (Ed.), *Present pasts: Urban palimpsests and the politics of memory* (pp. 138–157). Stanford, CA: Stanford University Press.

Huyssen, A. (2003b). Air war legacies: From Dresden to Baghdad. *New German Critique, 90,* 163–176.

Kennedy, A. L. (2007). *Day.* London: Jonathan Cape.

Kluge, A. (1978). Der Luftangriff auf Halberstadt am 8. April 1945 [The air raid on Halberstadt on April 8, 1945]. In A. Kluge (Ed.), *Neue Geschichten: Hefte 1–8* (pp. 33–110). Frankfurt am Main: Suhrkamp.

Latour, B. (1987). *Science in action.* Cambridge, MA: Harvard University Press.

Latour, B. (1995). The "Pedofil" of Boa Vista: A photo-philosophical montage. *Common Knowledge, 4*(1), 144–187.

Lindqvist, S. (2000). *A history of bombing.* New York: New Press.

Lovell, B. (1991). *Echoes of war: The story of H2S radar.* London: Taylor & Francis.

Lowe, K. (2007). *Inferno: The devastation of Hamburg.* London and New York: Viking/Penguin.

Mackenzie, S. P. (2001). *British war films: The cinema and the services.* London: Continuum.

Maier, C. (2005). Targeting the city: Debates and silences about the aerial bombing of World War II. *International Review of the Red Cross, 87,* 429–444.

Markusen, E., & Kopf, D. (1995). *Holocaust and strategic bombing: Genocide and total war in the twentieth century.* Boulder, CO: Westview Press.

Mavor, C. (2007). Blossoming bombs. In E. O. H. Slavick (Ed.), *Bomb after bomb: A violent cartography* (pp. 13–33). Milan: Charta.

Mendieta, E. (2007). The literature of urbicide: Friedrich, Nossack, Sebald and Vonnegut. *Theory & Event, 10*(2). On-line journal

Miller, D. L. (2006). *Masters of the air: America's bomber boys who fought the air war against Nazi Germany.* New York: Simon & Schuster.

Moeller, R. G. (2006). On the history of man-made destruction: Loss, death, memory, and Germany in the bombing war. *History Workshop Journal, 61,* 103–134.

Mumford, L. (1938). *The culture of cities.* New York: Harcourt Brace & Company.

Mumford, L. (1987). *The city in history.* London: Penguin. (Original work published 1961)

Nolan, M. (2005). Germans as victims during the Second World War: Air wars, memory wars. *Central European History, 38,* 7–40.

Nossack, H. E. (2004). *The end: Hamburg 1943* (J. Agee, Trans.). Chicago: University of Chicago Press. (Original work published in German 1948).

Olson, S. (1945, March 19). Underground Cologne. *LIFE,* p. 28.

Omissi, D. (1990). *Air power and colonial control: The Royal Air Force, 1919–1939.* Manchester: Manchester University Press.

Osborne, T. (2005). Literature in ruins. *History of the Human Sciences, 18,* 109–118.

O'Tuathail, G. (1996). An anti-geopolitical eye: Maggie O'Kane in Bosnia, 1992–93. *Gender, Place and Culture: A Journal of Feminist Geography, 3,* 171–185.

Overy, R. J. (1978). From "uralbomber" to "Amerikabomber": The Luftwaffe and strategic bombing. *Journal of Strategic Studies, 1,* 154–175.

Overy, R. J. (1981). *The air war, 1939–1945.* London: Europa.

Overy, R. J. (2005). Allied bombing and the destruction of German cities. In R. Chickering, S. Förster, & B. Greiner (Eds.), *A world at total war: Global conflict and the politics of destruction, 1939–1945* (pp. 277–295). Cambridge, UK: Cambridge University Press.

Peifer, D. (2004). Der Brand [The fire]. *Air & Space Power Journal, 18*(1), 121–124.

Pensky, M. (2004). Natural history: The life and afterlife of a concept in Adorno. *Critical Horizons, 5,* 227–257.

Presner, T. S. (2004). "What a synoptic and artificial view reveals": Extreme history and the modernism of W. G. Sebald's realism. *Criticism, 46,* 341–360.

Robbins, B. (2007). Comparative national blaming: W. G. Sebald on the bombing of Germany. In A. Sarat & N. Hussain (Eds.), *Forgiveness, mercy, and clemency* (pp. 138–155). Stanford, CA: Stanford University Press.

Satia, P. (2008). *Spies in Arabia: The Great War and the cultural foundations of Britain's covert empire in the Middle East.* Oxford, UK: Oxford University Press.

Schama, S. (2004, May 28). If you receive this, I'll be dead. *The Guardian* (London), n.p.

Sebald, W. G. (1982). Zwischen Geschichte und Naturgeschichte. Versuch über die literarische Beschreibung totaler Zerstörung mit Anmerkungen zu Kasack, Nossak und Kluge [Between history and natural history: Essay on the literary description of total destruction, with commentary on Kasak, Nossak, and Kluge]. *Orbis Litterarum, 37*, 345–366.

Sebald, W. G. (1998). *The rings of Saturn* (M. Hulse, Trans.). New York: New Directions. (Original work published in German 1995)

Sebald, W. G. (1999). *Luftkrieg und Literature* [Air war and literature]. Munich: Carl Hanser.

Sebald, W. G. (2001). *Vertigo* (M. Hulse, Trans.). New York: New Directions. (Original work published in German 1990)

Sebald, W. G. (2003). *On the natural history of destruction* (A. Bell, Trans.). New York: Vintage. (Original work published in German 1999)

Shelden, M. (1989). *Friends of promise: Cyril Connolly and the world of Horizon*. London: Harper & Row.

Sherry, M. (1987). *The rise of American air power: The creation of Armageddon*. New Haven, NH: Yale University Press.

Short, K. R. M. (1997). Bomber command's "Target for Tonight" (1941). *Historical Journal of Film, Radio and Television, 17*, 181–218.

Slavick, E. O. H. (2006). Protesting cartography: Places the United States has bombed. *Cultural Politics, 2*, 245–254.

Slavick, E. O. H. (2007). *Bomb after bomb: A violent cartography*. Milan: Charta.

Stewart, J. (n.d.). *Target for tonight, BFI screenonline*. Retrieved August 24, 2010, from, http://www.screenonline.org.uk/film/id/577991/index.html

Strachan, H. (2006). Strategic bombing and the question of civilian casualties up to 1945. In P. Addison & J. Crang (Eds.), *Firestorm: The bombing of Dresden, 1945* (pp. 1–17). Chicago: Ivan R. Dee.

Taylor, E. (2004). *Operation Millennium: 'Bomber' Harris's raid on Cologne, May 1942*. Staplehurst: Spellmount.

Taylor, F. (2004). *Dresden: Tuesday 13 February 1945*. London: Bloomsbury.

Thompson, H. L. (1956). *New Zealanders with the Royal Air Force* (Vol. 2). Wellington: Historical Publications Branch.

Vetlesen, A. J. (2006). A case for resentment: Jeam Améry versus Primo Levi. *Journal of Human Rights, 5*, 27–44.

Vonnegut, K. (2005). *Slaughterhouse five*. New York: Random House. (Original work published 1969)

Ward, S. (2006a). Responsible ruins? W. G. Sebald and the responsibility of the German writer. *Forum for Modern Language Studies, 42*, 183–198.

Ward, S. (2006b). Ruins and poetics in the works of W. G. Sebald. In J. J. Long & A. Whitehead (Eds.), *W. G. Sebald: A critical companion* (pp. 58–71). Edinburgh: Edinburgh University Press.

Webster, C., & Frankland, N. (1961a). *The strategic air offensive against Germany, 1939–1945: Vol. 1. Preparations*. London: Her Majesty's Stationery Office.

Webster, C., & Frankland, N. (1961b). *The strategic air offensive against Germany, 1939–1945: Vol. 4. Annexes and appendices*. London: Her Majesty's Stationery Office.

Wilms, W. (2006). Speak no evil, write no evil: In search of a usable language of destruction. In S. Denham & M. McCulloch (Eds.), *W. G. Sebald: History—Memory—Trauma* (pp. 183–204). Berlin: Walter de Gruyter.

Wyman, M. (1998). *DPs: Europe's displaced persons, 1945–1951*. Ithaca, NY: Cornell University Press.

Zehfuss, M. (2007). *Wounds of memory: The politics of war in Germany*. Cambridge, UK: Cambridge University Press.

Zinn, H. (1997). The bombing of Royan. In H. Zinn (Ed.), *The Zinn Reader: Writings on disobedience and democracy* (pp. 267–280). New York: Seven Stories Press.
Zinn, H. (2007). Foreword. In E. O. H. Slavick (Ed.), *Bomb after bomb: A violent cartography* (pp. 9–11). Milan: Charta.
Zuckerman, S. (1978). *From apes to warlords*. London: Hamish Hamilton.

Part IV
Postcolonial Cultural Memories

Violent Memories: South Asian Spaces of Postcolonial Anamnesis

Stephen Legg

When I delivered this material as a lecture in 2007, it risked eliciting nothing less than a surge of *déjà vu*. Its central themes of memory, violence, and postcolonialism had recently been, it seemed, endlessly debated in, and regarding, India. The symposium came at the end of, quite literally, an Indian summer[1] punctuated by two anniversaries of significant moments in Indian political history. May saw the celebration of what, in 1857, had been the initial events of a conflict that eventually became the largest uprising against the British Empire in the nineteenth century—a struggle variously known today as the "Great Revolt," the "Sepoy Mutiny," or the "First War of Independence." In August came the anniversaries marking the 1947 end of British rule on the subcontinent, the beginning of independence for India and Pakistan, and the eruption of violence accompanying the partition of those two new states. The anniversaries were held in India and the assorted territories that have been touched by the Indian diaspora. I spent December 2006 to January 2007 and March to April 2007 in Delhi and the summer in the United Kingdom, so had the opportunity to observe how the recollection of these events blurred the distinction between historical events and subjects of memory from two different geographical perspectives.

In Britain, British Broadcasting Corporation (BBC) correspondents filed accounts ab out the particular days on which the mutiny had started in 1857 and about the lowering of the Union Flag for the last time in New Delhi in 1947. But alongside these staccato notes picked out from the History of the subcontinent, there was also coverage of the repetitive, echoing murmurs of popular memories of these events. In Britain such memories were largely confined to the events of 1947 as presented on the BBC website entitled "India & Pakistan 2007."[2] The site contained links to a range of historical databases, including timelines of key historical events and narratives "From Empire to Independence: The British Raj in India 1858–1947."[3] The website also provided links to individual written accounts of "partition memories,"[4] an audio slideshow on partition,[5] and a special page of the

S. Legg (✉)
School of Geography, University of Nottingham, Nottingham NG7 2RD, UK
e-mail: stephen.legg@nottingham.ac.uk

P. Meusburger et al. (eds.), *Cultural Memories*, Knowledge and Space 4,
DOI 10.1007/978-90-481-8945-8_16, © Springer Science+Business Media B.V. 2011

BBC's "memoryshare" website devoted to India and Pakistan.[6] The memoryshare site enabled people to contribute their own memories of the events of 1947, democratizing the narrative of partition and introducing the voices of the interlocutors, often the relatives of persons whose memories were being channeled. Such memory work, as I seek to illustrate in this chapter, has already been expertly conducted in South Asia on the topic of partition. However, it also became clear during my time in Delhi that the events of 1857 were also being explored at the intersection of history and memory.

For instance, on January 6, 2007, an exhibition of photographs from 1857 was opened in Delhi with a lecture series entitled "On Hallowed Ground: Aftermaths of the Uprising, 1857." The word *hallowed* hinted at the way in which the uprising is viewed as an event that still haunts the places in which it occurred, just as the reference to "aftermaths" alludes to both the violent reprisals that followed the uprising and the difficulty of categorizing the "Mutiny" (a term which refuses to go away) as an event of the past. This troubled legacy was reflected in the lectures, with Professor Shahid Amin considering the historical narratives that sought to interpret the uprising and Professor Lahiri speaking on the memorialization of the uprising. Shuddhabrata Sengupta offered insights on how the photographs from 1857 might help make sense of images of political violence in present-day India. These photographs, notably those by Italian–British photographer Felice (Felix) Beato (1832–1909), have widely attracted comment not just for their value with respect to reconstructing a historical moment but also for their specific deployment at that time as a technology of remembrance to dictate how the events of 1857 would pass into memory. Beato's photograph of Sikander Bagh in Lucknow, complete with the decayed corpses of "mutineers" in the foreground, provides perhaps the most dramatic example (see Chaudhuri, 2005). The photograph, purportedly of the events of November 1857, was taken in April 1858 after the skeletons had been exhumed and theatrically rearranged to capture the might of colonial necropolitics (Mbembe, 2003). This photograph also definitively characterized the mutiny as *over*; as nothing more than a violent memory.

The ambiguous phrase "violent memories" strikes at two of the main conceptual matters that have been theorised by scholars of India: memories of physically violent acts; and the epistemic violence that recollection can do to those who are remembering, those who are remembered, and those who are forgotten. This theorizing does not suggest an epistemological division between representations of violence and nonrepresentational performances of violent acts, but it does hope to provide a methodological prompt to consider both aspects of the nature of violence. It also helps stress the significance of *participation*: be it the material or archival traces of those who participated in events being remembered, or be it contemporary participatory struggles to construct memories of events that are at risk of being lost to history.

This chapter provides an overview of the memory politics that have accompanied India's struggle for freedom from colonialism, both during the Raj (after 1857) and in the period since independence (after 1947). This perspective entails an expanded understanding of the violence in colonialism and imperialism but also of the spaces and means of remembrance that have accompanied them.

Pennebaker (1997) has argued that whereas wars, kidnappings, torture, and scandal have been told as the subject matter of history, the social dynamics and collective memories that have resulted from such acts have often been neglected. Researchers within the heterogeneous field of postcolonial studies have been working to examine the complex topographies of memory and forgetting that colonialism depended on and that postcolonial nations have inherited (see, for instance, Aldrich, 2005, on monuments and memorialization; Chattopadhyay, 2005, on memory and the city; Hall, 2007, on the legacies of the slave trade; and Healy, 1997, on museums, schooling, and history). Referring more specifically to work on Africa and South Asia, Gandhi (1998) has spoken of how anticolonial nationalists and postcolonial states sought to forget the past through a process of amnesia as the basis of historic self-invention and the erasure of what one may call violent memories. Usually, though, this repression has failed to overcome the past. With this general failure in mind, Gandhi (1998) has branded postcolonial theory "a theoretical resistance to the mystifying amnesia of the colonial aftermath" (p. 4) that encourages one to revisit, remember, and interrogate the colonial past.

Such theories have critically drawn on earlier work in ethnopsychiatry that inquired into the tenacious grip of colonial pasts (Mannoni, 1950/1990); on psychoexistential study of colonial domination (Fanon, 1965); and on politicopsychological investigations of the dependency relationships that developed between the colonized and the colonizers (Nandy, 1983). Drawing on these rich traditions of personal memory, postcolonial theory is increasingly recognized as a major contributor to contemporary theories of both individual and "social" memory (a binary system questioned later in this chapter). Rossington and Whitehead (2007) list postcolonial theory alongside Holocaust studies, False Memory Syndrome, and poststructuralism as an important factor informing the memory boom of the 1990s. Alongside Frantz Fanon, the two other referenced postcolonial scholars are Homi Bhaha and Gayatri Chakravorty Spivak. Bhaha has been influential with respect to colonial identities, mimicry, and hybridity; Spivak, through her association with the Subaltern Studies Group (SSG, also known as the Subaltern Studies Collective), has had a greater effect on the methodological debate among South Asian scholars regarding the question of how to retrieve memories from the colonial archive, interpreted in its broadest sense. After assessing these debates, I turn attention to memory work that has been conducted on the colonial state, anticolonial and communal nationalism, partition, and various political formations of postcolonial India.

Subaltern Memory?

The SSG continues to make an original contribution to research on history "from below" (see Chaturvedi, 2000; Guha & Spivak, 1988). The scholars in the original project sought to tell the story of "the subaltern"; the nonelite of the population; the people outside the grand, overarching narratives of Marxism, imperialism, and nationalism (Guha, 1982). Although jettisoning some of the structuralism of the latter three accounts, the SSG's early work retained a humanist notion of the subject

(the self-originating, self-determining individual, who possesses sovereign consciousness and reason and who is an agent in the power of freedom; see O'Hanlon,
1988, p. 191)—a controversial approach that quickly attracted criticism (Spivak,
1985). In the wake of this attack, the subaltern under study became a more frac-
tured and multiply situated subject, constituting various fragments of the nation
(Chatterjee, 1993). Although still interested in agrarian labourers, the urban poor
and the industrial proletariat, the SSG stressed that the experiences of middle-class
females or of members of the nonwealthy upper-caste could also now legitimately
be investigated as, in some senses, subaltern.

As something novel in colonial and postcolonial history, this project was also
a departure point for memory work on South Asia (for instance, see Amin, 1995,
on the blurring of historical account and memories of the violent events of Chauri
Chaura in 1922). The problem with focusing on the non-elite is not only that the
subjects of the research often were, have been, or are unable to write or to have
their written work preserved but also that they are unlikely to have been written
about. The subaltern subject is, in many cases, the subject of two violent memories.
First, where memories of the subaltern can be retold, they are often recollections
of the subjects of history who are most likely to have endured the violence of an
unjust society, be it against the person; against physical property; or against the ability to reproduce, cohabit, consume, or simply exercise personal freedom. Second,
subaltern memories are often the subject of epistemic violence in the sense that
such recollections and stories do not always exist in a form readily maintained by
the colonial or postcolonial archive. When these memories do figure, subalterns
are often spoken *for*, not *of*, hence Spivak's (1988/2000) famous question: can the
subaltern speak?

The methodological project of *anamnesis* attempts to challenge both kinds of
violent memories by seeking out the stories and experiences of the subaltern and by
critically interrogating the colonial and postcolonial archive. The word was originally used by Plato to refer to deliberate recollection rather than unbidden flashes of
memory (Samuel, 1994, p. vii). It has since been used in theology to recollect the
sacrifice of Jesus (Gross, 2000, pp. 51–52) and has been tentatively analyzed within
postcolonial theory (Gandhi, 1998, p. 8). Postcolonial anamnesis does not entail
abandoning the official archive as nothing more than a technology of government.
Rather, it involves working within and through the archive, re-reading colonial texts,
oral histories, memoires, dispersed moments, hidden memories, and subaltern languages. As Robert Young (2001, p. 386) has argued, subaltern discourses do not
exist separately from colonial and postcolonial discourses but emerge through the
fractures and contradictions of colonial modes of governance, representation, and
conduct. It is thus possible to view subaltern memories as always intertwined with
dominant discourses but as existing in a state of opposition or otherness to elite
norms. As suggested by M. Sarkar (2006):

> The study of popular memory is necessarily relational. It involves the exploration of two sets
> of relations: (1) that between dominant memory and oppositional forms across the public
> field, including academic productions; and (2) the relation between public discourse and a
> more privatized sense of the past generated within lived culture. (p. 139)

Expanding the second of these relations beyond the private realm, one can think of communities, social movements, or individuals both contesting and surviving dominant memory formations (Legg, 2005a), called *lieux de mémoire* by Nora (1989). Although privileged individuals and institutions can endorse the active forgetting of nonconformist histories and the commemoration of normative remembrance, these practices necessarily invoke acts of resistance and necessarily have a finite audience.

Remembering Founding Violence

Das (1995) has argued that the state, specifically in the context of colonial India, both enacted and spoke for violence, establishing the interpretation of the expert over that of the victim. This interpretation could span from the definition of what constituted the murder of a native subject (Bailkin, 2006) to the stipulation of the conditions that could justify colonial urbicide (Graham, 2004), a retributive type of urban demolition in which "the erasure of the memories, history and identity attached to architecture and place—enforced forgetting—is the goal itself" (Bevan, 2006, p. 8). Both interpretations were widely put into effect, to the advantage of the colonial state, after the uprising of 1857. Although the violence enacted in that year and during subsequent displays of colonial force tells much about the imperial apparatus, the constitutive role of indigenous agency underscores how superfluous it is to try and separate power from resistance or victim from victor. As the following account shows, however, there have been particular endeavors to create a narrative of colonial, nationalist, and communal recollections of the experience of violence at that time.

Regarding the interpretative debacle over the uprising/mutiny/war of independence, attempts to separate "history" and "memory" embrace a specious distinction that denies the very subjectivity of writing history, and demotes the significance of memory-work (Hutton, 1993). Indeed, the "historical" accounts of the mutiny that were formulated in the Victorian period were so filled with vitriol that their linear chronologies of events barely effaced the obviously traumatic memories that the authors retained of the uprising itself, whether directly encountered or mediated by the pathological reaction of the British press.

But there were also definite efforts to dictate how the uprising would be remembered. Photographs by Beato and others were used to depict the violence of the uprising and the comprehensive defeat of the mutineers. Paintings also depicted scenes of heroism, despotism, and sacrifice but could prove as malleable as memory itself. Sir Joseph Paton's 1858 painting *In Memoriam* depicted Indian sepoys bursting into a house containing a mother and her children (Procida, 2002, p. 111). The furor over an image so suggestive of the violence to which the Empire had exposed its womenfolk led to the sepoys being painted over as Scottish highlanders, transforming a scene of violent defeat into a victorious testimony to British resilience and heroism.[7] Vast swathes of cities that had been key sites for the uprising were destroyed, not just to facilitate military action in the case of future uprisings but to ensure that the residents of those cities would never forget the might of the colonial state (Gupta, 1981; Oldenburg, 1984).

Such modes of commemoration, being consecrated in sites of remembrance across northern India, were productive as well as destructive. Lahiri (2003) has documented the diverse manifestations of commemoration in Delhi, ranging from individual gravestones to plaques for key sites during the siege of Delhi to the Mutiny Memorial finally erected in 1863. The latter commemorates the British officers by name but partially forgets the contribution of Indian troops, mentioning them by regiment only. British people who died when Delhi was lost are also forgotten. The memorial is clearly dedicated to the people who retook the city, not to those who lost it. Such sites constitute part of what Baucom (1999) referred to as maps of the Mutiny by which it "survived its happening" (p. 104). The defeat of the Mutiny was perpetually re-enacted during the colonial period through tourist guidebooks that led visitors around the sites of the uprising, compelling the readers to recall the despicable violence of the mutineers and the justified violence of the British, yet ignoring the provocative injustices of the East India Company and the psychopathological violence of the state.

Such debates rumble on. Dalrymple's *The Last Mughal* (2006), a best-selling description of the uprising in Delhi, provides an exceptionally detailed and balanced appraisal of violence on both sides of the uprising. He has been charged, however, with conforming to long-standing trends of historiography and nostalgia. Levine (2005) had already accused Dalrymple of an overly nostalgic interpretation of eighteenth-century colonial India, and Prakash (2007) argues that a similar tone pervades *The Last Mughal*, which paints the period before the uprising as one of golden calm, not of continuous colonial exploitation and structuring power relations. It was within this wider project of recollecting both the extraordinary and the everyday nature of colonial violence at which anticolonial nationalists excelled.

Anticolonial (An)amnesia

The nationalist campaign in colonial India can be interpreted along the lines of simultaneous remembering and forgetting. The Indian National Congress, under the spiritual leadership of Mohandas Gandhi (1869–1948), encouraged the Indian population to recall their long and proud (though no less invented) traditions, not the crude orientalist stereotypes of their history, and to remember the physical and epistemic violence of the colonial state constantly. Countering these anamnestic measures were the injunctions of communal, or religious, nationalists. Both Hindu and Muslim nationalists urged the forgetting of histories that recalled the harmonious cohabitation of the two faiths and the hybrid cultures that had arisen from their interaction.

The emergence of these forms of nationalism force a consideration of social memory (see Fentress & Wickham, 1992; Middleton & Brown, 2005; Olick & Robbins, 1998). In the way they encouraged certain public acts of commemoration, protest, and popular recall and in the way they promoted private routines of bodily discipline and conduct, these nationalist movements not only sought to mobilize political ideologies but also to embed themselves in social memory. Radstone (2005) has, however, articulated the widespread concerns about the slippage of terms from the analysis of individual to social memory. She does not deny that there are publicly mediated representations of the past around which individual memories can coalesce (Halbwachs, 1925/1992). She does, however, argue that the use of metaphors (e.g., "anticolonial anamnesis" or "traumatized society") should be complemented by analyses of the "processes of articulation through which past happenings and their meanings are discursively produced, transmitted and mediated" (Radstone, 2005, p. 137).

Whereas there have been many studies on anticolonial nationalist overturnings of publicly accepted versions of Indian history, there are fewer studies of the ways in which articulations of public memory have been challenged. One possibility for such research is to look at immediate and very public contestations of attempts by the state to craft public memory. Such contestations could include the defacing of state monuments (see Wheelan, 2002, on colonial Ireland), the shunning of imperial ceremonies (such as the black-flag protests of the visit to India by the Prince of Wales in 1922), and the challenging of expert interpretations of violence. For instance, after a police shooting during the 1930 civil disobedience movement in Delhi, the local magistrate swiftly issued a report claiming that the shooting was not only "inevitable" but also "manly" (Legg, 2005b, p. 191). However, testimonials from the injured and the bereaved and detailed investigations into the number of bullets fired compiled graphic details of the scars, bullet wounds, and the overpowering grief in which the shooting had resulted. These findings, which were widely published, led the countercommittee established by the local Sikh community to insist that the shooting had been "indiscriminate, vindictive, and excessive" (p. 191), a conclusion that was commemorated by processions throughout the city in the years that followed. Rather than producing a mournful acceptance of the violence that had occurred, the accounts encouraged a melancholic refusal to forget it.

These points are cogent reminders that forms of collective memorialization and countermemorialization must be rooted in the body as both a physical site and an object of routinization and conduct (Connerton, 1989). Gandhi was keenly aware of this need for trans-scalar nationalist politics, which he propagated by minutely detailing the processions, flag-raisings, sexual habits, diets, songs, clothing, and modes of exercise that were to constitute the new nationalist body (Alter, 2000). Such practices had two aims: to create the impression that a certain space had survived colonial state-making and to stress that those spaces were to be intensely political (Chatterjee, 1989; Legg, 2003).

But this new sphere of the political was hotly contested. Forms of political affiliation based on faith and religious community had been growing during the nineteenth century, often as voluntary associations and reform groups. They became increasingly politicized in the charged atmosphere of the interwar years and were complemented by organizations established explicitly to defend their religious community and, later, to demand their own independent territorial homelands (Pandey, 1990; Veer, 1994). With the final outcome being anything but certain until shortly before August 1947, the horrific violence that erupted between Hindus and Muslims from 1946 to 1948 resulted in three "partitions of memory" (Kaul, 2001): of the subcontinent into India and Pakistan, the latter divided into East and West; of Bengal (divided Into East Pakistan and the Indian province of West Bengal) and the Punjab (which was divided between West Pakistan and India); and of local communities, families, and bodies, as result of (Pandey, 2001, p. 21). There has never been agreement on the number uprooted and killed in this violence. Didur (2006), for example, estimates eight to ten million migrants and 100,000–500,000 deaths; Butalia (2000), up to 1,200,000 migrants and one million deaths. Pandey (2001) observes that this violence "was not industrialised slaughter, directed from a distance, but a hand-to-hand, face-to-face destruction, frequently involving neighbour against neighbour. Its sites were more random. Its archives are more dispersed and imprecise" (p. 45). Just as other scholars have noted the localized brutality of postcolonial genocides (Mamdani, 2002), Pandey conspicuously calls attention to the "nonindustrialized" nature of this slaughter in order to differentiate it from the bureaucratized murder perpetrated in Germany and German-controlled areas under the Third Reich (see Gellately & Kiernan, 2003). Many commentators label the violence of partition as genocide (Brass, 2003); others have even tried to apply the word Holocaust to it (Godbole, 2006). Although the latter usage reflects failure to appreciate the specificities of that word, it does provoke comparisons between two peaks of violence in an exceptionally brutal decade.

With memory studies being able to extend beyond oral history to memoires, autobiography, and commemoration, a significant branch of this field of enquiry has been informed by efforts to comprehend the aftermath of the Holocaust. Since Yerushalmi's (1982) ground-breaking work on Jewish memory, Holocaust studies have grappled with notions of trauma, recall, witnessing, forgiveness, survival, representation, remnants, atonement, memorialization, and silencing (LaCapra, 1998). Although incomparable in many regards, the Holocaust and Partition can perhaps be compared as the two lodestars under which European and South Asian memory studies have picked their course. The founding amnesia of postcolonial states (Gandhi, 1998) was an active forgetting not just of colonial violence but also of the communal violence of self on self or, as it had come to be seen, self on internal other, that is, what Mamdani (2002) refers to as "politicised indigeneity" (p. 14). Once this powerful urge to forget had been overcome, however, the question remained of how to remember. Would the project be one of charting the incidences, causes, and consequences of communal violence? Would it be a categorizing of the morphology and function of violence? Or a process of classifying places by their degree of violence? Or should the project be more explanatory, that is, geared to examining cases of settling economic debt through communal violence or of institutionally orchestrating violence?

Srinivasan (1990) has argued that these categories would, in reality, work to normalize violence. Certainly, they may provide vital details for a thoroughgoing history of Partition, yet they risk ascribing a degree of finitude and pastness to questions that are infinite in their potential for interpretation and disputation and nothing less than present in the lived memories and political violence of contemporary South Asia. Srinivasan suggests that the study of violence focus on the "survivor" as an alternative interpretative category. The category itself would be analyzed as a nascent subject in post-partition India, but it would also be explored for its heuristic potential, as a channel for plumbing the traumatic, subaltern memories of violence itself. The archives would indeed be, as Pandey (2001) put it, more dispersed and imprecise than those of traditional historical research and would yield up accounts of witnessing that would throw into question the very concept of a history, or even histor*ies*, of partition.

Memory work on partition has been especially devoted to un-forgetting the experiences of women during and after partition. As Das (2000) has asked: "The violations inscribed on the female body (both literally and figuratively) and the discursive formations around these violations made visible the imagination of the nation as a masculine nation. What did this do to the subjectivity of women?" (p. 205). How do women become victims of ethnic or communal violence through gendered acts of violation? How do women live with this violence through domestication, ritualization, and renarration? How can one recollect the stories of the women who were abducted, the estimates of which range from 75,000 (Butalia, 2000) to 100,000 (Das, 1997)? These issues are part of the broader project of what Menon and Bhasin (1998) call gendered history, which reorients itself away from the objects of political history (making law, wealth, art, science, or war) from which women have traditionally been excluded.

One approach has been to look into women's writings (Didur, 2006). Although this kind of literature can challenge state narratives and represents a significant section of society, it has also been argued that this line of interpretation favors people able to have their words read and that it may rely on writing strategies that privilege nationalist imaginaries or traditional narratives. More popular has been work on oral histories of partition violence, notably Butalia's *The Other Side of Silence: Voices from the Partition of India* (2000). The focus of her investigations was Pandey's third type of partition, exploring how, for example, families were divided, friendships endured, people coped with the trauma, people rebuilt their lives, what resources were drawn upon, or how dislocation shaped survivors' lives.

> This collection of memories, individual and collective, familial and historical, are what make up the reality of Partition. They illuminate what one might call the 'underside' of its history. They are the ways in which we can know this event. In many senses, they *are* the history of the event. (Butalia, 2000, p. 8)

Studies of this sort highlight not just the experiences of generalized communal violence of partition but also the specifically gendered and sexualized violence enacted upon women. Menon and Bhasin (1998) insist that the retelling of this violence must not be through historical representations but rather through women's memories of violence, abduction, recovery, widowhood, women's rehabilitation, rebuilding, and belonging in the aftermath of sexual violence. This early emphasis on recollection does, however, neglect one of the chief contributions of these partition studies and others like them; namely, the fact that what is not said is often as telling as what is (on the contrast with Euro-American readings of silence as regressive, see Mallot,

2006, p. 168). The connotations of shame, guilt, betrayal, and pollution that were attached to rape, especially across communal divides, has pushed the experience of gendered violence beyond the realms of representation for many women. This experience does not lie in a land beyond representation, waiting to be recalled into the territory of speech; it is an experience that may be inherently beyond representation.

Of course, I do not mean to suggest that recall cannot contribute to memories of partition. Sinha-Kerkhoff (2004) has used oral histories to show how communities often categorized as either Muslim or Hindu have rejected such labels and their retrospective use to explain the past. Such accounts can also force one to address not only the bewildering range of sexualized violence but its inherent geography as well:

> The range of sexual violence explicit in the above accounts—stripping; parading naked; mutilating and disfiguring; tattooing or branding the breasts and genitalia with triumphal slogans; amputating breasts; knifing open the womb; raping, of course; killing foetuses—is shocking not only for its savagery, but for what it tells us about women as objects in male constructions of their own honour. . . . In the context of Partition, it engraved the division of India into India and Pakistan on the women of both religious communities in a way that they became the respective countries, indelibly imprinted by the Other. (Menon & Bhasin, 1998, p. 43)

Postcolonial Memory Politics

The fact that active forgetting of political violence has continued during India's independent era, has provoked a series of fascinating research projects into subaltern experiences of this violence. This work's methodological problems and interrogations of the archive have been similar to those of research on colonial memory politics, although the advantage of the postcolonial events being more recent is offset by the guardedness with which details of political violence are policed. Tarlo (2003) has placed the actual experience of seeking out memories of India's "Emergency" period, both archival and personal, at the center of her book, *Unsettling memories: Narratives of the Emergency in Delhi.* She inquires into the forced sterilizations and slum clearances that took place during India's partial suspension of democratic rule between June 1976 and March 1977, but she also underlines the challenges of locating recollections of an event that has been partially purged from the archive and wilfully forgotten by protectors of Indira Gandhi's legacy. As Tarlo says of the Emergency:

> Not only does it threaten the precarious image of India as 'essentially non-violent'—an image increasingly difficult to sustain—but it also implicates the state as the key agent of violence. More threatening still, the Emergency challenges the discourse of democracy which claims an unbroken hold over India's past from the present day right back to the attainment of Independence in 1947. (p. 22)

Roy (2008, 2009) has, likewise, reflected on the problems associated with retrieving memories of state violence against the Naxalbari movement in western Bengal in the early 1970s.[8] The notion of a narrative cure to traumatic experiences of custodial violence is critiqued as a process that can domesticate and discipline the radical and disruptive experience of rape or torture. The use of the body as both a trace of violence and a substitute for language during women's recollections of their experiences helped Roy explore how survival itself became the process by which violence has been comprehended.

Although memories of Naxalbari-related violence have not been addressed through commemoration, sites of violence that fit into nationalist narratives have been commemorated in India (including the New Delhi bungalows in which both Mohandas and Indira Gandhi were assassinated). Mookherjee (2007) has written about comparable sites in Bangladesh, which was formed on the territory of East Pakistan when the latter broke away from West Pakistan in 1971. During one incident in the war between East and West Pakistan, around 50 intellectuals were killed by occupying forces and their collaborators. This massacre has made these individuals, known as "martyred intellectuals," a focal point for commemoration of the war in Bangladesh. Mookherjee has examined the corresponding sites and monuments, remarking how they simultaneously sanitize the deaths and situate the melancholic sites within particular middle-class aesthetics and structures of nation-making (for reflections on violent memories in Pakistan, see Iqbal, 2008).

This chapter has stressed political violence that, especially in a country like Bangladesh, may well be remembered less than the violence done by floods, droughts, typhoons, or earthquakes. But environmentally wrought memories, too, can become politicized, as Simpson (2005) has shown in relation to the 2001 earthquake in the northern Indian state of Gujarat, an event estimated to have killed 16,500 people. Commenting on the urban politics of Bhuj, Gujarat's ravaged capital, Simpson has shown how various types of nostalgia emerged during reconstruction, both for the past royal state instead of the linguistically defined territory of Gujarat, and for previous kinds of community and social interaction. Yet these nostalgic urges were undercut by the altered social conditions resulting from the earthquake: The increased individualization spawned by the social anguish and mistrust caused by compensation claims undercut communitarian nationalist campaigns and shattered the institutions and practices that had engendered community cohesion and collective memory. Such dynamics prompted Simpson to reflect on Halbwachs's failure to consider the fragile connection points by which individual and collective memory are mediated (see also Radstone, 2005). One widely proclaimed material vehicle for this mediation is the monument, which in Simpson and Corbridge's (2006) reflections has a role as a means of dictating how the earthquake would be remembered in Gujarat. This process was orchestrated by high-caste Hindus, to the exclusion of other castes and religions, around a particularly nostalgic view of the past as part of a specific regional political agenda. The complex memory politics of this move are summarized by Simpson and Corbridge (2006): "The earthquake clearly is a break with the past, at least in terms of personal memory; but, because of the renewed importance of the past in a more general sense, there is now more past in the present than there was before the disaster" (p. 581).

Communal politics have been woefully prevalent in Gujarat, as expressed during communal riots in 2002, which killed 2,000 Muslims and made 150,000 homeless. The attacks were in reaction to the supposedly Muslim-incited burning of a train coach that left 58 people dead, mostly Hindus. Despite attempts by the Hindu nationalist government to dictate how the event was to be remembered, the extremity of the violence has led to its widespread designation as a "pogrom" because of the role played by the institutions of political society, either as bystanders or active participants. The nature of the violence set up harrowing comparisons and traumatic recollections:

> The use of systematic rape and sexual violence as a strategy for terrorizing and brutalizing women in conflict situations echoes experiences of women in Bangladesh in 1971, and in countries such as Rwanda, Bosnia and Algeria. In Gujarat, as in all these other countries, women have been targeted as members of the 'other' community, as symbols of the community's honour and as the ones who sustain the community and reproduce the next generation. This has become an all too common aspect of larger political projects of genocide, crimes against humanity and subjugation. (The International Initiative for Justice in Gujarat, 2003, paragraph 6)

T. Sarkar (2002) also forcefully spoke of the painful recollections that this violence elicited but claimed that the mobs of Gujarat had exceeded Nazi terror, Bosnian genocide, and even partition violence through the sheer intensity and sadistic exuberance of their cruelty, especially against Muslim women. Once again, the woman's body was territorialized, claimed, divided, invaded, and exposed as a site of almost inexhaustible violence. How this violence will be remembered, how its victims will survive, and how the designs of right-wing Hindu nationalists to forget the pogrom will be resisted are just some of the challenging questions facing scholars of contemporary India.

This brutality was driven by socially engrained memories of partition violence, but myths and traditions beyond the time scale of individual memory are also driving contemporary communalism in India, bringing out the explicit geographies of memory politics. The train carriage that was burned in Gujarat had been returning from Ayodhya, the city in which the Babri Masjid mosque had stood between 1528 and December 1992 (Bacchetta, 2000; Corbridge & Simpson, 2006). Hindu nationalists claimed that the mosque had been built on the site that marked the birthplace of Lord Ram, an incarnation of the Hindu god Vishnu. The mosque had been contested since the nineteenth century but was demolished by the gathered crowds only under the stewardship of the elected Hindu nationalist state government. The demolition sparked riots throughout India, for the official history of the site was contested by those who saw the mosque as a monument to an external, invading society and who mobilized ancient, violent memories regarding the site—with devastating results.

Conclusion

This review has necessarily been partial and exclusionary, and many of the events and debates covered will be dismissed by many readers as not being about memory at all. Though I have only alluded to a comparative approach, it is a research agenda that could be pursued to great effect. I have suggested certain similarities between Holocaust and partition studies and suspect that a methodological dialogue between these two vast scholarly enterprises would be incredibly productive. Debates on commemoration and postcommemoration (J. Young, 1993), trauma and witnessing (Edkins, 2003), and the city (Ladd, 1997; Till, 2005) surely have much to offer South Asian studies. Their focus on the reenactment of violent communal memories may, in turn, acquaint Holocaust scholars with stimulating lines of thought about the performative ways in which the past haunts the present. However, the dangers of exporting a European model, with its assumptions about the body, psyche, trauma, and memory, must be held in a productive tension with the possibilities of comparative work (Mallot, 2006).

People uncomfortable with a dialogue solely between the old imperial core and the colonial periphery will find fascinating work for comparison in Latin America (e.g., Bosco, 2004; Huyssen, 2003) and South Africa (Colvin, 2003), not to mention an innovative body of research on the memory politics of sites in Southeast Asia. This kind of inquiry has addressed issues of commemoration and scalar politics (Grace, 2007; Muzaini & Yeoh, 2007); the remembering of war and genocide (Hughes, 2003; Yoneyama, 1999); memory and new Asian urbanism (Chang, 2005); the unforgetting of sexualized colonial violence (Kim, 2005); and the survival of memories within rapidly modernizing landscapes (Noparatnaraporn & King, 2007). These studies could add another layer of intensity to the already remarkably diverse work on the violent memories of South Asia.

Acknowledgement I thank Peter Meusberger, Edgar Wunder, and all the staff at Villa Bosch in Heidelberg for the wonderful hospitality they offered during the symposia at which I originally presented the paper on which this chapter is based. It has since benefited from the helpful comments of an anonymous referee and from Srila Roy. Much of this material emerged from the "Geographies of Violence" lecture course I co-teach with Alex Vasudevan and Mike Heffernan. It has benefitted immensely from discussions with them and with the students who took the module.

Notes

1. I note the uncertain etymology of the term *Indian summer*, whether referring to South Asian or North American "Indians." However, this ambiguity seems appropriate in a chapter intended to challenge the notion of linear historical origins.
2. Retrieved March 11, 2008, from http://www.bbc.co.uk/indiapakistan/
3. Retrieved March 11, 2008, from http://www.bbc.co.uk/history/british/modern/independence1947_01.shtml
4. Retrieved March 11, 2008, from http://news.bbc.co.uk/1/hi/world/south_asia/6939997.stm
5. Retrieved March 11, 2008, from http://news.bbc.co.uk/1/hi/in_depth/629/629/6945591.stm
6. Retrieved March 11, 2008, from http://www.bbc.co.uk/dna/memoryshare
7. Retrieved March 11, 2008, from http://chnm.gmu.edu/wwh/modules/lesson8/lesson8.php?s=6#
8. This movement grew out of an incident that took place on May 25, 1967, when police in the northwestern Bengali village of Naxalbari shot and killed a group of villagers demanding their rights to harvest crops from a particular plot.

References

Aldrich, R. (2005). *Vestiges of the colonial empire in France: Monuments, museums, and colonial memories.* New York: Palgrave Macmillan.

Alter, J. S. (2000). *Gandhi's body: Sex, diet, and the politics of nationalism.* Philadelphia: University of Pennsylvania Press.

Amin, S. (1995). *Event, metaphor, memory: Chauri Chaura, 1922–1992.* Berkeley, CA: University of California Press.

Bacchetta, P. (2000). Sacred space in conflict in India: The Babri Masjid affair. *Growth and Change, 31,* 255–284.

Bailkin, J. (2006). The boot and the spleen: When was murder possible in British India? *Comparative Studies in Society and History, 48,* 464–493.

Baucom, I. (1999). *Out of place: Englishness, empire, and the locations of identity.* Princeton, NJ: Princeton University Press.

Bevan, R. (2006). *The destruction of memory: Architecture at war.* London: Reaktion.

Bosco, F. J. (2004). Human rights politics and scaled performances of memory: Conflicts among the Madres de Plaza de Mayo in Argentina. *Social and Cultural Geography, 5,* 381–402.

Brass, P. (2003). The partition of India and retributive genocide in the Punjab, 1946–47: Means, methods, and purposes. *Journal of Genocide Research, 5,* 71–101.

Butalia, U. (2000). *The other side of silence: Voices from the partition of India.* London: Hurst & Co.

Chang, T. C. (2005). Place, memory and identity: Imagining "New Asia." *Asia Pacific Viewpoint, 46,* 247–253.

Chatterjee, P. (1989). The nationalist resolution of the women's question. In K. Sangari & S. Vaid (Eds.), *Recasting women: Essays in colonial history* (pp. 233–253). New Delhi: Kali for Women.

Chatterjee, P. (1993). *The nation and its fragments: Colonial and postcolonial histories.* Princeton, NJ: Princeton University Press.

Chattopadhyay, S. (2005). *Representing Calcutta: Modernity, nationalism and the colonial uncanny.* London: Routledge.

Chaturvedi, V. (2000). *Mapping subaltern studies and the postcolonial.* London: Verso.

Chaudhuri, Z. (2005). Phantasmagoric aesthetics: Colonial violence and the management of perception. *Cultural Critique, 59,* 63–119.

Colvin, C. J. (2003). "Brothers and sisters, do not be afraid of me": Trauma, history and the therapeutic imagination in the new South Africa. In K. Hodgkin & S. Radstone (Eds.), *Contested pasts: The politics of memory* (pp. 153–167). London: Routledge.

Connerton, P. (1989). *How societies remember.* Cambridge, England: Cambridge University Press.

Corbridge, S., & Simpson, E. (2006). Militant cartographies and traumatic spaces: Ayodhya, Bhuj and the contested geographies of Hindutva. In S. Corbridge, S. Kumar, & S. Raju (Eds.), *Colonial and postcolonial geographies of India* (pp. 70–84). London: Sage.

Dalrymple, W. (2006). *The last Mughal: The fall of a dynasty, Delhi, 1857.* London: Bloomsbury.

Das, V. (1995). *Critical events: An anthropology of perspective on contemporary India.* Delhi: Oxford University Press.

Das, V. (1997). Language and body: Transactions in the construction of pain. In V. Das, A. Kleinman, M. Lock, M. Ramphele, & P. Reynolds (Eds.), *Remaking a world: Violence, social suffering, and recovery* (pp. 67–91). Berkeley, CA: University of California Press.

Das, V. (2000). The act of witnessing: Violence, poisonous knowledge, and subjectivity. In V. Das, A. Kleinman, P. Ranshele, & P. Reynolds (Eds.), *Violence and subjectivity* (pp. 205–225). Berkeley, CA: University of California Press.

Didur, J. (Ed.). (2006). *Unsettling partition: Literature, gender, memory.* Toronto: University of Toronto Press.

Edkins, J. (2003). *Trauma and the memory of politics.* Cambridge, UK: Cambridge University Press.

Fanon, F. (1965). *The wretched of the earth.* London: MacGibbon & Key.

Fentress, J., & Wickham, C. (1992). *Social memory.* Oxford, UK: Blackwell.

Gandhi, L. (1998). *Postcolonial theory: A critical introduction.* Edinburgh: Edinburgh University Press.

Gellately, R., & Kiernan, B. (2003). *The specter of genocide: Mass murder in historical perspective*. Cambridge, UK: Cambridge University Press.

Godbole, M. (2006). *The holocaust of Indian partition: An inquest*. New Delhi: Rupa & Co.

Grace, H. (2007). Monuments and the face of time: Distortions of scale and asynchrony in postcolonial Hong Kong. *Postcolonial studies, 10*, 467–483.

Graham, S. (2004). Constructing urbicide by bulldozer in the occupied territories. In S. Graham (Ed.), *Cities, war, and terrorism* (pp. 192–213). Oxford, England: Blackwell.

Gross, D. (2000). *Lost time: On remembering and forgetting in late modern culture*. Amherst, MA: University of Massachusetts Press.

Guha, R., & Spivak, G. C. (Eds.). (1988). *Selected subaltern studies*. New York: Oxford University Press.

Guha, R. (1982). On some aspects of the historiography of colonial India. In R. Guha (Ed.), *Subaltern studies I* (pp. 1–8). Delhi: Oxford University Press.

Gupta, N. (1981). *Delhi between two empires, 1803–1931: Society, government and urban growth*. Delhi: Oxford University Press.

Halbwachs, M. (1992). *On collective memory* (L. A. Coser, Ed. & Trans., with an Introduction by L. A. Coser). Chicago: University of Chicago Press. (Original work published 1925)

Hall, C. (2007). Remembering 1807: Histories of the slave trade, slavery and abolition. *History Workshop Journal, 64*, 1–5.

Healy, C. (1997). *From the ruins of colonialism: History as social memory*. Cambridge, UK: Cambridge University Press.

Hughes, R. (2003). Nationalism and memory at the Tuol Sleng Museum of genocide crimes, Phnom Penh, Cambodia. In K. Hodgkin & S. Radstone (Eds.), *Contested pasts: The politics of memory* (pp. 175–192). London: Routledge.

Hutton, P. H. (1993). *History as an art of memory*. Hanover, NH: University Press of New England.

Huyssen, A. (2003). *Present pasts: Urban palimpsests and the politics of memory*. Stanford, CA: Stanford University Press.

International Initiative for Justice in Gujarat. (2003). *An interim report*. Retrieved July 31, 2010, from http://www.onlinevolunteers.org/gujarat/reports/iijg/interimreport.htm

Iqbal, F. (2008). *Pakistan and violence: Memory, shame, and repression*. Retrieved March 13, 2008, from http://www.opendemocracy.net/node/35824/pdf

Kaul, S. (2001). *The partitions of India: The afterlife of the division of India*. Delhi: Permanent Black.

Kim, H. S. (2005). History and memory: The "comfort women" controversy. In T. Ballantyne & A. Burton (Eds.), *Bodies in contact: Rethinking colonial encounters in world history* (pp. 363–382). Durham, NC: Duke University Press.

LaCapra, D. (1998). *History and memory after Auschwitz*. Ithaca, NY: Cornell University Press.

Ladd, B. (1997). *The ghosts of Berlin: Confronting German history in the urban landscape*. Chicago: University of Chicago Press.

Lahiri, N. (2003). Commemorating and remembering 1857: The revolt in Delhi and its afterlife. *World Archaeology, 35*, 35–60.

Legg, S. (2003). Gendered politics and nationalised homes: Women and the anti-colonial struggle in Delhi, 1930–47. *Gender, Place and Culture: A Journal of Feminist Geography, 10*, 7–27.

Legg, S. (2005a). Contesting and surviving memory: Space, nation and nostalgia in Les Lieux de Mémoire. *Environment and Planning D: Society and Space, 23*, 481–504.

Legg, S. (2005b). Sites of counter-memory: The refusal to forget and the nationalist struggle in colonial Delhi. *Historical Geography, 33*, 180–201.

Levine, P. (2005). Review article: Britain's eighteenth-century empire. *Social History, 30*, 218–223.

Mallot, J. E. (2006). Body politics and the body politic: Memory as human inscription in what the body remembers. *Interventions, 8*, 165–177.

Mamdani, M. (2002). *When victims become killers—Colonialism, nativism, and the genocide in Rwanda*. Princeton, NJ: Princeton University Press.

Mannoni, O. (1990). *Prospero and Caliban: The psychology of colonization.* Ann Arbor, MI: University of Michigan Press. (Original work published 1950)

Mbembe, A. (2003). Necropolitics. *Public Culture, 15,* 11–40.

Menon, R., & Bhasin, K. (1998). *Borders and boundaries: How women experienced the partition of India.* New Brunswick, NJ: Rutgers University Press.

Middleton, D., & Brown, S. D. (2005). *The social psychology of experience: Studies in remembering and forgetting.* London: Sage.

Mookherjee, N. (2007). The "dead and their double duties": Mourning, melancholia, and the martyred intellectual memorials in Bangladesh. *Space and Culture, 10,* 271–291.

Muzaini, H., & Yeoh, B. (2007). Memory-making "from below": Rescaling remembrance at the Kranji War Memorial and Cemetery, Singapore. *Environment and Planning A, 39,* 1288–1305.

Nandy, A. (1983). *Intimate enemy: Loss and recovery of self under colonialism.* Delhi: Oxford University Press.

Noparatnaraporn, C., & King, R. (2007). Memory or nostalgia: The imagining of everyday Bangkok. *SOJURN: Journal of Social Issues in Southeast Asia, 22,* 57–82.

Nora, P. (1989). Between memory and history: Les lieux de mémoire. *Representations, 26,* 7–25.

Oldenburg, V. T. (1984). *The making of colonial Lucknow, 1856–1877.* Princeton, NJ: Princeton University Press.

Olick, J. K., & Robbins, J. (1998). Social memory studies: From "collective memory" to the historical sociology of mnemonic practices. *Annual Review of Sociology, 24,* 105–140.

O'Hanlon, R. (1988). Recovering the subject: Subaltern studies and histories of resistance in colonial South Asia. *Modern Asian Studies, 22,* 189–224.

Pandey, G. (1990). *The construction of communalism in colonial North India.* Delhi: Oxford University Press.

Pandey, G. (2001). *Remembering partition: Violence, nationalism and history in India.* Cambridge, England: Cambridge University Press.

Pennebaker, J. W. (1997). Introduction. In J. W. Pennebaker, D. Paez, & B. Rimé (Eds.), *Collective memory of political events: Social psychological perspectives* (pp. vii–xi). Mahwah, NJ: Lawrence Erlbaum Associates.

Prakash, G. (2007, April 30). *Inevitable revolutions* (pp. 25–30). New York: The Nation.

Procida, M. (2002). *Married to the empire: Gender, politics and imperialism in India, 1883–1947.* Manchester, England: Manchester University Press.

Radstone, S. (2005). Reconceiving binaries: The limits of memory. *History Workshop Journal, 59,* 134–150.

Rossington, M., & Whitehead, A. (2007). Introduction. In M. Rossington & A. Whitehead (Eds.), *Theories of memory: A reader* (pp. 1–16). Edinburgh: Edinburgh University Press.

Roy, S. (2008). The grey zone: The ordinary violence of extraordinary times. *Journal of the Royal Anthropological Institute, 14,* 316–333.

Roy, S. (2009). Testimonies of state terror: Trauma and healing in Naxalbari. In P. Roy, P. Chatterjee, & M. Desai (Eds.), *States of trauma: Gender and violence in South Asia* (pp. 141–171). Delhi: Zubaan Books.

Samuel, R. (1994). *Theatres of memory: Past and present in contemporary culture* (Vol. 1). London: Verso.

Sarkar, M. (2006). Difference in Memory. *Comparative Studies in Society and History, 48,* 139–168.

Sarkar, T. (2002). Semiotics of terror: Muslim children and women in Hindu Rashtra. *Economic and Political Weekly, 37,* 2872–2876.

Simpson, E. (2005). The "Gujarat" earthquake and the political economy of nostalgia. *Contributions to Indian Sociology, 39,* 219–249.

Simpson, E., & Corbridge, S. (2006). The geography of things that may become memories: The 2001 earthquake in Kachchh-Gujarat and the politics of rehabilitation in the prememorial era. *Annals of the Association of American Geographers, 96,* 566–585.

Sinha-Kerkhoff, K. (2004). Voices of difference: Partition memory and memories of Muslims in Jharkhand, India. *Critical Asian Studies, 36*, 113–142.

Spivak, G. C. (1985). Subaltern studies: Deconstructing historiography. In R. Guha (Ed.), *Subaltern studies* (vol. 4, pp. 330–363). Delhi: Oxford University Press.

Spivak, G. C. (2000). Can the subaltern speak? In D. Brydon (Ed.), *Postcolonialism: Critical concepts in literary and cultural studies* (pp. 1427–1477). London: Routledge. (Original work published 1988)

Srinivasan, A. (1990). The survivor in the study of violence. In V. Das (Ed.), *Mirrors of violence: Communities, riots and survivors in South Asia* (pp. 304–319). Oxford, UK: Oxford University Press.

Tarlo, E. (2003). *Unsettling memories: Narratives of the Emergency in Delhi*. London: Hurst and Company.

Till, K. E. (2005). *The new Berlin: Memory, politics, place*. Minneapolis, MN: University of Minnesota Press.

Veer, P. van der (1994). *Religious nationalism: Hindus and Muslims in India*. Berkeley, CA: University of California Press.

Wheelan, Y. (2002). The construction and destruction of a colonial landscape: Monuments to British monarchs in Dublin before and after independence. *Journal of Historical Geography, 28*, 508–533.

Yerushalmi, Y. H. (1982). *Zakhor: Jewish history and Jewish memory*. Seattle, WA: University of Washington Press.

Yoneyama, L. (1999). *Hiroshima traces: Time, space, and the dialectics of memory*. Berkeley, CA: University of California Press.

Young, J. (1993). *The texture of memory: Holocaust memorials and meaning*. New Haven, CT: Yale University Press.

Young, R. C. (2001). *Postcolonialism: An historical introduction*. Oxford, UK: Blackwell.

Spacing Forgetting: The Birth of the Museum at Fort Jesus, Mombasa, and the Legacies of the Colonization of Memory in Kenya

Denis Linehan and João Sarmento

Cornerstone Geographies

As the cornerstone of colonial expansion into East Africa, and, consequently, as one of the most important public buildings on the continent, Fort Jesus in Mombasa, Kenya, presents many opportunities to investigate the intersection of colonialism, memory, and power. The fort was built in 1594 by the Portuguese to help secure their foothold in East Africa and to provision and protect their expansive trading network in the Indian Ocean. With its caramel-colored rampart of hewn coral looming over the old-town district (Fig. 1) and its modern role as a hub of cultural activity and tourism in the city, the fort is listed by UNESCO as a potential world heritage site. It has a violent past and is shaped by multiple layers of history and memory. Over time it fell under and out of Portuguese control and operated for 300 years as the command center of the Omani Sultanate and, later, the Sultan of Zanzibar (Hinaway, 1970). It also functioned as a prison under the British from the late nineteenth century until a period in the 1950s that paralleled the Mau Mau revolt in Kenya, at which time the fort was converted into a museum. This conversion was funded with the assistance of the Portuguese government, which grasped the opportunity to restore the fort as part of that country's public commemoration of Prince Henry the Navigator, a paramount figure in Portuguese national and imperial identity. This chapter focuses on the transformation of the fort from a prison into a museum, a remarkable moment of colonial authority and anticolonial struggle that involved key figures of the Kenyan anticolonial movement, notably the trade unionist and nationalist politician Tom Mboya, and the leader of the East African Goan League, journalist Pio Gama Pinto.

D. Linehan (✉)
School of Geography and Archeology, University College Cork, Cork, Ireland
e-mail: d.linehan@ucc.ie

J. Sarmento
Department of Geography, University of Minho, 4800-058 Guimarães, Portugal; Centre for Geographical Studies, University of Lisbon, Portugal
e-mail: j.sarmento@geografia.uminho.pt

Fig. 1 Fort Jesus, Mombasa, 2007. Photograph Authors

Consulting archival sources in Nairobi, Kenya, and Lisbon, Portugal, we recover the history of the birth of the museum and analyze how the alliances, motives, and protests pertaining to the museum's creation were shaped by questions of memory, politics, and colonialism. We read against the grain of the colonialist archive, turning to strategies offered by Edward W. Said, the prominent Palestinian-American liter-ary theorist and culture critic, through contrapuntal critique of historical sources. We broaden his approaches from text to space in an "effort to draw out, extend, and give emphasis and voice to what is silent or marginally present ... in such works" (Said, 1994, p. 66). The architecture of the museum, like that of other colonial build-ings, was put to work to inscribe power and shape the identities and the narratives it projected onto the history of the Kenyan coast. It played havoc with African mem-ory, "initiating new forms of amnesia, nostalgia and false memories" (Mazrui, 2000, p. 87). These histories operated in colonial space and were constructed in "an arc of interests and concerns spanning the hemisphere" (Said, 1994, p. 101). At first glance these events may seem remote from the pressing social and political con-cerns in contemporary Kenya, but we propose that the memory politics that were at work in Fort Jesus in the mid–twentieth century remain relevant to debates about heritage and memory today. With a steady eye on what Gregory (2004) has defined as the "colonial present," we first consider issues of public memory and politics in contemporary Kenya and then reconstruct the arc of interest and concerns that cre-ated the museum in the 1950s. We concentrate on the construction of a colonialist perspective on the cultural landscape, the imperial memory work of the Portuguese, and the contestation of this process when the museum opened.

Memory Work and Disruption

Kenya is a challenging place to think about the cultural geographies of memory. Historical experience there has created a disruptive landscape in which to reflect on the relationships between public memory, the production of knowledge, and cultural self-definition. Public memory in Kenya is volatile; often politicized; and frequently subject to omissions, effacement, and amnesia. Both the legacies of colonialism and the inequitable social and political outcomes of the postcolonial settlement contribute to this volatility. In colonial times many aspects of Kenyan culture and history were systematically framed and subjected to western epistemological codes. Forms of knowledge found particularly in anthropology, archeology, and paleontology coded and categorized the Kenyan people from western perspectives. These forms of knowledge and the representations of land and culture embedded within them acted "as a form of epistemic violence to the extent that it involved immeasurable disruption and erasure of local cultural systems" (Simatei, 2005, p. 85). For that reason Kusimba (1996) has criticized the ways in which anthropologists and historians have "falsified the history of the Swahilis, presenting them as descendants of Asian colonists, [causing] irreversible damage to the community's perception of itself in relation to other Kenyans" (p. 201). This distortion has been used to legitimate the destruction of Swahili sites and monuments and the systematic misappropriation of sacred Swahili lands. Moreover, postcolonial criticism, despite its impacts in academic circles, has not effectively challenged such colonial modes of knowledge within the region. The ghosts of the colonial episteme, the range of discourses and fields of knowledge that constructed and maintained truth statements about the benefits of colonialism, still pervade many aspects of cultural heritage in Kenya, such as its museum and national monuments, which continue to exhibit an array of imperial traces and gloss over the horrors of colonization and slavery.

Compounding the issues raised by these legacies since independence, the Kenyan state has not actively pursued a coherent and sustained memory-making enterprise of its own as part of a nation-building exercise. Jomo Kenyatta, the first president of Kenya, exemplified this approach by instituting an overarching discourse of forgive and forget' in order to restore Kenya's international reputation, which had been undermined by negative representations of the Mau Mau revolt during the 1950s. More specifically, his aim was to maintain the commercial and political fabric of a neocolonial state: "It is the future, my friends, that is living and the past that is dead" (Kenyatta, 1964, p. 2). This decision to blot out the past from which independence was forged was probably unique among twentieth century states, for Kenya thereby officially disavowed its political origins. Since that period, Kenya has been diverging rather than integrating in civil and cultural terms: "Kenya has become a cesspool of all genres of political violence that have effectively confined its embryonic democracy to cold storage" (Kagwanja, 2003, p. 25).

In stark contrast to the nation-building orientation of the memory work of various postcolonial states in Asia (see Yeoh, 2002), debates and discussions about the past have often been evaded in Kenya, for engaging in them would disturb the neocolonial status quo and would question the motives of the postcolonial elites.

Memories of postcolonial injustice, inequity, violence, and abuse are still so strong in Kenya that the principal memory work of the state has been to promote their eradication. The Kenyan human rights lawyer Pheroze Nowrojee argues that "every office holder in Government" has "erased our history and moved to the [aggrandizement] of Presidents and rulers" (Nowrojee, 2002, p. 1). Whereas Nora (1989) contends that there are sites of memory (*lieux de mémoire*) because the lived environments of memory (*milieux de mémoire*) have dissipated, it arguable that the opposite is quite possibly the case in Kenya. The violence following the 2007 election demonstrates that Kenya is engulfed by the consequence of the memories of unresolved injustices—a political problem that remains unresolved and has impeded the effective operation of the Truth, Justice and Reconciliation Commission established in 2008. Together, the colonial and postcolonial conditions have disturbed a coherent version of the past and have thrown the process of public memory-making into turmoil. The dual origins of this condition, in turn, generate their spaces and outcomes, a process that has played into treatments of heritage and culture over the last 2 decades. The vacuum left by these disruptions has been filled by unfettered commercialization of culture, the lack of protection for national heritage (particularly cultural artifacts), an impeded treatment of history, and an unsustained policy of national commemoration.

Many of these conditions intersect at Fort Jesus, and the conditions of memory at work in the place may well be symptomatic of the condition of public memory in many parts of Kenya. Fort Jesus was declared a national monument under the Archaeological and Paleontological Interest Act of 1970, and the Old Town of Mombasa was designated a national monument in 1990. The fort houses a museum, a conservation lab, and an education department and is the nexus of a research program dedicated to the archaeological exploration of the coastal region. The Old Town Conservation Office, which is responsible for an area of roughly 33 ha (81½ acres), is nearby. The fort is open to the public daily from 9:30 A.M. to 6:00 P.M. It can largely be understood as a multifunctional space (see Wazwa, 2006), for its location near the business and commercial center of Mombasa and next to the old town serves many local and regional events: weddings, concerts, art exhibitions, corporate meetings, and social gatherings.

Inside the museum, active intervention in culture is limited and the exhibitions are static. The displays present the results of the archaeological excavations at Fort Jesus (essentially those conducted by British archeologist James Kirkman in the 1950s and 1960s), Gede, Manda, and Ungwana. They also contain donations by colonial collectors and artifacts raised in 1977 from the *Santo António de Tana*, a frigate that sank off the coast of Mombasa in 1697. Visitors walk through these exhibits of rocks, clay, and glass testifying to the cosmopolitan nature of the Swahili Coast, but a number of omissions largely prevent the exhibition from engaging in the dense spaces of struggle that the fort represents. These gaps operate on a number of vectors. For example, the fort must have had a primary stake in the slave trade— slavery was legal in Mombasa up to 1908, when there were over 4,000 slaves in the city—but the museum is silent on the subject. The passageway running down to the sea from the fort that guarded the movement of slaves to waiting ships is innocuously called "Passage of the Arches" rather than "Passage of No Return," the name such routes receive at many slave forts in West Africa. The cells and prison buildings were destroyed during the restoration of the fort in the 1950s, so its erstwhile function as a place of detention is downplayed. Nowhere is there any mention that the fort was used to incarcerate political dissidents who campaigned and fought against British colonial rule. To all intents and purposes the fort is a space for forgetting.

In this narrative void tourists sit for fun on the cannons, pose for photographs on the ramparts, and make scenic landscape shots of the harbor, framing the fort as an Oriental ruin. For about €75 (approximately $120 at 2010 exchange rates), they can take a sunset boat trip in a traditional Arab dhow, followed by a candlelight dinner on the ramparts of the fort. Billed as the Mombasa *Son et Lumière* (sound and light) show, this event converts the fort into a theater and restaurant. Statuesque figures in flowing white Kanzu gowns and kofia caps greet diners with flaming torches; drums beat in the distance, with actors posing as Arab Traders, Portuguese soldiers in sixteenth-century costume, and Omani aristocracy replete with head scarves and ornate Jambiya. The guests, served by waiters dressed as Portuguese naval officers, are treated to a flamboyant, choreographed rendition of the fort's history staged as a blend of the exotic and the arabesque. Telling something of the fort's and Mombasa's turbulent past, it is, in its style and omissions, undeniably interlaced with the legacies of imperialism. The tale excises the role of the British, who controlled Mombasa at the apex of European rule over East Africa and who converted the fort into a prison and then the museum. The past is overly romanticized for the patrons; it is subsumed in an exotic experience that shrouds colonialism in spectacle and nostalgia.

The pageant illustrates some of the dilemmas facing heritage and cultural memory in contemporary Kenya. McMahon (2008) suggests that when performers use the past imaginatively in theatrical productions, the changes they make in representations of race, colonial authority, and the agency of historical subjects relate closely to the way a nation remembers its past. The benign story of the colonial encounter and the framing of the fort and the people of the coast are indicative of the public treatment of colonialism and its ambiguous present in public memory. The present is charged with the legacies of the colonial past, but one of the principle consumers of this history, the western tourist, is spared feelings of guilt and offered instead a stereotyped image and experience of Africa. This cultural framing of the coast is deeply consensual, and given the contribution that tourism makes to the Kenyan economy, it is important to maintaining the *acuna matata* (no problem—be happy) image underpinning Kenya's international profile as a safe, secure, and trouble-free destination. Over the last decade, this image has been periodically damaged by acts of terror and political instability. The 1998 bombing of the US embassy in Nairobi, the suicide car bomb at the Israeli-owned beachfront Paradise Hotel near Mombasa in 2002, and the civil unrest after the 2007 elections have all undermined the Kenyan tourist industry.

As noted by Kasfir (2004), political history and discomfort are effaced by ubiquitous paintings of idyllic tribal village life, wildlife, and apparently "authentic" sculpture of native tribe people in souvenir shops and markets. The journey through Kenya is soothed by the aesthetics of safari style, colonial chic, and the self-consciously primitivist décor of the restaurants, bars, and hotels where tourists mix. This stylization of culture has been more recently enhanced though specialized encounters with "locals" that facilitate apparently ethical forms of consumption or contributions to the environment. Gomongo Village, near Mombasa, provides "a slice of life from about ten cultural groups in Kenya which include the Kikuyu, Turkana, Pokot, Maasai, Akamba … where tourists get to watch the preparation of food, feed crocodiles and meet witch doctors" (Gomongo Village & Ltd, 2008). These forms of ethnographic spectatorship bear an uncomfortable resemblance to the ways in which Africans were portrayed in the living dioramas of European and American exhibitions in the nineteenth and twentieth centuries. But it is clear that such forms of ethnographic and colonial chic have consolidated as a pattern of western cultural consumption of African heritage. The Swahili coast is increasingly dominated by upmarket hotels whose architectural and interior design not only stylize the apparent mystique of colonial times but also reproduce race relations similar to those of that era. Local people working in these exclusive hotel compounds are often dressed in costumes mimicking those that used to be worn by colonial servants. Embraced inside the legacies of imperial spectatorship, the notion of African heritage within these sites is constantly recycled in popular western representations of Kenyan culture. A notable example is a June 2007 issue of *Vogue*, in which British actress Keira Knightly poses in a series of photographs: one where she wears a flamboyant Yves Saint Laurent dress towering above a group of Masai tribesmen, another where she feeds milk in a bottle to a baby elephant wearing a blanket adorned with a large Louis Vuitton logo, and another where she poses as an Edwardian traveler on the Masai Mara. Like many Westerners drawn to Kenya on safaris, she acts out a colonial fantasy that could have been scripted from the pages of Karen Blixon's *Out of Africa* (Sykes, 2007).

These apparently benign memories of the colonial period are just a short step from the performance enjoyed by prosperous tourists on the ramparts of Fort Jesus. They also reveal the extent to which the experience of colonialism has been elided and how far Kenya has drifted from the aspiration of early post independence thinking about historical identity and cultural identity. In 1975 the eminence of culture, history, and heritage for national consolidation in Kenya was underlined in a report to UNESCO:

> The main objective of government cultural policy is therefore clear. It is the realization of national unity and cohesion and the creation of national pride and sense of identity among our people. Apart from the need to protect and preserve valuable assets, the part played by culture in national consolidation is recognized as one of fundamental significance since culture is the symbol of nationhood, the grassroots from which people spring. (As quoted in Ndeti, 1975, p. 35)

It is tempting to argue that the frustration of this dignified and politically astute aspiration is a symptom of the colonial and postcolonial condition in Kenya, which has conspired to disrupt the production and consumption of national heritage. Consequently, the manner in which these conditions influenced the construction of public memory at Fort Jesus offers insight into the origins of the legacies that seem to haunt the site today and indicates ways in which people might consider, and possibly contest, the memory of colonialism in Kenya. Close attention to the space of the museum and its memory work can effectively enable the observer to follow the nature of public memory and its forms, transformation, and meanings within civil society. As a western institution created in a colonial regime, museums in Africa are burdened with the politics of colonial memory and challenged by the reconstruction of new identities. The birth of the museum seems like the appropriate place to start with a critical history of the colonial legacies at Fort Jesus.

Colonialist Cultural Landscape and False Memory

After the physical appropriation of land, the process of laying claim to its history and memory by symbolically appropriating the past was a main ingredient of the colonial enterprise (Mudimbe, 1994). During the colonial period, the activities of white Kenyan historians and British archeologists repositioned Fort Jesus at the center of a cultural landscape and thereby constructed a distinctively colonialist understanding of the past. In the late 1920s, mirroring the goals of the Preservation movement in Britain, the colony of Kenya began legally protecting a number of key buildings and archaeological sites—18 monuments and antiquities in all by 1929. The significance of the Indian Ocean coastal region around Mombasa was clear from the beginning. Fifteen of the first protected sites, said to be Portuguese and Arab ruins, were recognized there, whereas just two tribal sacred sites were protected in the early years of the colony (Hart, 2007). During the 1930s and 1940s, Fort Jesus was increasingly identified as an important, but neglected, asset to the burgeoning tourist industry of the coast. In the 1940s and 1950s, the fort was reimagined as an iconic ruin in the middle of a cultural landscape "discovered" by British archaeologists. Under British rule, however, when Fort Jesus operated as a prison, its presence in the heart of the Mombasa, and more especially within sight of the Mombasa Club— the hub of social life for the British colonial set in the city—became increasingly unsatisfactory. From the correspondence in the archive, a strong opinion seems to have emerged in Mombasa that the fort had to become amenable to urban consumption and not "wasted" on disciplining the natives, who could be imprisoned far away from the city. Prominent visitors to Mombasa were sometimes permitted by the prison warden to tour the fort, but hoteliers and schools in the city were often spurned by the prison administration when they attempted to arrange organized visits.[1]

Through the efforts of the journalist and broadcaster Edward Rodwell, the fort's unsatisfactory status remained in the public eye. His *Gedi—The Lost City* (1946) was the first attempt to promote the archaeology of the region. This evocative book drew upon the *Lost World* literary genre and the text was filled with allusions to the mysterious origins and spectral qualities of the ruined city overtaken by the tropical forest: "The natives who live thereabouts talk of ghosts and weird cries in the night... the sinister silence of the city... pathways that disappear, trees that burst into flames" (p. 19). Rodwell also made clear that the city had its origins in Arab settlement and deemphasized its indigenous African qualities. He replicated this theme in his 1949 collection of essays entitled *Ivory Apes and Peacocks* (a clear allusion to the biblical story of Queen Sheba and Solomon), which focused on Persian, Arabic, and European incursions into East Africa.

In taking this approach, he was operating inside the colonial episteme constructing memories of an ancient kingdom reputed to have governed East Africa, guided in this case by the myth of Azania. (The Azanian thesis also attracted the backing of another British archeologist who played a seminal role in the archaeological exploration of Kenya, G. W. B Huntingford. He identified remnants of the Azanian civilization in his reading of the landscape of stone enclosures, hut circles, tumuli and cairns, earthworks, and irrigation systems; see Huntingford, 1933.) Like many European antiquarians, anthropologists, and archaeologists, Rodwell's work supported the Hamitic myth as well. Now largely understood as a European historical construct, the Hamites were depicted as a distinct population putatively from either Arabia or Asia and were at that time widely accepted as a historical fact (Dubow, 1995). According to anthropologist C. G. Seligman (1930), for instance, "the history of Africa south of the Sahara is no more than the story of the permeation through the ages, in different degrees and at various times, of the Negroes and the Bushmen by Hamitic blood and culture" (p. 19). Rodwell's work received wide praise in Mombasa, and it gave voice to a constituency of established Mombasa colonial families and businesses engaged in civic improvement. His work also encouraged the Royal Kenyan National Park to begin formal archeological excavation of the region.

Rodwell was hardly alone in either his efforts or his interests. In 1948, British archaeologist James Kirkman was made the Warden of Gedi National Park, an appointment that was to have profound impact on the archeology of the coast. His energy and a later visit to Mombasa by Princess Elizabeth II—an event that resulted in the construction of faux elephant tusk archways over what is now Moi Avenue in the city center—increased politicking about the status of the fort with some success. The Kenyan Legislative Council instructed the prison department to build (using prison labor) a new jail in Mtwapa to which the inmates at Fort Jesus could be transferred, and in 1951 the Council appropriated £10,000 for the restoration of the fort.

Kirkman was highly productive, keeping up a steady stream of excavations, reports, and international publications in journals such as *Antiquaries Journal*, *Current Anthropology*, and *Oriental Art*. He also ensured the legal protection of almost 40 new monuments on the coast between 1954 and 1959. After the excavation at Gedi, he completed work on other major sites along the Kenyan coast, including Takwa, Ungwana, and Mnarani. Through this work he denied the integrity of Swahili culture, consistently stating that the notable settlements in the region had their origins in earlier waves of Asiatic and Arab colonization. Kirkman (1964) claimed that "the historical monuments of East Africa belong not to the Africans but to the Arabs and Arabised Persians mixed in blood with the African but in culture utterly apart from the Africans who surrounded them" (p. 1). Without the influence of Islamic artisans, he added, the "coast would have remained a land of mud or grass huts like the rest of tropical Africa" (p. 19). To him, "Islamic as well as Christian art is descended from the adult, rational arts of the classical world or the equally mature art of Persia" (p. 51)—the clear implication being that African art was childlike, immature, and irrational.

Kirkman thus perpetuated a European myth that civilization came from outside Africa. His reports on leading sites tended to ignore the history and culture of local people and concentrated almost entirely on shoring up his hypothesis about the diffusion of Arab and Asian influence through the coastal areas, supporting, in turn, a historical narrative about the imagined country of Azania (Kirkman, 1960). He directed more attention to the architectural features of particular buildings or individual Chinese porcelain plates than to local tribes. His portrayal of Gedi made only the barest allusions to slavery; the settlements he discovered were portrayed in a vacuum; and his texts were riddled with Eurocentric and colonial bias, such as the term *cannibal* describing the sixteenth-century tribe that conquered the port of Kilwa.

With the creation of the British Institute of Eastern Africa in 1960, Kirkman's archaeological projects did much to lay claim to the land. They illustrate how the construction of historical narrative intersected with claims to knowledge about nature, place, and heritage, which were essential to maintaining the colonial gaze over the Kenyan landscape. Kirkman's work, to quote Gregory (2004), was as much about "making other people's geographies as it was about making other people's histories" (p. 11). Eventually living on the grounds of Fort Jesus, Kirkman pursued a scientific practice that was alien to local culture. It helped create a colonial edifice in the form of a museum, inside a colonial fortress, to present a colonial view of the coast, an account that accorded local African cultures only limited space. In this way Kirkman contributed to the construction of a knowledge regime that resonated strongly with the identity politics of the British colonial elite, whose way of conceiving the landscape diverged strongly from the values of the people working and living on the land. In representing the histories of the coast as non-African, and in establishing an imagined geography of invasion, diffusion, and improvement, Kirkman's archaeology acted as an instrument of colonial administration by providing the colonial mission with claims to truth and promoting specific colonialist ideas of history and racial superiority. In short, Kirkman epitomized the observations made by the historian Basil Davidson (1959):

> Africans, in this view, had never evolved civilizations of their own; if they possessed a history, it could be scarcely worth the telling. And this belief that Africans had lived in universal chaos or stagnation until the coming of Europeans seemed not only to find its justification in a thousand tales of savage misery and benighted ignorance; it was also, of course, exceedingly convenient in high imperial times. For it could be argued (and it was; indeed, it still is) that these peoples, history-less, were naturally inferior or else they were "children who had still to grow up"; in either case they were manifestly in need of government by others who had grown up. (p. ix)

This perversion of the relationship between history, knowledge, and place creates an unstable arena for the construction of memory. Kirkman constructed the heritage of the coast in a biased fashion. On the basis of that knowledge, the British could conceive of themselves as the latest and most powerful invader to civilize the coast, whose condition, had it been left to the indigenous tribes, would in the colonialist view would have remained backward and primitive. One of the governors of Kenya, Sir Philip Mitchell, reassured himself that "until about 500 years ago East Africa had probably been uninhabited . . . [b]etween the stone implements of some 30,000 years ago and Dr. Livingstone there is nothing . . . Nothing at all of African Africa: not a ruin, nor a tomb, nor an inscription; indeed not even a legend supporting anything resembling tribal history for more than a few generations" (P. Mitchell, as quoted in Sutton, 2006, p. 300).

Building a Museum and Celebrating an Empire

If the memory work of the British guaranteed the European's claim to the land and constructed a colonialist view of the cultural landscape that surrounded Fort Jesus, the involvement of the Portuguese, who funded the restoration of the site through the Calouste Gulbenkian Foundation, reinforced the European claim to Africa. In a remarkable convergence of colonial enterprises, the Portuguese enrolled Fort Jesus in their plans to celebrate the 500th anniversary of the death of Prince Henry the Navigator in 1960. They had begun planning for the Henry the Navigator celebration in 1956, but the Portuguese state had already been orchestrating various commemorations and other events for decades to promote the construction of the imperial nation. While the rest of Europe descended into war, Portugal celebrated its empire in the Portuguese World Exhibition in 1940. With the *Padrão dos Descobrimentos*, inaugurated in that year in Lisbon (and replaced by a permanent monument in 1960), the regime appropriated Henry the Navigator as the national hero, a figure who "contributed decisively to give the relations between European and non-Europeans, whites and colored people, a path singularly Luso-Christian (G. Freyre, as quoted in Léonard, 1999, p. 42).

Ironically, just as the Portuguese Prime Minister António de Oliveira Salazar, never set foot in Africa or in any of the overseas provinces, Henry the Navigator never participated in any of the adventurous maritime voyages for which he is renowned. Nevertheless, the Portuguese saw the 500th anniversary of Henry's death as a critical moment at which to assert their sense of nationhood and, more critically, to affirm Portugal's imperial identity, which was increasingly coming under siege by anticolonial liberation movements in Africa and Asia. Between 1956 and 1961, over twenty new African states became independent, with three of them—Senegal, Congo and Tanganyika (Tanzania since 1964)—bordering on the Portuguese territories. For the Portuguese state the celebration was therefore not just a "simple manifestation of historical nostalgia," but an "act of faith in the destinies of the motherland, deemed necessary at this time of incertitude in the world's life" (Ramos, 2005, p. 192).

Meanwhile, the British had been pursuing their own ideas about self-representation. Almost a decade earlier Governor Mitchell had concurred with proposals regarding the regeneration of the fort made to him from Mombasa and had given his support to the local representative on the Kenyan Legislative Council, C. G. Usher. To avoid competing with the Corydon Museum in Nairobi, the Governor had advised against the construction of an aquarium. What was needed, in Mitchell's opinion, was a museum "to represent the history, art and culture in its widest aspects on the Coastal areas, and including its ramification to the Persian Gulf, Karachi, Bombay, Europe, America and what-have-you."[2] He nominated Kirkman to lead the transformation of the fort.

However, the concerns of the colony quickly shifted to the Mau Mau uprising when a state of emergency was declared by Mitchell's successor as governor, Evelyn Baring, in October 1952. Soon the colony had neither the funds nor the political will to proceed with the fort's restoration, and the Legislative Council's £10,000 grant from the previous year was rescinded. The idea of a museum quickly lost support, especially because the prison at Fort Jesus played an important role in maintaining the security and judicial control of the coastal region during the Mau Mau period. Although the facility's proximity to an urban population kept it out of the colony's infamous "pipeline" of prison camps used to suppress the Mau Mau uprising, 75 individuals on remand, 287 prisoners serving sentences, and 80 others were still languishing there in May 1957—five years after the initial overtures for its restoration.[3] Fort Jesus at that time was also being used to detain psychiatric patients. Baring suggested to the Ministry of Defense that it assist in the evacuation of the fort by constructing A-frame structures to house prisoners at the maximum security prison at Shimo la Tewa, north of the city.

By this stage the Mau Mau rebellion had been brought under control at huge cost to life and liberty, and in 1958 the Kenyan government declared Fort Jesus a historical monument. Plans for the fort's restoration were given a new lease on life when it was established that the Gulbenkian Foundation was prepared to fund the restoration. According to a memorandum prepared by Baring, Louis S. B. Leakey, the palaeontologist and director of the Corydon Museum in Nairobi, informed him that Gulbenkian's was offering £1,000 for a library and a "research place," and a possible further £30,000 if the fort were evacuated.[4] Baring telegraphed Pedro Theotónio Pereira—the Portuguese ambassador in London and the administrator of the Gulbenkian Foundation in the 1950s—acknowledging his help and expressing "joy that it will be possible to renew and preserve a fascinating relic of the connection of this port of Africa with the famous Portuguese navigators of the past."[5] (Kirkman later learned that Pereira had masterminded the whole arrangement through the British Colonial Secretary, Alan Lennox-Boyd.[6])

The restoration of the fort was overseen by the Fort Jesus Advisory Committee, chaired by none other than Edward Rodwell. The committee membership consisted entirely of Mombasa's administrative elite, including one representative of the city's Goan community whose colonial connection to Portugal, as outlined below, was to become central to the commemoration of Prince Henry the Navigator planned for 1960. There were no Africans on the committee, and the archive does not mention their involvement in this restoration, save as laborers, night watchmen, or gatekeepers. The committee decided that the fort should be restored as closely as possible to its original construction of 1593. In other words, the principle alterations made during the Omani occupation were to be erased and the fort reinstated as an example of early modern European military fortification. However, in a decision playing as much on wistful longing for the past as on diplomatic niceties, it was agreed that the "old customs which had been handed over with the Fort should be preserved ...[;] the Sultan flag should continue to fly; a gun should be fired at the beginning and at the end of Ramadan and advice should be sought from the Provincial Administrator concerning the blowing of a horn when a ship was sighted."[7] As the work progressed, the committee also decided that the "prison period was of [little] interest."[8] Consequently, the prison store, the prison hospital building, and the walls around the women's jail were all demolished.[9] Almost a year later, the minutes of a meeting of the same committee reveal that it was found impossible to adapt any prison cells as public lavatories or ticket office and that these buildings, too, were neglected in the restoration.

"Outdoing Mr. Khrushchev": Protesting Imperial Memory Work

Upon the restoration of the fort, Pereira, by then vice president of Portugal, arrived in Kenya for a six-day official visit from October 27 to November 2, 1960, at the invitation of the new colonial governor, Patrick Renison. Pereira's itinerary was divided between two days in Nairobi, where he visited Goan Institutions and had several official meetings, and four days in the Coast Province where he opened the museum at Fort Jesus in Mombasa, met with representatives of Goan Institutions, and unveiled the Vasco da Gama memorial in Malindi, a coastal town 120 km (75½ miles) north of Mombasa. Although not anticipated when the agreement was concluded in the 1958, the realpolitik of decolonization and the emerging set of rules unfolding in the postcolonial world by time the Portuguese delegation arrived in the late 1960s encouraged the Kenya's colonial administrator to defuse any potential for controversy. On January 15, 1960, with Tom Mboya heading the Kenyan delegation, Kenya's timetable for independence was agreed upon at the Lancaster House Conference in London. The funding and the decision to invite Pereira to the opening ceremony in Mombasa set in motion various diplomatic negotiations and preparations that in themselves offer insights into the political sensitivities of the period. For example, Governor Renison was advised that Pereira should not receive representatives of the Goan community while he was staying at the Governor's Mansion, for the "Indians may be inclined to protest."[10]

Similarly, it was decided during the preparation of Pereira's visit to Fort Jesus not to invite the governors of Uganda and Tanganyika. Felix Dias, the Portuguese consul in Kenya, had pressed for these invitations, arguing that the event was very significant for Portugal and the Portuguese community in Kenya and should be accorded the highest honors. However, a note from the Governor's Office to the Provincial Commissioner of the Coast Province, John Pinney, advised Pinney to downplay the event, noting sardonically that "the Portuguese are addicted to the panoply of glory and would be inclined to make more of the occasion than we would."[11] Most likely aware of the political sensitivities around the visit, Pinney, vetoed Dias's proposal. Another blow to Dias was a decision by Renison not to accompany Pereira to the coast, even though the latter was a guest of the government of Kenya. The governor's exact motivations are not recorded, but it is likely that he was anticipating that Pereira's presence was liable to generate dissention both internally with the Kenya African National Union (KANU) and externally with India, neither of which he was keen to arouse given the decolonization talks and international diplomacy taking place at the time. The colonial administration in Nairobi was right to be concerned about the Portuguese visit; politically speaking, it had the potential to open a Pandora 's Box. Africa had entered an intense phase of political change, and Lisbon's trenchant opposition to decolonization made Portugal a frequent target of anticolonial protest.

One of the key areas where this vexing political question was to become apparent was the Goan community, whose diasporic identity and anxiety about its future in Africa were caught up in the political transformations and decolonization of the continent, which the British Prime Minister Harold Macmillan had famously termed the "winds of change" (MacMillan, 1960, p. 286). As Boxer and Azevedo (1962) point out, Goa's historical connections with the East African Coast run deep, especially in Mombasa. The Goan migrated to East Africa during the construction of the Uganda Railway at the turn of the twentieth century. But India's independence in 1948, the increasing pressure on Portugal to leave its "occupied" territories (Goa, Daman, and Diu), Portugal's rigid position under Salazar, and the rising nationalist movements in East Africa all contributed to escalating tension and uncertainty within the Goan community in Kenya, circumstances that encouraged them to reassert their relationship to Portugal. Reflecting the rift in Goa itself, Kenya's Goan community was divided into supporters of the Portuguese, as represented in several associations that Pereira visited in Nairobi and Mombasa (the Goan Institute, the Railway Goan Institute, the Goan Cymkhana, Santa Cruz Club, the Goan Taylor Society, the Goans Overseas Association, and the Goan Community), and people intent on seeing the cause of Kenyan decolonization succeed (the East African Goan League led by Pia Gama Pinto). The one group was eager to attend most events and become involved in the celebrations by organizing such things as dinners, visits to the local associations and Goan schools, and a local soccer tournament (the Henry the Navigator Football Cup, which raised money for the Vasco da Gama Memorial Fund). Nairobi Newspapers such as the *Mombasa Times*, the *East African Standard*, the *Sunday Post*, and especially *The Goan Voice* were used to promote Pereira's visit, boost the importance of Portugal, and underscore the significance and integration of the Goan community. This section of the Goan population sought Portuguese support and reassurance from Pereira's visit, especially because the future of the Asian community in Kenya was perceived to be in jeopardy. Members of the Goan community in the other group protested the visit, partly to criticize unceasing Portuguese colonization in India and partly to forge closer association with African nationalists and the cause for Kenyan decolonization.

Throughout the 1950s Pio Gama Pinto had been involved in the independence movement as a trade unionist and as a journalist promoting the cause for Kenyan liberation. As a young student in India, he had campaigned for the liberation of Goa, assisting in the activities of the Goa National Congress, but when faced with the possibility of deportation to the concentration camp of Tarrafal on Cape Verde, he returned to Kenya. In 1954, after his participation in Mau Mau-related activities in Nairobi, he was interned under special emergency powers during Operation Anvil, first briefly in Fort Jesus and then for three years in the Takwa Special Detention camp on Manda Island (Nowrojee, 2007). At that time, it was one of the severest and most isolated of the colonial concentration camps and was reserved for the hard-core Mau Mau (Elkins, 2005). When released in 1957, Pinto recuperated and soon went to work as a political organizer, using his skills as a journalist to write pamphlets, campaign materials, and letters to the press. He eventually established the KANU newspaper *Sauti Ya KANU*.

In statements made through the East African Goan League in the weeks before the official opening of Fort Jesus, Pio reiterated his opposition to Pereira's visit and contested the statement prepared by the Goan Overseas Association that "Goans look to Portugal as their Fatherland" ("Goans look," 1960). On Pereira's arrival the East African Goan League presented an open letter to Pereira complaining that the Portuguese government had failed to recognize the basic human dignity and rights of its colonial subjects. Pio argued that, in response to the "legitimate human urge of the indigenous peoples to free themselves from alien domination[,]. . . the Metropolitan government appeared to have turned a deaf ear and has resorted to repressive measures to sustain its authority" ("Pereira flies," 1960). Pio was supported by the small Asian Kenyan Freedom Party, which was broadly aligned with KANU and which condemned the invitation extended to Pereira, whom they regarded as a representative of what they called a fascist regime ("Portugal leader's visit," 1960). After this publication, a series of letters in the *East African Standard* condemned Pio's East African Goan League as unrepresentative and praised the fact that "the Portuguese world is an independent nation and not an empire" (Mascarenhas, 1960). One writer was so appalled that he suggested that Mr. Pio Gama Pinto had "outdone Mr. Khrushchev in leveling charges against the Portuguese Government" (Nunes, 1960). The *East African Standard* published just one letter supporting Pio's campaign, arguing that Pereira represented "a regime detested the world over" (Carvalho, 1960).

More significantly, Pio worked with Tom Mboya on a series of statement about Pereira's visit. At this stage Mboya was one of the most prominant figures in the KANU party. He also had a growing profile internationally and participating in the International Confederation of Free Trade Unions. In 1958 he and Julius Nyerere founded the Pan-African Freedom Movement for East and Central Africa. In response to Pereira's visit, Mboya condemned the labor conditions in the Portuguese colonies, which he likened to slavery. He argued that Portuguese colonial subjects were stripped of their dignity and that they lived in conditions worse than those under apartheid South Africa.

Clearly, such statements by Pio and Mboya were aimed at the nostalgic narrative about Portugal and its navigators as enacted at Fort Jesus, supported by Kirkman, and widely propagated by the Portuguese embassy. This media target was sizeable. Throughout 1960 numerous articles about Prince Henry, the celebrations of his 500th anniversary, Vasco da Gama, and the Portuguese impact on Africa appeared in the Kenyan press. And in June 1960 the Mombasa Town Planning Committee created Prince Henry Drive in the city ("Mombasa road names," 1960). The run-up to the autumn visit by Pereira also offered ample opportunity to cast Portugal in a positive light, with the press carrying dignified portraits of the diplomat and glowing accounts of the benefits of Portuguese civilization in Africa. In March, the Goan press published a report on the official visit to Portugal by the President of Brazil, Juscelino Kubitschek de Oliveira, including one noteworthy photograph of Pereira with the Pope John XXIII, taken on Pereira's way home after a "triumphal visit to Goa and Pakistan" ("His Holiness," 1960). In an article on a November banquet honoring Pereira, Dias praised Portugal for its "great contribution in bringing together the various races and creeds in the world" ("Portugal helped unity," 1960). Two months later Rodwell (1961) promoted the Portuguese celebration, arguing that Kenyan participation "would be a pleasant and polite gesture" (n.p.). In March, Kirkman (1961) also published a long tribute to Henry the Navigator in the *Kenya Weekly News*.

In challenging this colonial memory work, both Pio and Mboya drew directly on Davidson (1955), whose anticolonial text republished parts of a document—a devastating report on Portugal's African colonies—that had been secretly prepared by the Portuguese Inspector General of Colonies, Henrique Galvão. Mboya also raised the possibility of strike action in the port of Mombasa. This strike was a serious threat given the previous decade's history of labor unrest, which had prompted the colonial administration to commission the *Mombasa Social Survey*, a report on the economic and labor conditions of the city (see Rodwell, 1958). Moreover, Mboya had been instrumental in resolving a major dispute in the port in 1955 and was a key figure in the organization of the Dockworkers Union in Mombasa and the Kenyan Federation of Labour (Cooper, 1987). In 1960 Mboya also sanctioned physical protest against Pereira's visit and instigated both a public boycott of the public celebrations by Kenyans and a political boycott of private events to which African members of the Kenyan Legislative Council had been invited. Two Kenyan ministers who had recently been appointed to that body boycotted accordingly. The *Daily Nation* reported that six people had been arrested outside the Nairobi Goan Institute on October 27 after they had rushed at Pereira's car as it approached the institute ("Pereira flies," 1960). On the following day three more people were arrested for protesting at the Goan school ("Ginger Group," 1960).

The Portuguese daily *Diário de Notícias* predictably made light of these incidents and highlighted the vivid show of loyalty by the 1,500 Goan residents in the capital and the 500 schoolchildren who joined in the celebration. The coverage minimized the protest by "eight blacks exhibiting upside down banners" ("1500 Goeses," 1960). All the while, Pereira took every opportunity to tell journalists how the situation in the Portuguese overseas provinces was under control, stating, for example, "so far the situation within Portuguese territories is completely calm" and acknowledging "only minor incidents" ("All quiet," 1960). However, the protests persisted despite the highly polished media campaign to support the visit. At a political rally in Nakuru, Pereira's visit was condemned as a "danger to our freedom" ("Pereira petition," 1960). Action continued in Mombasa, where KANU applied for a license to hold a public meeting to exercise their right to protest the opening of the fort. The request was denied by the district commissioner, but one of the regional organizers of KANU's youth wing, Peter Lungatso, is reported to have "warned Africans to stay away from the celebration," instructing people to "keep off the streets when he [Pereira] passes" and adding that failure to do so would result in "their being regarded as 'the greatest enemy' of the African community" ("Gingers call off," 1960). Meanwhile, the Indian delegation in Kenya expressed their dissatisfaction more diplomatically. The Indian Trade Commissioner, Mr. V. V. Dev, requested the Mombasa city council to make certain that all Indian flags be lowered in the city on the occasion of Pereira's visit ("Indian flags," 1960).

"The Panoply of Glory": The Birth of the Museum

Against the background of these protests, Pereira inspected the Guard of Honour mounted by the Royal East African navy and thereafter solemnly entered Fort Jesus in Mombasa on October 29, 1960, as the Bamburi Band played the national anthems of Portugal, Zanzibar, and Britain. The Portuguese had lost the fort to the Omani more than 230 years before (November 26, 1729), but because of the financial support from the Portuguese Gulbenkian Foundation, it was the Portuguese vice prime minister who unveiled a plaque to declare the opening of the Fort Jesus museum. Representatives of the Sultan of Zanzibar were also present, as were the key figures of the colonial heritage administration: L. S. B. Leakey, Mervyn Cowie, the director of the Royal National Parks of Kenya; and, of course, Kirkman, the Warden of Fort Jesus and of Coastal Historical Sites. After the speeches, Kirkman took Pereira on a private tour of the museum.[12] The strike at the port had been called off, an unrelated dispute concerning pay for clerks at the Port having been resolved in the days before the visit. But newspapers did report that few "Africans" were seen at the celebration, suggesting that the boycott of the commemoration was successful. It is recorded also that another anticolonial protest was attempted that morning but that it was suppressed on Makupa road,[13] demonstrating that the police state created to suppress the Mau Mau rebellion took protests to Pereira's visit in stride.

Throughout these celebrations the Portuguese, like the British, took every opportunity to tell their history in very particular ways. Not only did they distort the harsh reality of conditions in Angola and Mozambique, they also used the opening of the Fort Jesus museum, among subsequent events, to present a wholly nostalgic portrayal of Portuguese history on the coast. At the local Goan school, the school principal, Mr. Ildefonse de Souza, was awarded the medal of the Portuguese Navy. Pereira also donated to the school a "dream book[,] . . . a lovely large volume bound in red with gold lettering on the cover containing some of the best maps made by the Portuguese since the early sixteenth century—entitled *Henry the Navigator*" ("Malindi Memorial," 1960). Later that day, Pereira decorated Kirkman, Rodwell,

Fig. 2 The Vasco Da Gama
Memorial, 1960. "It is
symbolic of the spirit of
discovery, and a motif of a
mast and full sail are set in
the surrounding pool of water.
The sail is decorated with the
Red Cross of the Order of
Christ." From "Malindi
Memorial Is Unveiled,"
October 31, 1960, *Daily
Nation* (Nairobi), p. 5.
Permission Nation Media
Group Kenya

and Dias with the Order of Prince Henry the Navigator, an honor specially created
in 1960 to mark the 500th anniversary of the prince's death.

The heroic sentiments represented in these gestures were reinforced soon afterward in Malindi with the unveiling of the Vasco da Gama monument, originally
conceived by Dias and Rodwell (Fig. 2). The monument was funded by monies
raised within the Goan community and designed by the Tanzanian architect
Anthony B. Almeida, of Goan origins. Eliding any reference to the Kenyan people,
Provisional Commissioner John Pinney stated that the memorial would be a symbol
of friendship not just between Britain and Portugal, but "between English people and
Portuguese nationals here in the Coast Province" ("Mr Dias," 1960). In Portugal,
the *Diário de Notícias* (1960a) noted that "this was further evidence of the profound
loyalty of Goese to the motherland, as well as to the duty that the Portuguese government has in giving national solidarity full support to the community in Kenya"
(pp. 1–2).

In its official version, the Vasco da Gama monument depicts a sailing ship
trimmed down to its elemental form: the mast, the sail, and the sea. As Brussens
(2005) observes, Almeida later argued that the monument could also be seen as an
abstract represntation of a sword. According to Brussens, this interpretation suggests
that Almeida aimed to subvert the ambitions of the Portuguese to memorialize Vasco
da Gama as a hero, for the monument could also act as a metaphor for "a history of

oppression, exploitation, and slavery" (p. 119). Whatever the effectiveness of this interpretation, which cannot be substantiated from the discourse around its opening, the monument lies in near ruin today, forgotten by many in a neglected location in Malindi. As a response to the aims of original colonial commemoration and as a suitable rebuke to the preservation of colonial myths at Fort Jesus, it is the derelict state of this memorial that is perhaps more authentic and critical than Almeida's post rationalization of it.

Orbits and Legacies

After leaving Kenya, Pereira toured Mozambique, Angola, São Tomé, and Guinea, arriving back in Portugal on November 18, 1960. On arrival in Lisbon, he informed the press: "Do you want to know what the Portuguese from Africa think? They are united and determined around the homeland flag" (Diário de Notícias, 1960b). For the British, too, the restoration of the fort saw to it that key colonial issues were addressed. It allowed them to pursue an imperial archaeology that made the colonial government of Kenya appear to be more progressive than it actually was. In the context of the Mau Mau revolt, it enabled a certain normalization of the colonial enterprise. This portrayal of Kenya starkly contrasted the coverage of brutality that enraged the Middle-England opinion from the late 1950s onwards, notably after the murder of detainees by colonial forces in the Hola concentration camp (Anderson, 2004). The barbarism of the colony could be partly washed away by the new fort and its museum. In the subsequent months, according to the Minister of Tourism, the future of the coast was bright. The advent of air travel, he argued, would enable coastal resorts like Malindi to become the "new Miami" ("Send girls," 1960).

These events illustrate that the restoration of Fort Jesus facilitated a convergence of two colonial enterprises that, despite their diverging strategies for the future of European colonization in Africa, manipulated, for their mutual benefit, the histories and memories of this site and its surrounding landscape. More broadly, we have commented on legacies of colonial knowledge about the political condition of public memory in Kenya. drawing upon postcolonial theory to recover the marginalized voices of the oppressed and the excluded. Close attention to the birth of the museum at Fort Jesus and its memory work has provided key insights into the politics of public memory and its forms, transformations, and meaning in colonial society. The recovery of these events is also important for understanding the orbit of colonial memory work that still afflicts the consumption of the past and of heritage both at this site and throughout Kenya.

Yet, despite the vast range of postcolonial criticism and ample scholarship that have recast the history of the coast (see Kusimba, 1999; Mazrui, 2002; Middleton, 2003; Wilding, 1987), the ghosts of the colonial episteme remain embedded in the fort. Although selected along with Mount Kenya as a national icon to be featured in school children's textbooks after independence, Fort Jesus, like most national monuments in Kenya, still mutes the story of colonization. The contemporary condition of memory enacted in the museum partly duplicates the process of forgetting and ensuring a particular form of consensual and regulated fiction first performed by the Portuguese at Fort Jesus in 1960. Our hope is that the history of the resistance to the restoration of the fort and the Portuguese diplomatic visit outlined in this chapter can serve as a platform for elaborating an alternative narrative at the site. This expectation takes on an extra dimension when it is remembered that the two key figures in the protest—Pio Gama Pinto and Tom Mboya—were both assassinated in the period after independence by still unidentified elements of the postcolonial regime lead by Kenyatta. As argued by Nowrojee (2002), the political significance of memory remains a potent force, for remembering acts of resistance in Kenyan history—such as those that occurred at the birth of the museum at Fort Jesus—"assures us that self-respect and dignity are possible in periods of oppression. It demonstrates the vulnerability of tyranny; it is an example against oppression" (p. 1).

Notes

1. Preservation of ancient ruins and visits to Fort Jesus, National Kenyan Archives (NKA), CA 17/79.
2. Letter to Hon. C. G. Usher from Sir Philip Mitchell, September 22, 1951, NKA, GH 10 20.
3. Memorandum to the Ministry of Defense from Evelyn Baring May 21, 1957, NKA, GH 10 20.
4. Memorandum to Ministry of Defense from Evelyn Baring, May 21, 1957, NKA, GH 14 24.
5. Telegram to Pedro Theotónio Pereira from Evelyn Baring, June 4, 1958, NKA, GH 28 19.
6. Letter from Alfred Vincent (Chairman of the Royal National Parks) to Evelyn Baring (Governor of Kenya), May 27, 1958, NKA, GH 26 17.
7. Minutes of a meeting of the Fort Jesus Advisory Committee, File 28(19), December 15, 1958, NKA, GA 3/1/2b.
8. Minutes of a meeting of the Fort Jesus Advisory Committee, File 28(19), December 15, 1958, NKA, GA 3/1/2b.
9. Fort Jesus National Park, Warden's quarterly report, June 30, 1960, NKA, NPK 16/12.
10. Letter from Roman Rostowsky to John Pinney, September 29, 1960, NKA, NPK 16/12.
11. Letter from Roman Rostowsky to John Pinney, September 29, 1960, NKA, NPK 16/12 2.
12. Itinerary of His Excellency Dr. [Pedro Theotónio] Pereira, NKA, GH 31/1.
13. Letter from District Commissioner John Pinney to the governor Patrick Renison, November 2, 1960, NKA, GH 31/55.

References

All quiet in territories says Pereira. (1960 October 29). *Daily Nation* (Nairobi), p. 2.

Anderson, D. (2004). *Histories of the hanged: Britain's dirty war in Kenya and the end of empire.* London: Weidenfeld & Nicolson.

Boxer, C. R., & Azevedo, C. (1962). *Fort Jesus and the Portuguese in Mombasa, 1593–1729.* London: Hollis & Carter.

Brussens, P. (2005). The (non)political position of the architecture of Anthony B. Almeida between 1948 and 1975. In *ArchiAfrika conference proceedings: Modern architecture in East Africa around independence* (pp. 115–126). Dar es Salaam: Archnet. (http://www.archnet.org)

Carvalho, M. (1960, October 26). Portuguese minister welcomed [Letter to the editor]. *East African Standard* (Nairobi), p. 17.

Cooper, F. (1987). *On the African waterfront: Urban disorder and the transformation of work in colonial Mombasa*. New Haven, CT: Yale University Press.

Davidson, B. (1955). *The African awakening*. London: Jonathan Cape.

Davidson, B. (1959). *The lost cities of Africa*. Boston, MA: Little Brown.

Diário de Notícias (Lisbon). (1960a, October 31), pp. 1–2.

Diário de Notícias (Lisbon). (1960b, November 18), p. 1.

Dubow, S. (1995). *Scientific racism in modern South Africa*. Cambridge, UK: Cambridge University Press.

Elkins, C. (2005). *Imperial reckoning: The untold story of Britain's gulag in Kenya*. London: Cape.

1500 Goeses. (1960a, October 29). *Diário de Notícias* (Lisbon), pp. 1–2.

Ginger group say—Go home Pereira. (1960, October 29). *Daily Nation* (Nairobi), p. 3.

Gingers call off big coast strike. (1960, October 29). *Daily Nation* (Nairobi), p. 2.

Goans look to Portugal as their Fatherland. (1960, October 26). *East African Standard*, p. 15.

Gomongo Village, Ltd. (2008). Advertisement. Mombasa Gomongo Village, Ltd.

Gregory, D. (2004). *The colonial present*. Oxford, UK: Blackwell.

Hart, T. G. (2007). Gazetting and historic preservation in Kenya. *The Journal of Heritage Stewardship, 4*(1), 1–7.

Hinaway, A. M. (1970). *Al Akida and Fort Jésus, Mombasa*. Nairobi: East Africa Literature Bureau.

His Holiness the Pope with Portuguese Presidency Minister. (1960, March 5). *The Goan Voice* (Nairobi), p. 3.

Huntingford, G. W. B. (1933). The Azanian civilization of Kenya. *Antiquity, 7*, 153–165.

Indian flags lowered. (1960, October 28). *Daily Nation* (Nairobi), p. 4.

Kagwanja, P. M. (2003). Facing Mount Kenya or Facing Mecca? The Mungiki, ethnic violence and the politics of the Moi succession in Kenya, 1987–2002. *African Affairs, 102*, 25–49.

Kasfir, S. L. (2004). Tourist aesthetics in the global flow: Orientalism and "warrior theatre" on the Swahili Coast. *Visual Anthropology, 17*, 319–343.

Kenyatta, J. (1964). *Harambee! The prime minister of Kenya's speeches, 1963–1964* (with a foreword by Malcolm MacDonald). Nairobi: Oxford University Press.

Kirkman, J. S. (1960). Ruined cities of Azania. *Outlook, 2*(3), 1–4.

Kirkman, J. S. (1961, March 3). Henry the Navigator. *Kenya Weekly News* (Nairobi), pp. 6–7.

Kirkman, J. S. (1964). *Men and monuments on the East African coast*. New York: Frederick A. Praeger.

Kusimba, C. M. (1996). Kenya's destruction of the Swahili cultural heritage. In P. R. Schmidt & J. M. Roderick (Eds.), *Plundering Africa's past* (pp. 201–224). Bloomington, IN: Indiana University Press.

Kusimba, C. M. (1999). *The rise and fall of Swahili states*. Walnut Creek, CA: Altamira Press.

Léonard, Y. (1999). O Ultramar Português [The Portuguese Overseas]. In F. Bethencourt & K. Chaudhuri (Eds.), *História da Expansão Portuguesa: Vol. 5. Último Império e Recentramento (1930–1998)* (pp. 31–50). Lisbon: Círculo de Leitores.

MacMillan, H. (1960). Winds of change. In B. McArthur (Ed.), *The penguin book of twentieth century speeches* (pp. 286–290). London: Penguin.

Malindi memorial is unveiled. (1960, October 31). *Daily Nation* (Nairobi), p. 5.

Mascarenhas, D. R. (1960, October 22). Visit of Portuguese Deputy Premier. [Letter to the editor]. *East African Standard* (Nairobi), p. 17.

Mazrui, A. A. (2000). Cultural amnesia, cultural nostalgia and false memory: Africa's identity crises revisited. *African Philosophy, 13*(2), 87–98.

Mazrui, A. A. (2002). *Africanity redefined: Collected essays of Ali A. Mazrui* (Vol. 1). Trenton, NJ: Africa World Press.

McMahon, S. C. (2008). Mimesis and the historical imagination: (Re)Staging history in Cape Verde, West Africa. *Theatre Research International, 33*, 20–39.

Middleton, J. (2003). Merchants: An essay in historical ethnography. *The Journal of the Royal Anthropological Institute, 9*, 509–526.

Mombasa road names changed by council. (1960, June 9). *Mombasa Times*, p. 3. (Article sourced in Arquivo Histórico Diplomático, Ministry of Foreign Affairs, Lisbon, File A 59 332)

Mr Dias pictured above with the Provincial Commissioner. (1960, March 26). *Mombasa Times* (Mombasa), p. 3. (Article sourced in Arquivo Histórico Diplomático, Ministry of Foreign Affairs, Lisbon, File A 59 332)

Mudimbe, V. Y. (1994). *The idea of Africa*. Oxford, UK: James Currey.

Ndeti, K. (1975). *Cultural policy in Kenya*. Paris: UNESCO Press.

Nora, P. (1989). Between memory and history: Les lieux de mémoire. *Representations, 26*, 7–25.

Nowrojee, P. (2002). Moral courage withers without memory: The acceptance speech by the recent Bernard Simons Memorial Award winner at the IBA conference in Durban. *Legalbrief Africa*. Retrieved October 21, 2008, from http://www.legalbrief.co.za/article.php?story=2002111480629999

Nowrojee, P. (2007). *Pio Gama Pinto: Patriot for social justice*. Nairobi: Sasa Sema Publications.

Nunes, I. (1960, October 22). Visit of Portuguese Deputy Prime Minister [Letter to the editor]. *East African Standard* (Nairobi), p. 17.

Pereira flies into petition by East Goans. (1960, October 28). *Daily Nation* (Nairobi), p. 7.

Pereira petition, The. (1960, October 29). *Daily Nation* (Nairobi), p. 3.

Portugal helped unity of races. (1960, November 2). *East African Standard* (Nairobi), p. 9.

Portugal leader's visit opposed. (1960, October 24). *East African Standard* (Nairobi), p. 4.

Ramos, R. (2005). A Erudição lusitanista perante a Guerra (c. 1960–c. 1970): Algumas observações sobre a polémica entre Charles Boxer e Armando Cortesão [The Lusitanian erudition in face of the War (c. 1960–c. 1970): Some observations about the controversy between Charles Boxer and Armando Cortesão']. In T. P. Coelho (Ed.), *Os Descobrimentos Portugueses no Mundo de Língua Inglesa 1880–1972* (pp. 189–218). Lisbon: Edições Colibri.

Rodwell, E. (1946). *Gedi: The lost city*. Mombasa: Mombasa Times.

Rodwell, E. (1949). *Ivory apes and peacocks*. Mombasa: Mombasa Times.

Rodwell, E. (1958). Labour unrest and Commissions of enquiry since 1957. In G. M. Wilson (Ed.), *Mombasa social survey* (pp. 231–261). Nairobi: Ministry of African Affairs.

Rodwell, E. (1961, January 15). Coast Causerie. *Kenya Weekly News* (Nairobi). n.p. (Press clipping sourced in Arquivo Histórico Diplomático, Ministry of Foreign Affairs, Lisbon, File A 59 332)

Said, E. W. (1994). *Culture and imperialism*. New York: Vintage.

Seligman, C. (1930). *The races of Africa*. London: Oxford University Press.

Send girls abroad. (1960, November 4). *East African Standard* (Nairobi), p. 1.

Simatei, T. (2005). Colonial violence, postcolonial violations: Violence, landscape, and memory in Kenyan fiction. *Research in African Literatures, 36*(2), 85–94.

Sutton, J. E. G. (2006). Denying history in colonial Kenya: The anthropology and archeology of G. W. B. Huntingford and L. S. B. Leakey. *History in Africa, 33*, 287–320.

Sykes, P. (2007, June). The chronicles of Keira; On a much-needed spring break, Keira Knightley hops the green hills of Africa in fittingly romantic, feminine looks. *Vogue*, pp. 179–186.

Wazwa, M. (2006). The Fort Jesus Museum in Mombasa: Its experience regarding social networks in urban and rural environments. *Museum International, 58*(1–2), 113–119.

Wilding, R. F. (1987). The Shore Folk: Aspects of the early development of Swahili Communities. *Mombasa Fort Jesus occasional papers*, No. 2. Mombasa: Unknown Binding.

Yeoh, B. S. A. (2002). Postcolonial geographies of place and migration. In K. Anderson, M. Domosh, S. Pile, & N. Thrift (Eds.), *Handbook of cultural geography* (pp. 369–380). London: Sage.

Part V
Pre-modern Cultural Memories

Landscape, Transformations, and Immutability in an Aboriginal Australian Culture

Robert Tonkinson

As social scientists, anthropologists are in no doubt as to the manifold functions of built environments in categorizing, organizing, and commanding space and in stabilizing and structuring human social and cultural systems. What, then, of nomadic societies, where there is little or no "built" environment in an architectural sense? Were hunter-gatherers in some way fundamentally disadvantaged by this lack? I address this question at the conclusion of the chapter, but, as a mode of adaptation, nomadism has indisputably served humanity very well for the great majority of its history, albeit within limits imposed by a need for mobility compelled by the ever-present prospect of diminishing food supplies (Sahlins, 1972).

Aboriginal Australian societies are notable for the persistence of their hunter-gatherer adaptation and for the seemingly contradictory co-presence among them of high mobility and very strong attachment to place. In their complex and pervasive religious system, "home" sites and estates were essential to both individual and group identities.[1] The grounding of identity in both "country" and totemic connections adds force to this attachment because the ancestral creative beings are closely associated with specific sites and tracts of territory. As Munn (1970) has ably demonstrated, country (the object world) not only anchors the human subject's consciousness and identity but also mediates relationships between the individual agent and the collectivity. In addition, certain acts of the living may be memorialized, inscribed, and objectified in landscape. Throughout Australia, a totemic geography (Strehlow, 1970) characterizes people's multiple linkages, as spirit and flesh, to place, and thence to the spiritual realm of the Dreaming and its ideologies of immutability.

Using examples drawn from Mardu people of the Western Desert (see Fig. 1), I argue that openness and flux in their social system are, in significant measure, consequences of broadly ecological variables. At a more fundamental level, however, a lack of closure in the religious system provides an essential space that accommodates dynamism and change, processes universal to human societies. Cultural

R. Tonkinson (✉)
Department of Anthropology, University of Western Australia, Nedlands, WA 6009, Australia
e-mail: bob.tonkinson@uwa.edu.au

P. Meusburger et al. (eds.), *Cultural Memories*, Knowledge and Space 4,
DOI 10.1007/978-90-481-8945-8_18, © Springer Science+Business Media B.V. 2011

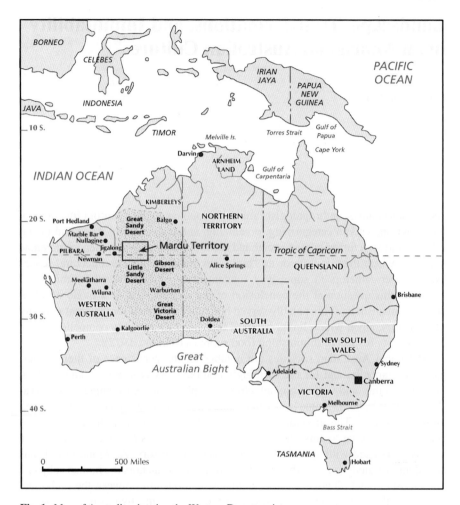

Fig. 1 Map of Australia, showing the Western Desert region

convictions about "immutability" and stasis are challenged both by the realities of life in a marginal arid environment and by religious institutions that absorb and sanctify innovation and change. In this chapter I also discuss the significance of identity politics, which are strongly—anchored by landscape, sites, kinship, and notions of home. They are more complex than ideology alone indicates and are significantly constrained by a religiously saturated and deeply spiritual worldview.

Transformations and the Institution of Immutable Order in the Creative Epoch

In Aboriginal religious thought, the arrival of the great creative beings on Australia's shores eons ago brought them face to face with a flat, featureless land. Those beings shaped the landscape, creating topographical features through the imprint of their actions, both intentional and by chance. They transformed it into what Aborigines today call country. This tumultuous era of sustained creativity is commonly known, among Aboriginal and non-Aboriginal Australians alike, as "the Dreaming." Most aptly, Stanner (1979) has dubbed it the "everywhen" (p. 24), a time that simultaneously encompasses not only the past but also the present and future. Ancestral acts of landscaping were, however, secondary to the vital world-creating activities of the superhuman beings. In addition to "putting" in place the first human beings, as a kind of life essence, the Dreaming creators imbued each group with its own distinctive dialect or language, laws, and culture, investing it with a unique socioterritorial identity. They also left behind an inexhaustible supply of animating spirits, plus the crucial ritual means for humans to perpetuate themselves and their natural environment.[2]

Just as anthropologists owe much of their understanding of Aboriginal religions, specifically the Dreaming, to the seminal insights that Stanner gained from his work with northern riverine groups (1965, 1966/1989, 1979), they have also benefited greatly from Munn's writings (1970, 1973) on worldview and religious symbolism among the Warlpiri desert people. Munn showed that, in Aboriginal thought, the founding epoch of desert society entailed a series of subject–object transformations entailing metamorphosis, imprinting, and externalization. The object world of landscape, or country, acts not only as an anchor for the consciousness and identity of the human subject but also mediates relationships between the individual and the collectivity and between society and the wider cosmic order.[3] In Aboriginal societies, objective knowledge of the natural world melds seamlessly with subjective revelation (Hiatt & Jones, 1988)—a point to which I return.

Knowing Country

Aborigines know country in two major ways. To begin with, there is obviously existential knowledge, which derives from the experience of seeing landscapes firsthand. From a Mardu perspective, such direct experience would include visiting it during dreams, in the birdlike form of a "dream-spirit" (*partunjarri*). Like other hunter-gatherers, Aborigines possess an encyclopedic knowledge of their physical environment and its resources. Then there is religious knowledge, much of which is imparted by adults, who constantly point out and explain how countless features in the landscape were created in the Dreaming by the transformational acts of creative beings: a salt lake made by the urine of Lungkurta, a lizard ancestor; distant hills seen as an outline of the head of Walawurru, the eaglehawk, and so on. The land is pregnant with such signs and possibilities, which are imprinted on human memories at a very early age and later elaborated upon with changes in status during the life cycle.

Additionally, people acquire knowledge of places not *directly* seen and experienced, but spoken, sung, and/or ritually dramatized, mainly via the media of mythology, song lines, story-telling, and ritual. Adults thus vicariously experience the travels of the famous creators and learn of the events that occurred at particular places along their ancestral paths. This knowledge allows them to talk confidently about places and events they may never have witnessed personally yet "know" through story and song. Country may therefore be intellectually grasped and assimilated from afar (R. Tonkinson & M. Tonkinson, 2001, p. 135). An audience can be taken on a journey of discovery and enlightenment without leaving the campfire, just as Mardu novices are "taken" riding, en masse during dreams, on the backs of serpents that plunge in and out of rain-making sites, in order to summon life-giving rain back to their homelands (R. Tonkinson, 1970, 2003). In Mardu worldview, these experiences are direct; they are never expressed as "I *dreamed* that. . ." but rather "I *went*. . ."

Space, Ecology, Memory, and the Religious Imperative

As much of their contemporary art depicts, Western Desert people perceive space less as a bounded entity than as clusters of points, most particularly named locations, joined by criss-crossing "paths" or "tracks" (*yiwarra*), many of which were those said to have been made by the creative beings during their Dreaming travels. Many important places are water sources of some kind, but a host of other sites also carry religious significance, collective, personal (as in the case of individual totems), or both. As Burridge (1973) fittingly observes, the Dreaming beings are credited with taking what might have been an eternal struggle between humans and their environment and transforming it "into a legacy of alliance and union" (p. 132). Landscape and skyscape alike were reined in by human imagination to become "an immense arena of relevance" (p. 136). Burridge also notes that "social and physical spaces became mnemonics of each other" (p. 136) because space was measured less in terms of distances than in the social categories that related people one to another. Over many millennia, webs of shared values, language, religious lore, kinship, social category, affinity, alliance, and exchange were forged across the vast Western Desert region (covering one sixth of the Australian continent), which is noteworthy for its high levels of cultural homogeneity (see R. M. Berndt, 1959). These complex interconnections helped compensate for the problem of very low population densities—a scattering of small groups throughout the desert—by uniting them into a single "society." This larger concept of shared belonging was only imperfectly and periodically realized, however, by way of the "big meeting" (*japal*), which brought together groups from a wide area. When water sources and food availability allowed it, they congregated to conduct the business of their society: the performance of rituals, particularly those connected with male initiation; the settlement of disputes; the exchange of information and ceremonial objects; the arrangement of marriages; the planning of future events; and the like.

The notable permeability of boundaries and relative openness of desert societies are underlain by an inescapable ecological reality: not the scarcity of water itself, but the unevenness and geographic unpredictability of rainfall. In other words, easy access to the territories and resources of neighboring groups is crucial to long-term survival (R. Tonkinson, 1988a, 1988b). Many cultural forms that have evolved over millennia suggest an intuitive awareness of the need to ensure an unhindered flow of human beings across the landscape by minimizing any tendencies toward restriction or closure.[4]

Memory is, of course, a central element in the transpositional processes of which Munn (1970, 1973) has written, for landscape becomes a mnemonic: not only for the world-creative acts and paths of the great Dreaming beings but also for recent events featuring the imprint of human actors upon the landscape. These contemporary happenings also contain creative potential for songs, rituals, and myths now and in the future; they are an integral part of the dynamism that keeps the religious system open and flexible. As I have noted in relation to the creation and eventual transmission of rituals around the huge Western Desert cultural bloc, the imprint of the here and now is rapidly transformed by distance and elapsed time into the eternal everywhen of the Dreaming (see R. Tonkinson, 1991, 2005).

In Aboriginal worldview, human life unfurls in emulation of the original world-creating and sustaining acts that set, once and for all time, the terms of life to which human descendants of the creative beings must submit themselves in order to perpetuate their entire cosmic order (see Stanner, 1979). A religious imperative (R. Tonkinson, 1978, 1991) commanded Aborigines to uphold and reproduce "the Law" (another English term commonly used among remote Aborigines to refer to the entire cultural edifice bequeathed them by their founding ancestral beings). By reproducing the Dreaming-ordained system, they ensured the continuing, automatic release of life-sustaining power emanating from the spiritual realm. Human life ran its course with vigilant scrutiny by, but no interference from, the creators, who had withdrawn after completing their earthly labors. Their eternal home is the spiritual realm, which lies beyond the powers of humans to reach them and is "here, there and everywhere, but nowhere to be seen" (Maddock, 1982, p. 106).[5] Another way to view the spiritual imperative is as an implicit threat that—should people turn away from the Law, thus reneging on their part of the "contract"—the automatic flow of life-giving power into the human realm will end. Little wonder that many older Mardu still attribute contemporary social ills and very high death rates to people's failure to follow the Law or properly hold on to it (see R. Tonkinson, 2007a, 2007c).

Totemism and Identity

A second key to the ancestor–human–landscape–cosmos nexus upon which Aboriginal religious life rests is totemism, which, in its Australian manifestations, is arguably more complex, integrated, and ramifying than anywhere else on earth. The notion of totemic geography has a long history in Aboriginal Studies and was prominent more than a century ago in the pioneering works of Spencer and Gillen (1899, 1904; see also Moyle, 1983; Strehlow, 1965). Aborigines inhabited a landscape alive with sites and areas of great spiritual significance. It was replete with meaning and implicit responsibility for their care and maintenance. One's homeland was a major focus of emotional attachment, and "homesickness" was, and remains, a powerful emotion, despite the necessity for nomadism on a continent lacking domesticable plants and animals—a way of life that precluded a sedentary life and permanent habitations. Aboriginal totemism was far more complex and significant than something merely "good to think with" (Lévi-Strauss, 1963; see also Hiatt, 1969; Maddock, 1997; and Morton, 1997 on totemism) particularly when considered at the individual level rather than that of the group or social category.[6]

Among the Mardu, two closely interrelated forms, conception totemism and what I have labeled "ancestral" totemism (Tonkinson, 1991, p. 68), were particularly important in grounding personal identity. Although other people may share the same conception totem (animal, vegetable, or mineral) or spring from the same creative being, every individual has a unique story of how she or he was "found" and then entered her or his mother. An instructive example is the contrast between a European view of Mardu territories as shown in Fig. 2 and the perspective shown in Fig. 3, drawn by a Mardu elder, Japurti, of his country, Kumpupintil (Lake Disappointment), in which he also depicts the location and identity (a snake) of his own conception totem. Japurti explained that he had been left behind in the form of a beard hair when a group of cannibal beings camped by the bed of a large creek. His mother had speared the snake with her digging stick while gathering food, but

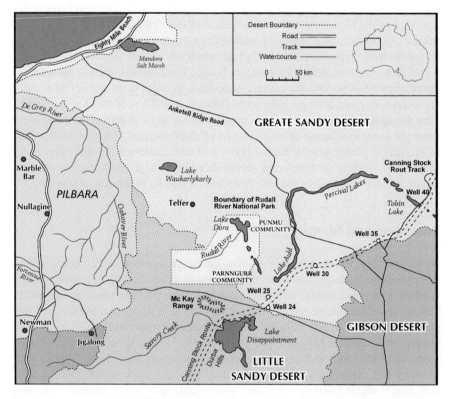

Fig. 2 Mardu territories, including Lake Disappointment, in the Great Sandy Desert, Australia

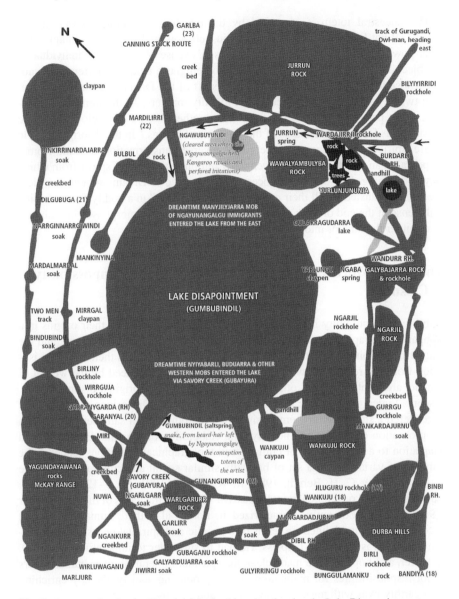

Fig. 3 A crayon drawing by Japurti, a Mardu elder, also showing the Lake Disappointment area

when she vomited after eating some of it she realized that it was a spirit-child in snake form (see R. Tonkinson, 1991, p. 81). Additionally, the location of this signal event simultaneously links a person to many others by means of ancestral totemism, which identifies the creative being or beings that left behind the life essence from which the particular totemic spirit arose.

The ancestral totem is identified by the question "*Ɖanalunta katiŋu, jurnu, yanu?*" (What [ancestral being] carried you, left you, and went on?). Imagine the sheer power of this notion for a Mardu person's sense of self: Every individual is an object of ancestral creativity, brought into being as a unique, differentiated subject whose identity is grounded in the very stuff of the Dreaming. No two people, even twins, will share an identical set of identity markers. At the same time, however, every person is identified with the many others across the region who share substance as fellow descendants of the same set of beings.[7] In the Aboriginal cycle of life, spirits born as humans undergo the reverse transformation at death, from a corporeal to an incorporeal state, eventually rejoining the pool of spirits from which they had sprung. It is the same process that happened to Dreaming beings, which, aged and exhausted by all their creative activities, "died" in a bodily (but not spiritual) sense at the end of their earthly exploits and then metamorphosed into objects on or under the land or into heavenly bodies.

Aboriginal Worldview: Assent, Activism, and the Impossibility of Closure

Stability and continuity in Aboriginal societies undoubtedly had their origins in a comparatively rapid spread of "settlement" across the Australian continent and the long-term exploitation of its resources. Another foundation was their complete isolation from the rest of the world for many millennia, as evinced by the weight of genetic, archaeological, and other evidence attesting to Aboriginal distinctiveness. It seems logical to conclude that the apparent absence of invasions and upheavals engendered a strong cultural emphasis on the reproduction of sameness rather than the promotion of change and novelty. The elaboration of regional differences and adaptation to a wide variety of climatic and topographical conditions tended to be a matter of variations on a set of basically similar social and cultural themes (see R. M. Berndt & C. H. Berndt, 1988; R. Tonkinson, 1991, pp. 5–12). Aboriginal worldview rested on a fundamentally passive "assent to the terms of life," as Stanner (1966/1989, p. 166) aptly characterized it, noting also that "human and social necessity was thus 'defined' in terms of a cosmic and spiritual necessity. The person himself was treated as helpless. He had to surrender to imperatives" (p. 166). However, as I hope to have made clear, the spiritual imperative gives human actors major responsibilities for maintaining and reproducing society, thereby enriching their earthly lives with meaning, motivation, and purpose.

Given the huge cultural stress on assent and immutability, why did Aboriginal society not fall prey to stasis, decay, and eventual implosion? In the first place, as I have indicated above, Aboriginal lives were lived in emulation of patterns set for all time in the Dreaming, and entailed the faithful maintenance of the religious system through correct and regular ritual performance. There was an inevitable tension between the dominant ideology of a static and immutable universe and the reality of dynamism in social and cultural forms (and in ecological relationships) (see R. Tonkinson, 2004c). In an ethnography describing Mardu "traditional" society and culture as lived and imagined immediately prior to initial contacts with Europeans, I attempted to show how such a massive contradiction between ideology and reality could be managed and perpetuated (R. Tonkinson, 1978, 1991). Stanner (1966/1989) had led the way with his insight that Aboriginal religious systems constantly strained toward closure but that, as if in recognition of its impossibility, their societies had evolved elements or mechanisms that enabled them to accommodate change. However, it was predominantly the kind of change that "would fit the forms of permanence" (p. 270), enabling these societies to attain stability yet avoid inertia.

The spirits of flora and fauna, which live in their billions within the landscape at "increase centers" (Meggitt, 1962, p. 221; R. Tonkinson, 1974, p. 75, 1991, pp. 117–118), usually respond to ritual acts performed every year by their living guardians to bring them out and become plentiful upon the land. Aboriginal religion, being strongly life-affirming, places high value on the worth of the individual, who is the medium through which new knowledge is channeled into the human realm. This flow is one-way, however, with the receiving individual being a passive medium whose creative acts are credited to the ancestral powers. Inequalities inherent in age and gender are the two most important differentiating criteria in the distribution of social and political power in almost all hunter-gatherer societies, where an egalitarian ethos tends to prevail. The Mardu belief that humans are merely channels for communication between spiritual and earthly realms rules out the accretion of power on the basis of individual difference, and this preclusion has significant political implications. Of course, people recognize and appreciate differences, such as artistic ability or verbal acuity, but they do not treat such attributes as a basis for status differentiation. The Mardu verbs that are used to depict the act of transmission between the spiritual and human realms affirm this denial of agency on the part of ego: the *jijikarrkaly* (spirit messengers, or go-betweens) "show," "teach," or "give" new information, songs, dances, body designs, sacred objects, and so on to human recipients (R. Tonkinson, 2005).[8]

Cultural Redundancy in the Religious System

What I have just described captures another important element of dynamism, one that is characteristic of Aboriginal Australia as a whole: the diffusion and transmission of ritual and associated songs, objects, and items for gift and exchange between groups. There is continual pressure to allow the release of newly revealed rituals, for example, into regional exchange systems like those of the Western Desert bloc. The sheer volume of new rituals being generated meant that at any given time certain older ones were falling into disuse to make room for the newly "revealed" rituals. Thus, the religious system's existing ritual repertoire was forever being enlivened by a measure of novelty.[9]

I say "a measure" of novelty, because one notable characteristic of Aboriginal religious systems, and a key to the seeming ease of memorization of religious lore (e.g., several thousand songs), is a kind of in-built cultural redundancy (Maddock, 1969; Stanner, 1966/1989; R. Tonkinson, 1978, 1991). New rituals will contain a few novel features but, for the most part, are recombinations of elements drawn from a preexisting repertoire of ritual "bits." In this sense there is almost nothing new under the sun. Stanner's (1966/1989) "forms of permanence" (p. 270) are manifest in these basic themes, which render the "new" always familiar and therefore easily assimilated and memorized via repeated performance.

The feats of memory exhibited by initiated men and by senior women are aided also by the overlapping nature of the major media through which religious meaning and understanding are transacted. Myth, songs, rites, objects, and altered states of consciousness are different, yet essentially interdependent, modes for the expression of the same profound truths about the constitution of the cosmic order and the maintenance of harmony among its human, natural, and spiritual realms.[10]

In this context, I allude to mythology as one other important conduit for the absorption of contemporary knowledge into an ideologically immutable cultural universe. I do so in order to show how new knowledge finds its way from individuals and the periphery into the core collective structures of Mardu culture, transforming both time and space into the eternal everywhen of the Dreaming. Ritual, dance, and song line are all major vehicles for the transmission of religious meanings, and Mardu place a strong emphasis on accuracy and faithful reproduction to ensure that these acts will be efficacious. In an oral culture, however, mythology is inherently flexible and open to individual interpretation and biases in the telling (within certain bounds, however, for it meshes with these other modes of imparting meaning). Myths, as statements about absolute truths of the Dreaming, are capable of extension and expansion. As noted above, newly revealed knowledge emanates from the ancestral creative beings by way of their spirit emissaries, but it also derives from the finding of objects and subsequent recognition of new linkages between particular sites in the landscape and the hitherto unknown intentions and activities of creative beings during the Dreaming. Needless to say, the political implications of such discoveries and interpretations may be considerable.

To explicate this point, I give a Mardu example. The discovery of a number of natural stone objects, easily identified by their color and shape, is known to have revealed that the major rain-making ancestor, Winpa, had traveled through Mardu territory. Once the relevant elders verified that the stones had indeed been left behind by Winpa, Mardu claims to proprietary rights in the major rain-making ritual associated with Winpa and his fellow serpentine ancestors were strengthened. The discovery also enabled the Mardu to reap the benefits in status that accrue to them as a "host" group. Mardu worldview rests on the assumption that new knowledge may be revealed at any given time and that this understanding is constantly being verified and reinforced—for instance, by the flow of newly composed rituals throughout the huge Western Desert region.

Undeniably, the absence of written history not only makes forgetting easy in Aboriginal culture but also creates an openness that conduces to the assimilation of valued new knowledge, which rapidly becomes "timeless," melding seamlessly into the all-enveloping Dreaming. Desert Aboriginal cultures have many features that compress genealogical time, such as taboos on using the names of people who die, shallow genealogies, and a kinship system that merges Ego's generation level with those of grandparents and grandchildren. A strong egalitarian ethos, plus the refusal to credit individuals for their creativity, does not provide for a rise of cults surrounding great leaders, artists, diviners, curers, warriors, and so on. Enduring cultural memories are focused strongly on religious lore, and the mnemonic provided by landscape and sites plays a vital role in constantly triggering and sustaining these memories. People interact in, and move through, a sign-laden world, and adults are empowered by the utter conviction that, through their ritual acts, continuing life and fertility are guaranteed.

Knowledge, Memory, and Contemporary Identity Politics

In this chapter my mixing of past and ethnographic present tenses is intended to signal the fact that Mardu lives today are a mélange of elements drawn from their traditional past and those emanating from decades of contact with the dominant Australian society in which the Mardu find themselves encapsulated.[11] What has remained important, though, despite ever-increasing Westernizing and assimilatory pressures, is their strong connection to place and the continuing significance of memory and practice concerning the Dreaming and their Law. Knowledge and memory are very much live issues, thanks to changes in legislative regimes at both state and federal levels. The most significant change has been the Australian federal government's Native Title Act (1993), following the High Court's 1992 landmark "Mabo decision." This Act conceded that the British had used a legal fiction, *terra nullius* ("unoccupied land"), to justify sovereignty and that native title was thus not everywhere extinguished by British colonization. Although much of the land in "settled Australia" has long been alienated by the invaders, native title still inheres in Aborigines' indigenous "laws and customs" and their continuing association with traditional homelands (see Brennan, 2005, p. 242; R. Tonkinson, 1998).[12]

For a variety of reasons, many Mardu are no longer living on their ancestral lands, but they remain highly mobile and frequently visit desert settlements to see kin and attend funerals, meetings, and ritual gatherings. Being "on country" still evokes strong feelings of attachment, security, and empowerment; as some Mardu have said, it "charges our batteries." Many older people are also at pains to take children and young adults back to ancestral lands in order to introduce them to sites in the landscape and impart the relevant stories.

The Mardu struggle for land rights and native title lasted more than a decade, and the process of mounting a claim required detailed documentation of their cultural knowledge and activities regarding their ancestral lands. As their consultant anthropologist for 10 years, and as the principal author of the "connection report" that constitutes the written evidence supporting their claim, I can vouch for the collectivity's prodigious knowledge and detailed memory of totemic geography, landscape, sites, myths, song lines, rituals, and objects. The Mardu claim was one of the strongest mounted so far in Australia, and in 2002 they were granted native title over a very large expanse of desert.[13]

The linking of oral traditions to landscape has legitimized connections via strong assertions of local and regional identity, which is one way to satisfy the legal requirements for claiming native title rights under Australian law. The Mardu underpinned their identity as a coherent entity having legitimate claims to country through the deployment of their knowledge of landscape, both practical and historical-mythical. Their outward looking, collectivist worldview counters tendencies toward local group parochialism or intergroup conflict (see R. Tonkinson, 2004b). At one stage since migration to the desert fringes, tensions grew between the Mardu and one group of their northern neighbors, who, led by a European, sought to assert political control over them. More recently, during the struggle over land rights, it became clear that a united front was necessary in order to achieve title, so the two groups ritually (and peacefully) settled their differences and formed a single claimant group. Aboriginal lives have changed, but the desert people have retained their highly valued sense of difference and autonomy. Protection of their territories remains a prime value, and through their continuing ritual activities they remember and reproduce country and themselves (R. Tonkinson, 2007a).

Conclusion

Although dealing ostensibly with the same set of subjects as the other chapters in this volume, this one appears to stand apart because of its subjects. The Mardu are, or were, nomadic hunter-gatherers, who traditionally had no built environment in an architectural sense. However, one could argue that the spiritual imperative central to Mardu society, which demands ritual activity to ensure the reproduction of society and resources, itself constitutes a "mode of production." As I have also noted above, Aboriginal belief is that when the great mythical beings of the Dreaming arrived on the Australian continent, they encountered a featureless land, which they modified (or "built") by creating its topographical features. So if one takes culture as the primary "builder," as social scientists are wont to do, then the human "descendants" of these mythical ancestors have, over a great many millennia, used their symbolizing capacity rather than architectural tools as the primary means of investing their environment (including the sky and its celestial bodies) with significance. In a sense, they have collectively built it as a massive repository of signs, on which they have imposed a multitude of meanings; and these meanings have, in turn, altered over time in response to social, cultural, and environmental changes.

From a cultural constructionist view, the desert environment of the Mardu may therefore be legitimately regarded for comparative purposes as built by virtue of the meanings invested in its existing features as part of a more general world-ordering imperative. Most fixed "monuments" and "memorials" are unmodified natural features, their cultural importance unrecognizable to non-Mardu and, in some of their detail, even to some Mardu themselves. Gender differences and the separation of secret-sacred knowledge mean that men and women may not read the same story into, or from, a given site or star cluster. Children are given simplified and nonsecret explanations, less elaborated than those of initiated adults.[14]

From the standpoint just explained, landscape features are comparable to the built environment as multivalent symbols for triggering and sustaining memory, as objects of veneration, as tools for learning, and as sites for ritual activities deemed essential for human and animal reproduction. Embodied in both the Dreaming and the Law, such sites stand as constant and ubiquitous reminders of the reality of the past, the necessities of the present, and the assurance of a future. They bring the Dreaming into the present and vivify it as a spiritual resource for the living, made immediate and relevant through the media of song, dance, ritual, and myth. In cultures without writing, people "read" land- and skyscapes for the meanings and proofs of what both underlies and substantiates the spiritual imperative.

Acknowledgement For her many helpful comments on this chapter, I thank Myrna Tonkinson. This chapter is based on anthropological field research carried out among the Mardu people of Australia's Western Desert region. Figures 1, 2, and 3 are based on those appearing as Maps 1 and 2 and as figure 5-2 in R. Tonkinson (1991), which is part of the Case Studies in Cultural Anthropology Series, published originally by Holt, Rinehart and Winston and currently by Wadsworth/Cengage Learning. As a Master of Arts student, I began fieldwork in 1963 at a remote Christian mission at Jigalong, on the edge of the desert in Western Australia, and wrote a thesis on intercultural relations (R. Tonkinson, 1966, 1974). My Ph.D. thesis (R. Tonkinson, 1972), which deals with Mardu ritual, was also based on material gathered at Jigalong. See R. Tonkinson (2007b) for a brief autobiographical sketch of my fieldwork in the Western Desert and Vanuatu.

Notes

1. Although I employ the "ethnographic present tense," the situation described in this chapter refers to "traditional" Mardu society and culture prior to the presence of Europeans (hence the use also of the past tense here and in analogous contexts throughout this chapter). Despite clear continuities from the past in many elements of their culture, the Mardu have undergone considerable transformation consequent upon their encapsulation as a small, relatively powerless minority within a large nation-state (see R. Tonkinson, 2007c).
2. As M. E. Tonkinson (1990, p. 191) has noted, the collective identity marker "Aborigines" was a British imposition of ethnicity on the Aborigines, whereas they identified *themselves* in localized, ethnocentric terms without any consciousness of national identity. In the Western Desert, for example, people recognized their regional homogeneity of custom and culture, but beyond the limits of their society they saw a dangerous landscape thought to be inhabited only by cannibal beings and malevolent forces.
3. Munn appears to have been inspired by the cultural constructionism of Berger and Luckmann (1967; see also Berger, 1967).
4. There is one important exception: boundaries essential to keeping secret-sacred places, objects, and activities inviolable from trespass by the young and the uninitiated. In the contact situation, the Mardu were at pains to keep their secret-sacred and core religious domain separate from that of the Europeans (see R. Tonkinson, 2004a).
5. This remoteness of the spiritual realm from human abilities to communicate with it explains why Aboriginal Australian religions were free of human attempts at suasion, manipulation, prayer, pleading, or sacrifice by individuals intent on swaying the powers residing there.
6. Aboriginal Australians are anthropologically famous for their complex category systems, traditionally existing throughout most of the continent. Congruent with, but different from, egocentrically constructed classificatory kinship systems, these overlying divisions into two,

four, eight, or sixteen named categories, membership of which is ascribed by birth, are useful as labeling devices and as general guides for pigeonholing people (see R. Tonkinson, 1978, pp. 54–60, 1987).

7. Some ancestral beings were sedentary, so their area of influence is more localized than that of ancestral beings who were great travelers. Recognizing that Aboriginal societies were replete with dualisms and cross-cutting classificatory systems, Burridge (1973) had the important insight that these schemes were "unitive." That is, they separated out and individualized people, creating unique social persons, yet were embedded within a broader "unifying" cultural framework that stressed cooperation and unity (R. Tonkinson, 1978, pp. 54–60).

8. Although people sometimes label new rituals by the place where they were "composed" or by the individual who dreamed most of the songs and associated ritual regalia, those who report their dream-encounters to others refer to themselves as *objects* of the revelation. These mediums are mature adults capable of interpreting their dream or daydream experiences, whereas children are said not to be subject to such revelations. However, what a person claims to have experienced and learned is never simply adopted unquestioningly. It must be shared with others who will discuss, ask questions, seek clarifications, debate as a group, and reach agreement as to the "real" significance of these indicative signs before the new knowledge becomes inscribed as an established social fact (see R. Tonkinson, 1970, 2003). If secret-sacred knowledge or objects are involved, subsequent meetings are restricted to fully initiated men, who have the right to attend but will leave the important conclusions to senior men of the highest grades in the ritual hierarchy. In the Western Desert, mature women also have rituals, songs, regalia, and the like that are secret-sacred to them, but on a much smaller scale than "men's business."

9. In a recent volume of papers on property and equality, one of the editors described my text on the Mardu as perhaps "the most distinctive case of interaction between ritual knowledge and political power in hunter-gatherer studies" (T. Widlok, 2005, p. 12). I showed how, in the political economy of Mardu religion, individuals are disengaged from their ritual creativity, which accrues as cultural capital to the local initiated male collective by virtue of its ability to enhance its prestige and influence and receive gifts. A local group does so by acting as hosts, an advantageous status enabling them to attract into their country other groups to be inducted into the new ritual. Eventually, through repeated visits, the visitors earn the right to receive associated sacra, which signify their attainment of performance rights and thereby enhance their political power, for they, in turn, become hosts able to attract yet other groups as novices for this ritual.

10. In a society lacking anything resembling formal instruction, learning is achieved through seeing, hearing, and repeated participation in ritual performances. Male initiation, which traditionally began around puberty with circumcision, was followed by a series of initiation stages over a period of about 15 years before a man was given his first wife. At this point, he achieved social adulthood. However, initiation into newly introduced rituals continued throughout one's life. There was always more to learn, even for senior members of the male ritual hierarchy, given the constant circulation of rituals throughout this vast culture area. Girls were not initiated and were given in marriage prior to puberty. They rose in the female ritual hierarchy as they grew older, but the major responsibility for social reproduction lay with the mature males (see Bern, 1979).

11. In Australia, Aborigines are a Fourth-World people who suffer considerable socioeconomic disadvantage. They and the country's other indigenous minority, the Torres Strait Islanders, make up less than 2% of the population (see R. Tonkinson, 1998).

12. Not only land rights and native title legislation but also state and federal heritage protection laws have had a significant impact on Indigenous identity politics in Australia. For a particularly remarkable example that generated nationwide media attention, see R. Tonkinson (1997).

13. Although a National Park on the western edge of their lands was regrettably not eligible for claim, it is the subject of continuing negotiations between Mardu and the state over a co-management plan.

14. For further details on Mardu ritual hierarchies and gender roles, see R. Tonkinson (1991, pp. 106–142). In some parts of Australia, Aboriginal people use the terms *outside* and *inside* to indicate public versus restricted domains of meaning (see Morphy, 2005).

References

Berger, P. (1967). *The sacred canopy: Elements of a sociological theory of religion.* New York: Doubleday.

Berger, P., & Luckmann, T. (1967). *The social construction of reality.* New York: Doubleday.

Bern, J. (1979). Ideology and domination: Toward a reconstruction of Australian Aboriginal social formation. *Oceania, 50,* 118–132.

Berndt, R. M. (1959). The concept of the 'tribe' in the Western Desert of Australia. *Oceania, 30,* 81–107.

Berndt, R. M., & Berndt, C. H. (1988). *The world of the first Australians* (Rev. ed.). Canberra: Institute of Aboriginal Studies.

Brennan, F. (2005). Land rights: The religious factor. In M. Charlesworth, F. Dussart, & H. Morphy (Eds.), *Aboriginal religions in Australia: An anthology of recent writings* (pp. 227–246). Aldershot: Ashgate.

Burridge, K. O. L. (1973). *Encountering aborigines—A case study: Anthropology and the Australian Aboriginal.* New York: Pergamon.

Hiatt, L. R. (1969). Totemism tomorrow: The future of an illusion. *Mankind, 7,* 83–93.

Hiatt, L. R., & Jones, R. (1988). Aboriginal conceptions of the workings of nature. In R. W. Home (Ed.), *Australian science in the making* (pp. 1–28). Cambridge, UK: Cambridge University Press.

Lévi-Strauss, C. (1963). *Totemism.* Boston: Beacon Press.

Maddock, K. (1969). *The jabuduruwa.* Unpublished Ph.D. dissertation, University of Sydney, Australia.

Maddock, K. (1982). *The Australian aborigines: A portrait of their society* (2nd ed.). Melbourne: Penguin.

Maddock, K. (1997). The temptation of Paris resisted: An intellectual portrait of a Sydney anthropologist. In F. Merlan, J. Morton, & A. Rumsey (Eds.), *Scholar and sceptic: Australian Aboriginal studies in honour of LR Hiatt* (pp. 39–63). Canberra: Aboriginal Studies Press.

Meggitt, M. J. (1962). *Desert people.* Sydney: Angus & Robertson.

Morphy, H. (2005). Yolngu art and the creativity of the inside. In M. Charlesworth, F. Dussart, & H. Morphy (Eds.), *Aboriginal religions in Australia: An anthology of recent writings* (pp. 159–169). Aldershot: Ashgate.

Morton, J. (1997). Totemism now and then: A natural science of society? In F. Merlan, J. Morton, & A. Rumsey (Eds.), *Scholar and sceptic: Australian Aboriginal studies in honour of LR Hiatt* (pp. 151–170). Canberra: Aboriginal Studies Press.

Moyle, R. (1983). Songs, ceremonies and sites: The Agharringa case. In N. Peterson & M. Langton (Eds.), *Aborigines, land and land rights* (pp. 66–93). Canberra: Australian Institute of Aboriginal Studies.

Munn, N. D. (1970). The transformation of subjects into objects in Walbiri and Pitjantjatjara myth. In R. M. Berndt (Ed.), *Australian Aboriginal anthropology* (pp. 141–156). Perth: University of Western Australia Press.

Munn, N. D. (1973). *Walbiri iconography: Graphic representation and cultural symbolism in a Central Australian society.* Ithaca, NY: Cornell University Press.

Sahlins, M. (1972). *Stone age economics.* Chicago: Aldine Atherton.

Spencer, W. B., & Gillen, F. J. (1899). *The Native Tribes of Central Australia.* London: Macmillan.

Spencer, W. B., & Gillen, F. J. (1904). *The Northern Tribes of Central Australia.* London: Macmillan.

Stanner, W. E. H. (1965). Religion, totemism and symbolism. In R. M. Berndt & C. H. Berndt (Eds.), *Aboriginal man in Australia* (pp. 207–237). Sydney, Australia: Angus & Robertson.

Stanner, W. E. H. (1979). *White man got no Dreaming: Essays, 1938–1981*. Canberra: Australian National University Press.

Stanner, W. E. H. (1989). *On Aboriginal religion* (with an Appreciation by F. Merlan and an introduction by L. R. Hiatt). Sydney: University of Sydney. (Original work published 1966)

Strehlow, T. G. H. (1965). Culture, social structure and environment in Aboriginal Central Australia. In R. M. Berndt & C. H. Berndt (Eds.), *Aboriginal man in Australia: Essays in honour of A. P. Elkin* (pp. 121–145). Sydney: Angus and Robertson.

Strehlow, T. G. H. (1970). Geography and the totemic landscape in Central Australia: A functional study. In R. M. Berndt (Ed.), *Australian Aboriginal anthropology* (pp. 92–140). Perth: University of Western Australia Press.

Tonkinson, M. E. (1990). Is it in the blood? Australian Aboriginal identity. In J. Linnekin & L. Poyer (Eds.), *Cultural identity and ethnicity in the Pacific* (pp. 191–218). Honolulu, HI: University of Hawaii Press.

Tonkinson, R. (1966). *Social structure and acculturation of Aborigines in the Western Desert*. Unpublished M.A. thesis, University of Western Australia.

Tonkinson, R. (1970). Aboriginal dream-spirit beliefs in a contact situation. In R. M. Berndt (Ed.), *Australian Aboriginal anthropology* (pp. 227–291). Perth: University of Western Australia Press.

Tonkinson, R. (1972). *Nga:wajil: A Western Desert Aboriginal rainmaking ritual*. Unpublished Ph.D. thesis, University of British Columbia, Canada.

Tonkinson, R. (1974). *The Jigalong mob: Aboriginal victors of the desert crusade*. Menlo Park, CA: Cummings.

Tonkinson, R. (1978). *The Mardudjara Aborigines*. New York: Holt, Rinehart & Winston.

Tonkinson, R. (1987). Aborigines. In M. Eliade (Ed.), *The encyclopedia of religion* (pp. 196–201). New York: Free Press/Macmillan.

Tonkinson, R. (1988a). Egalitarianism and inequality in a Western Desert culture. *Anthropological Forum*, *5*, 545–558.

Tonkinson, R. (1988b). 'Ideology and domination' in Aboriginal Australia: A Western Desert test case. In T. Ingold, D. Riches, & J. Woodburn (Eds.), *Hunters and gatherers: Vol. 1. Property, power and ideology* (pp. 170–184). Oxford, UK: Berg.

Tonkinson, R. (1991). *The Mardu Aborigines* (2nd ed.). Fort Worth, TX: Holt, Rinehart & Winston.

Tonkinson, R. (1997). Anthropology and Aboriginal tradition: The Hindmarsh Island bridge affair and the politics of interpretation. *Oceania*, *68*, 133–147.

Tonkinson, R. (1998). National identity: Australia after Mabo. In J. Wassmann (Ed.), *Pacific answers to Western hegemony* (pp. 287–310). Oxford, UK: Berg.

Tonkinson, R. (2003). Ambrymese dreams and the Mardu Dreaming. In R. Lohmann (Ed.), *Dream travelers of the Western Pacific: Sleep experiences and culture in Australian Aboriginal, Melanesian and Indonesian societies* (pp. 87–105). New York: Palgrave Macmillan.

Tonkinson, R. (2004a). Encountering the Other: Millenarianism and the permeability of indigenous domains in Melanesia and Australia. In H. Jebens (Ed.), *Cargo, cult, and culture critique* (pp. 137–156). Honolulu, HI: University of Hawaii Press.

Tonkinson, R. (2004b). Resolving conflict within the Law: The Mardu Aborigines of Australia. In G. Kemp & D. P. Fry (Eds.), *Keeping the peace: Conflict resolution and peaceful societies around the world* (pp. 89–104). London: Routledge.

Tonkinson, R. (2004c). Spiritual prescription, social reality: Reflections on religious dynamism. *Anthropological Forum*, *14*, 183–201.

Tonkinson, R. (2005). Individual creativity and property–power disjunction in an Australian desert society. In T. Widlok & W. Tadesse (Eds.), *Property and equality: Vol. 1. Ritualisation, sharing, egalitarianism* (pp. 32–46). Oxford, UK: Berghahn.

Tonkinson, R. (2007a). Aboriginal 'difference' and 'autonomy' then and now: Four decades of change in a Western Desert Society. *Anthropological Forum*, *17*, 41–60.

Tonkinson, R. (2007b). From dust to ashes: The challenges of difference. *Ethnos (Key Informants in the History of Anthropology Series), 72*, 509–534.

Tonkinson, R. (2007c). The Mardu Aborigines: On the road to somewhere. In G. Spindler & J. E. Stockard (Eds.), *Globalization and change in fifteen cultures: Born in one world, living in another* (pp. 225–255). Belmont, CA: Thomson Wadsworth.

Tonkinson, R., & Tonkinson, M. (2001). 'Knowing' and 'being' in place in the Western Desert. In A. Anderson, I. Lilley, & S. O'Connor (Eds.), *Histories of old ages: Essays in honour of Rhys Jones* (pp. 133–139). Canberra: Pandanus.

Widlok, T. (2005). Introduction. In T. Widlok & W. G. Tadesse (Eds.), *Property and equality: Vol. 1. Ritualisation, sharing, egalitarianism* (pp. 1–17). Oxford, UK: Berghahn.

Person, Space, and Memory: Why Anthropology Needs Cognitive Science and Human Geography

Jürg Wassmann

Establishing Persons Through Name Debates[1]

What's in a name? If one were to put this famous (Shakespearean) question to members of the Iatmul people living in the Middle Sepik region of Papua New Guinea (see Fig. 1), they would most probably answer "Everything!" In this chapter I aim to explain why this guess is plausible. The Iatmul knowledge about myths of origin, clans, totems, migration, and settlement is codified in an extremely complex system of myriad names. Names and the knowledge codified with them secure status, rights, and proprietary titles, among other things. It is no wonder that names are a matter of serious debate within this culture. Understanding the sophisticated Iatmul system of names requires not only sound anthropological research but also insights into human memory and learning capacities as well as competence in indigenous concepts of geography.

Among the Iatmul, conflicts over the rightful possession of a name are dealt with by having the opponents and their supporters meet in the center of the men's house for a special debate about the possession of the name (see Fig. 2). This event, which takes place near the ceremonial stool (*pabu*), is their most revered social form of intellectual discussion, for names are the very heart of the ramified Iatmul mythological system. Conflicts about land use, fishing rights, or rights to use personal namings are always about names and their mythological explanations.

Each speaker wants to prove that the name in dispute belongs to him or to his clan. He wants to prove in public to all the "old crocodiles"[2] present that he knows the mythological background of the name. He, therefore, must be able to mythologically "locate" the name in the landscape. This location is secret, however, and that is why the two litigating parties find themselves in a contradictory situation. On the one hand, they must prove their respective claims; they have to point to a connection. On the other hand, they do not want to divulge their mythological knowledge. As a consequence, they drop only veiled hints that test each other's mythological

J. Wassmann (✉)
Department of Anthropology, Heidelberg University, 69117 Heidelberg, Germany
e-mail: juerg.wassmann@urz.uni-heidelberg.de

P. Meusburger et al. (eds.), *Cultural Memories*, Knowledge and Space 4,
DOI 10.1007/978-90-481-8945-8_19, © Springer Science+Business Media B.V. 2011

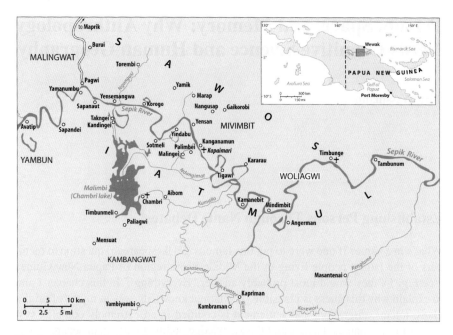

Fig. 1 The area of the Iatmul people, Middle Sepik region, Papua New Guinea

Fig. 2 Iatmul men's house, Papua New Guinea

knowledge. The result is an enigmatic and dynamic play of intimations and interpretations, which are either accepted or rejected. These exchanges about mythology
are not only presented verbally but are also partly staged and, in turn, may be interpreted with dramatic actions by an opposing speaker suddenly adorning himself

with a red hibiscus flower (which may signify an ancestor) or by something being represented mimetically (e.g., a bird or the movement of a crocodile).

The corpus of closely guarded information extends beyond location to include a bewilderingly large number of totems, thousands of names, and innumerable myths and fragments of myths with no readily apparent relation to one another. Knowledge of the links and ties between them is held by a small number of important men whose influence stems precisely from that knowledge (Wassmann, 2001). It is therefore not the mythological tales as such that are secret but rather their precise geographical locations in the space and the true identities of their protagonists.

With the debate taking place in a public arena, where moods are likely to change quickly, the atmosphere is heated. Political alliances and dependencies determined by kinship and social and financial debts are decisive, as are the prestige of the speakers, their rhetorical skills, and the ability to stage surprising changes. All these factors may result in a specific opinion among members of the public—without necessarily having this effect every single time. Some of these facets come across in the following excerpts from a verbal exchange in the men's house:

> *Kandim*: Now we are talking about this name [*Sisalabwan*].... A crocodile moves in the swamp, its tail forcefully beats the surface of the water, a sound is heard—and the birds *wundan* and *mbarak*, which have their nests in the grass swamp, are crying: wa-la! wa-la!...
>
> *Angrimbi*: So, you are using it?
>
> *Kandim*: There is no other thing that could be connected with this name. This is enough! You cannot insist on having the sole right to this name.
>
> *Angrimbi*:... If you cannot connect something else with this name, your claim is lost, over, the end! You may soon stop using the name, brother! Because it is really about a truly big and important thing [a crocodile].... Do you know about its [mythical] dwelling place?
>
> *Kandim*: It is enough if you have recited the string of names; it is the same issue.
>
> *Angrimbi*: No, not at all! My elder brother, you cannot talk like that. First you have to recite your line of names. First, we want to hear it!
>
> *Kandim*: It is enough if you have already recited Wani's string of names.
>
> *Angrimbi*: Now, I have listened to your string of names. Like a frog that clings to a different branch every night, you have put it together from different pieces!... He does not know anything! Come on, tell us the place! Name this place if you have learned something about it from your fathers.... Come here and tell us this place where they will build a village. I will not define the ancestral being. I am not going to recite the list of names of this place; do not count on me to enlighten you. (Stanek, 1983, pp. 259–260, translated and adapted by J. Wassmann)

The dominant lines of this debate are demands and statements such as "connect another thing with the name," "you have to recite your line of names," and, most significant, "tell us the place." Obviously, the true owner of the name is expected to be able to relate it to a mythological setting by linking the name line of the "crocodile" to specific places. Kandim fails to defend his case successfully because he is incapable of placing the name *Sisalabwan* within mythology and landscape.

To understand what *Angrimbi* was demanding of his opponent, consider the name *Patnawigumbangi*, for example. It is one of the names of the primeval crocodile that created the earth. The name is localized at the first station of a primeval wandering, the place of creation. It is part of the name pairs that are recited in a long string (Wassmann, 1991, pp. 231–232), such as:

1. *Pat-nawi-gumbangi* and
2. *Nganga-nawi-gumbangi*
   (*pat*: spittle; *nawi*: masculine ending; *gumbangi*: masculine ending; *nganga*: lower jaw;)
   These names may elicit a visual image: the place of creation, where there was, at the beginning, only water. The crocodile has spittle in its throat.
3. Lisi-nyo-mbu-ndemi and
4. Kasi-nyo-mbu-ndemi
   (*lisi, kasi*: shake, earthquake; *nyo*: mother of pearl, seashell; *mbu*: break open or to pieces; *ndemi*: masculine ending).
   The possible visual image derived from these two names concerns the time of origin and the place of creation. The crocodile = that is, the earth has just emerged from the sea and is rocking to and fro.
5. Lili-lipma and
6. Kwakwa-lipma
   (*lili*: slip away; *kwakwa*: stand up and fall down; *lipma*: coconut palm, a metaphor for place).
   These two names might evoke a visual image of the first place during creation.
   The newly created place = crocodile still rocks. The earth had come up, forming just a little marshy island.

Establishing the Space

In the Iatmul belief system water was everywhere at the time of origin, before creation. Suddenly, the water frothed and something small was washed up, a tiny creature with the skin, back, and legs of a crocodile and the face of a man. Its spittle sank to the bottom of the sea, then the crocodile moved and the spittle floated up to the surface of the water. The earth had come up, forming just a little muddy island still rocking to and fro. Time passed, and the crocodile split into two parts, its lower jaw becoming the earth, its upper jaw the sky. The sun *Nyagonduma* was thrown up, and there was light. This cleavage explains the subsequent division of society into earth and sky moieties.

Next, the first pair of brothers came into existence, and from them descended additional pairs of brothers by repeated processes. These pairs of brothers were the founders of the present clans. In the beginning, all the ancient people were gathered on the grass island, at the place of origin. Then the ancestral leaders and their relatives left the village, following in the tracks of crocodiles, which cleared the way for them. Thus came about the most important event of ancient times: the severance from the place of origin and the migration into the area of the present settlements (see Fig. 3). During this journey, always following the tracks of the crocodiles, whose moves shaped the hitherto nondescript landscape, the people took possession of tracts of land, parts of the bush, lakes, and watercourses, and villages and hamlets were founded. The land taken and the villages founded at that time determine present claims of possession. The scraps of food and the excrement left behind on the migration were the origin of the water spirits *wanjimout.*

Two facets are crucial. The two brothers in each pair behaved in different ways, and the migrations of the various clans had their own typical patterns. The second brother was the dynamic one, the one who first crossed the Sepik. The first brother, by contrast, initially remained close to the bushland and the place of creation. This contrast is expressed by the fixed terms *by canoe* and *on foot*, but both brothers ultimately covered the same route. A further point is that the ground covered by the migration of a clan centered on a particular area, in which it founded a particularly large number of villages. That space was either not touched at all by the other pairs

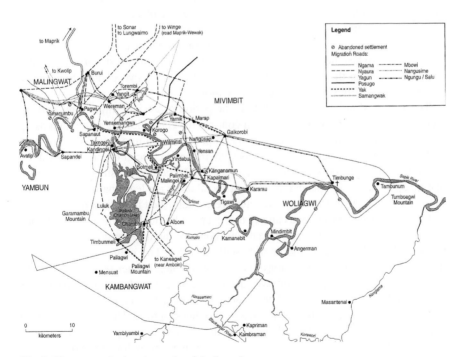

Fig. 3 The ancestral migration paths of the Iatmul

of brothers or was explicitly used only as a transit corridor. Each pair of brothers had its own area. It is typical that the regions of the fraternal pairs of the earth moiety lay mainly above (to the west of) the Middle Sepik and those of the sky moiety mainly below (to the east). These two features explain the correspondence between the earth moieties and the upper course of the river on the one hand and the sky moiety and the lower course on the other. They also explain the correspondence between the clans deriving from the first brother and the areas on the left bank of the Sepik (bushland) and the clans of the second brother and the areas on the right bank.

At each place visited during migration, the ancestors left behind a few men and women. They assigned to themselves an animal, plant, or some other object into which they could transform. Each place today therefore has its own "totem." In the Iatmul belief system this allocation of "totems" to clans means that all phenomena of this world are assigned to clans, with the earth, the fishes, and so forth belonging to the earth moiety; the sun, moon, and stars, to the sky moiety.

These totems and all the objects of the place receive proper names of their own, which are arranged in long strings of pairs. The inhabitants of the village are also given names—the names of their village's totem. The totems assigned in this way form the basis of the present totem system. Most important, the thousands of names used at that time are the stock of present names. This totemistic name repertoire is what defines the present-day Iatmul as persons.

Thus all persons and things of the present are closely identified with those of the past. Furthermore, both are associated with specific places on the mythological tracks. The person of today is defined by his or her ancient name in the sense that he or she figures as a reincarnation—albeit a frail one—of the primal namesake. The person also has the responsibility for each totem into which his or her ancestor could transform in the past. The use of names causes the two periods to coincide and expunges the linear genealogical succession.

The relationship between the past, as the period of ancient migrations, and the present can be conceived of as a spatial continuum. The following interrelationship can be readily visualized: The world and its people came into being at some time in the past, and the latter gave themselves their specific social order. According to the system, the present is nothing but a precise reflection of the situation created at that time, so the landscape and the present social order are legitimatized simply and solely by the fact that they originated and were established in ancient times.

Going one step further, one can say that every individual's name is polysyllabic. It is composed of two, three, or even four common nouns strung together and is followed by either a feminine or a masculine suffix. The nouns of a name pair, in turn, also form pairs. Etymology shows that the name either refers in a general way to the totem it designates or gives detailed information about the primal events around that totem at its place. The nouns constituting the name form a semantic reference. Each name "tells" a story in a kind of telegraphese. The names of a name string belong together because they belong to the same totem, place, and primeval event. There are hundreds of name strings. The question is how an old crocodile remembers the correct order of hundreds of highly structured names.

Establishing Memories

In many human societies the exceptional capability of the human mind to memorize and recall has always been regarded as an essential cultural feature. The Greek pantheon, for instance, included a muse of memory, *mneme*, daughter of *mnemosyne*, the personification of memory, through whom kings gained their power of authoritative speech. In Iatmul society, too, memory is connected to authority. It is also linked to learning—another process vital to the ability to establish persons and space. The nature of that interrelationship, at least in the context of this chapter, is partly explained by Squire (1987), according to whom learning in general is the process of acquiring new information, whereas memory refers to the persistence of learning in a state that can be revealed at a later time (cf. Anderson, 1983; Baddeley, 1994; McGaugh, 2000; Miller, 1956; Schacter, 1999). Tulving (1995) adds that memory seems time dependent: To remember means to represent something of the past in the present (mental time travel).

Human long-term memory, which is practically unlimited, can be divided roughly into episodic and semantic memory. Episodic memory deals with specific events or episodes from a particular time and place that one has experienced. It has two components: (a) familiarity with the past event and (b) recollection, or reexperience, of it. Semantic memory deals with facts, knowledge about the world and objects, knowledge about language, knowledge about oneself, and conceptual priming. Information is represented in long-term memory as a network of associations among concepts. Humans usually keep episodic and semantic types of memory well separated.

Cognitive scientists like those mentioned above draw attention to the fact that a person using no general memory-training principles will find it nearly impossible to store long mythological texts and hundreds of names in long-term memory both propositionally and in the correct order in a limited amount of time. Instead, a person tends to memorize prototypes of sequences in his schemata from which the actual story is then built up, and names then have to be reconstructed. General principles for training memory have been proposed. One is known as meaningful encoding, that is, the use of preexisting knowledge as a tool to store new information in memory (see the levels-of-processing [LOP] model by Craik & Lockhart, 1972; see also Ericsson & Staszenski, 1989). A second principle of skilled memory is the retrieval structure—the attachment of cues to new material for later retrieval of information (see, e.g., Ericsson & Kintsch, 1995). A third principle is the acceleration effect that practice has on the ability to learn material (see e.g., Hwang, Chang, & Chen, 2004).

Another tool for skilled memory is the use of mnemonic techniques. The long-known method of loci rests on the principle that the human mind remembers data attached to spatial information much more easily than it remembers data organized along some other lines. The method of loci, sometimes referred to as the "mental-walk" technique (e.g., Kosslyn, 1980, p. 88; see also Farah, 2001, p. 244; Harwood, 1976) is the method of visualizing items at different geographical locations and then mentally touring those locations to find the objects. Specifically, that exercise means—

1. selecting a series of vividly imagined locations,
2. memorizing those locations,
3. creating an image for each item to be remembered, and
4. placing those items, by using interactive images of them, in the selected loci.

Just how well these techniques can work is demonstrated by a study on individuals renowned for outstanding memory feats in forums such as the World Memory Championships (Maguire, Valentine, Wilding, & Kapur, 2003), Using neuropsychological measuring devices and structural and functional brain imaging, the authors showed that the subjects' superior memory capabilities were not driven by exceptional intellectual ability or structural brain differences but rather by a spatial learning strategy engaging brain regions that are critical for spatial memory in particular.

   With accurate memories being essential for the Iatmul to secure their rights in their society, how do *they* go about remembering what is necessary? Typically, the sole knowledge that participants in a name debate have acquired of mythological facts and ancestral names belongs to the semantic memory domain, for there is no a priori involvement of specific knowledge of events or episodes from a particular time and place that the subject has experienced. But using a purely semantic approach to the immense load of information that the Iatmul have to memorize would require an amount of training and rehearsal almost impossible to manage by any human being. In this situation the deep personal and emotional stakes that the remembering subject (LaBar & Cabeza, 2006) has in the string of names and cultural facts he reproduces—and the immense significance attached to the outcome of his performance—probably afford the speaker special access to the learned information. It seems likely that the Iatmul construct a kind of episodic or autobiographical representation of the myriad semantic facts and simultaneously organize great amounts of semantic information into complex spatiotemporal patterns. This procedure enables them to make use of memory systems other than those typically involved in purely semantic memory. Individual names and facts are cross-linked in various cognitive domains—spatial, temporal, and emotional—all of which provide mnemonic cues to the next level of information to be retrieved (e.g., the next name in the reconstructed line of ancestors that is being contested on a given occasion). This cross-linking technique is quite similar to the artificial cross-linking produced by the method of loci.

Mental Journeys

The landscape of the Middle Sepik is flat, monotonous, and quite amphibic. The river is prominent, and only a few hills emerge (see Fig. 4). This description reflects the impression of a non-Iatmul observer, of course. But imagine that the

Fig. 4 A Sepik landscape

old crocodiles, the big men, are assembling on a hill. They would see a landscape that is mythologically charged, a topography somewhat similar to what Strehlow (1947) described in his writings about the Aranda in Central Aboriginal Australia. Morphy (1993) has explained this perceptual difference in the following way: "A landscape-based cosmology is one way in which Aboriginal identity has been maintained, especially since the European colonists and the Aboriginals created such divergent landscapes out of the same pieces of geography. Landscape is a mnemonic for past generation" (p. 206). Writing of the Kwaio people in central Malaita, in the Solomon Islands, Keesing (1982), too, notes the divergence between western and indigenous understandings of the landscape: "To the Kwaio eye, this landscape is not only divided by invisible lines into named land tracts and settlement sites, it is seen as structured by history" (p. 76).

One could present additional examples of the dissimilarities between western and nonwestern perceptions of landscape. Gow (1995) is referring to an indigenous people in the Amazon region when he notes that "what the Piro 'see' when they look at the land is kinship" (p. 56). The research by Weiner (1991) on Papua New Guinea's Foi people describes a topography where "a society's place names schematically image a people's intentional transformation of their habitat from a sheer physical terrain into a pattern of historically experienced and constituted space and time. ... The bestowing of place names constitutes Foi existential space out of a blank environment" (p. 32: cf. Basso, 1988; Feld & Basso, 1996; Fox, 1997).

The Iatmul perceive the Sepik River as the original sea of creation, the grass islands as the contemporary world, the small surrounding creeks as features carved by the original crocodiles, and the Palingawi mountain as something erected by two cannibalistic eagles. They see places and parts of the bush as being connected to animals and plants, for each place enacts their myths. These people see embodied mythology. It is as though one were looking upon the real events surrounding the ancestral wandering, as though one were seeing image schemata that help one take what has been witnessed and verbalize it in texts, songs, names, and staged in ritual performances. I have good reason to assume that the person undertakes in the *pabu* ritual a mental journey. Emplacement is thus the most basic medium of mnemonics.

In the Iatmul case under consideration in this chapter, the memorizing of hundreds of names in the correct order is presumably structured by a mythology equal to countless "mental walks" in the primeval space. Landscape for the Iatmul people serves as a medium for cultural memories.

There is no doubt that every human being has a memory. In addition, it is supported by outside dimensions external to the brain (Assmann, 1992). Each culture develops something that could be termed its connective structure. This structure links people together, promoting a space of shared experiences, expectations, and practices that leads to trust and orientation through its binding force. It connects past and present by incorporating images and stories from other times into the present—as the Iatmul example has shown. This aspect of culture resides in mythological and historical narratives. Both aspects—the normative (directive) and the narrative—ground belonging and identity.

Belonging to an external dimension of human memory, the notion of cultural memory goes beyond that of tradition. It is stored in a variety of agents, including specialists, experts, shamans, griots, priests, and "old crocodiles"; in systems of notations such as *churingas*; or writings. This cultural memory must be seen as separate from the "communicative memory." It contains only those memories that relate to the recent past and goes back only about four generations.

The Iatmul visually and orally represent the events that took place in the past. The external visual representation takes the form of the *kirugu*, or knotted cords (see Fig. 5). Each cord has a length of 6 to 7 m (6½ to 7½ yd) and knots of different sizes at regular intervals. Each *kirugu* represents one of the ancient migrations and bears the name of the crocodile that cleared the path for the clan group founder. Each of the large knots in a *kirugu* represents a place along the migration route; the smaller knots contain the secret names of the totem associated with each spot. Orally, the past intended for the public is recited in song cycles (*sagi*). Each cycle consists of a fixed sequence of songs and lasts between 12 and 16 h. Each song relates a short tale in which a particular act is accomplished by the totem of the place along the ancient migration route. The texts recited in the song are simple, small, harmless extracts from the secret myths.

Delimitations

The fate of general concepts such as "clan," "tribe," "boundary," "lineage," or "cultural pattern" is uncertain, and there is growing evidence that many traditional concepts taken for granted in anthropology are fuzzy. The kind of identity that inheres in such connections seems to be most aptly described as belonging to country rather than to the notion of containment within a solidary group. But

Fig. 5 A knotted cord, the visual representation of an ancient migration of the Iatmul people, Papua New Guinea

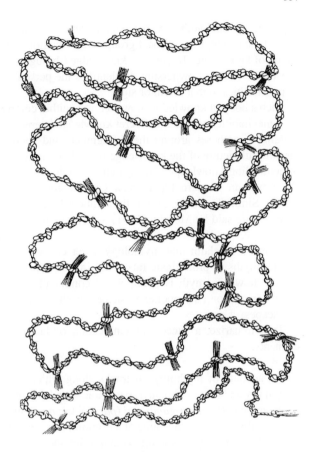

this "belonging to country" does not necessarily imply spatial delimitations in the western sense with their fixity, absoluteness, and systematics. Instead, it means a substantial core of people who indisputably have rights to specific spatial fixed points in the topography (Sutton, 1995). Cores, not social or spatial boundaries, are the focus.

The Iatmul seem to be very definite in their social organization, which is highly structured and stable. Their social organization as a whole is legitimized through religion and cosmology inscribed in the environment. One might gain the impression that the "idea" of the system is constantly present, that people try to represent it in the social structure and outline of the villages.

Distributions

The foundation of knowledge varies from people to people. "In Aboriginal societies knowledge is land-based" (Rose, 1996, p. 2). Among the Iatmul it is based on names, which are connected to places in the environmental space. In both societies, however, personal authority, personal achievement, the authority of elders, and the integrity and autonomy of local groups are a function of restrictions on the dissemination of knowledge. To perform knowledge (through song, dance, story, and name debates) is to assert ownership. It identifies the person as someone with rights and responsibilities to that totem or side.

Such a body of knowledge, however, is a neither complete nor fixed whole. There is an inevitability of leakage. Secret knowledge keeps seeping out, and people keep building hypotheses around these fragments and keep trying to piece together a meaningful picture of the knowledge from them. In response, societies invent ways of controlling knowledge. The system for doing so as practiced by the Mountain Ok groups in Western Papua New Guinea, for example, is described by Barth (1987). Similarly, the Yolngu in the Arnhem Land Region of Australia's Northern Territory are said by Morphy (1991) to have an almost constant fear of losing vital knowledge.

Iatmul men claim that mythology never changes and that someone who tries to alter myths or promulgate false ones invites affliction by the totemic ancestors. In fact, however, myth is manipulated continually. Whether or not it gains currency depends on its proponents' success in the debates about names, persons, and landscapes.

To summarize, a successful vindication of Iatmul myth needs the following elements:

1. An account of mythological tracks along which ancient people moved across country and thus established space (traced and documented by anthropology). An example is *Pat-nawi-gumbangi* (*pat*: spittle; *nawi*: masculine ending; *gumbangi*: masculine ending), the name of a primordial crocodile that created the earth from a dribble of spittle in the primordial water and then enlarged the shapeless earth, from which the first pair of brothers emerged. They subsequently followed the migratory route of the crocodile, creating today's social structure and division into an earth hemisphere and a sky hemisphere.

2. The *pabu* ritual, during which present-day Iatmul undertake a mental journey, whereby emplacement is the most basic medium of mnemonics (traced and documented in cognitive science). *Patnawigumbangi* leaves the first place of origin and migrates into the present day settlements, cleaving a path for the first people. At certain places along this path, settlements are built and the totems distributed. Migrations of different clans are memorized as mental journeys along the primordial paths. Events around the journeys of the ancestors are stored in prototypes that serve to reconstruct names and myths on demand. The knotted chord serves as a mnemonic aid.

3. The perception of present-day landscape as the primeval space (traced and documented by the discipline of human geography). Through the past migrations of *Patnawigumbangi* and other crocodiles (other clans), the contemporary world has been created, including the central Sepik river and the area's creeks, lagoons, hills, and villages. Looking at today's landscape, people see a primordial "frozen" landscape and their own cultural memories.

Notes

1. Some of the ethnographic data were published in Wassmann (2003).
2. The Iatmul use the expression "old crocodiles" to refer to "big men" in their culture.

References

Anderson, J. R. (1983). Retrieval of information from long-term memory. *Science, 220*, 25–30.

Assmann, J. (1992). *Das kulturelle Gedächtnis. Schrift, Erinnerung und politische Identität in frühen Hochkulturen* [Cultural memory: Writing, remembering, and political identity in ancient civilizations]. Munich: C. H. Beck.

Baddeley, A. D. (1994). Working memory: The interface between memory and cognition. In D. L. Schacter & E. Tulving (Eds.), *Memory systems* (pp. 351–367). Cambridge, MA: MIT Press.

Barth, F. (1987). *Cosmologies in the making*. New Haven, CT: Yale University Press.

Basso, K. (1988). Speaking with names: Language and landscape among the Western Apache. *Cultural Anthropology, 3*, 99–130.

Craik, F. I. M., & Lockhart, R. (1972). Levels of processing: A framework for memory research. *Journal of Verbal Learning and Verbal Behavior, 11*, 671–684.

Ericsson, K. A., & Kintsch, W. (1995). Long-term working memory. *Psychological Review, 102*, 211–245.

Ericsson, K. A., & Staszenski, J. J. (1989). Skilled memory and expertise: Mechanisms of exceptional performance. In D. Klahr & K. Kotovsky (Eds.), *Complex information processing: The impact of Herbert A. Simon* (pp. 235–267). Hillsdale, NJ: Erlbaum.

Farah, M. J. (2001). The neuropsychology of mental imagery. In F. Boller & J. Grafman (Series Eds.) & M. Behrmann (Vol. Ed.), *Handbook of neuropsychology, Vol. 4. Disorders of visual behavior* (pp. 239–248). Amsterdam: Elsevier.

Feld, F., & Basso, K. (Eds.). (1996). *Senses of place*. Santa Fe, NM: School of America Research Press.

Fox, J. (1997). Genealogy and topogeny: Towards an ethnography of Rotinese ritual place names. In J. Fox (Ed.), *The poetic power of place* (pp. 92–103). Canberra: Australian National University.

Gow, P. (1995). Land, people and paper in Western Amazonia. In E. Hirsch & M. O'Hanlon (Eds.), *The anthropology of landscape* (pp. 43–62). Oxford, VA: Clarendon Press.

Harwood, F. (1976). Myth, memory and the oral tradition: Cicero on the Trobriands. *American Anthropologist (New Series), 78*, 783–796.

Hwang, W.-Y., Chang, C.-B., & Chen, G.-J. (2004). The relationship of learning traits, motivation and performance—Learning response dynamics. *Computers and Education, 42*, 267–287.

Keesing, R. (1982). *Kwaio religion: The living and the dead in a Solomon Island society*. New York: Columbia University Press.

Kosslyn, S. M. (1980). *Image and mind*. Cambridge, MA: Harvard University Press.

LaBar, K. S., & Cabeza, R. (2006). Cognitive neuroscience of emotional memory. *Nature Reviews Neuroscience, 7*, 54–64.

Maguire, E. A., Valentine, E. R., Wilding, J. M., & Kapur, N. (2003). Routes to remembering: The brains behind superior memory. *Nature Neuroscience, 6*, 90–95.

McGaugh, J. L. (2000). Memory—A century of consolidation. *Science, 287*, 248–251.

Miller, G. (1956). The magical number seven, plus-or-minus two: Some limits on our capacity for processing information. *The Psychological Review, 63*, 81–97.

Morphy, H. (1991). *Ancestral connections: Art and an Aboriginal system of knowledge*. Chicago: Chicago University Press.

Morphy, H. (1993). Colonialism, history and the construction of place: The politics of landscape in Northern Australia. In B. Bender (Ed.), *Landscape: Politics and perspective* (pp. 205–244). Oxford, UK: Berg.

Rose, D. (1996). *Nourishing terrains: Australian Aboriginal views of landscape and wilderness.* Canberra: Australian Heritage Commission.

Schacter, D. L. (1999). The seven sins of memory: Insights from psychology and cognitive neuroscience. *American Psychologist, 54,* 182–203.

Squire, L. R. (1987). Memory: Neural organization and behavior. In J. M. Brookhart & V. B. Mountcastle (Eds.), *Handbook of physiology: The nervous system, Vol. 5. Higher functions of the nervous system* (pp. 295–371). Bethesda, MD: American Physiological Society.

Stanek, M. (1983). *Sozialordnung und Mythik in Palimbei.* Basel: Wepf.

Strehlow, T. G. H. (1947). *Aranda Traditions.* Victoria: Melbourne University Press.

Sutton, P. (1995). Atomism versus collectivism: The problem of group definition in Native Title cases. In J. Fingleton & J. Finlayson (Eds.), *Research monographs: Vol. 10. Native title: Emerging issues for policy, research and practice* (pp. ix–xxii). Canberra: Centre for Aboriginal Economic Policy Research.

Tulving, E. (1995). Organization of memory: Quo Vadis? In M. S. Gazzaniga (Ed.), *The cognitive neurosciences* (pp. 839–847). Cambridge, MA: MIT Press.

Wassmann, J. (1991). *The song to the flying fox: The public and esoteric knowledge of the important men of Kandingei about totemic songs, names and knotted cords (Middle Sepik, Papua New Guinea).* Port Moresby: Institute of Papua New Guinea Studies.

Wassmann, J. (2001). The politics of religious secrecy. In A. Rumsey & J. Weiner (Eds.), *Emplaced myth* (pp. 43–72). Honolulu, HI: University of Hawai'i Press.

Wassmann, J. (2003). Landscape and memory in Papua New Guinea. In H. Gebhardt & H. Kiesel (Eds.), *Heidelberger Jahrbücher: Vol. 47. Weltbilder* [Heidelberg annuals: Vol. 47. Images of the world] (pp. 329–346). Berlin: Springer.

Weiner, J. (1991). *The empty place: Poetry, space, and being among the Foi of Papua New Guinea.* Bloomington, IN: Indiana University Press.

Abstract of the Contributions

Communicative and Cultural Memory

Jan Assmann

Abstract Like consciousness and language, human memory is acquired through communication, socialization, and acculturation. It is, therefore, about both one's brain and one's social and cultural relations and comprises three dimensions: the personal, social, and cultural. Human memory is "embodied" in living personal memories and "embedded" in social frames and external cultural symbols (e.g., texts, images, and rituals) that can be acknowledged as a memory function insofar as they are related to the self-image or "identity" of a tribal, national, and/or religious community. Whereas the social or "collective" memory comprises knowledge commonly shared by a given society in a given epoch, cultural memory in literate societies includes not only a "canon" of normative knowledge but also an "archive" of apocryphal material that may be rediscovered and brought to the fore in later epochs. The formation of a canon of "classical" or sacred texts requires techniques of interpretation to keep accessible the meaning of the texts that may no longer be altered or multiplied. At that stage of cultural evolution, cultural memory changes from ritual to textual continuity. Cultural memory becomes complex, splitting into the "classical" and the "modern," the "sacred" and the "secular."

Memory and Space in the Work of Maurice Halbwachs

David Middleton and Steven D. Brown

Abstract This chapter examines the intellectual legacy of French sociologist Maurice Halbwachs (1877–1945) in order to address three research questions. First, how are individual and collective memories formed, retained, and manipulated? Second, what accounts for the persistence and changes of cultural memories? Third, how do spatial and cultural contexts influence memory? Despite his reputation as a theorist of how *groups* remember, Halbwachs's real contribution to the study of social memory is his comprehensive account of the structure of the collective frameworks in which recollection is situated. The notion of a collective framework by itself helps to clarify what Bartlett (Remembering: A study in experimental and social psychology, 1932) describes as an "organised setting," namely, a structured set of meanings that stands in advance of a given act or remembering. However, Halbwachs adds an additional "physiognomic" dimension. The spatial locations occupied by communities become etched by frameworks in such a way that their particular perspective on the past comes to appear timeless—a "larger and impersonal duration" that marks the thought of individual members. Space becomes territorialized by collective memory. It then becomes apparent that remembering is profoundly shaped by the mutually responsive relationship between social groups and the places they inhabit. The greater the range of memberships held by an individual, the more complicated the nature of personal memory becomes.

Knowledge, Cultural Memory, and Politics

Peter Meusburger

Abstract After categorizing different types of collective memories, the author discusses tensions between collective memories and the knowledge of individuals. He notes that collective memories are often based on Manichean morality and that "memory industries" try to manipulate well-informed and highly educated societies in ways similar to those used by emerging nineteenth-century nation-states to manipulate their undereducated or illiterate societies. It is argued that designers of monuments and exhibitions should increase the attention they pay to the knowledge of the audience and the reception of exhibitions by visitors. The interpretation of texts, politically loaded images, and monuments depends more on the observer's prior knowledge, ideology, and emotions than on the intentions of the producer of images and monuments. The final section deals with the nemesis represented by collective memories based on Manichean morality.

The Rütli in Switzerland: Minor Memory—Major Ambitions

Georg Kreis

Abstract The Rütli is the place where Switzerland is said to have been founded at the end of the thirteenth century. It is, on the one hand, a real place in the geography of Switzerland and, on the other hand, a symbolic place in the mental landscape of the Swiss society. Three major problems are discussed in this chapter. First, how has this place gained its importance? Second, what is the status of this specific place in the larger field of cultural memories? Third, what is the substance of the Rütli, and how has the importance of its different contents changed in changing times? The two main answers are that national memory and group memory are not opposites in this case, a conclusion that may be explained by the long democratic tradition of Swiss society; and that the Rütli is a vessel for various types of content.

Sharing Space? Geography and Politics in Post-conflict Northern Ireland

Brian Graham

Abstract In pursuing the idea that cultural memory is central to the recognition that any present must have a past, the author contends that the peace process in Northern Ireland has largely elided both the role of culture and its cognates—memory and identity—and the symbolic realm of meaning, which, ultimately, is the force that validates the notion of citizenship and thus the legitimacy of any polity. The author first explores the question of identity, politics, and territoriality before moving on to examine the British government's rhetoric of a "shared future" and of "shared space." He then uses the example of "the past that is not the past" to illustrate limitations of this rhetoric. Lastly, he argues that the political invisibility of geographical and cultural processes—especially memory work—is compromising and undermining the attainment of a peace process that might extend beyond the limitations of power-sharing between the two antipluralist political parties.

Memory—Recollection—Culture—Identity—Space: Social Context, Identity Formation, and Self-construction of the Calé (Gitanos) in Spain

Christina West

Abstract Knowledge, recollection, and memory are the basics for the construction and characteristics of a cultural identity, which is built on a "me-" and a "we-identity" and which is fixed in the collective memory. According to J. Assmann, the collective memory is composed of the communicative and the cultural memory, the operational modes of which depend on the level of a society's orality and literality. The Calé (Gitanos)—the Romani people in Spain, who are in transition between orality and literality—are chosen for an analysis of the importance that the different types of memory have for the formation and change of culture and cultural identity. Flamenco as an oral mode of expression and distinction is shown to be a fundamental link in the identity construction of the Gitanos.

Seven Circles of European Memory

Claus Leggewie

Abstract Europe is mainly a common market, a free zone for private and business travels, and partly a common currency. Against this conventional wisdom the author argues that Europe is more than the Euro (and the Champions League) and that it can function only with a shared memory of its conflicting past during the twentieth century. The author develops seven circles of European memory, starting with the unbalanced remembrance of totalitarian crimes (Holocaust and Gulag). He focuses then on ethnic cleansing particularly in the European periphery—the Turkish genocide against the Armenians, the civil war in former Yugoslavia, and the massacres under the colonial period in Africa. A particular aspect is the remembrance of forced and voluntary migration processes into Europe. "European" is not an artificial consensus on these aspects but a civilized way to deal with disparate views.

Halecki Revisited: Europe's Conflicting Cultures of Remembrance

Stefan Troebst

Abstract In the early 1950s, the Vienna-born US–Polish historian Oskar Halecki developed a model of "the limits and divisions of European history" from antiquity to the Cold War. Using cultural and religious criteria, he identified four historical mesoregions: Western Europe, West Central Europe, East Central Europe, and Eastern Europe. Post-1989–1991 cultures of remembrance, too, reveal a Europe of four mesoregions, ones that closely resemble those of Halecki's historical Europe. In the Western part of the European Union, an "Atlantic," victory-based remembrance prevails. In West Central Europe (i.e., in partly postfascist, partly postcommunist Germany), 1945 is remembered ambivalently as defeat *and* liberation. In East Central Europe, which has been part of the EU since 2004, the Yalta syndrome and the Molotov–Ribbentrop Agreement of 1939 shape collective memory. In Eastern Europe, that is, the Russian Federation and some other parts of the Commonwealth of Independent States (CIS), 1945 functions as a new founding myth replacing that of 1917.

Remembering for Whom? Concepts for Memorials in Western Europe

Rainer Eckert

Abstract In this chapter World War II in Western Europe is seen as a formative part of the construct of Europe. The collective and differing individual historical experiences of thirteen European countries are analyzed. Comparisons between different "Western" countries of the continent reveal a group whose historical remembrance after 1945 concentrates primarily on the members' own suffering under the German terror during World War II (e.g., Belgium and Austria). Other cultures of remembrance (e.g., Denmark and France) are shown to be rooted more strongly in a tradition of resistance. The author points out the long time it took for most European countries to begin coming to terms with the Holocaust and wartime collaboration. He notes both change in the self-images of the countries that had not been occupied and the different memory that Germany's wartime allies have of their role in the conflict, their relationship with the Germans, and the conduct of the war.

Family Memories of World War II and the Holocaust in Europe, or Is There a European Memory?

Harald Welzer

Abstract This chapter deals with the question of how personal memories of the National Socialist past in Germany are passed on to younger generations. Rather than viewing this process as a unidirectional handing down of memories from generation to generation, the author examines how memories are negotiated and recreated in intergenerational discourse. Drawing on a series of case studies, he discusses how the meaning of past experiences is construed and organized within particular narrative genres.

Annihilating—Preserving—Remembering: The "Aryanization" of Jewish History and Memory during the Holocaust

Dirk Rupnow

Abstract Since the end of World War II, but especially over the last 20 years of debate about memory and representation, there has been suspicion that Germany's National Socialists had planned not only to annihilate the Jewish people physically but also to obliterate them from history and memory—together with the traces of the persecution and the mass murder they had to suffer. Thus, the notion of genocide was occasionally modified and reinforced byconcepts intended to describe an alleged obliteration of memory and "murder of memory." In contrast, projects and phenomena openly countering efforts to render the victims totally forgotten have received only isolated and inadequate attention. These projects are aimed instead at achieving a more advanced functionalization of the victims, one that goes even beyond extermination.

History/Archive/Memory: A Historical Geography of the U.S. Naval Memorial in Brest, France

Michael Heffernan

Abstract Memorials, like texts, escape the intentions of those who create them. Designed to recall past events or personalities, memorials are sometimes radically reinterpreted as a consequence of later political or military conflicts, acquiring new layers of meaning as a result and engendering different, often unanticipated memories. The chapter examines this process with reference to a specific, deeply contested *lieu de mémoire*: the US Naval Memorial in the French city of Brest. This imposing tower has a complex history that reveals both the creative and the destructive impacts of twentieth-century warfare on European urban environments and underlines the uneasy relationship between the United States and its European allies. Originally constructed in the early 1930s to commemorate the achievements of the American Expeditionary Force in World War I, the memorial was destroyed during the German occupation in World War II, only to be rebuilt in the late 1950s. Using published official histories, unpublished archival materials in France and the United States, and the oral testimonies of some of the city's residents, this chapter examines the politics behind the surprisingly varied interpretations of the memorial's construction, destruction, and reconstruction.

Places and Spaces: The Remembrance of D-Day 1944 in Normandy

Sandra Petermann

Abstract With World War II having razed vast parts of Europe by 1945, many citizens of the continent's war-torn countries hoped they would soon leave behind the effects of turmoil, destruction, and trauma. The author examines the commemoration of D-Day (June 6, 1944), exploring why war commemoration rituals still captivate thousands of people and illustrating attempts that have been made to shape a peaceful future in postwar Europe. She draws on concepts of action theory to demonstrate how rituals create, in a single place, various kinds of space informed by ideology, beliefs, and knowledge and how they can help people come to terms with a harrowing past. The chapter is based on more than 100 qualitative interviews with participants in rituals, tourists of battlefields, and people who redesign former war zones for commemorative purposes. The interviews underwent qualitative content analysis and were studied together with extensive archive material.

"Doors into Nowhere": Dead Cities and the Natural History of Destruction

Derek Gregory

Abstract W. G. Sebald's lectures on "Air war and literature" have been criticized on two fronts. His claim that the Allied bombing offensive against Germany was erased from public memory has been challenged, and his appeal to a "natural history of destruction" to account for that lacuna has been condemned for its "naturalization" of military violence. Read differently, however, Sebald's inquiries identify a crucial link between trauma and the rupture of language, and they can be elaborated in ways that reveal the indispensable role of abstraction in the construction of a "kill-chain" through which cities are converted into targets. Visualization is a central modality of this process, in which targeting is made to appear as a purely technical and perfectly rational exercise. Seen thus, the kill-chain is an apparatus that enframes and entrains all those caught up in it. Conversely, its performative power can be called into question by novelists, artists, and others who draw attention to the process of abstraction in their re-presentations of bombing.

Violent Memories: South Asian Spaces of Postcolonial Anamnesis

Stephen Legg

Abstract The ambiguous phrase "violent memories" strikes at two of the key conceptual matters about which scholars of India have theorized: memories of violent acts and the violence that such recollections can do to those who remember them, those who are remembered, and those who are forgotten. The author seeks to provide an overview of the memory politics that has accompanied India's struggle for freedom from colonialism, both during the Raj and since independence. The main events and processes that scholars of postcolonial and subaltern studies have investigated in India are reviewed, including anticolonial violence and nonviolence, the memory politics of the "Mutiny" of 1857, gendered and sexed politics and violence, the partition of 1947, communal riots, Indira Gandhi's "Emergency," and natural disasters. The author positions these reviews within relatively broad theoretical trends in postcolonial studies from which they have drawn and to which they have a great deal to contribute.

Spacing Forgetting: The Birth of the Museum at Fort Jesus, Mombasa, and the Legacies of the Colonization of Memory in Kenya

Denis Linehan and Joao Sarmento

Abstract This chapter discusses public memory in Kenya through an analysis of the restoration of Fort Jesus, Mombasa, Kenya, and the contemporary role of the fort as a site of memory. Drawing on the political uses of erasure, fiction, and omission, the authors reveal continuities in the production of memory at Fort Jesus that have been politicized in colonial and postcolonial contexts. An analysis of the British and Portuguese motives in converting the fort into a museum shows how the transformation supported their imperial projects in Africa in face of growing calls for decolonization. The chapter also analyzes the resistance to the restoration led by two figures in the Kenyan anticolonial movement, Tom Mboya and Pio Gama Pinto. Although reaffirming how their resistance to the museum provides a critical alternative to the nostalgic narratives currently in vogue at the site, the authors conclude that the memory work around Fort Jesus actively neglects the colonial experience.

Landscape, Transformations, and Immutability in an Aboriginal Australian Culture

Robert Tonkinson

Abstract Aboriginal Australian societies are notable among hunter-gatherers for the seemingly contradictory co-presence of high mobility and a deep emotional attachment to their homelands. Totemic geography underlies people's multiple linkages to place, and certain acts of the living may also be memorialized, inscribed, and objectified in landscape. Using examples drawn from a Western Desert people, I show that, despite a dominant ideology that stresses "immutability" and stasis, there is a lack of closure in their richly complex religious system, allowing the accommodation of an inevitable dynamism. Openness and flux are, in significant measure, consequences of broadly ecological variables in one of the world's most marginal environments for human survival. Among these desert people, identity politics, though more complex than ideology alone suggests, are significantly constrained by a religiously saturated worldview.

Person, Space, and Memory: Why Anthropology Needs Cognitive Science and Human Geography

Jürg Wassmann

Abstract Among the Iatmul of the Sepik River in Papua New Guinea, conflicts over the rightful possession of cosmologically significant names are decided by having the opponents and their supporters meet near the ceremonial stool (*pabu*) in the men's house for a special debate. The thousands of secret sacred names of persons and places that may be involved are central to the ramified Iatmul mythological system, which is anchored in the landscape and which combines the past and present. Demanding elaborate feats of rhetorical skill and memory facilitated by localized mental representations, such encounters involve mastery of highly complex intellectual activities that draw on comprehensive knowledge of Iatmul myths of origin, clans, totems, migration, and settlement. This chapter first presents excepts from such debate and explains that an anthropologist's understanding of this complex system requires insights into research on human memory and learning capacities as well as competence in indigenous concepts of local geography.

Landscape Transformations and Immutability in an Aboriginal Australian Culture

Robert Tonkinson

Abstract Aboriginal Australians' conceptions of landscape transformation reconcile seemingly contradictory conceptions of high mobility and a dogma of attachment to place and certain areas of the life space ...

Person, Space and Memory: Why Anthropology Needs Cognitive Science and Human Geography

Jürg Wassmann

Abstract Among the Iatmul living in Papua New Guinea, conflicts over the rights of possession of totemic and its significant names are decided by having the opponents and their supporters name the centennial most (place) in the ...

The Klaus Tschira Foundation

Physicist Dr. h.c. Klaus Tschira established the Klaus Tschira Foundation (KTS) in 1995 as a not-for-profit organization conceived to support research in informatics, the natural sciences, and mathematics and to foster public understanding of these sciences. Klaus Tschira's commitment to this objective was honored in 1999 with the "Deutscher Stifterpreis," the prize awarded by the National Association of German Foundations. Klaus Tschira is a cofounder of SAP AG in Walldorf, one of the world's leading companies in the software industry.

The KTS provides support mainly for research in applied informatics, the natural sciences, and mathematics and funds educational projects for students at public and private universities and schools. The resources are used largely for projects initiated by the foundation itself. It commissions research from organizations such as the Heidelberg Institute for Theoretical Studies (HITS), formerly known as EML Research, founded by Klaus Tschira. HITS focuses on new theoretical approaches to interpreting the rapidly increasing amounts of experimental data. In addition, the KTS invites proposals for projects that are in line with the central concerns of the foundation.

The seat of the KTS is Villa Bosch in Heidelberg (Fig. 1), the former residence of Carl Bosch (1874–1940), the Nobel Prize Laureate for Chemistry. Carl Bosch, scientist, engineer, and businessman, joined BASF (Badische Anilin- & Soda-Fabrik) in 1899 as a chemist and became its CEO in 1919. In 1925 he was appointed CEO of the then newly created IG Farbenindustrie AG, and in 1935 he became chairman of the supervisory board of this chemical conglomerate. In 1937 Bosch was elected president of the Kaiser Wilhelm Gesellschaft (later renamed as the Max Planck Gesellschaft), the premier scientific society in Germany. Bosch's work combined chemical and technological knowledge at its best. Between 1908 and 1913, together with Paul Alwin Mittasch, he solved numerous problems in the industrial synthesis of ammonia, drawing on a process discovered earlier by Fritz Haber (Karlsruhe), who won the Nobel Prize for Chemistry in 1918. The Haber-Bosch process, as it is known, quickly became the most important method of producing ammonia—and remains so to this day. Bosch's research also influenced high-pressure synthesis of other substances. He was awarded the Nobel Prize for Chemistry in 1931, together with Friedrich Bergius.

In 1922 BASF erected a spacious country mansion and ancillary buildings in Heidelberg-Schlierbach for its CEO, Carl Bosch. The villa is situated in a small park on the hillside above the Neckar river and within walking distance from the famous Heidelberg Castle. As a fine example of the style and culture of the 1920s, Villa Bosch is considered one of the most beautiful buildings in Heidelberg and has been declared a protected cultural site. After World War II, it served as a domicile for high-ranking military staff of the United States Army. Thereafter, a local enterprise used the villa as its headquarters for several years. In 1967 Süddeutsche Rundfunk, a broadcasting company, established its Heidelberg studio there. Klaus Tschira bought Villa Bosch as a future home for his planned foundations toward the end of 1994 and had the building restored and modernized. Combining the historic ambience of the 1920s with the latest infrastructure and technology, Villa Bosch reopened in new splendor in mid-1997, ready for fresh challenges. The former garage, located 300 meters west of the villa, now houses the Carl Bosch Museum, Heidelberg, founded and managed by Gerda Tschira and dedicated to the memory of the Nobel laureate, his life, and his achievements.

For further information contact:

Klaus Tschira Foundation gGmbH
Villa Bosch
Schloss-Wolfsbrunnenweg 33
D-69118 Heidelberg, Germany
Tel.: (+49) 6221-533-101
Fax: (+49) 6221-533-199
beate.spiegel@klaus-tschira-stiftung.de

Public relations:
Renate Ries
Tel.: (+49) 6221-533-102
Fax: (+49) 6221-533-1986
renate.ries@klaus-tschira-stiftung.de

www.klaus-tschira-stiftung.de

Fig. 1 Villa Bosch (© Peter Meusburger, Heidelberg)

Fig. 2 Participants of the symposium "Cultural Memories" at Villa Bosch in Heidelberg. (© Thomas Bonn, Heidelberg)

Index